THOMAS BECKET

THOMAS BECKET

Defender of the Church

Father John S. Hogan

Our Sunday Visitor
Huntington, Indiana

Our Sunday Visitor Publishing Division
Our Sunday Visitor, Inc.
200 Noll Plaza
Huntington, IN 46750
www.osv.com
1-800-348-2440

ISBN: 978-1-68192-582-0 (Inventory No. T2452)
1. RELIGION—Christianity—Saints & Sainthood.
2. RELIGION—Christianity—History.
3. RELIGION—Christianity—Catholic.

eISBN: 978-1-68192-583-7
LCCN: 2020939796

Cover design: Amanda Falk
Cover art: *The Martyrdom of St. Thomas Becket, Archbishop of Canterbury* by Jean-Baptiste Marie Pierre (French, Paris 1714–1789 Paris); Public Domain Image
Interior design: Amanda Falk

PRINTED IN THE UNITED STATES OF AMERICA

In memory of my father,

Tom Hogan

(1939–2017)

Contents

Introduction

S aint Thomas Becket is a saint known only to a few in this current age. As his optional memorial appears on the Church's general calendar during the Octave of Christmas, he can get lost in the festivities of the Lord's nativity. He may also be overshadowed by another English martyr, his namesake Saint Thomas More. Yet, this twelfth-century archbishop of Canterbury, slain by knights in his own cathedral, is a man who has extraordinary relevance for Christians in every age, and most particularly for the time in which we now live. In the area of medieval scholarship, far from considering him a distant figure from the past, modern historians must come to terms with Becket. Indeed, the Becket controversy continues to challenge, and people find themselves almost being forced to take sides today as in the 1160s. His life is one of the most recorded of medieval saints. A wealth of contemporary biographies, hundreds of letters (his own and those of others), and Church and state documents plot the course of his dispute with King Henry II of England, revealing that almost everyone had an opinion on him and his struggle.

Thomas's murder in his cathedral in Canterbury just after Christmas in 1170 sent shockwaves throughout medieval Europe. It seemed to be the extreme result of a struggle between Church and state as manifested in a very personal struggle between two men who had been friends. The killing stopped the belligerents in their tracks. As the details of the archbishop's death emerged, many were gripped with horror, while others were inspired to devotion. Those who had known him in life may well have understood why in the end he had a violent death, and those who knew Henry II may have ceded that he was the very man to carry it out. Thomas's murder and the revelation of secret penitential aspects of his life had a chastening effect on many and led them to wonder who this martyred archbishop actually was: Had they known him at all? That is a question that still occupies historians, and it is one that should occupy us even as we venerate this man as a martyr-saint of the Church. In coming to understand him, we will come to understand what the Church is and what her role in the world ought to be.

Thomas Becket did not live as a saint for most of his life. As a young man he was vain, lazy, and wild; devoted to his mother yet a wastrel; a lover of the high life but also a loner. A charmer, he had heartbreaking charisma. He was said to be handsome; and yet, he was not known to have had an amorous relationship. Highly intelligent from his youth and ambitious, he was a late starter. As an archdeacon and royal chancellor of England, he was diligent and capable, loyal to the king, sometimes gauche, and often the butt of the king's jokes. Simply devout, he was chaste, but also worldly and materialistic. He was not above pulling a fast one and maneuvering people and situations to yield a desired result.

As archbishop, he became more penitent and devout. He spent hours studying the Scriptures, a development from his simple piety; but his character did not change too much, not at first. He was still ambitious, but now for the rights of the Church. Implacable and immovable, he was prepared to employ any means necessary to achieve his aims. He wielded his powers with skill and sometimes brutality. With no hesitation, he imposed penalties, excommunications, and interdicts. He was a fierce combatant, much to the chagrin of Henry II and the fears of a pope who was trying to find some sort of peaceful settlement to a controversy in England while in the midst of his own crisis. Thomas was a man who stood for his rights and would permit no trespass, nor turn a blind eye to transgressions, even for the sake of picking his battles to win a war. Was this out of personal pride or vigilance for the sake of the Church and her flock?

That question has been asked many times down the centuries and is still being considered; the answer can only be found in the life and words of Thomas himself. Historians have studied him, his words, the dispute, the people around him and their views of him; as one might expect, they have come to differing conclusions. Today, many historians do not like Thomas. Some of these are admirers of Henry II, a notable king indeed, for them the archbishop was an ambitious man intent on preventing the reform of the English political and judicial system. Others dislike him because he was a defiant defender of the Catholic Church, one who insisted on the Church's rights over and against the secular. There are those who see him as a self-obsessed man who would not back down in a crisis for the sake of peace, a radical who prolonged the agony of a nation rather than embrace a more conciliatory and pastoral position.

And then there are some — perhaps a few today — who see a hero, a warrior, flawed as he may have been; a man who felt he had to do what he thought was right. In the past, Catholic authors have been generous with Thomas, painting the man and his struggles in black and white: the Augustine of Hippo figure, the convert who fought for the Church in the face of an evil king's tyranny. That picture does not do justice to either Thomas or the king. Becket would be the first to say that Henry was not an evil man; after all, the archbishop loved his friend, and their dispute brought with it a great deal of personal suffering.

As scholars have examined every aspect of Thomas's life, interestingly, in recent works, too little emphasis has been placed on his faith. Indeed, it is this lack of emphasis that has, in my view, led some to misunderstand Thomas and his motivations. Many misread his actions as simply those of an arrogant man who was prepared even to die to preserve his honor. The historian W. L. Warren, for example, in his magisterial biography of Henry II, says that Thomas "was fundamentally a proud self-centered man."[1] Warren is not alone in this view. Is it true? In my opinion, no; for one thing, it is too simplistic — at the very least,

Thomas was complicated. What leads such fine scholars to conclude that he was simply arrogant? According to Warren, it was "his prohibition of the bishops performing their duty to the king."[2] Warren was no friend of Thomas; like many others, he held Thomas more responsible for his own death than those who killed him.[3] Like many others, Warren does not understand Thomas Becket. This is because, in failing to understand Thomas's faith — which was real and sincere — we cannot fully understand his motives.

For all his ambition, ability, pride, and humiliation, Thomas Becket — or as he would prefer to be called, Thomas of Canterbury — was a man of faith. He was lukewarm in the beginning; but through time and suffering, he embraced a deeper living of the Gospel, imperfect as it may have been at times. While he was conscious of his dignity (a problematic issue in his struggle), Thomas gradually came to understand that he had a greater master than any earthly king or even pope. This sinful and often difficult man came to realize that the Church, and religion in general, was not a department of state. While bishops and clergy owed fealty to their king in many areas, in the end, their first and most important master was Christ — and the Church was Christ's, not Henry's. Perhaps scholars see Thomas through an Erastian lens, presuming that the Church must be subject to the state.[4] In that context, if Thomas was only a minister of the king, certainly his actions would seem to be disloyal. But he was not a minister of the king; he was a minister of the Church and meant to be, first and foremost, a servant of Christ. His refusal to concede may be seen as arrogance and pride by some; but in reality, it sprang from his loyalty and obedience to Christ. Interestingly, almost every martyr of the Church, from Saint Stephen to Saint Oscar Romero, who died in opposition to the state, has been criticized by those who do not understand faith.

This biography seeks to examine Thomas and his actions in the context of his faith, a faith that was deepened through a gradual transformation that took place following his appointment as archbishop. Two keys help us to understand how this transformation took place: the simple piety his mother taught him as a child, and a sense of duty that at first served his ambition and allowed him progress through work well done, but later led him to serve another and greater Master. That progress from self-ambition to an ambition to serve God, marked by the four sections of this biography, was gradual. It is a spiritual drama in which, over time, and through various struggles, one master gave way to another, as Thomas increasingly died to self, as Jesus urges us in the Gospel. Some have considered Thomas an enigma — and he may have been one, even to himself, but not to heaven. Something about his life, his final struggle, and his death won favor with God. We know this because — to the astonishment of king, courtiers, Church officials, and even his friends — miracles abounded from the moment of his martyrdom. What did God see in this man? What did he make of his stubborn stand against his king? What was the meaning of his death? Without doubt, the answers to these questions can be seen in the fact that God made him a saint, as the miracles testify; the Church, in humble obedience, would confirm this even as her clergy scratched their heads, mystified. Thomas's glorification was a sign that God approved of his struggle, both his personal struggle and that with the king; and that his death was a true martyrdom

As the battle between Church and state resumed and rolled on in the years to come, Thomas's sainthood would certainly prove useful. But what of his life? Thomas's friends and enemies, scholars, and theologians would spend centuries poring over every deed, every word spoken or written, and every event to discover what made him acceptable to God. Was it simply his death? Was Thomas a victim or a martyr? Does God raise up victims, or was Thomas indeed one of the Church's great heroes whose relevance extends well beyond their time and personal situation?

In *A Short History of England*, G. K. Chesterton describes Thomas as "a great visionary and a great revolutionist."[5] The saints have relevance for every age, and though some ages may forget certain saints, other ages realize how poor they are without them and turn once again to these heroes of the faith to intercede for us and to help us make sense of the Gospel in the age in which we live. Thomas is more relevant now than ever as secularism leans over faith and seeks to destroy it. Chesterton suggests that Thomas was an impractical man living in a practical age and that his impracticality came from the Gospel, where mercy and pardon outweigh the burden of justice.[6] In Chesterton's eyes, the dispute was between the state, which could only work with the machinery of punishment, and Thomas's Catholic Church, which worked with the machinery of pardon. This is certainly one way of looking at the dispute — as a case of two visions clashing as much as two individuals fighting on a deeply personal level. But it was more than that.

Both Thomas and his nemesis, King Henry II, were baptized Christians; both claimed to be Catholics and faithful sons of the Church, and yet the quarrel between them concerned the Church, its way of life, its relationship with its members, and its relationship with a state that also claimed to be Christian. How was a dispute possible? In Thomas's life and experience, we see how it was possible and indeed necessary. The Christian Thomas clashed with the Christian Henry because Thomas finally understood what the Gospel was all about and what it meant to be a Christian, a disciple of Christ. In wisely calling him a visionary and a revolutionist, Chesterton points to the radical nature of Christian discipleship. Speaking of Thomas as impractical, Chesterton is saying that the kingdom the Christian disciple must inhabit is not of this world. The values of this kingdom are utterly impractical in the eyes of the world — they are otherworldly — and that is why they are the only values that will work here to create a more just and human society. These values raise the mind, heart, and soul of a person to God, the Creator. Thomas understood this as a canonist, but he grew to understand it even more as a Christian and most radically as a priest. In analyzing the conflict with Henry, one must never forget that Thomas was a priest, because becoming a priest changed everything for him.

One aspect of Thomas's life that has fascinated historians and writers alike is the nature of his friendship with Henry. For many, the story of Thomas and the king is a story of two men in conflict. There is no doubt that the dispute between the two was aggravated by an intensely personal dimension, and it may have been the cause of the dispute, as Henry expected Thomas to conform to his will for the sake of their friendship as much as for the sake of his being a subject. One author in the twentieth century, the playwright Jean Anouilh, reflected on this in particular. His play *Becket*,[7] the basis of the 1964 movie of the same name,[8] explores the exterior conflict between archbishop and king. However, both play and movie are flawed because Anouilh's work is historically inaccurate. For one, he thinks the issue of the dispute was not only personal in terms of a broken friendship but also a clash between the Anglo-Saxons, which he believed Thomas to be, and the Normans, represented by Henry.[9] When later informed that Thomas was a Norman, Anouilh did not correct his error but left the play as it was; and though he acknowledged that it contained historical inaccuracies, he was quoted as saying that history might eventually "rediscover" that Thomas was a Saxon after all.[10] Another inaccuracy leads to Anouilh's ultimate failure to understand Thomas: Despite the piety and strength he portrays in his protagonist, he does not delve deeper and sees only a man in conflict with another man, the destruction of a close friendship. Without question that did happen, but there was a lot more going on. There is always the danger of concentrating only on the external and superficial when trying to understand Thomas — a complex man who, with every passing year, was delving more deeply into profound mysteries, sometimes despite himself.

Another notable work of the twentieth century is the poet T. S. Eliot's drama *Murder in the Cathedral*, written for the Canterbury Festival in 1935.[11] This work delves much deeper than does Anouilh's. This is a spiritual drama in which Eliot tries to understand Thomas's inner conflict as he faces martyrdom. The theme of the play is pride and the character of the archbishop as he struggles with temptations to pride, first in fleeing martyrdom but then in succumbing for the wrong reason. Eliot sums up this tension in these famous lines: "The last temptation is the greatest treason: / To do the right deed for the wrong reason."[12] Eliot also offers his version of Thomas's Christmas Day sermon and allows the four knights time at the end of the play to explain why they killed the archbishop. They at first appeal to the audience's sense of honor to hear their side of the story, but end by ordering the audience to disperse quietly to their homes and do nothing that might provoke any public outbreak.[13]

Eliot is correct to reflect on Thomas's inner conflict. When Thomas became archbishop, he had to die to self. The simple piety that had sustained him until then was no longer enough. Sterner stuff was required now, and that was radical holiness. As he returned to England in December 1170 after six years of exile to face what he knew was coming —

martyrdom — he may have remembered Saint Paul's words that it is not easy to die, not even for a good man (see Rom 5:7). Yet he, Thomas of London, made archbishop of Canterbury, would have to face such a fate. As he crossed the water from exile to martyrdom, he may have mused on his life, seeking to understand the years that had been given to him, their significance, and how they would culminate.

This biography, an introduction to his life, aims to consider Thomas, his background, his influences, his progress in ambition and office, and his struggle to a new generation of Catholics who may not know him as well as other saints. Thomas's life and the controversies in which he was immersed are complex. This biography tries to offer to the general reader a sense of what was going on. There are many biographies of the man, and many of them are as complex as the dispute; this aims to offer a simple chronological narrative in as far as it is possible. In this regard, I found John Guy's chronology, unfolding of events, and discussion of the historical milieu around Thomas in his biography[14] the most successful and most accessible, and I have drawn upon this work as a major resource and used his chronological sequence. Other biographies that have proved most beneficial are those by Frank Barlow[15] and Anne Duggan.[16] In terms of the original medieval biographies, Michael Staunton has provided some excellent translations of extracts from those works, and while I have drawn on the original texts, I also consulted these extracts.[17]

To understand Thomas and his struggles, one must understand the time he lived in and the people and events that surrounded him. He was no solitary, detached saint; he was a man of his times, and those times formed the man now venerated as a martyr. This author aims to take his readers to meet Thomas by setting them down in the middle of twelfth-century Europe, with all its grandeur and chaos; its complex familial relationships; its political intrigue and instability; and the mischievousness, virtues, and sinfulness of its inhabitants. It is only in the crowded heart of that "chaos" that we can understand the influences that formed Thomas; the people he loved, respected, and struggled with; and the events that raised him to high office, pushed him against a wall, and forced him to fight. His work in defense of the Church was not a simple affair; it was so complex that it divided good people and devout Catholics. The trouble started with a problem of succession and the need for political reform and stability. It came to its climax as the blood of the primate of England was spilled on the floor of his cathedral.

This is the story of a man who wrapped himself in power and luxury, and then was gradually stripped bare through suffering, betrayal, repentance, and even foolishness — a man who was forced into exile so he could prepare to die in his cathedral, proclaiming to the world that the vision that transformed him is worth dying for, as is the One who confers that vision. He learned, often in great bitterness, that true liberty and freedom can be found only in Christ. In a sense, this is the story of every Christian; though the time and circumstances may differ, the struggle remains the same. For this reason, contemporary Catholics need to rediscover Thomas Becket. He is indeed a man and a saint for our times, someone we modern Christians have much to learn from. It falls to every generation of Catholics to engage with the saints anew, to discover what the saints have to say to them about their own concerns and about the state of the Church and her relationship with the world. Thomas of Canterbury is one whose time has come again, who is emerging from the shadows even as it seems the Church has entered into them. He seeks to engage with us.

Thomas's shrine at Canterbury was a place of pilgrimage for more than three hundred years before it was destroyed during the English Reformation. In that time, countless men and women came to his tomb, entrusting their concerns and needs to his wisdom and his prayers. In the devotional life of the Church, this should continue unabated. Faithful disciples of Jesus Christ are invited to see in Thomas a companion on the pilgrim path of fidelity, a wise teacher, an ardent intercessor, and a fatherly figure who can help us stand firm amid the storms that all too often assail the Church and her faithful members. In the providence and plan of God, Christians have discovered time and time again that when trouble comes, Saint Thomas Becket can be found standing with us, with the poor and afflicted, with those who may have been led to believe that there is no hope.

There is always hope, even in the greatest crisis, even in the most profound darkness, even when those who were supposed to be faithful have run away. Thomas did not run away. While his exile may have seemed to be his abandoning his see and his cause, in reality it was the means of ensuring he was free to continue his struggle, as previous archbishops of Canterbury had taught him. As he came to discover, he was first and foremost a pastor and shepherd, a father of souls, a faithful and true bishop whose concern was for the flock and their passage in holiness to the fulfillment of God's promises. This is his story, an introduction to his life that this author hopes will engage, fascinate, and, above all, inspire.

Prologue

The day — July 7, 1220 — promised to be hot. Conscious of this and perhaps surrendering to festivity, given the joy of the occasion, the archbishop of Canterbury, Stephen Langton, had barrels of wine placed at each of the city gates to quench the thirst of the crowds of pilgrims making their way to the cathedral for the day's great events. An act of generosity that may well have led Stephen to turn a blind eye to the arch-diocesan bursar's raised eyebrow, it proved a popular decision. Whether the queues at the barrels surpassed the queues into the cathedral is not recorded by historians, but spirits were high, even riotous, for the solemn translation of the body of the martyred archbishop Saint Thomas Becket.

It had taken two years to prepare for this day. The cathedral was finally restored after a disastrous fire in 1174 — thankfully, the tomb of Saint Thomas in the crypt had escaped the flames. A new, magnificent chapel dedicated to the Holy Trinity had been built onto the east side of the cathedral, behind the high altar. Two craftsmen, Walter of Colchester and Elias of Dereham,[1] had been working feverishly to construct a magnificent shrine in this new chapel. A great stone plinth with an open arcade rose up from the paved floor of the chapel, its summit empty for the moment but destined to hold an ornate reliquary. Above the plinth hovered a painted wooden canopy, carefully designed to protect — and at various times, to be solemnly raised to reveal — the resting place of the martyred archbishop.

Some days before (the accounts differ — some say the day before, others a week before), Archbishop Stephen, his prior Walter, the monks of the cathedral monastery, and other officials had descended into the crypt, to the tomb covering the stone sarcophagus where Thomas of Canterbury, also known as Becket, had been laid to rest by monks in late December fifty years before. Expecting reprisals from the knights who had killed Thomas, the monks in great fear had quickly cleaned his body, dressed it in pontificals, and interred it. The body had remained undisturbed all those years. Though Thomas had been canonized three years later in 1173, there had been no *recognitio*,[2] no relics taken, just a finer tomb constructed over the original one for the edification of the pilgrims. Now, that tomb was to be taken apart and the body exhumed and made more accessible for the veneration of the faithful. The monks themselves would carry out this solemn task.

Two accounts suggest that the body was found intact and that the monks, with tears in their eyes, lovingly carried it out of the tomb to be placed in a more appropriate casket.[3] Another account, with weightier evidence perhaps, differs: It relates that the body had or was decomposing, leaving only frail bones; these had to be handled with great care, as some disintegrated easily.[4] Archbishop Stephen took some bones for relics, not only for distribution in England, but to fulfill numerous requests from all over Europe.

In the fifty years since the martyrdom, the cathedral had received numerous gifts and offerings for the shrine, an enormous quantity of precious gems included, and these were employed by craftsmen in the construction of a new casket. Covered in gold plate and trellised, the casket was studded with gems — diamonds, sapphires, rubies, emeralds, pearls, and other jewels such as cameos, agates, cornelians, and onyx. One of the most spectacular jewels was the great Régale de France, a most extraordinary ruby that King Louis VII of France had given to the shrine during a pilgrimage he made in 1179 — an act of homage from one of Thomas's most ardent supporters during his exile. What the shrine was to contain, however, was even more precious. Following the *recognitio*, the skull and bones of Saint Thomas were placed in an iron urn, a "feretory," which was sealed in the new casket and then taken away to a private place in preparation for the translation.

Bishops, priests, religious, pilgrims, and officials traveled from all over England and Europe to be present at the translation. The numbers were so vast that there was soon no room in the inns, and a sea of tents rose up in the fields surrounding the city. A papal legate, Pandulf Verraccio, was present.[5] No stranger to grand occasions, Pandulf, now also bishop of Norwich, had been present at Runnymede in 1215 when King John was forced to sign the Magna Carta. Not the most humble of men, Pandulf had seen off the legate who had been sent to replace him when his term of office was over. Once the rival was routed, he took up the position again; his confidence and overbearing nature were trying the patience of England, Church and state. As Archbishop Stephen greeted him with the kiss of peace, Pandulf had no idea that the archbishop was plotting to oust him again, this time for good, and that the plot would prove successful.

Young King Henry III, King John's son, was also present. The participation of this grandson of Henry II, the king who had clashed with Thomas, symbolized reconciliation and peace. Just four years into his reign, the thirteen-year-old king was very much under the governance of his regent and mentor, Hubert de Burgh, who was also present. The young king would assume governance in 1227 but would remain highly influenced by de Burgh, then Earl of Kent, and launch out into what would be a very unpopular reign. Though he was personally pious, Henry III's early reign would be marked by debacles and revolts, his later reign by crises, conflict, and defeats. Ironically, he would prove a poor substitute for his grandfather in his governance; but in terms of his faith, he was a more amenable man who needed the Church to help him out of tight spots.

The archbishop and his entourage approached the place where the casket rested. Bishops took hold of the casket, and the great procession began. To a glorious chant, the body of the saint slowly made its way through the crowds into the great nave of the cathedral and then ascended a mighty staircase into the Chapel of the Holy Trinity. Brought before the new shrine, the casket was carefully raised up and placed atop the plinth. The summer sun shone through the windows, and the assembled congregation marveled at the colors of the gemlike panes in the light now reflecting off the casket; the whole cathedral was filled with what seemed a celestial celebration of light. Beneath the casket, on one side of the plinth, an altar had been constructed for Mass, and so the Holy Sacrifice was offered, the first of many for the next three hundred years. After Mass and Office had been sung and the dignitaries withdrew to their own festivities, the pilgrims ascended the steps and crept under the arches of the arcade, which now seemed to resemble an ark of refuge, to touch the tomb above and offer their prayers. The miracles that had begun at the old tomb in the crypt would continue from this splendid setting.

The Shrine of Saint Thomas of Canterbury was one of the most magnificent in all of England. The pilgrims gazed in awe at the magnificence of the new tomb, but the magnificence of the life and witness of the man who rested within was of even more significance. Greater again, perhaps, were the miracles and favors that poured out like sweet wine or soothing oil upon the sick and the troubled, the fearful and the desperate. The humble men and women of England and Europe knew that in Saint Thomas of Canterbury they had an intercessor, one who was powerful with God because he had stood up to the powerful of this world; a man who knew exile and abandonment, pain and calumny; a man who had stood alone for what was right. Whatever cause the pilgrim brought to Canterbury, Thomas would know what to do, how to help and even obtain a grace from God. No longer occupied with the affairs of Church and state, Saint Thomas took up the affairs of his devotees — and he was so successful in this endeavor that his shrine became the third most important pilgrimage destination in medieval Europe, after Rome and Santiago de Compostela.

For 318 years, this shrine was the jewel in the crown of English Catholicism. But in 1538, it was violently dismantled, the ark of the intercessor for the people torn down, the relics burned as another King Henry sought to wipe out the memory of a man he considered an enemy of the realm, a treasonous subject, a stumbling block to the freedom and dignity of England.

This man was Thomas Becket, Thomas of London, Thomas of Canterbury: deacon; priest; archbishop; sometime royal chancellor; friend of the king; troublemaker; penitent; exile; turbulent enemy of the king; unyielding, ungrateful wretch; shepherd; murdered priest; martyr; saint; wonderworker; enigma.

Part I

Ambition's Servant

1
The Ship

The trouble began with the sinking of a ship. Quite apart from the appalling loss of life, such disasters often bring endless problems, with varied tribulations surging out from the original calamity. This was certainly the case with the sinking of the *White Ship* off the coast of Normandy on November 25, 1120. Dan Jones, in his history of the Plantagenets, describes the events.[1] The owner and captain of the ship, Thomas FitzStephen, had rented the vessel to William the Ætheling,[2] Duke of Normandy and the only legitimate son and heir to the throne of Henry I, king of England.[3] With his half-siblings Richard of Lincoln and Matilda, Countess of Perche,[4] and dozens of the young set of the Norman realms, William was leading a pleasure cruise across the English Channel from Barfleur in Normandy to the English coast. Dashing and gregarious, William was seventeen, recently married, and the hope of his father and kingdom. William was returning to England from having paid homage to the king of France. His father had just conferred the Duchy of Normandy on him, and as a duke of the realm of France, William owed an act of obeisance to his feudal lord, King Louis VI, nicknamed "the Fat."[5]

At the moment the ship raised anchor, William was drunk, as were his guests and, much more worryingly, the crew. There was a good wind. The *White Ship* was a large vessel capable of dealing with choppy waters, so the crossing promised to be nautically uneventful, if not so in other ways. The captain, who had already imbibed too much alcohol to offer a sound proposition, never mind steer a ship in any direction, swore they would fly across the channel, even overtake the other boats that had already set sail. Priests arrived to bless the boat, but the carousers jeered at them and waved them away. There was no need for holy water, for the roisterers had a more potent liquid to fortify them, and besides, surely this ship was unsinkable.

With passengers in such high spirits, the ship was ready to set off at high speed. One passenger, however, was getting nervous: Stephen of Blois, William's cousin. Catching a whiff of the wind and the unruly celebrations on board, he excused himself and disembarked — a ship sailing at top speed with a well-oiled crew and a wild party in full swing seemed too much like tempting fate. He and a few companions would set sail on a more sober vessel. One contemporary historian maintains that Stephen was actually struck with a case of diarrhea and needed urgent relief, which was unobtainable at that particular moment on the *White Ship*, so he quietly excused himself.[6] No matter whether Stephen's departure was in response to a premonition or to afflicted bowels, it changed the course of history.

It was after midnight when the ship weighed anchor and, at full speed, launched headlong into the bay to the cheers of its intoxicated passengers, three hundred in all. Determined to race the other vessels to England as the captain had promised, all sails unfurled to catch the full force of the wind, and the crew drove the ship toward the channel and right onto the Quillebeuf, a submerged rock at the mouth of the harbor, tearing an enormous hole in the prow. Water poured into the ship, and as a quickly sobering crew desperately attempted to bail it out, panic broke out among the passengers. Those with their wits about them realized that few might survive this disaster, and one of them must be the heir to the throne. As passengers fell into the icy waters, inebriated and unable to swim, their fine, thick clothes pulling them down into the depths, a single lifeboat was launched with a small crew to take William back to shore.

Whatever his state, William showed some courage and chivalry. As he looked back at the sinking ship, he spied his half-sister Matilda desperately treading water and about to go under. She was screaming for her life, and William could not ignore her. He ordered the boat back to pick her up. As they approached her, other desperate souls attempted to scramble onboard, causing the lifeboat to capsize, and William, Duke of Normandy, heir to the throne of England, was tossed into the icy waters and disappeared down into the abyss. For all his efforts, Matilda also drowned, as did their brother Richard and everyone else except one man: a butcher from Rouen who had stepped onboard ship to collect monies owed to him and had been waylaid by the revelers.[7] He had a lucky escape, but England and Normandy did not.

When news reached King Henry I, he was distraught. His heir was dead; who would succeed him? The dynasty was now on shaky ground. Stephen of Blois, stepping safely off his boat in England, was one candidate; he was Henry's nephew, his closest legitimate male relative. Another possible heir was William's elder half-sister, another Matilda (Henry would call four of his daughters Matilda).[8] The eldest and only legitimate daughter of King Henry I and his first wife, Matilda of Scotland, this Matilda was the wife of the king of Germany and Holy Roman emperor, Henry V. She was now the heir apparent, but given that she was a woman, this was not apparent to all, and certainly not to Stephen. Henry had another child, Robert, Earl of Gloucester, who was capable enough to assume the crown, but he was illegitimate, born of an affair the king had had with a woman from Oxfordshire. Indeed, Robert was the eldest of twenty-two illegitimate children Henry had sired with numerous women, several others of whom also came from Oxfordshire. The king would not prove so fortunate in the childbearing stakes with his wives, not even with his new teenaged wife, Adeliza of Louvain, whom he married just weeks after the tragedy. She bore him no children, though she later bore seven children for the Earl of Arundel, whom she married in her widowhood. Robert of Gloucester was accomplished, but the stigma of illegitimacy would be too much for the barons to accept, though many of them had brought unacknowledged children into the world through extramarital affairs.

King Henry concluded that the succession would have to fall to Matilda. In 1120, she was eighteen years old and celebrating the tenth anniversary of her marriage to the Holy Roman emperor Henry V. Sadly, that marriage had not produced any children; her husband would die in 1125 without an heir. Henry then called his daughter, who had no role in the empire, back to England. As it was then obvious that Adeliza was not going to bear him a son, the king realized that he had to ensure that Matilda's accession to the throne would be as painless as possible; to do so he would have to bind his barons to an oath. Oaths in the Middle Ages were of supreme gravity; their witness was God himself, and breaking an oath was considered a serious offense against God.

At Christmas 1126, Henry summoned the barons to court. Enthroned with his daughter at his side, he called the barons forward and received from each of them an oath of allegiance to Matilda — to uphold her claim to the throne upon Henry's death and to do all that was necessary to ensure a secure succession. Among those who took the oath was Stephen of Blois. Forcing the barons to take this oath was an extraordinary measure, and some found it most irregular, as Stephen would maintain later in his effort to legitimize his claim to the throne. Female sovereigns were not a good idea, many of the barons complained among themselves — they brought instability and weakness to a dynasty, perhaps even war. Even if he resented the grumbling, Henry was not immune to the opinions being voiced behind his back. If Matilda was to have any chance to hold on to the throne, she would need a strong husband to assert her rights, and so the king arranged a match with Geoffrey, nicknamed "Plantegenest,"[9] then the eldest son of the Count of Anjou. He was an adept and ambitious man, and even if love never blossomed between the two, the prospect of being consort to a powerful queen would keep the young man onside.

Matilda and Geoffrey were married on June 17, 1128.[10] When the twenty-six-year-old bride saw the groom, she was not impressed. Eleven years her junior, he was lanky, ginger-haired, giddy, and bursting with energy; he also liked to wear a flower in his hair.[11] Matilda was a much more sober character, imperious and dismissive, and she found much to dismiss in her new consort. To celebrate the marriage, Geoffrey's father, Fulk, abdicated as Count of Anjou and went to the Holy Land to assume the crown of the Kingdom of Jerusalem. Geoffrey was now count, so at least Matilda was consort to a ruler. However, this was no boon to Matilda; she detested Anjou and regarded her new husband's family as nothing short of murdering savages. The marriage did not start well, and it continued as it began, with arguments.[12] Soon after their espousal, the couple separated and would remain apart for five years. Still worried about the future of his dynasty, Henry first counseled and then threatened the couple to fulfill their conjugal and dynastic duty. The couple would do so on at least three occasions, bringing three sons into the world. The first was born on March 5, 1133, and he was called after the man he was destined to succeed: Henry.

Henry I could not have been described as a doting grandfather, but he was a happy and relieved one: He had a male heir to follow on from his daughter. In June of the following year, the spare arrived — Geoffrey — and an emergency heir would arrive in July 1136: William. However, the days were growing short for Henry. In November 1135, he arrived at one of his hunting lodges in Normandy for a few weeks of sport before Christmas, but he fell ill the next day — it was said that he was afflicted with food poisoning after eating lampreys against his doctor's advice. He was not to recover; he died on December 1 with his son Robert by his side. His remains were prepared for burial — his entrails interred at a local priory and his embalmed body transported back to England to be buried at Reading Abbey.[13]

Henry seems to have died in peace. The succession was settled. Matilda was secure because his faithful barons would ensure that she was crowned and would reign in relative peace until Henry II was ready to ascend the throne, be it on her death or on her abdication, whichever was deemed more politically expedient. However, neither course of action was deemed expedient by many, and there was one who was keen to throw all of Henry's plans to the wind and plant himself on the throne of England: Stephen of Blois. Trouble was about to begin in earnest.

2
A Boy from London

Though of Norman stock, Thomas Becket was, above all, a Londoner, and that is of vital importance. Londoners were, and still are for the most part, a people set apart from the rest of the English. Though often of mixed ancestry, Londoners gel into a single, determined will, and though they might fight among themselves, should danger come from without, they stand as a single entity. This "plucky" attitude has seen them through various disasters, from the plague and the Great Fire of 1666 to the Blitz during the Second World War and the terrorist attacks that threaten London today. Londoners do not surrender easily. For much of their history, the threat from without was monarchical.

Londoners were wary of kings. They considered London an independent city. That spirit of independence so marked its denizens that monarchs felt the need to tread carefully. During the Norman invasion, following the death of the Anglo-Saxon King Harold at the Battle of Hastings in October 1066, the triumphant William the Conqueror was quickly relieved of any fantasy he might have entertained of walking into

London and claiming his capital. Before his coronation at Westminster, he would have to lay siege to the city.[1] The winter of 1066 saw William up against stiff resistance as he tried to bring his capital to heel. His victory at Hastings might have decided the fate of England, but not of London. The city would eventually fall, but William took note of the lesson: Londoners were proud and ready to make any sacrifice necessary to keep what they saw as their autonomy; it would be best to keep them onside. Though William built a defensive castle, the White Tower (now the Tower of London), to keep an eye on the Londoners and subjugate them, he dared not build it in the city, but erected it instead on land beyond the city limits. The Londoners still resented it as an affront to their liberty. And though William and later kings granted them charters,[2] they resented those, too, since they implied that the king of England had the authority to grant them.

So Thomas, son of Gilbert and Matilda Becket, was a Londoner — a man who cherished his autonomy and freedom and, if necessary, was prepared to fight to preserve what he believed was his. His proud Norman blood may well have enforced that determination. His father, Gilbert, hailed from Thierville, a town southwest of the city of Rouen, and was from the knightly class; his mother, Matilda, was a native of Caen.[3] Gilbert had made a career for himself as a textile merchant in Rouen, and he may have met the young Matilda there. There is speculation that Matilda may have been from a wealthy family and of a higher social standing than Gilbert;[4] if so, he improved his prospects in marrying her. They are believed to have been in their early twenties when they married sometime before 1110, young enough to leave Normandy and immigrate to London to start a new and prosperous life, as had many other Normans who were settling there since the invasion. The couple found a home in Cheapside, not far from Saint Paul's Cathedral; there, Gilbert continued to work as a textile merchant until he found a new interest and income in the property business.

Thomas was born in the family home in Cheapside on December 21, most likely in 1120,[5] and was baptized later that day at the Church of Saint Mary Colechurch, which was just next door to the Becket home. Given that babies were usually baptized a few days after birth, Thomas's quick baptism may be an indication that he was sickly, or at least that his parents feared he was. As it was the feast of Saint Thomas the Apostle,[6] he was given that name. It must be noted that though Thomas is often referred to as Thomas Becket, he never actually used what is now regarded as his surname; indeed, there is evidence that he may have disliked it. The name *Becket* derives from the diminutive of the French word *bec*; its origin is not certain, though there are three theories.[7] The first, not the most pleasant one, maintains that *Becket* referred to a physical trait within the family — a rather prominent, beaklike nose. *Beak* in French is *bec*, so "Beaky." Thomas did indeed have that feature, and the fact that he did not use Becket and his enemies did may lend credence to this theory, or at least to Thomas's and his enemies' belief in it. The second theory is less embarrassing, in that *Becket* may refer to the Norman name for a brook, *bec*. A third theory suggests that the name may be derived from a town or area in France called Bec, of which there are many. Thomas's father would have had connections with Bec in Normandy,[8] and his family may have had its ancestral origins there. The truth may never be known. What is known is that Thomas never used the name, though his father did. During his lifetime, he was known as Thomas of London until his appointment as archbishop, when he became known as Thomas of Canterbury. The form à Becket was never used by or of Gilbert or Thomas; it is, in fact, a later invention, perhaps contrived in imitation of Thomas à Kempis, author in the fifteenth century of *The Imitation of Christ*.

Thomas was one of four surviving children born to the couple; his three sisters were Agnes, Rose (or Roheise), and Mary.[9] As the couple's only son, he was the apple of Gilbert's eye, but Matilda was particularly devoted to him, and it was his close relationship with his mother that would prove most influential in his life. Contemporary biographies of the martyr present Matilda as an extraordinary figure. She is, for example, credited with various dreams or visions that seemed to foretell her son's future glory. In his biography of Thomas, written a year or so after the martyrdom, which he witnessed and tried to prevent, Edward Grim[10] details some of these phenomena.[11] He relates, first of all, that after she conceived Thomas, Matilda had a vision in which she saw the River Thames, which flows through London, flowing within her. Fearful,

Matilda believed this was an evil omen, but when she sought counsel from a man of God, she was told that one born of her would rule over many people. Another wise person offered a supplementary insight: She would soon receive a stream of graces that would be like a river irrigating the land in the manner of the Gospel teaching that the one who is thirsty should come to Christ so that fountains of living water should flow out of Christ into him (cf. Jn 7:37–38). Matilda was deeply comforted by these explanations, but more visions were to come.[12]

Grim recounts a second vision in which Matilda is brought to Canterbury, and as she tries to enter the cathedral there, her womb begins to swell with her child to such an extent that she cannot enter the building. Again, she was distressed — did this mean that she was unworthy to enter a church?[13] A subsequent vision given to her, Grim explains, banished this fear. As she was preparing for the birth, she had a vision of twelve stars of extraordinary brightness falling from the sky onto her lap. Grim interprets this vision not only as prophesying Thomas's greatness but also a sign that Thomas will preside over the world at the Last Judgment with those twelve elect lights of heaven.[14]

A final vision related by Grim seems to signify Thomas's prominence. In this dream, Matilda sees her son lying in his crib naked. Rebuking the nurse caring for him, Matilda is told by the nurse that he is covered; there is a noble purple cloth folded over him. To make sure that he is covered properly, Matilda and the nurse attempt to unfold the cloth, but discover that the room is too small for them to do so; they try to unfold it in other rooms, but they are also too small. Eventually, they go out into Smithfield, a large open space in London, but that place is not big enough either. Failing to find a large enough space, they hear a voice from heaven that tells them that all their efforts are in vain — not even all England is large enough to contain this purple cloth.[15]

These visions and dreams have to be regarded with caution. While they cannot be completely dismissed, they are recounted by a biographer who not only wished to understand and celebrate the life of a martyr but also sought to defend a man whose life at that point in time posed more questions than it answered. Many medieval hagiographies employed such mystical phenomena to hail both God's singular blessing on their subject from infancy and their subject's future greatness, so Grim or others may have invented these stories to add luster to the archbishop. That said, it is not beyond the realm of possibility that these stories contain a germ of truth, preserving some less prophetic dreams Matilda may have had during the course of her pregnancy. There are historians who are of the opinion that these dreams are just fanciful elements of medieval hagiography and there is a sound basis for that opinion.[16]

Whatever her mystical experiences may or may not have been, Matilda Becket was a pious woman who took her responsibilities as a Christian mother seriously, and her efforts in this regard would prove fruitful, instilling in her son a simple but authentic piety that would remain even in his most extravagant years. In this, Matilda almost certainly set her son on the road to holiness and prepared him for the conversion that lay ahead. Whatever doctrines he learned as student, deacon, priest, and bishop, it was Matilda's own living of her faith and her deep devotion to the Mother of God that most profoundly affected Thomas. Many years later, he would speak most fondly of her, once saying to his friend John of Salisbury that it was from her lips that his first lessons in godliness came. He also mentioned her love of Our Lady, a love that had instilled itself in his heart through her example.[17] Some of Thomas's biographers have speculated that though he was surrounded by women, in his life, he had a close relationship with only two: his mother and the Mother of God.[18] The nature of those relationships may well have preserved him in the years to come.

Matilda was Thomas's first teacher. Being of noble stock and a draper's wife, she would have had a rudimentary education to assist her husband in the day-to-day running of their business. If she came from a family socially superior to her husband's, she may have been better educated than he was. She passed these skills on to Thomas, who proved to be an amenable and able student. While reading and arithmetic formed part of her curriculum, Matilda's primary focus was the fundamentals of the Christian faith and teaching her son how to pray. Thomas and his sisters were brought to Mass each Sunday, and the family prayed every day. A love for the poor and the practice of charity were urged on the children. When he was three, his mother weighed Thomas and from then on would give the value of his weight in alms, often urging him to go out to visit the poor and give the alms himself.[19] He was taught that the measure of who he was as a person and a Christian depended on the measure of his charity. For the rest of his life, Thomas would hold to his mother's example; even when immersed in the ways of the world, he remained true to prayer and charity, regularly seeking out those in need and giving alms, often lavishly.

Though there were tensions between the native Londoners and the Normans, Thomas and his generation seemed to marry the two traditions quite successfully. The family home was notably Norman and comfortable by contemporary standards. The family members spoke French among themselves at home but used English when speaking to the servants and for relationships and business outside the house.[20] As a property owner and landlord, Gilbert had some standing within the community, and he was so well respected that he was elected to serve as a sheriff in the city. Thomas would have grown up with a sense of privilege thanks to his father's success, and as he grew older, he would have expected to become important and influential himself.

By the time he was seven, Matilda had exhausted all she could teach him, and the decision was made to send him to the local parish elementary school, called a "song school."[21] There, under the master, Thomas improved his literacy and arithmetic and learned Latin, which was the language of learning and the language of the Church; almost all documents at that time were written in Latin. The curriculum for such schools also included basic logic and rhetoric, and perhaps other subjects such as geometry and music. Given Thomas's position in society, his teachers would have tried to equip him for a career in business or law, so rhetoric, grammar, and logic were indispensable.

When Thomas was ten, Gilbert enrolled him in the newly founded school at the Augustinian Merton Priory in Surrey, fifteen miles southwest of London.[22] He was most likely a boarder, since the journey to the priory would have been too long to accomplish twice a day.[23] While the Augustinians were still engaged in constructing their buildings at the time he was there, the school had already earned a considerable reputation. The priory was founded in 1114 by a sheriff of Surrey, Gilbert Norman, with the permission and assistance of King Henry I. In 1117, the Augustinian Canons Regular of Huntington took possession of the priory and founded the school.[24] Among its early students was Nicholas Breakspear, who entered the school five years before Thomas in 1125; he would be more famously known as Pope Adrian IV (reigned 1154–1159), the only Englishman to be elected to the papacy.[25]

If Gilbert wanted his son to excel, then his attending one of the new, prestigious, and fashionable schools was a necessity. Matilda was also anxious to ensure that Thomas had the best education they could provide, so perhaps a school renowned for its rigor and away from London seemed ideal. At Merton, the young student received a classical education, and it seems he thrived; his singular talents were uncovered. He had a retentive memory and a brilliant mind. His biographer "Roger of Pontigny"[26] relates that Thomas at this time had a singular grace and a powerful intellect. As he grew strong in body, his mind advanced even further. He developed an ability to work out difficult problems and understand complex ideas, surpassing his fellow students with a particular sharpness of mind. Though he suffered from a stammer, which he would have all his life, for Thomas it was not an impediment at all, but an aid to his growing charm. Gifted with subtlety and keen perception, he was admired by many.[27] That said, for all his ability, he was, like many students before and after him, inclined to laziness, depending on his natural giftedness to get him through, which it did a little too often, much to the chagrin of his teachers.

After two years at Merton, Thomas returned to London to attend grammar school.[28] There were three of these in the city: Saint Paul's, Saint Mary-le-Grand, and Saint Mary-le-Bow. It is mostly likely that he attended Saint Mary-le-Bow, which was not far from his home, though Saint Paul's, attached to Saint Paul's Cathedral, was not too far away either. These schools were highly respected and known for their professionalism regarding study; they also promoted a certain freedom, even headiness, in the lives of their students, who were encouraged to engage in friendly rivalry as a means of preparing them for the world. Disputations and competitions were the order of the day as students were urged to work hard in order to excel and triumph over their rivals. Humor, wit, and play were nurtured, and though certain extremes usually went unchecked in the spirit of freedom, each young man was expected to be able to respond to jests poked against him and give as good as he got. It was an atmosphere Thomas would have reveled in. Rather than earning a reputation of unleashing young, wild men about town, these schools were admired by the officials and citizens of London and their students often envied for the fun and opportunities they had.

Growing up in the city, Thomas would have had a hectic social life. The eternal bustle of the medieval capital of England held many curiosities and pleasures for young men.[29] As the son of a well-to-do businessman, Thomas had every opportunity to engage in these diversions. Through his father, he was acquainted with a number of notable and wealthy figures, and these formed his social circle. Londoners engaged in various sports and games in their free time. Sundays were days of particular amusement, and the city dwellers often went out to the fields outside the city walls to engage in sports not permitted by the city authorities. Thomas was part of that migratory crowd and would have enjoyed the various sports. The young men were particularly fond of military-style games, mock tournaments, wrestling, and fencing. Horseracing was another obsession, and it was at Smithfield, then outside the city, that Thomas was introduced to riding.

One curious incident, noted by his secretary and biographer Herbert of Bosham,[30] occurred at this time in Thomas's life: a vision of the Blessed Virgin. This story may well serve the same purpose as Grim's accounts of Matilda's prophetic visions or dreams, but it is worth noting. According to Herbert, Thomas was laid low in bed with a fever when he perceived a woman standing at the side of his bed. Holding two keys in her hand, the woman offered them to him, saying, "These are the keys of paradise of which you shall have charge hereafter." Herbert maintains that he heard this from Thomas himself, and he may have.[31] Whatever the veracity of the story, the vision certainly reflects his destiny, and as he grew to maturity, Thomas developed a deep faith in that destiny, though it would differ greatly from that destiny revealed in Herbert's story of the vision. But for now, life was good for Thomas of London. Everything was going according to plan — be it Thomas's plan or Gilbert's. A good life of success, influence, and wealth lay ahead of him.

3
Our Friend Richer

Thomas was growing into a very tall, dark, and handsome young man — he would be well over six feet in his maturity. The nose that made him self-conscious at times and led his enemies to call him "Beaky" did not distract from his fine features; indeed, it lent him an air of sophistication and nobility. His stammer enhanced rather than diminished his charm and elegance. He had engaging, bright eyes and was pale in complexion. Though he was devil-may-care in his attitude and becoming more confident as he grew older, drawing people to him, there was always something distant about him. The historian Dom David Knowles[1] has noted that while Thomas was well respected and deeply admired by those who knew him — even his enemies knew there was something formidable about him — few spoke of loving him, the exceptions being Theobald of Bec, archbishop of Canterbury, and Henry II.[2] There seems to have been something in him that kept people somewhat at a distance. This distance lent him an enigmatic air and, over time, would lead people to misunderstand him and his motives.

Despite his stature, Thomas's health was mediocre. From an early age, he developed a problem with digestion, a common ailment given the health hazards of the time, particularly when it came to food and its preparation. Thomas would have to keep an eye on what he ate and drank, as he discovered in one incident that almost cost him his life — one bad drink could trigger a serious reaction. He learned to steer clear of cider and wine, rarely imbibing them and preferring beer, which was less risky.[3] While his biographers note that Thomas was modest and pleasant in his speech, they also relate that he loved a good time. Despite his budding nobility, he had a weakness for frivolity and fine garb. He was gregarious, enjoying the company of others, and was always at the center of buffoonery and pranks. This joie de vivre brought him to the attention of another wild spirit, Richer II, Lord de L'Aigle, a Norman nobleman more commonly known as Richer de L'Aigle.

Richer was an aristocrat to his fingertips and reveled in the life and influence of the minor nobility. He was also a restless and turbulent man involved in numerous disputes and political machinations. Born in L'Aigle, Normandy, sometime around 1095,[4] he was the eldest son of Gilbert, Lord de L'Aigle, and his wife, Julianna of Perche. The family was wealthy and well connected: Not only was Richer the descendant of the noble Barons de L'Aigle, but also his mother was the daughter of Geoffrey II, the Count of Perche, a veteran of the Battle of Hastings, a prominent landowner in England, and the founder of a leper colony. As respected courtiers, the de L'Aigle family seem to have had their fingers in a number of pies and, not content to remain in the background serving greater lords, made forays into royalty themselves. Richer's sister, Marguerite, would marry the king of Pamplona (later Navarre), García V, and become the mother of King Sancho VI. However, the de L'Aigle family influence waned in Navarre thanks to Marguerite's extramarital affairs before her early death in 1141. While her widowed husband and his realm may not have mourned her deeply, her daughter Marguerite remembered her with great fondness. It seems adventure, unpredictability, and a refusal to conform were essential traits of the de L'Aigles.

Richer's family had a tradition of service to the Norman dukes. His paternal great-grandfather Engenulf had been in service to William the

Conqueror during William's invasion of England in 1066 and given his life for the duke's cause at the Battle of Hastings. His father, Gilbert, had been in service to Henry I, for which he was given Pevensey Castle and its estates in Sussex to add to lands he already possessed in Normandy. When he inherited the English lands on his father's death, Richer had clashed with Henry I, who had expressed his preference that Engenulf and Geoffrey, the two younger de L'Aigle brothers, take over their father's English lands. In response, Richer defied the king and nurtured a relationship with King Louis VI of France, Henry's rival, to gain a royal ally to his cause. Not afraid to play rough in the game of politics, Richer eventually led a rampage against King Henry, attacking his neighbors and laying waste to their land. Richer's uncle had to intervene to resolve the dispute, but Richer emerged the victor. Another scrap with King Stephen — Stephen of Blois — during the Anarchy[5] would see him lose his Sussex estates again; but his was a charmed life, and he eventually won them back. He would remain for many the proof that it was possible to face down a king, though a cool head, clever stratagem, and the nerve to risk it all on the venture were necessary in the fray.

Richer also knew tragedy: His brothers Engenulf and Geoffrey had both perished in the sinking of the *White Ship*. As the horrors for the doomed passengers unfolded, Geoffrey was managing to hold out in the waters; but just before he could be rescued, he succumbed to hypothermia and slipped down to his death. Even in the midst of the tragedy that would cause such chaos in England, the de L'Aigle family had its part to play.

Richer held lands near Thierville in Normandy, near the Abbey of Bec; it was perhaps through these possessions that he came to know Gilbert Becket, and it was through his father that Thomas became acquainted with the dashing Norman lord. Richer was a regular visitor to the Becket house in Cheapside, staying with the family whenever he was on his way to or from Normandy and his Sussex estates.[6] During evening conversations, young Thomas, entranced by the exuberant aristocrat who seemed wild and honorable at the same time, drank in Richer's stories of his exploits and family history. Richer may have recognized a kindred spirit in Thomas, for the two became fast friends even though

L'Aigle was probably in his mid- to late thirties at this time and Thomas in his early teens.

The nature of this relationship has been questioned: Why would a successful and wealthy lord take an interest in the young son of a former draper and landlord?[7] By the time the two met around 1131, Richer was a married man with children. Though some have recently seen a less-than-savory interest here, there is no evidence of it. Without doubt, Richer saw a young man who reminded him of himself, one who was as ambitious but lacked the privilege of a noble family. He saw a possible protégé, which Thomas would indeed become. The Becket scholar Frank Barlow suggests that Thomas may have acted as a substitute for his two dead brothers — Richer may have desired a brother figure to share his interests and sports.[8] It is also possible that Richer saw in Thomas a young man who could go far and thought it might be wise not only to guide him in his path but also to make a connection that could prove useful in the years ahead. Whatever the reasons, there seems to have been a genuine affection between the two. As for Thomas, he was completely dazzled by the baron and saw in him a model for his own ideals.

As much as he found it necessary to engage in the sport of politics and king baiting, Richer loved country sports even more, and Thomas came to enjoy this entertainment as passionately as his new mentor. He may have loved the temptations of the city, but Thomas soon found these country pursuits vastly more exciting and engaging than any game at Smithfield. On his estates in Sussex, Richer introduced Thomas, on holidays from school, to hunting and hawking, games that would thrill and entertain him for the rest of his life. He became very fond of horses, and it was noted later in his life that he was a fine horseman; his skills were no doubted perfected during these forays into the landscape of the Sussex estates. Thomas not only embraced these country pursuits but also acquired a fondness for the life of ease — the lordly life and all its attendant pleasures. Richer was only too keen to form what he may have seen as a fellow pilgrim in this lifestyle, much to the discomfort, it seems, of Thomas's parents.

Matilda and Gilbert may well have had cause for concern. Under Richer's influence, their little boy was changing. Matilda would have noticed a less pious streak appear in her son, one that was undermining the humility she had tried to instill in him.[9] As he grew in confidence, he may have become more aristocratic in his bearing. That might not be an advantage to the son of a London landlord who would have to make his way in the world; it could win him enemies. Time away from study may also have been a problem, and although the trips to the country occurred during holiday time, he may have been prone to distractions when in school, which would not have helped his inherent laziness. While Gilbert may have reveled in his son's new connection, he would have noticed that this relationship was one centered on pleasure and not vocational advancement. If Becket senior had any reservations, it may have been the fear that Richer's mentoring would not be confined to the horse and the hawk.[10]

The couple would have been more concerned if they had known their son was getting into serious scrapes during his time in the country. His keenness for the hunt had led him to take risks in pursuit of his prey. One incident is recalled in the biographies. While out hawking with Richer one day, Thomas ended up in a millstream and almost drowned, much to the horror of his mentor. One account maintains that he fell off his horse as he was crossing a narrow bridge. Another version has him actually jumping into the water to save a prize hawk. According to this version, Thomas's horse stumbled, and the hawk fell into the millstream, caught up in its cord and unable to free itself. Loath to lose the bird, he dived in after it. Though the versions differ, both are possible, given his budding unruliness. He found himself in difficulty as the stream pulled him toward a millwheel.[11] He was rescued in time, but this incident reveals the dangers he willingly risked for his sports; there was a streak of recklessness in him that others would comment on later in his disputes.

Despite such incidents, Thomas loved his time in the country. Falconry would become one of his great loves, and the thrill of the chase excited him. He came to life in the camaraderie of his fellow hunters and with the chatter of the retainers. He was fit and young, and the hunt provided him with the means to relish his strength and develop his skills. He learned to wrestle and fence; he was successful and often triumphed over his opponents. He also grew to love the life of privilege — rubbing shoulders with the nobility, sampling the treats of a life that was beyond his father's means. The presumption of a higher status in society appealed to him. In Richer's company and with his set, the world offered new possibilities, sweeter things, and a greater freedom.

It was not to last. Either due to their concern, or as part of their plan for his life, around 1139 Gilbert and Matilda decided to send Thomas off to Paris to continue his studies. It was the end of the halcyon days in Sussex and of the intimate relationship with his dangerous and exciting mentor. But the two would meet again, most crucially in 1164 during the crisis over the Constitutions of Clarendon;[12] then, Thomas and Richer would be on opposite sides. Richer would go on to survive his former protégé by six years, long enough to see him canonized. Was he, like many others, amazed at Thomas's stubbornness and refusal to give in to the king? Did he perhaps see himself and his own rebellious disposition at play in the archbishop? And what did Richer make of the miracles at his tomb? We shall never know.

Richer continued to live his life of rebellion and pleasure. His relationship with King Henry II was tense, and he fell afoul of the monarch on more than one occasion. In 1173, he was in revolt against Henry's son, Henry the Young King, and though his rebellion failed, he managed to hold onto his possessions. He married Beatrix d'Estouteville, by whom he had four children. In his later years, Richer became quite religious and began to lament his wayward life. In his remorse, he turned to charitable activities and endowed priories and monasteries. He died on August 24, 1176, and was buried in the Benedictine priory of Saint Sulpice-sur-Risle near the family seat at L'Aigle. His eldest son, also Richer, inherited the titles and estates, but when his grandson, Gilbert, died without heirs in 1231, the de L'Aigle Norman estates were taken by the crown.

4

The Anarchy

On December 22, 1135, Stephen of Blois, nephew of the recently deceased King Henry I, had himself crowned king of England in Westminster Abbey; a couple of weeks later he attended the burial of Henry I at Reading Abbey.[1] While he was supported by many lords and barons of England, the country held its breath: How would the other person who claimed the throne react? The idea of a woman reigning was not a comfortable one for some of those concerned with political stability; to them, Empress Matilda, though daughter of King Henry, widow of the Holy Roman emperor and now wife of the Count of Anjou, did not have what it would take to govern a tetchy and often chaotic realm like England.

Son of William the Conqueror, Henry I had been an extraordinarily competent king. Though he had had his problems, he had brought stability, peace, and security to his realms, Normandy and England, and sought to establish a strong dynasty; the *White Ship* tragedy, though, put an end to that. No mere autocrat, he had been intelligent and a little educated, and he had tended to avoid excess (except when it came to women and cruelty), which was a major bonus among monarchs. He had taken whatever steps were necessary to safeguard what he saw as his God-given right to rule, and anyone who had opposed him in any way had been dealt with mercilessly, regardless of who they were, as Saint Anselm, archbishop of Canterbury,[2] found to his cost. Henry's running such a tight ship had augured hope for the future, but when the heir to the throne is lost and the subjects have divided loyalties over a successor, a peaceful future is not assured.

As Henry had made a point of acknowledging his daughter as his heir, he did not expect any opposition.[3] Matilda was his flesh and blood, and he may also have recognized that if pushed, she could prove herself to be her father's daughter; but England did not know that yet. However, once he was dead and sealed in his tomb at Reading Abbey, it was up to others to decide who should occupy the throne. Stephen made a dash for it and made sure that the oil of anointing was poured over him with what some regarded as unseemly haste.[4] While some forces within England saw him as a stronger candidate and were happy to see him crowned, other forces — armed forces — were gathering on the continent to press Matilda's claim. The stage was set for civil war, for what historians would later call the Anarchy, and though it was a war between potential monarchs, it would affect the lives and destinies of countless souls, both English and Norman, including Thomas, still a young boy in school in London.

Stephen's claim, Matilda's supporters insisted, was infamy and treachery. He had promised to uphold her right of succession and to support her should she have trouble establishing her reign. Instead, he rushed to England, called a mass meeting of the citizens of London, and, painting a picture of dire political unrest, urged them to elect him as king. He was aware that he had to have the support of London if his campaign to claim the crown was to be successful.[5] They elected him king; the city's citizens took an oath to help him with their resources and to protect him, and they would remain his loyal subjects in the years to come.[6] Following a hasty coronation, Stephen issued a charter of liberties to repay his supporters, promising them that he would respect all the laws and customs of the kingdom that had been established during the reign of their beloved and saintly King Edward the Confessor, the Anglo-Saxon who reigned from 1042 to 1066. It was a wise move because Stephen needed allies. His brother, Henry of Blois, the bishop of Winchester, tried to smooth things over by attempting to convince the barons who had made oaths supporting Matilda that these oaths could, in good conscience, be set aside for the sake of the realm. Meanwhile, Stephen was preparing a charter guaranteeing the liberties of the Church in the hope of keeping the bishops onside.

At this time, Matilda was in Anjou, occupied with family life and unable to drop everything and hurry to London to stake her claim; she did not think she needed to do so since Stephen had pledged his loyalty to her. When news of Stephen's betrayal reached her, she was furious. She was indeed Henry's daughter, and she was not prepared to allow her cousin to usurp what she knew was hers. Her husband, Geoffrey, was as equally put out. He was a schemer, and he had hitched his ambitions to his wife's wagon. Why be Count of Anjou alone when you could also be consort to a monarch, an influential consort — perhaps even a king consort? Stephen could not be allowed to get in the way of his hopes. However, as revenge is a dish best served cold, the scheme to overthrow the treacherous cousin would need to be carefully planned and carried out. For the time being, there was little Matilda and Geoffrey could do, so they merely moved to claim disputed dowry castles and bided their time.[7] In the meantime, Geoffrey took up his eldest son's claim to the Duchy of Normandy and thereby put the next generation on a sound footing to drive home any successes Matilda would have in her campaign. Safe in England for now, Stephen could do little to prevent Matilda from taking the Norman possessions, but he would have been a fool to think she would leave it at that.

Stephen reigned in relative peace for three years, but they were revealing years. While he had been quick off the mark, he lacked the ability to reign effectively. His leadership skills were tenuous, and though he seemed capable, generous, and gregarious, he was in reality mistrustful of others, weak, and manipulative. He relied on a small group of barons for advice; these were his personal friends on whom he lavished favors while alienating the other barons, freezing them out of the life of the court. Stephen made enemies of powerful men who could have supported him and lent legitimacy to his reign. He was a man who nurtured appearances — protocol was strictly enforced — but he was deficient in many areas of the craft of statesmanship. His divisive reign had a destabilizing effect on England, and as Normandy appeared to be lost to him, he seemed to forget this major territory of his supposed realm. For the first fifteen months of his reign, he did nothing with Normandy; when he did return there with an army of mercenaries to stake his claim, he discovered he had lost any chance of a foothold.

One of those he alienated was Robert, Earl of Gloucester, Matilda's half-brother. Interestingly, though Robert took an oath to his father King Henry to support his sister's claim to the throne, when the king died, he initially wavered rather than publicly stand by his half-sister. He had made the homage to Stephen, albeit reluctantly.[8] Robert was one of the most important peers in England and would have been an ideal ally, but Stephen's botched attempt to assassinate him, according to Robert, finally pushed the earl over to Matilda.[9] Penitent for his disloyalty, he would prove to be her chief and fiercest supporter in England, as she would have expected all along.

The only party to benefit from Stephen's reign was the Church, which was able to gain liberties and properly enforce the reforms of Pope Saint Gregory VII, who had tried to limit the role of monarchs in the governance of the Church.[10] In 1136, Stephen granted the Church a charter in which he ceded into the hands of the bishops all judgment and power over ecclesiastical persons and their possessions and all ecclesiastical appointments.[11] This was an extraordinary concession from the perceived royal prerogative, one that would prove problematic for Stephen's successors, but it fulfilled the requirements of Pope Gregory's reforms. The charter further decreed that candidates for the episcopacy were to be chosen without royal interference; that no act of fealty to the monarch was required from new bishops, not even for their lands and estates; and that there were to be no restrictions on appeals to the pope. Bishops were also free to travel to Rome to meet the pope, where previously such journeys were restricted. Finally, Church councils could be called without royal consent. The bishops could not believe their luck when he promulgated this charter. Perhaps some were saying to themselves that his reign could not last; they would be proved correct in that.

Another who held such sentiments regarding Stephen's reign was the Empress Matilda. She was wise to wait; her patience and continued insistence on her claim won her allies among the barons. When Robert of Gloucester came to her cause in 1138, she knew it was time to strike. Submitting a formal appeal to Rome, she asked the pope to intervene and ensure that Stephen be held to the solemn oath he had taken. When Stephen heard of this move, he realized he needed to consolidate support within the court, and so began a purge of officials who had served Henry and could therefore no longer be trusted. He purged barons and bishops alike, seizing their property, looting their coffers, and adding to the list of his enemies.[12] Meanwhile, on September 30, 1139, as Thomas was on his way to carefree days in Paris, Matilda, arriving from the continent with her army, set foot on a beach just south of Arundel Castle in the South Downs in England; the civil war had begun.[13]

Matilda's invasion truly initiated anarchy. England was already unstable and divided; her presence made things worse. A number of disaffected barons joined her cause, but they were few, and many of them wanted to unseat Stephen rather than support the legitimate candidate to the throne. England split in two. Matilda had a number of successes at first; as her army advanced up the country, Stephen's forces were unable to hold their ground or recapture what she had taken. However, she did not have the strength to defeat Stephen and take control of England. While she had her first major victory in 1141, capturing the city and castle of Lincoln and kidnapping Stephen himself, the effort was doomed to failure.[14] With her nemesis in captivity, she dubbed herself "Lady of the English" and began to make arrangements for her coronation in Westminster. Interestingly, Stephen's brother Henry of Blois, bishop of Winchester, came over to her side, as did many of the king's barons, who may have concluded that the end had come for the usurper.

Flush with victory, Empress Matilda did not reckon on one force that could be turned against her: Stephen's wife, Queen Matilda,[15] a woman scorned who roused what was left of Stephen's forces and made a spirited attack on Empress Matilda's army. Meanwhile, Empress Matilda was now arguing with the bishop of Winchester, and she did not impress her new-found allied barons with her arrogance. It was when she refused to grant the independent-minded Londoners financial concessions that things really turned sour. They chased her out of the city; she was reclining on a couch, waiting for dinner when the bells of London began to ring, announcing the attack of Londoners. She had just fled her accommodation when a mob broke into her apartment and began to loot it. She fled for the safety of Oxford. [16] If that were not enough, her brother Robert tried to settle scores with the bishop of Winchester by besieging the bishop's diocesan seat and was captured in the attempt. When a request for a prisoner exchange arrived, Empress Matilda knew her situation was unraveling. As she traded King Stephen for Robert, she likely saw that she was losing whatever grip she had on power.[17] By November 1142, under siege in her castle in Oxford, she knew her campaign was in tatters.

Her husband, Geoffrey, was faring much better. His campaign in Normandy was meeting with success as he conquered one city after another, pressing his son Henry's claim.[18] That he left devastation in his wake and rendered Normandy a wasteland seems to have been lost on him. His accomplishments allowed him to come to his wife's rescue, and so he promised to send three hundred knights to her aid; however, she was still waiting for them at Christmas in 1142. No doubt frustrated by cabin fever and the tardiness of her husband, Matilda made a risky decision — she would slip out of the castle in Oxford and make her way to Abingdon. In the dead of night, covered in a white cloak, she managed to creep out past the guards, and, camouflaged in the snow, she traipsed the eight miles to friends who were waiting for her.[19] Spirited away to the West Country, Matilda lived to fight another day and prolong England's agony.

Gathering fresh troops, she reengaged Stephen, but she was too weak to overcome him, and he was too weak to defeat her. England descended into a stalemate as two courts emerged with a claimant to the throne in each. Public order dissolved into chaos; the rule of law stood for nothing. England was divided three ways: those loyal to Stephen, those loyal to Matilda, and those loyal to no one but themselves. It was indeed anarchy.

Taking advantage of the situation, King David I of Scotland[20] invaded the north of England, annexing Westmorland, Cumberland, and Northumberland. Foreign soldiers invaded various areas of England, attacking and ravaging the people, as there was no real army to defend them. Flemish mercenaries arrived and seized castles with their estates and assets. Hordes of violent ne'er-do-wells terrorized and robbed the simple folk of the country. In an attempt to safeguard their homes, possessions, and livelihoods, landowners took whatever measures were necessary to defend themselves.

While England was falling around their ears, Stephen and Matilda tried to lend legitimacy to their administrations. Both set up official governments, issued decrees, and passed laws — to no effect. They minted their own coin, ran their own courts, and established their own systems of patronage. They even sought to establish diplomatic relations with other realms. It was all a charade, a delusion. Finally, at the beginning of 1148, Matilda decided to return to Normandy.[21] She was not giving up on her claim, but she had had enough; it was time for someone else to take up the cause. She made her way to the priory of Notre-Dame-du-Pré, just outside Rouen, to spend her remaining years in peace and quiet. Stephen may have thought that he had won, that he had finally rooted her out through an exasperating stalemate. But it was not to be so. Matilda passed the baton to her eldest son, Henry of Anjou, who was now sixteen and often called FitzEmpress after his mother.[22] His father had successfully pressed his claim for Normandy, but the young prince could now take up his own campaign for England. Stephen would not know what was coming until it hit him. Henry of Anjou was no Matilda; he aimed to be Henry II, his grandfather's true heir in every respect, and he could be just as brutal and unforgiving.

5

Paris

As Thomas was romping around Sussex, his father, Gilbert, was planning how to prepare his only son for a life of work. His mother,
Matilda, also harbored dreams of greatness for him, while growing ever
more concerned for his well-being. Ambitious for Thomas, and perhaps
all too aware of his inherent laziness and his new love for the privileged
life, they plucked the young man from his life of pleasure, with all its attendant foibles and dangers, and packed him off to Paris to continue his
education, most likely in the fall of 1139. Less fortunate contemporaries
were already engaged in earning a living, perhaps married and struggling to raise families; Thomas had had a much easier life.

Paris was the ideal place for an ambitious father to send a bright
and promising son.[1] Even in medieval times, it was a glamorous city. A
cosmopolitan hub, it attracted people from all over Europe for business
and pleasure. Among the most fascinating institutions within the city
were the emerging schools where scholars took up positions to teach the
brightest minds in Europe. The University of Paris would become one of

the most renowned academic institutions in the world and a major theological center for the Church for many centuries. It would educate vast
numbers of young men — popes, theologians, saints, and royalty among
them. Among its greatest teachers would be Saint Albert the Great and
his student Saint Thomas Aquinas, who would write much of his *Summa
contra Gentiles* during his first stint as a master in the university in the
middle of the next century. When Thomas of London arrived in Paris,
the formal foundation of the university was still sixty years away; what
he found was a constellation of renowned schools, some centered on an
individual master, situated in various places around the city and suburbs
and educating about 2,500 students.

The schools and the eventual university were ecclesiastical foundations, so their students came under the direction of the Church. Those
attending them were tonsured, not to indicate that they had entered
the clerical life, though many of them would, but to signify that they
were now under the protection of the Church. It is not certain whether
the tonsure applied as early as Thomas's sojourn, but his experience of
education in Paris was certainly ecclesiastical, and many of his teachers would have been priests. The quality of the education was second
to none, and the academic life of the city was exciting and innovative,
though not without controversy. Teachers, or masters, were theologians
in their own right, developing their ideas in lectures and composing
treatises that were read throughout the Church. Many of these thinkers
would become highly influential not just in their day but for centuries,
and the writings of a number of these masters laid the foundations of
many of our theological positions today.

Among those educating the future leaders of Europe were Peter
Lombard, the compiler of the *Sentences*, which formed the basis of theological education for centuries; and Peter Abelard, a theologian whose
personal life is now more famous than his theories. Lombard arrived in
Paris in 1134 and was teaching at the cathedral school of Notre Dame;
he was renowned as a theologian by 1144. He would be elected bishop of Paris in 1159. Peter Abelard was a very different sort of man. As
Lombard progressed in the ecclesiastical life and was renowned for his
innovative orthodoxy, Abelard's life and genius were mired in scandal

and accusations of heresy. He had arrived in Paris in 1100 and was taught in the cathedral school of Notre Dame before teaching in various places in France. He had returned to Paris in 1108 to take up a position as master at the cathedral school. From there, he engaged in a number of disputes. It was his affair with a young woman, Hélöise, that led to his downfall. Scandal surrounded their torrid relationship, which produced a child, and even greater infamy awaited Abelard as he faced trial and condemnation for his theological positions. Saint Bernard of Clairvaux was involved in the formal process that eventually led to Abelard's excommunication in 1141. Abelard would die in 1142, but not before the excommunication was lifted and he was reconciled with Bernard.

It is not known where Thomas studied or under which teachers, but it is unlikely that he studied under Peter Lombard, and he certainly did not study under Abelard, though Paris would have been abuzz with news of his trial. It would have been unusual to study in Paris at that time and not seek out the great lights, so even if he was not studying there, Thomas may have gone to the cathedral school to hear Lombard, who was gaining a reputation for his singular method of teaching. But there were other great teachers of note, and if Thomas had had the wit to realize it, he could have attained in Paris all the knowledge, influence, and contacts he needed to carve out a successful and profitable career. One of his early biographers, Guernes de Pont-Sainte-Maxence, a writer known for his meticulous research who wrote his life of Thomas in French and published it four years after the martyrdom, maintains that Thomas did not study theology but rather took courses in the arts.[2] Of the four academic areas in the schools — arts, medicine, law, and theology — arts was considered the lowest. Anne Duggan suggests that Thomas went to Paris not to study the arts curriculum in its entirety, but rather to "cherry pick" some of the advanced courses.[3] Biographers indicate that he may have studied under the great Robert of Melun;[4] his later recommendation for Robert's elevation as bishop could be offered as evidence to suggest that he did. Robert's career would prove interesting and influential for Thomas.

Little is known of Robert's origins, though it is known that he was born in England around 1100. The title he bore, Melun, refers to the town in France where he taught between 1142 and 1147. He was in Paris for most of his career and was considered one of the great *disputatores* of the time.[5] A student of the Parisian schools himself, Robert had studied under Peter Abelard; while he admired Abelard, Robert was strictly orthodox in his writing and teaching. Hugh of Saint Victor, the theologian of the mystical life, had also taught Robert and would influence his work. In 1137, Robert succeeded Peter Abelard as a teacher in the school on Mont Sainte-Geneviève on the Left Bank of the Seine; there he taught and influenced a number of scholars, Thomas's future friend John of Salisbury among them.[6]

Robert was in great demand as a theologian, and because of his orthodoxy and brilliance, he was trusted to adjudicate the questionable works of other scholars. In this role, he opposed the teaching of the bishop of Poitiers, Gilbert de la Porrée, who in his commentary on the work of the early sixth-century Roman theologian Saint Severinus Boethius offered an interpretation of the mystery of the Holy Trinity that seemed to contradict Church teaching. Peter Lombard had raised the alarm about this work, with Saint Bernard of Clairvaux sharing his concerns; the matter was referred to the pope. In 1148, when Pope Eugene III came to Reims to preside over a council — one that Thomas would also attend with Archbishop Theobald of Canterbury — Robert, Saint Bernard, and others were called to a consistory to contest Gilbert's theology. Saint Bernard already had his suspicions about Gilbert, since he had been a defender of Peter Abelard; indeed, he regarded Gilbert as a heretic. Robert was just as vociferous in his opposition to Gilbert's writing. However, while Gilbert was required to recant and change the offending passages in his work, he was not formally condemned as a heretic, much to Robert and Saint Bernard's chagrin, and he returned to his diocese with his reputation unsullied.

Robert would teach in France for forty years, after which he was recalled to England to take up the position of bishop of Hereford in 1163, an appointment in which Thomas was instrumental. Robert would become an uneasy ally of Thomas's in the disputes that lay ahead; but apart from his support, wavering as it would prove to be, there was something vital in one of his works that may have proved valuable for Thomas, though the student may not have noticed it until he was archbishop. His *Quaestiones de Epistolis Pauli*, a commentary on Saint Paul's theology, reflecting on the issue of kings and their subjects' obedience to them, had something interesting to say. While it was accepted that Christians had a duty to submit to secular power — Saint Paul suggests this in his Letter to the Romans (13:1–7), Robert notes that royal power does not excuse tyranny, and Christians must distinguish between the monarch in their person and royal power. If a monarch acts as a tyrant, he then acts impotently.[7] There is no evidence to show that Thomas drew upon this teaching during his conflict with Henry; it would be interesting to know whether he was aware of it and whether it colored his response to Henry in their dispute.

Thomas's life in Paris remains a mystery. Only two people in the historical record claimed to have known him in Paris — the first is Everlin, abbot of Saint Lawrence at Liège. Following Thomas's canonization, Everlin dedicated an altar to him in his abbey church and spoke of their time together in Paris.[8] The second, Ludolf, archbishop of Magdeburg, claimed to have been one of his students.[9] Thomas was never a teacher, so Ludolf must have meant that they were fellow students. One of Thomas's later friends, John of Salisbury, was in Paris at the same time, and though the two often shared memories of the city in their conversations and knew people in common,[10] there is no evidence that they knew each other then — they did not meet until both were working for the archbishop of Canterbury.

Whatever hopes and dreams Matilda had for her son, Thomas had other ideas. Instead of removing him from an aimless life of pleasure, his parents had inadvertently sunk him in the motherlode. While Paris was indeed a fervent grove of learning, it was also a heady center of excess. If Thomas was sulking as he crossed the English Channel, he certainly perked up when he found himself plunged into the vibrant social life of the city; and given his fondness for the high life, he may have been as or more regular a student of the Parisian world of festivity as he was of the lecture hall. Students generally gathered in the various taverns and inns of the city to discuss their day's work, to eat, and to drink. Those who were looking for something more intimate could find it in the taverns or in certain spots outside the city where ladies of the night loitered for business.

There is no doubt that Thomas jumped right into this life. Paris held many temptations, and young men succumbed to them. Yet, for all his love of pleasure, his contemporary biographers note that he remained chaste:[11] Thomas was with the others up to a point, but there were limits, and it seems that casual sex may have been one of them. Some modern biographers believe that he engaged in these pleasures, too[12] — that his contemporary biographers, rather than offend the dignity of the new martyr, spared his blushes in this regard. However, while the early biographers did not concentrate a great deal on these years, they did accept that his student life was less than perfect and hardly virtuous. If he had been as rakish as his fellow students in Paris, these biographers' admitting that he had had sexual experiences in his youth would have enhanced the impact of his conversion and the penitential nature of his life as archbishop; it would have made him another Saint Augustine of Hippo. Also, given that many of Thomas's contemporaries were still alive when the early biographies were written and knew all too well that he had been no saint for much of his life and demonstrated many faults, it would have been counterproductive for his biographers to maintain that he was chaste if it was known he was not.

How he was able to remain chaste when everything seemed against it is unknown. Perhaps his distant and at times cool personality, as noted by some,[13] prevented him from forming close relationships with others and militated against sexual intimacy. He may have been too awkward to engage a prostitute or not particularly interested; it may have been too seedy for his liking. Perhaps his mother had left her mark; his piety drew a line in the sand that he would not cross, though he had crossed many others. Whatever the cause, his refusal to succumb is noteworthy and reveals an aspect of his personality and nature that, though hidden in the years of excess, boded well for the future.

Whoever taught Thomas during his time in Paris and whatever he did, it is obvious that he did not learn a great deal, for when he entered the service of Archbishop Theobald of Canterbury a number of years later, he needed further tutoring to give him the skills to advance. While the schools in Paris gradually developed into the university, taking a degree was not yet heard of in Thomas's day; however, students would reach a point in their education where they could qualify to teach and so would be called *magister*, or master. Clerks who had spent a certain period of time in these schools would normally be addressed as *magister*. Thomas was never styled *magister* in his later employment, and educated colleagues sometimes looked down on him; indeed, his advancement caused jealousy among some because he was deemed unfit, partly because of his lack of education.

That said, Gilbert did not intend his son to be a teacher; he had other plans for him. Thomas was intelligent and possessed natural gifts, so a little education went a long way. He could speak and write Latin; he was fluent in French before he ever set foot in Paris; and he had the basics of a medieval education. Frank Barlow in his biography suggests that Thomas, when royal chancellor in 1155, had the same level of education as an average bishop.[14] It is unclear how much of that education was from Merton Priory and later studies in Canterbury as archbishop's clerk and how much was from his time in Paris, but it may be that his time in Paris was not of great educational benefit to him.

Thomas remained in Paris for about two years. At some point in 1141, when he was twenty-one, devastating news arrived by means of a messenger: His mother had died.

6
Return of the Wastrel

Thomas left Paris, but by the time he returned to London his mother was already buried, and he had to content himself with solitary moments of grief at her tomb. The house seemed empty; everything had changed. Roger of Pontigny in his biography says that Thomas became careless in his studies as a result of Matilda's passing,[1] suggesting that he may not have returned to London upon hearing of his mother's death, but only when the zest of the student life was gone. The period of mourning would prove to be a dark one for father and son; it was also a time of decision for both.

Thomas made up his mind not to return to Paris. Whether that was his initial intention is unknown. Certainly, his mother's death meant that some of the pressure for him to continue was gone, but subsequent events may also have relieved him of whatever urge remained. Gilbert had retired by now, and if he had hopes of living from the rents he charged his tenants, those hopes were quashed as he fell victim to a series of misfortunes, including fires in a number of his properties.[2] Money was not as plentiful as before, and there was not enough in the family coffers to send Thomas back to Paris. The tuition fees might have been manageable, but the son and heir had not been living hand to mouth: Gilbert could no longer afford to keep a young socialite living the good life in Paris.

At the age of twenty-two, Thomas was indeed a young man with prospects. However, in the year after his mother's death, despite his father's hints and then urgings, he made no effort to benefit from his natural abilities. He lazed about at home and around London, intent, as his friend and biographer Herbert of Bosham noted, on the kind of things that are sweet and fashionable.[3] Thomas's only cares at this time were for clothes and his appearance — he wanted to look more fashionable than anyone else. Modern psychologists might see this behavior as a means of coping with his mother's death, and perhaps it was, but it was also entirely in keeping with his character. If, in the wake of his wife's death, Gilbert was exercising patience with his son, then he was a very patient man indeed. However, that patience came to an end after a year. The pressure was on Thomas to grow up and start earning his keep. At his father's insistence, job hunting started and negotiations to find him an employer began. Thomas would now have to pull his weight; his working life was about to begin.

Around 1142, thanks to his father's influence, Thomas was given a position as a clerk in the business of a London banker and sometime merchant, Osbert Huitdeniers, whose last name means "Eightpence," though he was worth considerably more than that.[4] Contemporary biographers refer to Osbert as a relative of Gilbert Becket,[5] and that may explain how Thomas got a position. Osbert remains a shadowy figure in history. Having served as a justiciar, an administrator of justice, he had also been one of the sheriffs of the city (as had Gilbert), and his term of office had just come to an end around the time Thomas came on the job market.

The nature of Osbert's banking is not known. He had made a number of important contacts through his business, and he had connections with the royal court. He was known to have had links with the Angevins — the House of Anjou, that of the future Henry II and his father, Geoffrey. He held land in Kent received from Henry I's son Robert, Earl of

Gloucester; and Empress Matilda is known to have given him land. These gifts indicate that he had won the royal favor, most likely for his service to Matilda and her son's cause during the Anarchy. In fact, he was among a delegation representing London citizens that came to Matilda in 1141 as she was attempting to win the capital to her cause. Osbert, as an associate of her brother Robert, was already in her camp; some even identify him as the head of the pro-Angevin faction in the city, engaged in trying to swing notable citizens to support Matilda's claim. When she lost London's favor and King Stephen was again ascendant, Osbert was forced to find refuge with the Earl of Gloucester on his estates. As he was a refugee from the city for supporting her claim, Matilda granted him a stipend of twenty pounds per annum. By the time Thomas arrived, Osbert was back in business, whatever it was, legal or otherwise.[6]

According to some biographers, Thomas was given the position of secretary to Osbert, coupled with the task of keeping accounts.[7] Some biographers maintain that he did not work for Osbert personally, but rather that Osbert, as sheriff, got him a position in the municipal offices.[8] He would remain in this employment for two or three years, deriving a great deal of experience, particularly in the area of finance, that would prove useful for the positions he held later. Working for a man immersed in the political scene, Thomas would no doubt have been keenly aware of what was happening in England and Normandy.

These years in Osbert's employ would prove important. For one thing, the work and the exposure to the business and political life of England gradually pulled Thomas out of the life of pleasure and enkindled in him an interest in the world. Though little is known about this time, it was one of the most formative in his life, opening new horizons and convincing him that he had ability and that he must get up and use it. He would have become acquainted with the workings of financial affairs, both in the general market and in the civic realm. He also participated in transactions with the royal exchequer and he would have learned a great deal about the system of taxation, the reforms that were already under way in that arena, and perhaps even the financial mollification of kings.

Although he had an income and was busy, Thomas's ambition had returned, and keeping accounts for a banker was gradually losing its sheen — the work did not have enough meat to satisfy his growing hunger for advancement. To his love of fashion and leisure, he now added determination. He wanted to go places, and a clerk's desk in a relative's business was not a springboard to any kind of prestige. It provided only an honest day's work, and even that was questionable if some historians are correct that Osbert's business was more inclined to the shadows than to the light.[9] Thomas was, in short, bored, and he began the search for another, more lucrative position that would enhance his prospects.

Perhaps impressed with his son's newfound enthusiasm for advancement, Gilbert offered his advice and assistance: It was time to move on. This time, he would pull out all the stops, and he could do so because his son was finally hungry for an improvement in his career. But where could Thomas go? For an ambitious man, there were two roads to take. The first was to join the service of the monarch at court. Given that the kingdom was in the midst of the Anarchy and an utter mess, divided between two claimants to the throne, even applying for a position was a political statement and a risk. If Thomas backed the wrong horse, it could be fatal for his prospects. The second road was safer and within reach: the service of the Church, and for the ambitious clerk it had to be the court of the primate of England, the archbishop of Canterbury. That was not an impossible reach for the Beckets because the incumbent, Theobald, former abbot of Bec, was a friend, a fellow native of Thierville, and perhaps even a relation of Gilbert's. Two of Theobald's associates, brothers from Boulogne — Baldwin, archdeacon of Sudbury, and Eustace — were frequent guests at the Becket household, and their support was easily won. All that was required was a quiet word in the ear of the archbishop.[10]

7
Theobald

If Gilbert's[1] advances toward finding a position for his son in the household of the archbishop of Canterbury were successful, Thomas would enter the service of one of the most remarkable men in medieval England, a man who would play an important part in finally bringing the Anarchy to an end. From humble origins, the former monk and abbot of Bec who now occupied the primatial see of England would leave his mark, not just on England and her history but on one destined to become one of England's greatest martyrs.

Theobald of Bec was elected to the see of Canterbury on December 24, 1138, and consecrated archbishop on January 9, 1139, by the papal legate Alberic, cardinal bishop of Ostia. His journey to the primacy of England was an interesting one. He was supported by King Stephen, who chose Theobald over his own brother, Henry of Blois, bishop of Winchester. Stephen feared that Henry, who coveted the office, would use it to control him, and he had enough influence as it was. Perhaps Stephen also understood that Henry was not entirely to be trusted; in 1141, when

Stephen was captured, Henry would go over to Matilda's side in the civil war. Indeed, the king ensured that Theobald's election took place while his brother was in Winchester ordaining deacons.

Theobald was born in Thierville,[2] the same area of Normandy from which Gilbert Becket hailed; the exact date of his birth is unknown, but it is reckoned to be around 1090. Almost nothing is known of his family, but his father is believed to have been a knight, and at least one of his brothers also entered service in the Church: Walter, who became a deacon and later bishop of Rochester. Theobald discerned a vocation to the Benedictine life and entered the Abbey of Bec, which was not far from his home. He lived the life of a regular monk and may have held various offices within the monastic community. He first comes to attention in 1127, when he was appointed prior of the abbey; ten years later, he was elected abbot, though his election did not proceed smoothly. Archbishop Hugh of Rouen, the local bishop, refused to give his consent, claiming that he had not been consulted on the election. Until Theobald had made a profession of obedience, Hugh would not grant the abbatial blessing. The new abbot refused to comply — none of his predecessors had done this; neither would he. For fourteen months both sides held their ground. In the end the abbot of Cluny, Peter the Venerable, negotiated a compromise — Theobald would offer a verbal profession of obedience, and Hugh, forgoing a written profession, would accept it.

The new abbot revealed a strong personality and innate stubbornness, personality traits that would serve him in his work but also create difficulties and enemies. Following his abbatial blessing in 1137, he would serve just one year as abbot before being nominated by King Stephen to the see of Canterbury. Why he was chosen is a mystery. His short tenure as abbot was not enough to allow a proper assessment of his ability to govern anybody, never mind a primatial see. He was pious, learned, and efficient, but there was nothing special about him to recommend him, and he had no family connections. Perhaps his principled stand against Bishop Hugh was seen as a qualifier and marked him out as one who could fulfill the often difficult demands of high office — he might be a strong leader. Theobald could also have been chosen as archbishop because of his abbey's reputation. Bec had provided two archbishops for Canterbury — Lanfranc and Anselm — and both had been outstanding. Lanfranc had been a great servant of the Church and a pillar of support for the new Norman monarchy. The same could not be said of Anselm, who spent most of his administration in conflict with kings over the liberties of the Church, but he had been an extraordinary pastor, renowned for his learning and holiness. So, it seems, Bec had a knack of electing singular abbots who later proved effective as bishops. Given that the monks elected him unanimously and, when that election was threatened with nullification, battened down the hatches in order to keep him, it may have been concluded that there must have been something extraordinary about him.

As soon as he was consecrated archbishop, Theobald traveled to Rome to receive the pallium[3] from Pope Innocent II. While there, he participated in the Second Lateran Council, which took place in April 1139, joining almost a thousand prelates called to deal with issues that had emerged following a recent schism, excommunicate King Roger II of Sicily, and draw up measures to enforce ecclesiastical discipline and morals. When the council concluded, Theobald returned to England to take the helm of the archdiocese and face the numerous difficulties, both ecclesiastical and political, emerging in a kingdom languishing in civil war.

Upon his election, Theobald swore fealty to Stephen and, in doing so, declared where his loyalty lay. He would play a vital role in the Anarchy and its resolution in the years to come. For all his piety, he was not beyond nepotism; as soon as he returned to his archdiocese, he appointed his brother Walter as archdeacon of Canterbury. At this stage in his episcopate, while he could not escape political issues altogether, he was resolved to keep his political participation to a minimum, remaining neutral.[4] But his rival for Canterbury, Henry of Blois, also known as Henry of Winchester, was a much more political animal, and he was intent on making life difficult for Theobald. When the pope made Henry papal legate, things got more complicated for the archbishop. In the legatine office, Henry had a power that exceeded Theobald's in various areas of the Church's life, including the power to call councils, which could be troublesome forums. However, while he was not inclined to dip his toes too often into England's political waters, Theobald would prove himself a force to be reckoned with in his own realm of Church governance. If Stephen thought he had appointed a weakling to the see of Canterbury, he soon discovered his mistake. Though he had served as abbot for only a year, Theobald slipped quite comfortably into the archiepiscopal shoes.

Whatever fears the king may have had, he saw that Theobald was a man of honor. In 1141, when Stephen was in captivity and his brother was sitting at the feet of a triumphant Matilda, the archbishop did not switch allegiance and rush to the camp of the victor. He had taken an oath of fealty, and that could not be discarded for political convenience. He made his way to Bristol, where Stephen was being held, and spoke with the king in person regarding what had to be done. Stephen gave his permission for Theobald to go to Matilda's side; given the circumstances and the archbishop's position, it was the most prudent move for now.[5] When Matilda fell again and her brother Robert was captured, Theobald took a leading part in the negotiations that led to the exchange of Stephen for Robert. Bishop Henry of Winchester then switched sides again and called a council to legitimize Stephen as king, perhaps in an attempt to save himself. It was Theobald who crowned Stephen king at Canterbury Cathedral that Christmas of 1141.

Theobald and Henry of Winchester did not get on, and their dealings with each other were always strained. This had a positive aspect for Canterbury, and for Thomas himself, in that the archbishop had to invest time and resources in gathering a competent and hardworking staff around him to help him deal with a workload that was continually growing, as well as various situations, both ecclesiastical and political, that were intensifying in complexity. Theobald had to fight for his corner of the Church, both in England in the midst of a war of succession, and also in Rome as Bishop Henry unveiled his plans to have Winchester elevated to an archiepiscopal see and a rival to Canterbury. In his more than twenty years of service, Archbishop Theobald would never find rest or even a moment to distract himself from trouble and machinations.

Bishop Henry of Winchester's legatine powers came to an end with the death of Pope Innocent II in September 1143. The election of a new pope, Celestine II, gave Theobald an opportunity to solidify his position by seeking the position of legate for himself. Traveling to Rome, he met with Celestine in March 1144, but failed to secure it. Henry would not be successful either. Celestine died a few days after meeting Theobald and was succeeded by Lucius II. Though his reign was short, he managed to appoint a legate to England. It was neither Theobald nor Henry, however, but an Italian: Cardinal Imar, bishop of Tusculum. Lucius did accede to Henry's request to raise Winchester to an archiepiscopal see and dispatched Imar to oversee it. However, the pope died on February 15, 1145, and with him Henry's chance to become an archbishop, much to Theobald's relief. Imar himself moved on, up, and eventually down as he not only supported an antipope, Victor IV, but also consecrated him, earning an excommunication for his trouble.[6]

The organization of Theobald's service and household was complex.[7] Though Canterbury was his principle residence, the archbishop had other castles and estates that he visited at various times of the year. The archbishop's court, like that of a monarch, was almost nomadic in its constant progress from one residence to another. These residences were situated in the vast estates owned by the see of Canterbury in Kent and in Sussex, Surrey, and Middlesex. Saint Anselm had acquired a property in Lambeth, across the Thames from London, and the archbishop used this when he needed to be near the royal palace at Westminster. Theobald did not use this residence too often, preferring to stay at his manor house at Harrow, just a short ride from London.

The archbishop's entourage was considerable. A crossbearer went before him — this was an important ceremonial and liturgical office that proclaimed the authority and dignity of the archbishop. He had a chancellor; two chaplains, usually monks; and a butler who ran the domestic affairs of the household. Dispensers, a chamberlain, and a steward completed the upstairs domestic staff. Below stairs, the household operated as any feudal lord's service did: cooks governed by a master cook, a baker, ushers, porters, grooms, janitors, numerous kitchen staff, and servants to clean and wash. As a feudal lord and an owner of vast estates that were to yield sufficient income to meet the annual expenses of the palace, chancery, and other offices, the archbishop also employed servants to manage his estates and collect rents from his tenants.

Theobald's archiepiscopal court consisted of clergy of various ranks, his clerks, and officials. The archdeacon was the most senior of the arch-bishop's household, in charge of the administration of the archdiocese, governing in Theobald's name with jurisdiction delegated from the arch-bishop. Below the archdeacon were myriad clerks of various ranks and seniority who carried out the day-to-day running of the archdiocese and household while also fulfilling duties related to matters of the primacy. The church courts also fell under the jurisdiction of the archbishop, and his staff had to manage these also. The archbishop would normally hear the important cases in these courts, but some of the more senior clerks presided over lesser matters and delivered binding judgments. One of the skills Theobald looked for in his servants was diplomacy, coupled with a thorough knowledge of canon and civil law. He expected them to deal not only with their many duties but also with other issues, awkward or otherwise, that would have emerged on a daily basis. As Theobald was called upon to intervene in state affairs, his clerks understood the need for studied diplomacy, and their master expected competency, ability, and a certain creativity.

The archbishop's clerks were nominally clerics, but these men were not following a vocation to priesthood. While they were tonsured, they occupied the lower ranks of the clerical hierarchy: lectors, acolytes, and, at most, subdeacons. The lower ranks were not bound to the rule of cel-ibacy, nor did they take religious vows or serve any liturgical function beyond being readers or minor servers at Mass and the Divine Office. Because they were working for bishops and the Church, many men in England at that time were considered clerics, even married men who occupied the lower ranks, and this designation affected their rights and answerability under the law. They were, in fact, subject to canon law, and if accused of a crime, they were to be tried in ecclesiastical rather than civil courts under English law. This had been a bone of contention between the state and the Church for some time.[8]

As noted, diplomacy was a vital skill among those in the archbish-op's employ. Diplomacy was necessary not only for dealing with external affairs and disputes and the foibles, ambitions, and intrigues of fellow staff, but also for keeping on the right side of the archbishop. Theobald, for all his piety and fairness, had a quick temper and could be rash; he was well known to throw out blunt statements and could be hard on his servants, though he always valued their service and loyalty and rewarded diligence. He could be extremely sensitive and, given his humble origins, was prone to insecurity. The archbishop's servants would have known that they had to boost their master's confidence at times, particularly when he was being attacked by enemies or under pressure from the king.[9]

This world that Thomas was about to enter required skill to negotiate. It was at some point in 1145 that Thomas arrived at the archbishop's manor at Harrow for his interview with Theobald. He met with an experienced and even war-weary man now fully immersed in the affairs of Church and state. The young man before him was yet an unknown entity to the archbishop; but Theobald, it seems, was impressed with what he heard and saw in the interview. Thomas was charming and used every opportunity to reveal his natural intelligence and experience to date, while hiding the holes in his education; he must have displayed his abilities and his unwavering enthusiasm. And Theobald was given to nepotism. In addition to having awarded his brother Walter the post of archdeacon of Canterbury, he had given junior roles in the household to a plethora of nephews. If Thomas was indeed a relative, Theobald would have been inclined to give him some form of employment in the archiepiscopal court. At any rate, the archbishop accepted Thomas immediately as a clerk. Whether Thomas knew it or not, his life's work was to begin in earnest with this humble position of junior clerk.

8
Archiepiscopal Servant

Life in the archbishop's household was hectic. Like many ecclesiastical centers in England at the time, it was a mix of diocesan chancery, monastery, and secular court, all sharing the same buildings and coexisting in relative peace — but with intrigue. Thomas struggled at first in this new environment. There was a hierarchy among the clerks; some were very well educated, and these would have considered Thomas an inferior. But rather than stunt the young man, the situation actually stirred his ambition. He saw how clerks had risen up the ranks, some being appointed archdeacons of various dioceses so they would, in time, easily slip into the episcopacy. Thomas may or may not have had designs on holy orders, but his ambition was growing, and the first step toward advancement was to enter the ranks of the clerics, as was normal for those who served the Church in a professional capacity. He received minor orders soon after he was appointed clerk, and as he entered the clerical state, his status changed. In accordance with the much-disputed custom, he was now subject to ecclesiastical rather than civil jurisdiction in many areas.

Thomas's whole world changed. No longer a resident in London, he now lived a peregrinate existence, moving with the archiepiscopal court from Canterbury to the various manors Theobald occupied in accordance with his business. Working for the official Church then, as now, was challenging in many ways, including morally; it was not, perhaps, the best place to see the Gospel at work. There were those who sought to serve the Church and the archbishop, but there were others who saw every action, every decision, every development, in terms of moving up and down ladders, making or breaking careers. The game of power occupied many in the archbishop's household, and in the daily activity of the archiepiscopal court, politics was as much a motivation for them as the Church's mission. The court teemed with all the emotions of men who were seeking to make something of their lives. In that context, alliances were made and broken, friendships formed, individuals noted and marked. A way of doing things in terms of procedure, law, and custom became a status quo that was carefully adhered to, not only to ensure that things were done right but also to keep peace, to keep certain individuals in check, and to unite the whole body ecclesiastical as one whenever a threat came from outside.

Such was the way of life in any court, but in this one, the hardworking and committed archbishop, a man of faith, made all the difference. He inspired loyalty. Dropped into this clerical soup, Thomas had to hit the ground running and find friends among the staff. One prominent member of the court, however, may not have been initially inclined to a positive relationship with him: Roger de Pont L'Évêque. Roger was a native of Normandy, born around 1115. Upon his entrance into Theobald's service, it was obvious that his ability matched his ambition, which was far-reaching and intense. Thomas's early biographer William of Canterbury relates that Thomas formed an alliance with Roger and another clerk, John of Canterbury. The three, William insists, made a pact to protect and help one another advance their interests and careers. Given that it was rare for the three to be absent from the household at the same time, there was always at least one to keep an eye on what was happening and inform the others when they returned.[1] Frank Barlow in his modern biography suggests that Roger was suspicious of the newcomer from the moment Thomas arrived and that he regarded the manner of the young Londoner's arrival as irregular.[2] That Theobald quickly developed an affection for Thomas did not help matters, and so whether or not Roger and Thomas were allies, close or otherwise, their relationship soon became bitter and confrontational.[3] Perhaps Roger, as an ambitious young man, was indeed wary of Thomas, but judged that for the time being, it was more conducive to his career to form an alliance with this new arrival. As Thomas advanced, however, Roger's ambition may have overcome whatever affection for Thomas or initial pragmatism he may have had. Later events would lead Roger to despise him even more.

Thomas had few qualifications for his position. He was probably hired because Theobald wanted someone with experience in financial matters, which Thomas had thanks to Osbert, and saw in him a young man who could be trained for greater things. As he would have expected, Thomas started at the bottom as the junior clerk assigned the lowliest of tasks: filing, taking statements, doing odd jobs, being ordered about by his seniors. He watched his steps in the first few weeks, taking careful note of how things were done and how people worked and reacted. He aimed to be helpful and competent; and as he completed his work in an exceptional manner, not only was Theobald vindicated in his decision, but others noticed this young man's ability. One of those was Theobald's brother, Walter the Archdeacon. Walter was always happy to have someone help him with his duties, particularly when he had to stand in at the court while Theobald was away on business. For Walter, Thomas gradually became that clerk who was always willing to help; this was a smart move on Thomas's part.[4]

To bring his education up to the standard required of a clerk, Theobald assigned Thomas to study with a tutor, who would not only teach him the knowledge he needed for his day-to-day work but also help develop his natural skills and fit him for tasks the archbishop already had in mind for this new protégé. The tutor was already teaching Theobald's nephews, so Thomas was more than likely included in classes that had already been arranged. These lessons were not a leisurely familiarizing of oneself with Church law and practice; rather, as soon as he was appointed to mentor the new clerk, the tutor arrived with an armful of works for Thomas's attention, prominent among them works on canon law.[5] One of the important tasks of the primate's court was dealing with legal matters, and for this Theobald needed capable advisors and clerks who were well versed in the law. As Thomas was seemingly marked out for legal work, Theobald had to ensure that he not only grasped the fundamentals of canon law, but also knew his way around the complexities of the Church's legal system in order to harmonize it with, and at times challenge, the system of civil laws. Experts on canon law and other matters pertaining to the life of the Church would have been regular visitors to Canterbury, and Theobald may have given Thomas the opportunity to speak with them and thereby supplement his studies. Thomas would doubtless have become acquainted with the reforms of Pope Saint Gregory VII,[6] since they had recently affected relations between the Church and the secular powers in various realms. As a servant of the Church, the new clerk would need to understand not only the law of these reforms, but also the response with which they had been met.

Thomas was doing well. Theobald was not given to fawning over his servants, but he was impressed with his new clerk. He started planning great things for Thomas, who was finding himself by the archbishop's side more often as time passed. Meanwhile, Roger de Pont L'Évêque was festering with malice and discontent; it may have been he who dubbed Thomas *Baillehache*, or "Hatchet Man." As time progressed, the two were considered rivals, and bitter ones at that. Roger was given to conspiracy, and he began to use his skills to undermine Thomas before he achieved too lofty a role in the archbishop's service. On two occasions, Roger was able to stir up trouble, making false accusations against Thomas to the archbishop and providing evidence that seemed to confirm the truth of his claims. On both occasions, Theobald was convinced and dismissed his protégé from his service and his presence. Both times, Thomas took refuge with Walter, Theobald's brother, for whom he had done many favors; and, convinced of the clerk's innocence and perhaps even of Roger's malice, Walter interceded with his brother each time and won Theobald around, helping to restore Thomas to his position and to favor. Roger's triumph was short-lived on both occasions, but his contempt for the "lowborn clerk" never waned.[7]

As he returned to the court after each of his banishments, it may have seemed to his nemeses in the archiepiscopal household that Thomas, the upstart, had a charmed life. By this stage, Thomas was well aware of the dangers and pitfalls that lay around him, and now he was ready for a fight and willing to do what he could to rise above those who tried to bring him down. Thomas was too clever and too ambitious to be caged in by those who wanted to destroy him. He may have felt insecure at first due to his lack of education and his "lowborn" status compared with many of those around him, but he was gifted and competent. The wastrel of the Paris years was gone; now, he was intent on going as far as he could. His ambition would prove to be a great motivator, and while collegial and supportive of his fellow clerks, Thomas relished competition and pushed himself. He kept an eye on his enemies and was very careful in his dealings with Roger.

In the meantime, around 1147, another ambitious and highly skilled clerk came into Theobald's service: John of Salisbury. This young man arrived with a reference from none other than the highly esteemed and venerated Saint Bernard of Clairvaux.[8] Thomas might have seen another rival, but his first impressions of John were favorable; this new clerk, while obviously gifted and highly capable, was very different from Roger. Thomas offered the hand of friendship to John, and it was gladly accepted. Not only would the two become fast friends, but their friendship would prove to be one of the most providential relationships in Thomas's life. John would be a friend, an ally, and a confidant; a sure support in the years of suffering and exile that lay ahead; a champion following Thomas's death; and one of his biographers. John would become one of the foremost intellectuals of his age and would also know exile, which for a man of his sensitivity would be a very bitter experience. In time, he would be raised to the episcopate and, on his death, leave an important body of work.[9] Entering Theobald's service as the archbishop's secretary, John would hold the post for seven years — years he and Thomas would cherish and often reminisce about later in their lives.

As Thomas progressed in his studies and served his master well, Theobald made the decision to send his clerk abroad to continue his studies in a more formal environment. Though he was often hard on his clerks, Theobald was generous. Recognizing their gifts and abilities, he sought to give them every opportunity to perfect their skills and interests, realizing that these skills would be beneficial to the Church, both local and universal.

Thomas was sent first to Bologna,[10] the great university in the north of Italy. Founded in 1088 and still in existence, it is the oldest continuously functioning university in the world. In Thomas's day, it was just over fifty years old but already an important center for learning. Having gained a notable reputation for canon law, it was the obvious place to send Thomas. One of its first professors had been Irnerius, a native of Bologna, who founded the school of jurisprudence at the university. Often called *lucerna juris*, the "lantern of the law," Irnerius is credited as the founder of the medieval Roman law tradition for his recovery of the *Codex* of the sixth-century Eastern Roman emperor Justinian I, a revival that would prove revolutionary for European law for centuries to come. Irnerius had died long before Thomas arrived, but Thomas would have studied under men well versed in Roman and canon law, some of the best legal minds in Europe at the time. Among these were the "Four Doctors" of Bologna: Bulgarus, Martinus Gosia, Jacobus de Boragine, and Hugo de Porta Ravennate. These were towering figures who not only brought their brilliant minds to bear on the study of law, but were also involved in the various disputes and controversies of the twelfth century.

Thomas would spend a year at Bologna, and it would be very different from his last foray at university. Now a serious student and a cleric, he would not have put frequenting the local taverns on his list of priorities, if on any of his lists at all. He threw himself into his studies, not merely for the sake of academic interest, but also because the law he was studying and the cases his teachers were considering might well have a direct bearing on his own career and decisions he might have to make in the future. The method employed by the law school of Bologna was that of the "glossators." This was a detailed study of the laws with copious explanations of the text added in the margins — glossing, after the method of Irnerius. This method led Thomas to a deep familiarity with the law, its sources, and the many nuances it held that would allow wide application.

Bologna was known as the university where future archdeacons were educated; among Thomas's fellow students would have been men who had just been appointed and ordained archdeacons and those who had reason to consider themselves archdeacons in waiting. Thomas may well have seen Theobald's plan for his life in this choice of school. But Theobald had another reason: Bologna was at the heart of a legal reform, one that Theobald himself was promoting and would introduce into England in the next few years with his appointment of the renowned legal scholar Roger Vacarius to a position at Oxford teaching Roman law in 1149. That decision would upset the royal masters of England, who liked to see themselves not only as the fount of all honor but also as the fount of all law. Theobald was a revolutionary in his own way, ensuring that the Church in England was in the vanguard of intellectual knowledge, with well-educated clerics to advance and protect the Church. Following Thomas's studies in Bologna, Theobald arranged for him to be enrolled for a short time in the law school of Auxerre in France, where the courses he attended completed his legal education.

During his time of service, Thomas had already been on missions with Theobald, whose skills were now variously employed in the service of the state as well as of the Church. Certainly by the time he was in Auxerre, Thomas was deemed one of Theobald's personal assistants. When Pope Eugene III called a council to be held at Reims in France in March 1148, Theobald sent word to Thomas in Auxerre to make his way to Reims to join him there. Pope Eugene had originally called the council to meet at Trier, in what is now Germany; however, an unfavorable reaction from the locals forced the pope to change the venue to Reims. Over the council's eleven days, the pope intended to bring an end to debates on a number of canons that had been promulgated at the Second Lateran Council in 1139. One of these canons forbade clerical marriage. When the canon was pronounced, it was greeted by the council bishops with much hilarity in the hall — the clergy already knew about the law of celibacy, but it seemed that some offenders against the canon were feigning ignorance and still holding out for a change. Other matters included the condemnation of a heretic, Éon de l'Étoile, a Breton who thought he was the Messiah; a further condemnation of the supporters of the antipope Anacletus II (Anacletus had died in 1138, but his supporters were still making a nuisance of themselves); and other various disputes that needed to be settled.

At this point, Theobald was going through a bad patch with King Stephen. Feeling more comfortable on the throne with Matilda weakened, the king had begun to reverse some of the liberties he had yielded to the Church. To consolidate his position, Stephen had appointed various bishops to support him; including, it was said, William FitzHerbert, his nephew, to whom he granted the see of York, England's second metropolitan see and often a rival to Canterbury. Though aware that the king might not approve of his leaving England, Theobald was not prepared to miss the council — he needed to consult the pope about important matters. Escaping Stephen's spies, the archbishop commandeered a smack, a traditional fishing boat, and stole across the English Channel in the midst of a storm to plead his case with the pope. When Theobald arrived at the council, Pope Eugene took one look at the newly arrived archbishop and gleefully commented that the journey seemed more of a swim than a sail, and he was correct. Theobald and his crew looked worn and bedraggled like survivors of a shipwreck and were still suffering the effects of seasickness.[11]

Thomas met up with his archbishop at Reims and, working with his friend John of Salisbury and Roger de Pont L'Évêque, made ready the archbishop's case against Stephen.[12] Theobald had already suspended the bishops the king had instructed not to attend the council, among them Theobald's nemesis, Henry of Winchester, because word of this had reached Stephen, the archbishop knew he was in dangerous waters. As they worked, Thomas found himself in the midst of the great and the good of the Church. For the first time, he set eyes on a pope and could see how a papal court operated, even if out of its natural forum in Rome. He saw some of the Church's renowned contemporary theologians, and without doubt he would have spoken to Saint Bernard at least once, even if superficially, given that he was now a close friend of one of Bernard's protégés. His old master from Paris, Robert of Melun, was also there, and perhaps some of his former student acquaintances. The council opened up the world of the Church to Thomas, and as clerk and close assistant of the archbishop of Canterbury, who was there on high-ranking business, he was at the center of it all.

Theobald argued his case persuasively and won the pope to his side. William FitzHerbert was formally deprived of the archbishopric of York on the grounds that the king had rigged the election, and his replacement, the Cistercian abbot of Fountains Abbey, Henry Murdac, was confirmed. William's opponents also maintained that his personal life was far from ideal. Even Saint Bernard claimed to be aware of his unchaste lifestyle and ambition; in a letter to Pope Innocent II, Eugene's predecessor, he had described William as being "rotten from the soles of his feet to the crown of his head."[13] While the same could be said of many a cleric then and now, the accusation proved useful for Theobald's case, even if it was untrue. Saint Bernard of Clairvaux had gotten many things right in his life, but his opinion of William FitzHerbert was as far off the mark as could be. The man was, in fact, a saint, and the Church would confirm it by canonizing him in 1227. William's chief opponents in York were Cistercians who were aggrieved at not being included in the episcopal election that saw William elevated and were displeased that their man was passed over for the archbishopric. They may have filled Bernard with lies, which led to his rash judgment of a man whose holiness was similar to his own. Saints make mistakes, too, and they can be misled by those who are not themselves saints.[14]

For Pope Eugene, confirming these decisions was not enough; he had to deal with Stephen. He proposed to excommunicate the king of England and ordered preparations to be made for the ceremony. To everyone's astonishment, Theobald knelt before the pope and begged him not to excommunicate Stephen.[15] Eugene was dumbstruck. He interpreted Theobald's gesture as Christian charity and, in acknowledgment of the plea of mercy, reversed his decision. However, Theobald's gesture was mostly political. He knew Stephen all too well — defying a pope was not beyond the realm of possibility for him. Stephen was unpopular with many, but an excommunication imposed without the king having a chance to defend himself might win many to his side and make the civil war, which was already wreaking havoc in the kingdom, much worse.

The council ended on April 1, but the pope and others remained to deal with what for Saint Bernard of Clairvaux was the main business of the council: the case of Gilbert de la Porrée. Theobald may have remained for that and witnessed Eugene's compromise on the issue. He returned to Canterbury, again traveling discreetly to avoid the king's spies, to receive a hero's welcome as the people heard of his magnanimity in asking the pope not to excommunicate the king. Stephen was not so impressed. As soon as he heard Theobald was back, he sent one of his stalwarts to demand the archbishop's submission to the crown. Theobald refused and not long after was deprived of his property, taken into custody, delivered to a ship bound for Flanders, and unceremoniously told to get out and never come back to England.[16] The archbishop took refuge at the Benedictine Abbey of Saint Bertin at Saint-Omer and began his efforts to get back to England. Thomas may have made his way back to Auxerre to finish his studies, or he may have returned from the council with Theobald and gone into exile with him. Later in his life, Thomas would describe these events in great detail to a cardinal in the Roman curia,[17] and the detail is so vivid that he may well have been with his archbishop and experienced them personally.

Life was not too bad for Theobald at Saint Bertin's. His friends were able to visit him, bringing provisions and news of what was happening in England. It was obvious that Stephen had forced the archbishop into exile even in the face of Theobald's great act of charity toward the king in preventing his excommunication. In a sense, the exile was beneficial to Theobald's cause, even if it was irksome. Various negotiations took place, but when these failed and news of Theobald's exile finally reached the pope, he was furious. He issued a papal edict demanding that Stephen recall the archbishop; if Stephen refused to heed it, England would be placed under interdict.[18] If Stephen persisted in his obstinacy, then he would be excommunicated, and with that, his subjects' loyalty to him would be absolved.

Seemingly unaware of the advantage it may have given Matilda's side, weak as it was at that time, Stephen disregarded the edict and continued to defy both pope and archbishop. In response, Eugene opted for the interdict, but directed Theobald to impose it in order to make a point. Though he imposed it in obedience to the pope, Theobald was doubtful as to its effectiveness, and he was proved correct — the interdict had no effect, because many feared it would resurrect the civil war. Indeed, the ever-independent Londoners lodged an appeal with Rome to have the interdict lifted. The clergy of Canterbury, however, obeyed, though some in the monasteries held out. Watching from Saint Bertin's, Theobald realized by the spring of 1149 that he would have to take drastic action to resolve the issue. Despite the risks to his own safety, he had to return to England. Adopting a disguise, he hired a boat at nearby Gravelines in Flanders, sailed to Gosford in Sussex, and then rode to Framlingham to the castle of Hugh Bigod, a onetime supporter of Stephen who had since defected to Matilda's cause.[19] There, safe behind the walls of the impenetrable fortress, Theobald very publicly resumed the work of the archiepiscopal court, once more asserting his authority over the Church in England. When Stephen heard of Theobald's return, he thought better of his position and realized how far he had gone. Now that Theobald was in the fortress of a former supporter who was now an enemy, Stephen suddenly realized that Theobald could well become a powerful proponent of the empress's cause, and that could well mean the end of his reign. Stephen reached out to the archbishop and settled the dispute; Theobald's lands were restored, together with compensation for lost earnings and damage to the property.

Back in Canterbury, Theobald may have pondered the events of the last year. He had won and brought a king to heel for his transgressions against the Church and her rights; his predecessors would have been pleased, and perhaps he had set a precedent for his successors. But more needed to be done. Stephen's position was precarious, and so, too, England's. Matilda had withdrawn, but the issue of the throne was not resolved; though there was peace for now, it was uneasy and fragile. Theobald knew that the most awkward task of all lay ahead. For now, life at the archbishop's court had returned to normal, or at least as normal as it could be, given the political climate, but it would not remain so for long.

As for the clerk, when Thomas returned to Canterbury, Theobald made a surprise announcement: Thomas was to be his spokesman, and he was to be sent on various missions on the archbishop's behalf. It was obvious that Thomas possessed great skills of diplomacy and tact, and recent events had honed those skills further. Theobald could be rough and dogmatic in his directives, but Thomas was a clerk who was able to translate his master's intentions in a subtler manner. A good communicator who could now carefully control his stammer, he could spin a persuasive argument. It was another good decision on Theobald's part; Thomas would excel as his spokesman. Theobald may also have mused that his young protégé might prove useful to the Church in England.

Now Thomas would be thrust in earnest into the heart of English political life and the maelstrom that was tearing the country apart — the Anarchy had woken up and was breathing fire again. Closer to home, Walter, Theobald's brother, was elevated to the see of Rochester, no doubt due to his brother's influence, and was consecrated bishop on March 14, 1148. The archdeaconry of Canterbury was now vacant, and Theobald did not wait long to appoint to the office his most able and senior clerk: Roger de Pont L'Évêque. It was a decision Thomas's enemy greeted with glee, and Thomas with caution.

9

Peace

In March 1148, Matilda returned to Normandy to find peace in the priory of Notre-Dame-du-Pré. Having had enough of war, she just wanted to pray and live a quiet life among the nuns for the years that were left to her. She passed the scepter, impotent as it was for now, to her son Henry Angevin. This young man, son of two noble houses, heir through his mother to the realms of England and Normandy and through his father to the dukedom of Anjou, had all the assets to become one of the most powerful monarchs in Christendom; he also had the ambition and ability. Stephen was well aware of this, and he realized that he needed to take action to prevent Henry from gaining a foothold in England. The time had come, he surmised, to crown and anoint his son Eustace, the Count of Boulogne, as junior king of England to settle the matter of succession and provide for a smooth transfer of power when he died.

In 1147, hungry for victory for his mother and himself, fourteen-year-old Henry landed in England at the head of an army. While the English were concerned a new front had opened up in the civil war, and there were rumors that the young commander led a large army, their fears were unfounded as Henry's army, not as impressive as the rumors would have it, quickly abandoned him and his cause when the money ran out and no wages were paid. Henry appealed to his mother and his uncle Roger to assist him financially, but they refused — they may not have been keen to finance what they might have seen as a foolhardy venture.[1] With a display of bravado, however, Henry appealed to King Stephen, offering to withdraw his army if the king would send him money. Astonishingly, Stephen agreed, and Henry returned to Anjou.[2] Henry's second attempt occurred in 1149, this time with the support of his great-uncle, King David of Scotland. With a newly minted knighthood, thanks to the Scottish king, Henry set his sights on York and took it, before heading south. Stephen was not prepared to repeat his generosity this time. Sending a formidable army, joining with that of his son, Eustace, they created enough resistance for Henry that he was forced to return to Normandy.[3]

In the meantime, Geoffrey, Henry's father, was growing in power and influence, and this worried King Louis VII of France. Having deprived Stephen of his Norman domains, Geoffrey had Henry proclaimed Duke of Normandy, an action that further alarmed the French king. Henry governed as duke for the next few years, developing his administrative skills. To pacify Louis, who could become a serious enemy, and to win him as an ally in the claim for the English throne, Geoffrey advised Henry to do homage to Louis as his feudal lord; Henry agreed to do so, and Louis formally acknowledged him as duke in 1150.

Henry's ambition was growing, and planning for an invasion of England was under way. Geoffrey was at the heart of the planning, but on September 7, 1151, he died suddenly of a fever. Knowing his son all too well, and recognizing the real possibility that he might deprive his younger brother of an inheritance, Geoffrey had made arrangements for Henry to inherit the title of Count of Anjou and Maine only until he was king of England, at which point he would be legally obliged to pass the title and domains to his younger brother, also called Geoffrey. At his father's death, Henry promised to do so, though he would regret the promise, and had his brother Geoffrey not been offered the title and domains of the County of Nantes a few years later in 1156, Henry would have reneged on his promise to his father and done what he had to do to prevent his brother claiming his right. Though he challenged Henry and made trouble for him, Geoffrey took Nantes, Henry kept Anjou and Maine, and they finally settled down to an amicable, if tense, relationship.

Meanwhile, Theobald was petitioning Rome for the office of papal legate in England; once again, his rival in this issue was King Stephen's brother Henry, bishop of Winchester. Thomas was now being sent on missions for Theobald, some of them to Rome, where he was reacquainted with the workings of the curia. In 1149, Theobald sent Thomas to the pope to deliver his petition, and it met with success. That Henry of Winchester had already held the office and had used it to assail the see and archbishop of Canterbury proved an advantage for Theobald's request — Rome had learned its lesson. Thomas's advocacy before the pope was a powerful piece of persuasive oratory, and while Bishop Henry had rushed to Rome himself to plead his case, he was no match for Thomas, who wiped the floor with him, figuratively speaking. Thomas came back to England with the official bull appointing Theobald papal legate, the pope's representative in England, invested with papal authority.

King Stephen was furious. His brother had lost the one office that could be most useful in his claim to the throne, and now it was in the hands of the archbishop whom he had exiled and who was on the verge of going over to the young Angevin. A further complication for the king was that any power Bishop Henry might have claimed to crown and anoint Eustace was well and truly gone; now only Theobald, as both archbishop of Canterbury and papal legate, had the authority to preside over a coronation. Theobald would have argued that the power belonged to the archbishop of Canterbury alone anyway, but it was sweet to have legatine powers to reinforce his point. He was also aware that Stephen was looking for a way out of his predicament. No sooner was Thomas home from Rome than he was sent back to the pope, this time with a much more impressive entourage — the formal delegation of a papal legate — to petition Eugene for a decree forbidding Eustace's coronation. Again, Thomas met with success: The pope agreed and issued the decree.

As Thomas returned to Canterbury, Stephen's own delegation arrived in Rome to plead his case; the king had appointed none other than the archdeacon of Canterbury, Roger de Pont L'Évêque, as his spokesman. Roger argued that the decree be withdrawn, but Eugene refused to rescind it, citing as one of his reasons Stephen's breaking of his oath of fealty to Matilda. Eugene's decision caused ripples in both England and France. The pope had called Stephen an oath breaker and had come down, at least tentatively, on Matilda's side. This finally vindicated Matilda and gave her son Henry the political legitimacy that even a successful war could not confer. The question for the Angevin was how to use this papal pronouncement to push his cause in England.

On a personal level, Thomas's own rivalry with Roger had deepened. That Roger had agreed to plead for the king revealed that his ambition outweighed his loyalty to his archbishop. Perhaps he was just a canon lawyer arguing a case for a client who just happened to be a king pushing a cause contrary to that of his archbishop — and every client is entitled to be heard — but Thomas would have taken note of Roger's attitude. This man was capable of disloyalty to further his own aims. In the years ahead, Thomas would become more than well acquainted with this streak in Roger.

Stephen was not to be outdone. In the spring of 1152, he called a council in London to discuss the possibility of proceeding with Eustace's coronation regardless of the papal decree. Bishops and lords attended the council to hear the king give the reasons why the ban had to be ignored. Eustace was also present in full view of all; any refusal to agree would be deemed a personal affront to the heir to the throne. Turning to the bishops, Stephen demanded that they consent to the coronation and then asked them to nominate one to do it. To a man, they looked to Theobald; he had the right as primate to preside at a coronation, and none of them was willing to usurp that right. Now sure of his brother bishops' support, Theobald stood and faced the king. The pope had forbidden this coronation, he said, and therefore it would not happen.

King and son were incensed. They ordered that all the bishops be incarcerated in a nearby house and provoked with threats and hardship; they would remain there until they consented. Some bishops backed down, but most held the line. Theobald, seizing a quick opportunity, fled the assembly with Thomas and others in tow and made for the River

Thames with the king's knights in hot pursuit. As providence would have it, a boat lay idle; commandeering it, the fleeing company set sail down the Thames as the king's knights pursued them, seeking to assassinate the archbishop. They reached Dover in time to catch a boat to the continent, and Theobald and his faithful clerks sailed across the channel to Flanders, arriving on April 6, 1152. Theobald's second exile had begun.

This exile would prove to be short; he returned a few months later, in August. Stephen quickly repented of his rage and realized the foolishness of his actions. He had just driven the archbishop of Canterbury and papal legate into the arms of the Angevin, and with him many of his supporters in England, the hierarchy included. Stephen realized he needed to back down if he or Eustace were to have any chance of keeping the throne. Henry Angevin had gathered enough allies already, the most recent being the king of France, Louis VII, who had just formally recognized the young man as duke of Normandy, thereby depriving Stephen of those realms for good. Little did Stephen know that as Theobald was fleeing toward Flanders, ships facing toward England were already lining up in the ports of Normandy: Henry Angevin was preparing to invade. It was only the possibility of a desired marriage that distracted Henry from immediately carrying out his plans.

Louis VII of France had just obtained an annulment from his consort, Eleanor of Aquitaine, one of the most extraordinary women of the medieval period, and Henry was very interested in a match with her. Henry was not interested so much in Eleanor's abilities and strength, which he would come to despise in time, but in her vast fortune and estates as the only heir to her father's duchy. She was also a direct descendant of Charlemagne; marriage to such a woman brought prestige to any royal house. Henry was nineteen, and Eleanor thirty; she was the mother of two children for the French king — both daughters, to Louis's disappointment. She was feisty and ultimately unconquerable. She had had a number of public arguments with Louis, and the relationship was so strained that at one point even the pope had had to intervene to seek reconciliation. Louis and Eleanor were also related within the forbidden degrees of consanguinity, so a marriage should never have been permitted — hence the decree of nullity.

Henry was enamored of her, though probably not for the reasons one contracts a modern marriage. Eleanor was also taken with Henry, though again probably not out of love. In this young and ambitious duke and possible king, Eleanor saw the means of restoring the glories of her duchy, which had declined since the death of her father, William X. Her grandfather, William IX, had been an effective ruler, a man who loved life and women — he had a reputation as a lecher. He was as daring on the battlefield as he was in his affairs, but he also fostered a love of learning and literature; he was, it seems, a competent lyric poet. Eleanor's father, William X, nicknamed "the Saint," was not as gregarious as his father, though he had been involved in a number of campaigns, notably against Normandy. Initially a supporter of Antipope Anacletus II, he was converted by Saint Bernard of Clairvaux to orthodox Catholicism. Upon his death in 1137 on a pilgrimage to Santiago de Compostela, William X left his eldest daughter and heir in the care of King Louis VI of France, who married her off to his son and heir.

Sizing Henry up, Eleanor may have thought he could help her restore the honor of her house; in this, her wits had abandoned her.[4] Any notions she may have harbored of being able to dominate Henry Angevin were seriously deluded, but it was an effective delusion that saw them march up the aisle together on May 18, 1152, eight weeks after the annulment had been granted and not long after two attempts by ambitious suitors to kidnap the bride and marry her themselves.

As the couple honeymooned, King Louis fumed — not only had Henry married his former wife, and in unseemly haste, but as Duke of Normandy and a subject of the king of France, Henry had not honored the custom of seeking permission to marry from his feudal lord. In revenge, Louis attempted to scuttle Henry's plans, backing the cause of Louis's sister's husband, none other than Eustace, Count of Boulogne and prince of England. Eustace had married Constance of France in 1140. Louis invited Eustace to come to Normandy and preempt Henry's invasion of England. Eustace duly arrived and joined Louis in a campaign against the Angevin, laying siege near Dieppe. However, despite the distractions of a new wife, Henry was well able to meet the challenge and ran Eustace out of Normandy to Paris. Six weeks after he started his campaign, the young count went back to England with his tail between his legs.

The initial pleasures of marriage honored, Henry realized the time was ripe for his invasion. His ships were waiting, and his knights were tired of twiddling their thumbs; it was time to begin his campaign. In the second week of January 1153, his fleet left Barfleur for England.[5] The boats faced a cold winter gale, but the army of 140 knights and 3,000 infantry landed safely at Wareham and made for Malmesbury, seizing the town and laying siege to its castle. In the meantime, Henry made his way around England, arriving in Gloucester, where, on April 19, he held court for Easter and proclaimed himself by his new title, Duke of Aquitaine. He then began his campaign in the midlands — laying siege to castles, capturing them, and forcing their occupants to surrender to him — all the while looking to that moment when he could claim another, loftier title.

Thomas was facing battles of his own in Canterbury as an uneasy peace with Roger de Pont L'Évêque seemed to make life just about bearable. However, an incident occurred that brought Thomas to Roger's defense in the hope that some sort of reconciliation could be effected. John of Salisbury in his biography records accusations made against Roger during his time as archdeacon — that he was involved in a relationship with a young man in Theobald's household. The young man, Walter by name, began to spread rumors of this relationship, and when Roger heard of this, he pursued proceedings in court against him. The court found in Roger's favor, and as punishment for what were now regarded as false allegations, Walter had his eyes gouged out. Walter continued to make accusations against Roger in defiance of the court's judgment; in responding to them again, the archdeacon allegedly persuaded a civil court to condemn Walter, and the young man was hanged.[6]

In 1152, the case was made public, and Roger found himself in hot water. Though Roger's enemy, Thomas knew that Roger was entitled to a fair hearing, and so he enlisted the help of colleagues, legal experts among them, to deal with the matter. Theobald heard the case and was persuaded to accept a "purgation" from Roger, in which he denied under oath that any of the charges made by Walter were true. The archdeacon then had to travel to Rome to defend himself before the pope. Following a hearing at the papal court, he was cleared of the charges. He returned to his office, and his career advanced unaffected. In future disputes with Thomas, Roger would conveniently forget what his nemesis had done to help him. Biographers have tried to confirm whether these events occurred or whether John of Salisbury invented them to settle a score with an implacable enemy of Thomas's who had benefited from his innate magnanimity. Most are inclined to believe that Roger was accused of something and might even have been guilty of an illicit relationship, though John may have exaggerated it in some respects.[7] As to whether Thomas's assistance tempered relations between Roger and himself in real terms, it is doubtful.

By the winter of 1152, Stephen and Eustace were entrenched in a siege at Wallingford, Henry's base in Oxfordshire; the Angevin was forced to meet them in battle to relieve the castle. The barons, however, were not so keen to see bloodshed. They had much to lose in terms of their holdings in both England and Normandy; regardless of who won this battle, they would have offended one of the two rulers, Henry or Stephen, to whom they owed feudal loyalty. They feared the price they would have to pay for their perceived disloyalty. Eustace berated his barons, as he knew his only chance of wearing the crown was victory in battle, but they ignored him. Henry and Stephen would be forced to negotiate. The two agreed to talk, shouting at each other across the River Thames and trying to agree to a solution. The efforts failed, and both parties rode off, Henry to attack Stephen's possessions at Stamford and Nottingham, and Stephen to attack Henry's at Ipswich. Eustace sulked his way to the abbey at Bury St. Edmunds, where he demanded food and money from the monks. When they refused it, the irate count ordered the abbey to be pillaged and the church to be desecrated. On August 17, 1153, Eustace suddenly collapsed and died. He was about twenty-four years old, and while the cause was a heart attack, many interpreted his sudden demise as God's response to his actions at Bury St. Edmunds. As his marriage to Constance of France was childless, Eustace left no heir.

Eustace's death seemed an evil omen and removed any hope Stephen had of keeping the throne. The last obstacle to finally ending the Anarchy was removed.[8] The king was also battling depression following the recent death of his wife — Queen Matilda, whom he regarded as his strength and most ardent supporter, died of a fever on May 3, 1152. Theobald took the initiative. In the previous months, he had already been in contact with both sides, urging negotiations. They were difficult months, as neither side fully trusted him. Stephen wondered how much of the old loyalty remained after all that had happened; Henry was not quite sure whether the archbishop had really come over to his side. Theobald needed extraordinary tact and prudence — one false step and not only would the little progress he had made be reversed, but the whole venture could come crashing down, soaked with the blood of countless innocent men and women.

In that summer of 1153, Theobald and his entourage, with Thomas at his side, had come looking for Stephen and Eustace to see whether they could be persuaded to agree to some form of negotiation. Later, Theobald met with Henry to see if he, too, could be coaxed to meet Stephen. By this time, Henry was more inclined to listen to Theobald; the archbishop had mediated a quarrel Henry had had with the bishop of Salisbury, so he had proven himself. Theobald had come to the decision that Henry must end up with the crown, regardless of how that was negotiated. In his efforts, Theobald found he had an unexpected ally: Stephen's brother, his old nemesis Bishop Henry of Winchester. Perhaps through the wisdom of old age or a dawning realization that it was the only way to peace, Bishop Henry had come to regret his part in assisting his brother to seize the throne, and he was now a willing and generous servant of the archbishop in his efforts to bring the whole sorry episode to an end.

For six months, Theobald, with Thomas's able assistance and shrewd diplomacy, went back and forth from Stephen to Henry. Stephen, heartbroken after Eustace's sudden death, was no longer as fiery and insistent. At this stage, it seemed he just wanted to keep the crown for himself; he was no longer concerned about the succession. This opened the way to reconciliation. With the agreement of both parties, Theobald arranged a meeting. On November 6, 1153, Stephen and Henry met face-to-face at Winchester and there agreed to end hostilities and settle their differences. Theobald proposed a compromise that might satisfy both parties.

The peace was carefully choreographed. In a grand procession, Stephen led Henry through the streets of Winchester to his palace, where a great council had gathered. Before them, Stephen declared Henry to be, for all purposes of the law of succession, his son and his heir, the lawful successor to the throne. In doing this, Stephen excluded his younger son William from any claim. Henry would require an oath from Stephen and his supporters to confirm William's exclusion. The agreement, which Theobald had brokered, would allow Stephen to reign until his death, when Henry would succeed him. In terms of property that had been seized by either side during the civil war (castles and lands), these were to be returned to those who had held them during the reign of Henry I, thus establishing a principle Henry Angevin would seek to use to his advantage during his reign.

It took six weeks to formalize the agreement in writing, and the treaty enshrining the new arrangement and succession was signed when the royal court met for Christmas at Westminster Palace.[9] Stephen took his oath excluding William from the succession, and William did homage to Henry as his father's heir and future king. Stephen's knights did likewise, with the proviso that their fealty lay with Stephen until his death. Important castles such as the Tower of London and those at Windsor, Oxford, Lincoln, and Winchester were given into the temporary possession of neutral parties until Henry succeeded. The bishops then took oaths of fealty to Henry.

Officially and legally, there was no mention of Thomas during these conferences; he was a mere clerk. Yet, his part in the negotiations was indispensable. Theobald had relied upon him and trusted him implicitly, and Thomas had excelled. The archbishop was, once again, vindicated in his decision to hire this Londoner and invest so much in him; he had received a mighty return. At the first opportunity, Thomas would be rewarded with even greater responsibility and greater trust. There was another who noticed this clerk's ability — Henry — and perhaps he, too, filed away what he had seen for future reference.

As negotiations to end the civil war were being conducted, Henry Murdac, archbishop of York, died on October 14, 1153. Having failed to win the loyalty of the clergy of his archdiocese, he had had a difficult tenure. He was succeeded by his rival, the much maligned but innocent

William FitzHerbert. William had traveled to Rome to plead with the new pope, Anastasius IV, to restore him to the see. The pope agreed, and William was reappointed archbishop on December 20, 1153, returning to York in May 1154. William's period of office was to be short; he died suddenly a month later, on June 8, Trinity Sunday, after offering Mass. Initial investigations into his death revealed that he had been murdered — the chalice at Mass had been poisoned, and a culprit had been identified: the archdeacon of York, Osbert de Bayeux. Osbert had been a supporter of Henry Murdac and opposed to William's succeeding to the office. Murder charges were brought against Osbert, and he stood trial in 1156 when the case was transferred to the papal courts, but no record of judgment exists. God's judgment of William FitzHerbert's life and character was revealed by the miracles that began to occur when he was invoked by the ordinary people of the archdiocese who had always supported him.

With York vacant for the second time in a year, a neutral candidate was needed. Thanks to Theobald's efforts, one was found in his archdeacon: Roger de Pont L'Évêque was elected to the second most important see in England. He left Canterbury and traveled to York, where he was consecrated archbishop on October 10, 1154. The office of archdeacon of Canterbury was now vacant.

10

Archdeacon

With Roger on his way up north, Theobald now had a position with which to reward his most able clerk and ensure that his talents could be used to greater effect within the Archdiocese of Canterbury and the Church in England. Thomas had been reaping the rewards of his labors in other ways; of late, he had been gathering benefices from a number of churches.[1] This had been supplementing his income and was beginning to provide him with a comfortable lifestyle. His first benefice came from the abbot of St Albans who conferred the church of Bramfield in Hertfordshire on him; later, a grateful bishop of Worcester also conferred the church of Saint Mary-le-Strand in London on him for his assistance in various matters.[2] Theobald then granted him the benefice of Otford in Kent as a reward for his work at the Council of Reims. A number of others followed, including one from St. Paul's Cathedral in London. These "livings" provided Thomas with additional income, which became more necessary as he rose up through the ranks and his expenses increased. Now, with Roger out of the way, he was called into the archbishop's presence to learn that he would receive the greatest office in Theobald's gift: the archdeaconry of Canterbury. Apart from being a promotion to an important position, the archdeaconry brought with it a very generous income and the hope of even more benefices to come. Life was good for Thomas.

Already in minor orders, Thomas now needed to be raised to the subdiaconate and then ordained to the diaconate in order to take possession of his office.[3] The exact date of his ordination is not known, but it is believed to have happened around October or November 1154. When he was in minor orders, marriage was still possible; but now Thomas had to embrace a life of celibacy, though that was not a barrier for some who held such offices. Roger de Pont L'Évêque, for example, is known to have fathered a child at some point in his career. To Thomas's credit, though he was ambitious and was very happy to accumulate wealth and enjoy the lifestyle he could now afford, he would remain true to the promises he made at his ordination. As he donned the dalmatic, Thomas's ambitions were finding fulfillment at last.

In terms of dignity, the archdeacon of Canterbury, the most senior archdeaconry in England, was almost on a par with bishops and abbots. The office came with an income of more than one hundred pounds a year, which was a serious sum of money in 1154 and, ironically, was more than the archbishop of York would receive — Roger had to take a cut in salary with his move to the higher office. While the office brought great prestige, it was usually seen as a "suggestive" appointment — the one appointed to the office was marked out for even higher office. Thomas knew without a doubt that unless some disaster should fall upon him, he would in time become a bishop. As his predecessor had become an archbishop, that too was a real possibility. Thomas brought a wealth of experience to the office and, by now quite adept at meeting whatever challenges arose, was quick to gain even more experience in the daily exercise of this high ecclesiastical position.

Like every deacon, Thomas had a role to play in the sacramental life of the Church. While he could not offer Mass, hear confession, or administer the Sacrament of the Sick, he could baptize, marry, preach, and preside at various ceremonies. While historians correctly plot Thomas's progress in status and wealth, his spiritual response to these steps in his elevation is not usually highlighted. For all his ambition and love of mammon, Thomas never lost the simple piety his mother had taught him or forgot his duties to the poor as his lot in life improved. His resolve to stay true to his promise of celibacy when many others in his position were happy to forget it in the throes of passion and opportunity reveals that his simple piety was made of stern stuff and could steer this young man in the right direction morally. As an archdeacon, Thomas was not merely an ecclesiastical official and an administrator; he was also an ordained minister, with duties and responsibilities that were as much spiritual as they were political and administrative. The key to understanding the complexities of Thomas Becket's character lies in realizing that his Christian faith mattered to him even when his adherence to some of its tenets may not have been ideal.

On October 25, 1154, around the time of Thomas's ordination, King Stephen died. His peaceful reign was short, just ten months; he contracted what appears to have been dysentery while staying at Dover Priory. He was buried at Faversham Abbey with his wife and son Eustace. The king's death would prove to be an advantage for Henry; his position in Normandy was not as secure as he would have hoped, and any number of events could have weakened his position. A long, peaceful reign for Stephen could well have seen a reversal of fortune for the beleaguered king and his young son William.

When Stephen died, Henry was in France assisting Louis VII, who was now pacified after his rant over Henry and Eleanor's hasty marriage. As a feudal subject of France, Henry was fulfilling his duty to stand with his king in a war with some of Louis's unruly vassals. When news came to him that Stephen had died, he immediately proclaimed himself Henry II of England and enjoyed the victory not only for himself but for his mother, still living her life in the monastery; she was finally vindicated in her claim, though she would never wear the crown herself. Despite his pleasure at his succession, Henry was in no hurry to get to England. He tarried in France and made arrangements to sail back in early December. In the meantime, Theobald took the reins and governed as regent until Henry condescended to gift England with his presence.

King Henry and Queen Eleanor arrived in England on December 7, 1154, landing near Southampton and making their way to London, where preparations for the coronation were already advanced.[4] On December 19, Henry and Eleanor were anointed and crowned by Theobald at Westminster Abbey;[5] Henry was twenty-one years old, his queen thirty-two. They already had a son and heir, William, Count of Poitiers, just over a year old, and Eleanor was pregnant again — a second son was due in February. It seemed a new dynasty was about to be founded and secured. Flush with victory, Henry was confident in his ability to rule with skill and security. He sought peace and unity, and assured his new subjects that he would restore England to her former glory after almost two decades of war, strife, and death. A new age had begun; he hoped the days of tyranny were over.

Such too were the hopes of the people of England, who were worn out after civil war and the tense reign of the usurper. They were sure that they now had a great prince, and Henry was keen to confirm that impression. He wanted peace and stability, and he planned to deliver them. In his coronation charter, the new king made his subjects no promises, but he assured them that he would grant them all the concessions, liberties, and freedoms that his grandfather, Henry I, had allowed them.[6] That in itself should have rung warning bells — Henry I had been more an autocrat than a generous libertarian. The new young king looked back on his grandfather's reign as halcyon days when the iron fist, neatly nestled in a velvet glove, ensured that the crown jealously guarded its rights, liberties, and assets — with an uncanny ability to dip into the assets of others when the need arose.

Among those serving at the coronation was the new archdeacon of Canterbury, assisting the archbishop in the various liturgical actions of the ceremony. Henry would have noticed Thomas, now dressed splendidly in the dalmatic and no doubt as professional in his liturgical role as he was in the vital role he had played in the tense negotiations of 1153. Did Henry muse on the fact that he in large part owed the crown he was wearing to the deacon now standing before him in the abbey? He may well have done so, perhaps even speculating that this servant of the archbishop might prove an effective servant of the crown. Henry would need help to usher in this new age and to bring about that restoration of royal power and privilege he desired; he needed formidable and able counselors and advisors, and he saw before him the newly ordained archdeacon of Canterbury, who had been so deft in the negotiations for peace.

As the palace at Westminster was deemed uninhabitable, having suffered damage during the Anarchy, Henry and Eleanor spent Christmas at the Cluniac Bermondsey Priory on the southern bank of the River Thames, holding court there for the first few months of their reign. The priory provided accommodation for the royal family and their servants until a suitable residence was ready; it was close enough to London, and it provided some peace and quiet, which the new queen appreciated for the last days of her pregnancy. On February 28, 1155, Eleanor gave birth to the couple's second son, Henry. The succession now seemed secure.

Meanwhile, in January 1155, Thomas received a summons from the royal court — he was to present himself at Bermondsey for an audience with the king. Henry had made up his mind. He had seen Thomas at work, and now he wanted him for royal service. This competent and dutiful man would be at Henry's side — if the king got his way, not as clerk but as royal chancellor.

Part II

The King's Servant

11

Henry

The first thing to note about Henry II is that he was a restless man.[1] Never content to stay in one place, he had to be on the move, preferring his saddle to his throne; perhaps he saw the two as one and the same, given who was astride them both. This restlessness revealed his personality. Happiest on the back of a horse, he lived, like many a warrior, on the edge; he was a man who wanted to be in control, a man of action, a man for whom tolerance might be a sign of weakness. There is always the temptation, among Catholics in particular, to see Henry Angevin as a wicked man, a precursor to Henry VIII who sought to bring the Church under his control and was prepared to liquidate whoever he needed to — even the archbishop of Canterbury — in order to achieve that aim. That would not be the whole truth any more than is the narrative that, rough as he was, he was put upon by an ambitious and angry Catholic cleric and backed into a corner out of which he had to come fighting to preserve his kingdom and his just plans for renewal and stability.

Henry was a complicated man with a lot of baggage, a king who knew what he wanted and was prepared to make tough decisions to achieve his aims. He had had to fight for his crown, a crown he should have inherited from his mother; and once he had it, he had to fight for his rights as monarch of England and Normandy. He inherited a worldview very different from ours; he failed to understand the developments in the Church as she sought to free herself from secular control. It is no offense to Thomas Becket to accept that Henry Angevin, king of England, seen by some as the founder of the House of Plantagenet, was indeed an extraordinary man and a notable king, and to see the ungodly row between him and Thomas as a tragedy born of the character not only of the archbishop but of the king himself. Henry's inner turbulence would foster conflicts not only with his archbishop but with his wife, his sons, and any number of unfortunate souls who dared to cross him. As a contemporary historian who knew Henry, the archdeacon Gerald of Wales, once noted in his writings, because of his personality Henry "found strife instead of safety, ruin instead of repose, ingratitude instead of constancy, and the utmost confusion instead of peace and tranquility."[2]

Though he often described Thomas as a lowborn clerk, Henry's own origins were not so exalted. He was the great-grandson of William the Conqueror, who was, in fact, illegitimate. William was born of a woman called Herleva, who was mistress to his father, Robert, Duke of Normandy. Herleva hailed from a family of leather workers in Falaise in Normandy, and it has been noted more than once that Henry's rough ways may have been a throwback to his humble ancestry. Once, for example, as Henry was sewing a leather plaster onto his wounded finger with particular proficiency during a meeting with another bishop with whom he was in conflict, the bishop noted the skill he had inherited from his "cousins of Falaise." To his credit, Henry roared with laughter; he was able to take a joke even at his own expense and let the bishop off the hook for his wit, to the surprise of the assembled courtiers.[3]

Henry was born in Le Mans in the county of Maine, in what is now France, on March 5, 1133. Maine was disputed territory, as both Normandy and Anjou claimed it. The marriage of Geoffrey of Anjou and Empress Matilda of Normandy seemed to settle the dispute, as their joint heir, Henry, would claim Maine unopposed. Henry's earliest years were spent with his mother at her court in Normandy, but when he was about seven years old, he went to live in Anjou at his father's court while his mother tried to stake her claim to the throne of England. When he was nine, his father sent him to Bristol in England to live with his uncle Robert of Gloucester, Matilda's half-brother, to be educated in his household.[4] Sending children to be educated in the household of a relative was a common medieval practice, but Henry's presence in Bristol, an important center of opposition to Stephen, was no accident; it was a political move to consolidate support for Matilda and put Stephen on edge. In about 1143, Henry returned to Anjou to continue his education, remaining there until he was about fourteen.

Henry was a bright young man who loved reading, a passion he inherited from his father and maintained throughout his life.[5] While he gave greater priority to hunting, reading came a close second in his affections. He was known to carry scrolls with him wherever he went and was often seen reading while astride his horse during sieges and other idle moments. He was educated by a number of reputable scholars who awakened in him an interest in many areas of learning. Adelard of Bath, for example, would dedicate his treatise *On the Astrolabe* to him, and it was not an empty gesture: Henry would have been inclined to read it, particularly as it dealt with a practical scientific instrument.[6] His reading preference was, unsurprisingly, for works concerned with law and government. Linguistically, he was also proficient, developing an understanding of a number of languages, though he only spoke his native French, Latin, and occasionally a little English.[7]

Physically, Henry developed into an athletic young man. He inherited his father's red hair and freckles and had blue-gray eyes whose natural gaze was a piercing stare. His head was large and round, propped up on a short neck. He was short and inclined to be stocky; aware of this, he was careful of what he ate as he grew older and exercised, though it did not prevent him from developing a paunch in later life.[8] His legs were at first strong and athletic, but over the years became bowlegged thanks to his continual riding. He wore his hair closely cropped, and he dressed shabbily — he never had an interest in sartorial elegance. As a child, he could be sullen, and this attitude often recurred in adulthood, particularly when he could not get his way. His father, Geoffrey, possessed a charm that his son did not inherit; Henry was more inclined to his mother's temperament, for good or bad, though he was not as reserved as she could be. He wore his temper very close to his skin, and he had a natural inclination for bullying.[9] It seems he was never taught table manners as a child, or at least the lessons were not reinforced in any meaningful way, because he never possessed them as an adult; his eating habits were rough and far from those expected of a king, usually scandalizing his more exalted dinner guests.

Henry was religious in a conventional sense.[10] He attended daily Mass, as was the custom for Catholic monarchs at the time, though he was often to be found conducting state business in the chapel during the liturgy. He lacked an authentic piety and was given to sacrilege in his casual approach to the sacred.[11] He is known to have been an oath breaker. The solemnity of taking an oath meant little to him; when required to do so, he happily agreed but really had little intention of honoring what he had promised — an attitude he refused to tolerate in others. His moral life was also problematic and did not reflect that expected of a Christian. Like many Catholics before and after him, Henry did not make faith the priority in his life; it came second to his role as king and statesman. Henry saw everything as subordinate to the state and government, and as he saw himself as the state, everything — even the Church — had to be subordinate to him. This was at the heart of his dispute with Thomas. In this clash, he encountered a man who was gradually realizing that Christ and the Christian faith took precedence over everything else, including the king and the state. Subordinating faith to politics affected both Henry's worldview and his relationships, yet his faith was important to him. He was easily offended should anyone suggest that he was not Christian. He was, in his own view, a very Christian king; indeed, he saw himself as having an important governing role within the Church, and he was prepared to take that role very seriously.

In terms of his personality, Henry was a very complex man. While he bore no great eminence — he was a rough man by nature and in appearance — he was a brilliant statesman and seemed naturally inclined to govern, which he did with great aptitude. However, he was a flawed man whose temperament, as noted by Gerald of Wales, created problems for himself and for those around him. He tended to see relationships in terms of loyalty to him and his reign, showering his favor on those he saw as being devoted to him and coming to hate those he perceived to have betrayed him. Once he had formed an opinion of an individual, he rarely changed it. He could joust, reach agreements with, and form alliances with his enemies and those who challenged him — his relationship with Louis VII of France being a case in point. With those under his authority, he was not so generous. He was irrational and ungovernable when he fell into a fit of rage, but he could also be lovable, gentle, and friendly. In company he enjoyed, he was affable, witty, and polite. He was very accessible, even to the lowliest of his subjects. Though he is often compared with Henry VIII, the two men in fact had little in common. Both were men of great ability and could inspire admiration and loyalty, and both could be ruthless. However, Henry Angevin lacked the nihilistic qualities of Henry Tudor. He certainly lost control when he was angry and was bitter toward those he felt had offended him, but Henry VIII was more calculated and savage. While both men could be imperious, Henry VIII, a man possessed by power and lust, was so because of willfulness and perhaps even wickedness; Henry Angevin was simply a man controlled by his passions and flawed personality. For all his faults, he was admired not only by barons and lords but by bishops and even saints. Saint Ælred of Rievaulx[12] and Saint Gilbert of Sempringham,[13] for example, both contemporaries of Henry and Thomas, held him in high regard.

There seems to have been an emotional deficit in Henry that skewed how he saw those around him. This defect can be seen in his marriage with Eleanor and his relationships with his children and, of course, Thomas. There was an irrational persistence in Henry, a rage and childishness that drove him demented at times as he reacted unreasonably to various challenging situations; as Guy notes, Henry's greatest weakness was his temper.[14] He often found it difficult to forgive when he came to hate someone, as he did Thomas in time. In his eyes, nothing could redeem the one he hated.[15] Not even his wife and children escaped this bent of Henry's. It must be noted, however, that the king was not entirely to blame for the family strife that lay ahead. If he had been married to a saint, such a wife might have quelled the unruliness in him; but he was married to a woman who was as calculating and as ruthless as he was. It is no wonder that the children resembled the parents.

As king of England and Duke of Normandy, and married to the Duchess of Aquitaine, Henry was as powerful as the king of France. After Louis and Eleanor's annulment, he had wooed one of the most powerful women in Christendom and won her. The couple would have eight children to add to a son Henry had had with a mistress in about 1152. That son, Geoffrey, was destined to become archbishop of York in 1189, succeeding Roger de Pont L'Évêque. A second illegitimate son would be born to another mistress in about 1176, possibly Ida of Tosny, wife of the Earl of Norfolk; that son would become William, Earl of Salisbury.[16] Of his legitimate children with Eleanor, three sons would be kings: Henry the Young King, Richard I ("the Lionheart"), and John. Another son, Geoffrey, became Duke of Brittany, while their three daughters married nobles: Matilda became Duchess of Savoy; young Eleanor, queen of Castile; and Joan, queen of Sicily.

Once Henry took the throne, his reign (his dispute with Thomas aside) was positive for England. While he wanted to restore the many laws, customs, and arrangements that existed under his grandfather, he initiated many new laws and customs that were to the benefit of the kingdom and the people.[17] He sought to increase the power of the English royal courts, producing a more coherent system of laws and the means to implement them by appointing good administrators and making wider use of juries. He challenged not only Church courts but also the role of the barons in dispensing justice. Inheriting an abysmal financial system, Henry made it one of his first priorities to stabilize the currency and rejuvenate a poor economy while establishing financial institutions to undertake reforms and improve accounting. His reforms not only achieved these aims, but also led to a significant increase in royal revenues, assisted by new taxes and new sources of income from fines and amercements.[18]

Politically, he consolidated his English territories against the Scots, fortifying the north, and gradually brought Wales into submission to England. He also secured his realm on the continent, and after going to war to secure his wife's duchy, he governed to various degrees territory stretching from the English Channel to the Mediterranean, controlling more of France that any ruler after the Carolingians. Historians often refer to his realm as the Angevin Empire. In 1171, he invaded Ireland with the assistance of the king of Leinster, and though he would have to appoint and recognize Rory O'Connor as high king of Ireland in 1175, in reality Henry was lord of Ireland. He would intervene more directly in Irish affairs from 1177 onward; though ultimately, according to Warren, his policy in Ireland was a failure — his one major failure.[19] However, the troublesome Irish to one side, Henry was an emperor in all but title.

In January 1155, much of this lay in the future, mere ambition in the heart of a young king. To begin his work, Henry needed solid support and experienced, faithful servants to help him achieve his aims. In their meeting, Henry did not mince words with Thomas as he laid his plans before him. A new age was dawning for England, and he wanted the archdeacon to assume the office of royal chancellor and serve both this new and ambitious project and its master.

12
Royal Chancellor

Thomas accepted the king's offer. With Thomas a mere three months into his role as archdeacon of Canterbury and Henry a mere six weeks into his reign as king, the two would form an alliance to work together to rebuild England and restore the monarchy. Given their abilities, their ambitions, and their determination, it seemed like a marriage made in heaven.

Theobald had recommended Thomas to Henry as royal chancellor.[1] The archbishop would have seen the advantages of having his loyal protégé at the heart of the royal court, privy to the king's plans and decisions, perhaps even a trusted confidant. With Thomas as his servant — dare one say spy — in the corridors of secular power, Theobald would have hoped to secure the Church's interests; a likely necessity, as the wily and prudent archbishop would have already suspected that Henry was not entirely to be trusted. As Henry was a young man already known for his restlessness and passion, the archbishop may have likely felt that a calming influence would be needed now that Henry had charge of England. It has also been suggested that the archbishop, aware of the barons' animosity toward the Church, sought to have an advocate with Henry to prevent their influence on the king's policies regarding the Church.

This new king had spoken of returning England to the state it was in when his grandfather reigned, and any wise churchman would have feared that trouble lay ahead and would have tried to make provision for it. But there was also an opportunity for the restoration of peace and order. If a good relationship between the Church and the crown was established, Theobald could "retire" to pastoral duties and intellectual pursuits. As both archdeacon of Canterbury and royal chancellor, Thomas may have been, one historian surmises, a symbol of working cooperation between the Church and the crown.[2] If this was Theobald's plan, he did not expect that his archdeacon would truly become Henry's confidant and shift his allegiance. The archdeacon must have been overwhelmed at Henry's offer: two premium appointments in such a short time. While he was no doubt thrilled, he may well have been a little shaken. But he was not going to pass up this extraordinary opportunity. He accepted, and with that came a new master, a new plan of action, and new ambitions.

The office of the royal chancellor of England, the *cancellarius regis*, was an important one within the realm, but its importance lay more in what it could be than in what it was.[3] The holder of the office could make it great, and during his time as royal chancellor, Thomas did exactly that. It was a position second only to chief justiciar, the medieval equivalent of prime minister; at the time of Thomas's appointment, that office was held by Richard de Lucy and Robert de Beaumont. The royal chancellor, later lord chancellor, was at that time a royal chaplain, indeed the chief ecclesiastical officer in charge of the Chapel Royal; hence, the holder was always a cleric. However, that was the chancellor's only ecclesiastical responsibility; the other duties of his office were secular and administrative.[4] He was the keeper of the Great Seal, the king's official seal, so he had an important part to play in drawing up and confirming the legislative acts of the reign. Supervising royal charters, writs, and orders, he was in a sense a secretary of state for the various strands of the king's government. He was also in charge of the scriptorium, where official documents were written and copied, and the custodian of all state archives. The office also had legal responsibilities, as the royal chancellor would be called upon to act as a judge in the king's courts.[5]

The royal chancellor also had financial responsibilities, fulfilling various duties at the royal exchequer. He collected and controlled the revenues from vacant dioceses and abbeys, as these revenues came to the crown for the duration of the vacancy — a situation that often led to abuses and delayed ecclesiastical appointments if the monarch found himself in need of funds. Unscrupulous chancellors often conducted this "pillaging of the Church" — which Saint Anselm, when archbishop of Canterbury, Theobald, and other bishops complained about — by regularly advising kings to keep certain wealthy bishoprics and abbatial offices vacant for as long as possible in order to replenish straitened royal coffers. Chancellors were also charged with finding other ways of meeting the expenses of king and government.

The chancellor normally traveled with the king as advisor and clerk. Immersed in the affairs of state, he stood by the king's side at court, attended the king's various meetings, and lived the life of a senior courtier. This was a role Thomas surely embraced with pleasure and gusto. Under his administration, the office achieved a prominence and prestige it had never had before, mainly because of Henry and Thomas's growing friendship. Thomas was now thirty-four, still fit and young. He stood taller than the king, and he carried himself with a nobility that Henry lacked. Given his confidence, ability, and bearing, it might be more correct to say that the office of chancellor grew into him rather than that he grew into it. If ever a man was ready for the affairs of state and its trappings, it was the new archdeacon of Canterbury. When he arrived at Henry's court to begin his work, Thomas brought his ambitions with him, and while he had attained high office, he would enhance that office as much as it would enhance him. Those around him noted that he was a singular individual.

The new chancellor was thrown into a flurry of activity right away. Henry unveiled his plans, and Thomas was to make it his mission to ensure that those plans came to fruition — that the king got what he wanted with the least amount of trouble. Waiting for him as he took his place were letters of congratulation and advice, among them one from

Bishop Arnulf of Lisieux.[6] A rather slippery character even though he was a bishop, Arnulf tended to put the king's interests before anything else in his life — sometimes even the Church. Even then one could not be sure if this was for the king's benefit or for Arnulf's. The bishop offered Thomas advice on how to serve the king — he himself had served Henry for four years at that point, so he knew all the pitfalls, and he claimed that he was seeking to help Thomas negotiate them.[7] No response from Thomas is extant; perhaps he knew better than to respond in writing to such an epistle. Given his experience so far, he probably discerned that this prelate could not be trusted. Thomas knew full well that the way ahead was littered with traps and unscrupulous sycophants.

The first year of Thomas's administration saw him on horseback trailing Henry as he undertook the pacification of England.[8] Drafting treaties, charters, and other documents, he played the straight man to a tentative monarch trying to woo potential challengers to his reign to become allies and supporters (or at least, render them harmless). One of the first challenges to negotiate was the presence of the late King Stephen's mercenaries, men who had fought Henry on the battlefield. Thomas was involved in ushering them out of England back to Flanders, a mission that required just the right amount of tact and a steady hint of threat. Another thorny issue concerned property. After the Anarchy, numerous castles had to be returned to their rightful owners, and many other castles, which had been built illegally, had to be torn down. Thomas was in the thick of negotiations that would see some dispossessed and others disappointed. Once that process was under way, Henry launched his plan to obtain land and begin building his own castles and fortifications; this would also have created additional headaches for the chancellor, as he had to draw up the necessary documents and somehow obtain the necessary signatures or seals as a confirmation of consent, sometimes from very unwilling subjects. Not everything went smoothly; serious trouble emerged with one particular baron, Hugh de Mortimer, who illegally held a royal castle in Shropshire, that of Bridgnorth. De Mortimer and a number of other barons were prepared to fight for their cause, forcing Henry to lay siege and eventually bring them to heel. A council was then held at Bridgnorth on July 7, 1155, to formalize the barons' submission, and Thomas and his staff had to deal with the paperwork.[9] Henry's battles always ended with lots of paperwork.

As the months passed and England was lulled into peace, Henry began to feel much more comfortable. His Norman possessions, however, were becoming a cause for concern. His brother Geoffrey was threatening revolt, and King Louis VII of France, despite their reconciliation, was still harboring resentment at his marriage to Eleanor. Having failed to give Louis a male heir, Eleanor had by December 1155 given birth to two sons for Henry — the heir and the spare — and she was pregnant again. To make a point, Louis refused to acknowledge Henry as Duke of Aquitaine.[10] This was not just a personal gripe against Henry; there was also a political issue at play. If Eleanor had failed to provide Henry with male progeny, then the two daughters she bore Louis would have had a claim to Aquitaine, and Louis could have claimed jurisdiction and the duchy's wealth. Henry, fearing an alliance between his brother and Louis, left England in early 1156 to engage with Geoffrey, arriving in Rouen on February 25 with Thomas in tow. Henry would engage in a campaign against his brother, and the chancellor would be forced to settle down to all the paperwork the dispute generated.

Henry's little war against his brother cost Thomas more than time drawing up papers; he was now confronted with the need to raise money to finance a campaign that could end up being a long and drawn-out affair, if this spat followed the pattern of other royal family feuds. These wars were usually fought by professional soldiers and mercenaries, so a deep purse was required to hire, replenish, and feed troops; the raising of this purse fell to Thomas. He came up with a lucrative proposition: to revive an old form of taxation called "scutage" (shield money).[11] Scutage was a tax that knights who had been granted land by the king paid in lieu of military service, which was usually required of them whenever their feudal lord needed to raise an army. Henry I had been the first English king to use this exemption tax to finance mercenaries. The knight-tenants paid a set figure, and the king would buy whatever personnel or equipment he needed. Thomas would prove quite zealous in resurrecting the tax, imposing a fee that was above the historic rate; not a fee based on how many soldiers were owed to service, as tradition dictated, but rather the same fee for all the knight-tenants. This new scheme of taxation, which was in essence unequitable but highly profitable, raised the hackles of the knights. They protested vigorously, but as Thomas's scheme was bound to raise more than enough money to fill Henry's war chest, the king was not inclined to listen. Among those who objected most strongly was Archbishop Theobald, himself bound to pay scutage — Duggan notes that Canterbury's scutage was charged for 84 ¾ fees.[12] He lodged a petition to be exempted from the payment, but Thomas refused it; Theobald was not happy.

Henry's campaign proved successful. Louis was not inclined to fight and made peace on February 5, 1156, acknowledging Henry as Duke of Aquitaine as long as Henry performed the customary homage to Louis as his feudal lord in this respect.[13] Eleanor, by all accounts, was not delighted with this outcome, as she saw her husband usurp what was her duchy and the French king confirm that usurpation. With this agreement between the kings, Geoffrey was eventually forced to back down. Meanwhile, Henry set his sights on the Duchy of Brittany, and particularly the port city of Nantes, which he claimed as a feudal dependency.[14] In a brilliant political move, Henry exploited a civil war in the duchy and had the denizens of Nantes declare Geoffrey, Henry's brother, as their count, while persuading the Breton barons to declare one of his Norman lords, Conan, Earl of Richmond, as their new Duke of Brittany. Geoffrey was pacified with Nantes, future trouble there was diverted, and Henry now had an ally in Brittany. It seems that the idea of diverting Geoffrey to Nantes was Thomas's.[15]

After Eleanor gave birth to a daughter, Matilda, in June 1156, she joined Henry on an excursion throughout their realms on the continent. Thomas went back and forth, accompanying the royal couple for a time, then returning to England for work. As the king was away from England, it fell to Thomas to carry out a number of duties on his behalf, including greeting ambassadors, holding court, and entertaining. His encounters with various officials worked to his advantage, as his charm, generosity, and courtesy won their approval and, in turn, gave foreign representatives a positive opinion of the new king and his court. In such meetings, Thomas also sharpened his diplomatic skills.

Those skills would prove crucial as Henry faced his next crisis, another spat with Louis, this time over the territory of the Vexin. This area in northwestern France, traditionally associated with a tribe known as the Veliocasses, was the subject of dispute between the two crowns for a number of years. At this point, Henry possessed it, but Louis was under the impression that when Henry gave homage to him as French king for his possessions on the continent, this territory was to be ceded to France. The dispute remained unresolved until Louis's second wife, Constance, gave birth to their daughter Margaret in the spring of 1158. At that stage, tentative diplomatic negotiations were under way, but the birth of the little princess opened a new possibility for a resolution: Little Henry junior, by now the heir apparent following his elder brother William's death in December 1156, and little Margaret would be engaged to be married, and the Vexin would form part of the marriage agreement. It fell to Thomas to negotiate this proposal with Louis.

For this important diplomatic mission in early 1158, Thomas would have to use every resource he had in the service of Henry's cause. He was, in essence, charged with forging a dynastic alliance. The embassy he put together was legendary, "of oriental magnificence" as one historian notes,[16] a statement of Angevin power and prestige, but perhaps also to display the eagerness of a self-made man for the trappings of status and the privilege of rank.[17] He assembled an enormous entourage: a large number of knights, clerks, and servants of all ranks dressed in the most stylish and expensive livery.[18] A large number of wagons transported what each department of his household needed for the negotiations and entertainments. His makeshift office, kitchen, and chapel, and all that was required for their efficient functioning, were transported together with the great tents he and his retinue would need for accommodation, meetings, and entertainment. Whole wagons carried his vast wardrobe of clothes; it was noted that he had twenty-four changes of clothes of the finest quality, most of which he wore once and perhaps a few twice. The best tableware and linens, along with superlative delicacies and wines, were secured. The embassy would have to replenish supplies along the way, sometimes surreptitiously in order to circumvent a ban Louis had imposed on markets and other suppliers, lest Thomas's embassy ravage resources and leave the French king with little for his own banquets. Louis did not want the English to surpass him in hospitality in his own country.

As the embassy progressed across the north of France to its meeting with Louis, passing through towns and villages, the natives were astonished by the progression of pages, knights, wagons, and animals organized into a grand procession to impress. At the end of the cavalcade came the chancellor in all his finery, leading people to gasp in wonder: If the chancellor of England is so great, then the king himself must be extraordinary.[19] This was the impression Thomas had aimed to create — a mystique for Henry that, in turn, created one for himself. As he made his way through these towns and villages, Thomas gave liberally to the locals: money, food, clothes, and beer were distributed generously, and as always he remembered the poor; with his mother's example in mind, he was profligate with the beggars he met on his way.

Despite his best efforts, Louis failed to outdo Thomas in hospitality. The chancellor organized extravagant banquets and entertainments, conferring gifts upon the members of the French court and others as tokens of his goodwill.[20] His diplomatic skills were as well tuned as his hospitality was lavish; he persuaded Louis to agree to the espousals and successfully negotiated the terms. It was agreed that the Vexin would be ceded to France until the day young Henry and Margaret married, when King Henry would take possession. In return, Margaret, as the wife of the heir to the English throne, would receive the revenues of the cities of Lincoln and Avranches, together with lands to support an army of five hundred knights as her personal retinue, thereby providing her with both an independent income in compensation for the Vexin and independent security. When the conferences were over and Louis and his retinue had been sufficiently dazzled by English abundance, Thomas returned to England in a state of triumph. He had proven that he was not just a high-ranking clerk; he was a man of state, the king's most trusted official, a diplomat of great resources who had safeguarded his king's domains and laid the foundation for a dynastic alliance that could establish peace between these two important realms for generations, or so he hoped. Thomas also gained a new friend and admirer, one who would prove useful in the years ahead: the king of France.[21]

Later, in the summer of 1158, following the death of Henry's brother Geoffrey, Henry's presumed ally in Brittany, Duke Conan, seized Nantes, forcing the king to take up arms on the continent once more. He made his way to Paris to confer with Louis, who gave him custody of little Margaret. When Henry turned toward Brittany, Conan surrendered. For all his bravado, the duke knew he had no hope of victory. Henry decided to be magnanimous. While he took possession of Nantes, he recognized Conan as duke but subject to him.[22] Conan may have breathed a sigh of relief. Having called that individual to heel, Henry found time to take a leisurely tour of Normandy, inviting King Louis to join him and also extending an invitation to Thomas as a reward for his superlative diplomacy. Making his way to join the kings in their diversions, Thomas seemed to be an inseparable part of Henry's administration — indeed more: a personal friend.

13
The Trappings of Power

With the office of royal chancellor came expectations of a particular lifestyle, not merely for the sake of a chancellor's dignity but also for his lord, the king's. In medieval times, the majesty of the king was to be seen in his closest collaborators, and as a senior servant of the monarch, Thomas would have to oblige — not that he needed any persuasion. Much has been written about Thomas's lavish lifestyle; but in reality, extravagance was expected from a man in his position, even if he enjoyed it a little too much. Yet, in the midst of it all, a hidden piety kept a leash on the archdeacon, even if he pulled against it at times. A magnificent household was necessary to establish his power within the realm; he entertained not for mere pleasure but as a means of carrying out state business, brokering solutions to problems, and bringing malcontents, possible enemies, and high-ranking figures into an amicable relationship with the king. As chancellor, Thomas would also have had to keep a hospitable table for the king, his family, and friends. His generosity and extravagance were an obligation of the office.[1]

There is no doubt that Thomas warmly embraced the lifestyle his position brought. It had always been his ambition to have a good life, to have wealth and status; and now that he had it, he meant to enjoy it. It is not known exactly how much he owned or how much he earned. He continued to draw his ecclesiastical benefices, and he would have had other sources of income given his position at court. He was also able to draw upon the royal treasury to meet his expenses; while this was allowed, it would later provide Henry with ammunition to castigate Thomas. However, he also incurred debts because his lifestyle exceeded his income, as would become obvious later. His household was second in size only to the king's.[2] He had a number of ships at his disposal, always ready to take him across the English Channel. He had a retinue of knights — it is thought about 150 — and his responsibility to support them and their households along with his own is an indication as to his financial situation. He dressed well, keeping a stylish wardrobe that included silks and furs of the finest quality and of which he was very proud. He also had a menagerie, a little zoo, which traveled with him on his journeys and was used for the entertainment of his guests. The furnishings in his home were of the highest quality, and his dinner service the best that money could buy. Thomas lived in luxury.

He also ate well, insofar as his digestive ailments would allow. He enjoyed fine wines, though he was never known to be excessive — his health problems made sure of that. He developed a sensitive palate and relished the finest delicacies, the more exotic the better; rare foods, served on gold and silver plates, would become regular dishes at his table. His cooks were among the best in the kingdom, and they were given free rein to produce what was most delicious and, at banquets, what would most dazzle his guests. Thomas was ostentatious in showing that he had the trappings of power and wealth, and his table was on the frontline of this spectacle. He was a lavish entertainer, sparing nothing to ensure that his guests were well treated and well fed. While courtiers were used to royal chancellors being generous at table, Thomas seemed to take their breath away.

Some believed that he was trying too hard, that he was too ostentatious, that he behaved as if he had something to prove. His enemies regarded this excess as compensation for his low birth, as his attempt to be better than everyone else, or as an expression of the inadequacy he felt in the presence of men who were socially superior.[3] While he may have gone overboard in his indulgence, Thomas was always courteous and kind toward his guests, and this won him approval. Those who were invited to dine with him were treated royally, and this would be a constant for him both as chancellor and as archbishop. There was an aspect to his character that sought not just to win the approval of others, but also to be good to them. As during his great embassy to the king of France in 1158, he was liberal in giving gifts, and he never forgot the poor. Though swimming in luxury as chancellor, he did not forget his mother's lessons on providing for the needy; as his wealth increased, so, too, did his almsgiving.

His household was a marked contrast to the king's. As Thomas's was ordered, tidy, and carefully managed, Henry's was unruly and chaotic, reflecting the king's own manner of life.[4] Henry did not keep regular hours; he came and went as he pleased all hours of the day and night. He had no time for etiquette, but expected his servants to be there when he needed them, whenever that was. He would often work late into the night and then sleep late in the morning. He loved his food and was very fond of his wine, drinking copious amounts each day. His servants and guests, however, did not fare as well, often dining on inferior quality meat, stale bread, and sour wine or beer. The king was renowned for his yelling, the chief means through which he instructed his officials and servants. As he was apt to change his mind frequently, his household was in a perpetual state of flux and panic. The chancellor's household was much more refined and, while busy, it was a saner and gentler place to be. The servants were well cared for, and guests were treated not just to lavish hospitality but also to an extraordinary degree of courtesy and kindness by the chancellor himself. Thomas never lost his gift of charm. The stability and organization of the chancellor, his staff, and his household may well have balanced out the king's and managed to keep some decorum within the official organization of the realm.

Despite his busy life as clerk, archdeacon, and now chancellor, Thomas never lost his love for country sports. As a clerk, he had carefully built up his collection of hunting birds and horses, but now as chancellor he finally had the resources and opportunities to rival his friend Richer in his pursuits. He kept hawks, falcons, and hounds, maintained fine stables, and, whenever he had time, was out hunting on the lands and estates surrounding his residence. He usually had a number of companions with him on these forays, most notably Henry himself, who loved the sporting life. It is likely this mutual love sealed the friendship between king and chancellor. In the evenings, as work was complete for the day, Thomas would relax with company for dinner and engage his love for chess. He was a brilliant chess player; his good memory and skilled tactics usually meant he triumphed over his opponents.

Given the time and practice of many men of power, it would not have been surprising if Thomas had taken a mistress or engaged in sexual relations with women. Even though he was a deacon and bound to celibacy, others before him had succumbed to the weakness of the flesh, and as it was one of the most common vices of the nobility and the powerful, such illicit pleasures seemed to have been overlooked and even expected. The king, though married to the most desirable woman in Europe, was promiscuous, as were many other nobles, clergy, and even popes. However, this was one area of transgression in which Thomas did not indulge. For all his faults, Thomas maintained his purity. Contemporary commentators said of him that he was a chaste man who hated indecency and depravity.[5] Given the often riotous nature of life at court, particularly during banquets and celebrations — when alcohol was flowing freely, and with it opportunities for casual sex, it would have been difficult for Thomas to avoid compromising situations. Prostitutes were almost unofficial courtiers, usually residing not far from the royal palaces and offering their services to nobles, soldiers, and servants. When the court was traveling, the ladies of the night followed the royal wagons in a wagon of their own and set up camp not far from the main site. Yet, Thomas was adamant. One man who knew him once said of him that though he may have been proud and given to worldly vanities, he was chaste in body and healthy in soul.[6] His biographer William FitzStephen[7] noted that no lechery polluted him.[8]

Thomas did everything he could not to fall into sexual temptation. One story related by biographers describes how Thomas managed to escape from one awkward situation.[9] Henry had discarded one of his mistresses and, to free himself of her, tried to pawn her off on his chancellor. She was not put out by the suggestion at all, as Thomas was a very handsome man. She sent suggestive messages to him, offering her company. A clerk who was staying with Thomas discovered the notes and read them. He saw a chance to blackmail the chancellor. He intended to catch him in bed with the king's mistress and blackmail him for his silence. During the night, the clerk, supposing Thomas and the lady to be in the throes of passion, sneaked into the room, only to find the bed empty and the sheets undisturbed. Further investigation led him to find the chancellor fast asleep on the floor, wrapped only in his cloak, with his bare legs and feet exposed to the cold. Thomas had spent hours in prayer and had fallen asleep exhausted yet still offering penance for his sins, choosing the cold floor rather than a soft, warm bed. The lady had not been invited to his lodgings; in fact, he had never even engaged with her — the messages had gone unanswered. As Thomas would not succumb to sexual temptation, he maintained a similar standard in his household. He not only encouraged good living among his staff, but also put measures in place to ensure that they would not be led astray, at least not under his roof. Should staff commit misdemeanors, he dealt with them, even dismissing them if necessary. In one case, he dealt with one of his clerks who had seduced another man's wife by putting him in chains in the Tower of London.[10]

It is a testament to the complexity of Thomas's character that though he loved an opulent lifestyle, the faith his mother taught him still directed the fundamental aspects of his life. He coupled his increasing generosity to the poor with a chaste lifestyle while encouraging those in his employ to do the same. But that was not all. As the incident above reveals, he was given to acts of penance. His staff noted that after a day of self-indulgence, he would often spend the night in penitential acts as a means of reparation. He continued to pray each day and nurture his relationship with God. Thomas never forgot that though he may often have lived and acted like a secular official, he was a deacon of the Church, and he realized that he had to overcome his weaknesses if he were to observe the manner of life expected of a man in holy orders.

Thomas knew he was paying a high price for the honor Henry had bestowed upon him. He was seen as the king's creature; he made enemies of former friends in his attempts to provide the king with what he wanted, and he struggled with that. Another who struggled with Thomas's situation was Theobald. The archbishop was aware that his archdeacon served a difficult king who pulled him in one direction as Theobald tried to keep him focused on the Church. He had not been impressed by Thomas's refusal to grant his petition for an exemption to the scutage, though he could understand it. But other decisions gratified the archbishop, and one was Thomas's policy of trying to make sure Henry filled vacant bishoprics and abbatial offices quickly rather than take advantage of vacancies to enhance the royal coffers. He had some success there. Seeking worthy candidates for these offices, Thomas would attempt to steer Henry toward them for the good of the diocese or abbey. In one case, Henry was about to appoint a questionable candidate to the Diocese of Exeter; when Theobald heard of it, he was horrified — he had another candidate in mind, one he judged better suited. The archbishop made his views known to Thomas, the chancellor pursued the matter with Henry, and to Theobald's delight, Henry chose his candidate.[11]

Dealing with Henry on such matters required great tact, and Thomas was usually shrewd enough to know what would work and what would enrage the king. But he was not always successful. When the matter of a scandalous marriage arose in 1160, Thomas found himself on the wrong side of the king.[12] The issue concerned canon law and the requirement of consent for a valid marriage. In an attempt to seize control and influence in Boulogne and Picardy, Henry decided that his cousin Matthew of Alsace would be married to the heir of William, Count of Boulogne. However, there was a problem. This heir, Marie of Blois, the daughter of the late King Stephen, was a nun; in fact, she was the abbess of the Abbey of Romsey in Hampshire, and quite happily so. Such trifling matters did not worry Henry. Once the two were married, Matthew would control Boulogne and Picardy through his wife, and Henry would control Matthew. As far as Henry was concerned, it was easily achieved.

However, Mother Marie did not agree. She was quite happy living her religious life and was not prepared to sacrifice her religious vows to marry a stranger in order to fulfill the king of England's ambitions. She refused to agree to the marriage. In a fit of rage, Henry ordered her to obey;

once again, the good abbess refused. At this point, Thomas intervened. Calling the proposed union profane and abominable, he asked Henry not to violate Marie's religious vows and her free will, quoting canon law to consolidate his argument. Turning his wrath on his chancellor, the king rebuked him fiercely. Determined to force his plans through with sheer violence, he sent his men to the abbey to kidnap Marie and drag her to the altar, where she was forced to take the marriage vows. The marriage was, of course, invalid and would be annulled in 1170, though Matthew would hold on to the title and estates. Marie bore Matthew two daughters who would be as independent as their mother. Once free of Matthew, she returned to religious life, to the Benedictine monastery of Saint Austrebert in Montreuil in what is now the north of France. In this matter, Henry revealed his attitude toward the Church, toward her laws, and toward the will of those who opposed him, and it was deeply disturbing. Thomas took note, as did Theobald.

When he had to deal with a similar issue — this time the king's anger toward John of Salisbury due to his close relationship with the pope — Thomas realized he had to be shrewder.[13] John had been sent to Rome to represent Theobald's interests at the papal court, just as Thomas was meant to do at the royal court. The pope at the time was the Englishman Nicholas Breakspear, who reigned as Adrian IV. He and John had been friends for a long time, so when John arrived, he was welcomed warmly and given a privileged place at the papal court. When Henry's ambassadors arrived in Rome to request the pope's permission to invade Ireland, they noticed John's singular favor, and one of them, the inimitable Bishop Arnulf of Lisieux, sent back slanderous reports; Arnulf and John became enemies.

John had heard that Arnulf was spreading lies about him, and in an attempt to undermine Arnulf and annoy Henry, he persuaded Adrian to grant the petition but with conditions. Henry found these conditions intolerable and reacted badly, blaming John for the partial failure of his petition. As he resented the pope's jurisdiction in England, Henry considered John's close relationship with Adrian to be treasonous, and decreed that the clerk would be put on trial for treason as soon as he set foot back in England. John was appalled and fell into a state of serious anxiety —

he knew this trial could yield only one judgment: death. He appealed to Thomas to help him and Thomas agreed, stepping into the midst of the fray to find some solution. Having learned from his previous entreaty for Marie of Blois, Thomas tried another means of getting around Henry — he appealed to Queen Eleanor to assist him. Together, chancellor and queen persuaded Henry to relent. The king agreed not to hold a trial, but John was to be banished from his presence. Fearing that John would lose all his benefices and be impoverished, Thomas also managed to convince Henry to allow the clerk keep his post in Canterbury and his salaries.

Thomas may have reveled in the trappings of power, but they came at a price that was often high, personally and professionally. Despite his great power and influence, he was at the mercy of a young king who was a slave to his anger and possessed an extraordinary pride. In the early years, this was not a problem; and though it would become challenging in the later years of his chancellorship, Thomas's close relationship with Henry covered over much that was unpleasant — for a time, at least.

14
Master and Servant

From the moment of his appointment as chancellor to the day he left for Canterbury, Thomas spent much of his life, apart from particular missions, in the company of the king and his court. For most of that period, as Henry was resident in Normandy for the greater part of his first eight years as king, the chancellor spent little time in England. Given his office, he had privileges others did not have, including access to the king — others usually required permission to be in the royal presence. He was one of Henry's most trusted advisors and perhaps the closest to the young monarch. Thomas was twelve or thirteen years older than Henry. He was also four inches taller, and more noble in his bearing. Though the two would not have been expected to get along beyond a professional level, over time Thomas and Henry developed a deep personal friendship, a friendship that seems to have been the most intimate either of them would have in their lives. Thomas's biographer William FitzStephen noted that there was never in Christian times two greater friends who were more of one mind.[1]

Henry trusted Thomas implicitly, and while they had disagreements, the king, hardly a man for bureaucracy, was content to leave business to his chancellor, financial matters included. Thomas was allowed extraordinary freedom when it came to the royal treasury, a treasury he helped enrich; he would live to regret this freedom. Henry was shrewd and careful, and though he allowed Thomas a long leash, the chancellor was still on a leash, and the king understood that there could be times when he might deem it necessary to tug Thomas back into line, as future events would reveal. In these halcyon days, however, king and chancellor worked happily together for the good of England. While Henry was the architect of the restoration of good order in the kingdom, Thomas played his part in helping these plans come to fruition; his king had complete confidence in him.

Much has been made of this friendship between Thomas and Henry; their future conflict would be so bitter because it was deeply personal. As the daily business of government brought the two into close quarters, each recognized something in the other, perhaps a kindred soul. While Thomas was a bureaucrat and Henry was a warrior, they shared a love of the outdoor life. Each brought out something in the other. Henry satisfied Thomas's ambition, and his appreciation of his chancellor's expertise enhanced his government. Thomas found in Henry a replacement for Richer, a boon companion on the hunt and in conversation. He was now an accomplished sportsman and a match for Henry in horsemanship. The two would often ride off into the forests with hawks, falcons, dogs, or in Thomas's case, wolves, to engage in a few hours of the hunt, returning for dinner and an evening's conversation over chess and wine. Many times, Henry would stop by Thomas's rooms for a quick conversation. On frequent occasions, Thomas would host the king for dinner — the food in the chancellor's household was, as noted, well fit for a king. Though Thomas was extravagant and enjoyed luxury, Henry was happy to turn a blind eye; he was aware that his chancellor liked nice things, and while he knew the royal treasury was funding a lot of it, he was happy to leave things be since Thomas, through his charm and generosity, also brought honor to him.

As the years passed, their familiarity with each other grew, and a comfortable rapport was established, but Thomas always had to be conscious that Henry was the king. At the end of the day, the friendship was always weighted in the king's favor. As he got to know his master well, Thomas learned when to speak and when to stay silent. If he needed to intercede for anyone, he would first work out what tactic he would use. While Henry would be inclined to hear him, he could fly into a rage if he had made up his mind on a matter and Thomas tried to make him think again. Though Thomas and Henry were friends, they were always master and servant.[2] Henry could never regard a servant as an equal, but Thomas came as close as it was possible for the king. A man who held genuine affection for those he had come to regard as close companions, Henry could indeed be said to have loved Thomas; the depth of his later hatred would prove that. As the years passed, the character flaws of both men and their different views on a number of things often led to awkwardness and tensions. While good humor flowed between them, at times Henry liked to use it to assert he was in charge, putting Thomas into difficult and embarrassing situations on purpose to remind the chancellor who was the superior and who was the minion. The king did not want to be in his servant's shadow even if he regarded that servant as a friend.

One incident, related by an eyewitness, William FitzStephen, reveals the real dynamic at the heart of Thomas and Henry's relationship. On a cold winter day, Henry and Thomas were out riding in the City of London when they came upon a poor beggar shivering with the cold. Henry asked Thomas if it would be a great act of charity to give him a thick, warm cloak. Thomas agreed that it would and commended the king for seeking to act in such a manner. Henry asked the beggar if he would like a new cloak and then, turning to his friend, informed him that the deed of charity would be his and made a grab for Thomas's cloak. Thomas refused to part with it and held on — it was a new cloak lined with fur, and it had cost him a lot. Henry continued to try to force the cloak off, and a tussle ensued. When Henry's guards tried to intervene, he pushed them away and persisted until Thomas finally relented. Henry joked as he gave the cloak to the beggar, and all but Thomas laughed at his expense.[3] Humiliated, the chancellor was now wiser about his master, his demands, and how he was prepared to treat others, even those closest to him.

Other issues caused tension in the relationship, one being the king's immoral lifestyle. Though somewhat restrained during Thomas's lifetime, the king was prone to extramarital affairs and bouts of debauchery. As noted, while Thomas was worldly, he was not promiscuous or inclined to tolerate it in others, and certainly not in a man he considered his friend. There were said to be incidents where Henry put Thomas into embarrassing and morally dangerous situations, forcing the chancellor to try to wriggle himself free and slip out of temptation's way.[4] Thomas would have tried, insofar as he could, to keep Henry faithful to his wife, and he may have had some success, given that it was after Thomas's death that Henry's serial infidelities began in earnest.

Henry's terrible temper was also a problem. While Thomas would have tried to maneuver himself and whatever matters he was discussing with the king around his potential rage, he was not always successful and often felt the brunt of Henry's wrath. The king's personal manners may have annoyed Thomas, who was careful and dignified in how he conducted himself. Thomas would have had to accept that there was little he could do, consoling himself with the fact that kings are given greater indulgence by others for their failings.

Another matter that would have caused tension was Henry's inclination to irreligiosity. Though Thomas was not perfect himself, he maintained a sense of decorum around sacred things and events, particularly the Mass and the environs of the Chapel Royal, which was under his care as royal chancellor. He may have been impressed with Henry's attachment to the collection of relics he owned and took everywhere with him, although the king probably had more interest in their perceived miraculous powers than any sense of authentic devotion to the saints. Likewise, Henry was keen to push the cause for canonization of King Edward the Confessor perhaps not so much to recognize the beloved king's sanctity as to affirm the sacral mystique that surrounded kingship. Had Thomas been a more pastoral deacon, he might have applied some effort to convert the king, but that might have been quite difficult for a man who conducted state business during Mass, was happy to break oaths, and was an expert at adultery.

However, though a deacon, Thomas was primarily an administrative servant, and as such he continued to meet with great success in his work. Due perhaps to his friendship with the king as much as to his ability, Thomas won many of the barons and clerks to his side. His generosity and charm were important instruments in his winning friends and allies, and while he could be tough, Thomas was usually very fair in resolving conflicts. His fondness for giving gifts won him friends, but his close relationship with the king also brought him enemies, as some at court who sought preferment resented the attention and affection given to the "lowborn clerk." Many of these malcontents would come out of the woodwork when Thomas and Henry clashed, but for the period of his chancellorship, they restrained themselves and had to be content with gossiping, inventing little intrigues, and making life difficult for him while hiding their malice, lest the king become aware of it.

As Henry admired Thomas, he rewarded him well. That the king would later seek the highest preferment for his chancellor is an indication not only of how much he trusted Thomas, but also of how much he held him in affection — and how convinced he was that Thomas was his man. Both Thomas and Henry seem to have been men who had difficulty with intimacy, and yet sought some form of companionship. While as a layman Henry might have been expected to find this intimacy in marriage, his marriage to a strong, ambitious woman was for the benefit of his kingdom and dynasty, and it may have lacked what Henry was looking for, if he was even capable of finding it. In those times, it seems, only the poor could afford to marry for love; kings, magnates, and great men married for other reasons. His various affairs did not last long and seemed no more than physical relationships, though one later on seems to have been something much deeper.

Thomas, too, may have sought a companion. With the exception of Richer, there is no one else in his life who could be identified as a close friend; indeed, he always seemed somewhat aloof and distant. Henry, for all his faults, was more than a feudal lord and patron. The two men were very different, yet Thomas found in Henry someone he could relate to and befriend. Some recent historians have tried to find something sexual in the relationship, just as some have wondered whether Thomas's earlier friendship with Richer might have been a youthful exploration of his sexuality.[5] There is no evidence to suggest this at all, and given Thomas's approach to things sexual, he might have been appalled at the idea; not because he was trying to hide something, but because he was chaste. Thomas and Henry, chancellor and king, were most likely good friends despite their inequality, serious personality issues, and different viewpoints.

Another relationship that was changing at this time was that between Thomas and his archbishop, Theobald — another who held him in deep affection. Thomas's work as chancellor often brought him into conflict with the archbishop and the Church. In his biography of Thomas, Frank Barlow maintains that while Thomas was loyal, his was a type of loyalty that was "markedly egocentric": When he left an employer, he moved to the next without regret, discarding old friends fairly easily as he made his way in the world.[6] While this view may be somewhat cynical and harsh, it contains a grain of truth in the sense that Thomas seems to have been a pragmatist when it came to relationships at this time. He was not inclined to let them get in the way of his business if he could help it. As chancellor, he was completely loyal to his new master, and though he was a deacon of the Church, he gave precedence to Henry rather than to Theobald. Theobald would discover to his cost in the years to come that Thomas was the king's man.

One case may have shattered the archbishop's illusions regarding Thomas's loyalty. In 1157, the bishop of Chichester, Hilary, was involved in a long-running dispute with the Benedictine Battle Abbey, built on the site of the Battle of Hastings. The bishop, like many other bishops at the time, was trying to bring order to his diocese and establish his authority. This project was often resisted by religious communities, which sought to assert their independence from the bishop. The abbot of Battle Abbey was claiming exemption from the bishop's jurisdiction, asserting that the abbey was founded by royal charter; waving the charters in the face of the bishop, the abbot declared that the abbey was therefore independent. Hilary was an exceptional canon lawyer, and he knew that the charters were not authentic and that some of them had recently been faked to meet objections to the abbey's independence. Fortunately, Hilary had the backing of the pope and his metropolitan, Theobald himself, who came to his defense. In 1155, King Henry had confirmed the charters, though he would have suspected, if not actually known, that they were of doubtful authenticity.

In May 1157, the row escalated again, and a case was brought to a hearing at Colchester before the king himself. Thomas was appointed to represent the abbot of Battle Abbey, putting him in direct conflict with Hilary and Theobald. The hearing was controversial, and Henry took grave exception to Bishop Hilary's questioning of the validity of royal authority in ecclesiastical affairs. Thomas's response and defense of the abbot were ruthless and successful, and Bishop Hilary was forced to submit to a judgment against him. Thomas was doing his job and doing it well, but it caused Theobald much concern and pain to witness one he hoped would represent the Church's efforts to maintain her liberties and rights in the forefront of denying them. Frank Barlow suggests that, in all of this, Thomas probably never felt as much as a twinge of conscience.[7]

If Thomas blithely returned to the other demands of his office and tried to move on from the Battle Abbey affair, this case would come back to haunt him. Later, when he was struggling with Henry himself over the same issues, he cited this case in a letter to the pope as one in which royal authority was a threat to papal authority in ecclesiastical matters.[8] He would also have remembered a flippant remark made by the king during one of the exchanges in court. Hilary had challenged Henry's authority, saying that the king could not deprive a bishop of his see. Henry agreed, but in reply put out his arms and said, "Very true; he can't be deposed; but look, he can be given the push," while giving a forceful thrust with his hands.[9] Thomas had laughed heartily at the jibe, little knowing that he would later come to regret his amusement.

While little is known of Thomas's interior life at this time, his friend and biographer John of Salisbury notes conversations the chancellor had with Theobald and other friends in which, contrary to Barlow's suggestion above, he expressed deep misgivings and weariness. The constant stress, the intrigue at court, the demands of the king, his being torn between Henry and the Church — all these contributed to his despair. He wished for eternal life, John writes, to be free from the bonds of court without being branded a traitor. Yet he was forced to continue, to make a special effort to fight the "beasts" at court, to carry out his business while trying to deal with the struggle. He was aware of all the flattery and allurements of those who wanted his attention and patronage, but he was cautious of them. John also claims that Thomas said that all too often he was forced to contend with the king as much as with his enemies. The chancellor was well aware of the limits of his relationship with Henry — and of the fact that one day his world could come crashing down upon him.[10]

15

Thomas the Warrior

Under Thomas's direction, the office of royal chancellor attained a singular prestige. His personal relationship with Henry assisted him greatly in this regard. When he arrived, the office of the chancellor had a small staff, including a handful of clerks; Thomas would bring that number up to more than fifty,[1] drawing skilled men from the courts and the Church and spotting talent himself among ambitious and able applicants. These clerks were well trained under his guidance, as Thomas realized — as did Theobald at his court — that competency in finance, diplomacy, and the law was crucial if he were to carry out his work effectively, raise the status of the role of chancellor, and fulfill his own ambitions.

Thomas assumed even more stature when a new area of activity opened up for him. In his service to Henry, Thomas had discovered another dimension to his personality when he became involved in the king's wars. He was a good clerk, financier, and judge and had also proven himself as a diplomat. He had been with Henry when he had launched his campaign to pacify England, though as a servant and companion rather than as a warrior. However, when Henry set out to deal with the most powerful of Welsh princes, Owain of Gwynedd, following a council at Colchester in 1157, Thomas had a new role to play.[2]

Owain was king of Gwynedd in northwest Wales, having succeeded to the throne upon his father's death in 1137. His father had intended that Owain share the kingdom with his brother Cadwaladr, but after a series of unfortunate events, Cadwaladr fled into exile, and Owain took his possessions. During the Anarchy, Owain took advantage of the political turmoil in England to push the boundaries of his territories to the east, defeating Madog, the Prince of Powys, and taking his principality, while causing problems for English settlers. In the summer of 1157, Henry decided it was time to erase what could become a serious threat: He announced a campaign to crush Owain. Thomas was keen on the war and helped Henry organize the feudal army that was required. Standing with Henry's troops were Owain's enemies: his brother Cadwaladr, and Madog.

Thomas threw himself into the business of war and, in an extraordinary measure, consulted fortune-tellers to advise him on the best time to attack. Heeding their advice, king and chancellor directed a fleet to sail along the coast of the Dee estuary, shadowing a land army making its way toward the island of Anglesey, the heart of Owain's territory. However, the fortune-tellers proved false, as they usually do — the fleet was attacked when it landed on the island, and the king and his land army were ambushed by the Welsh. Henry managed to prevent a massacre and, quickly recovering, advanced the army to Snowdonia. Realizing that he was unable to meet the challenge, Owain sued for peace, doing homage to Henry and returning Powys to its prince. He would remain king of Gwynedd until his death in 1170. After Henry returned to England, Owain would eventually see another opportunity present itself; with Madog's death in 1160, he invaded Powys and claimed it for himself.

Though that campaign was short lived, having been at the king's side Thomas now had the taste of blood in his mouth, and he would seize another opportunity to play the warrior in one of Henry's incessant disagreements with King Louis VII of France, this time over the claims of Aquitaine in 1159. Henry had his eye on the County of Toulouse, in what is now southern France, over which the Duchy of Aquitaine maintained a claim.[3] The Count of Toulouse, Raymond V, naturally rejected this claim. Given that Eleanor's entitlement had not been pressed and Raymond had not been brought to heel, Henry felt it was time to do both; no doubt, Eleanor was the main driving force behind his decision. Victory in this campaign would extend the Angevin Empire to the Mediterranean Sea. As Henry arrived in Poitiers, his forces were gathering and preparing to invade Toulouse. Many feared that Louis would enter the fray, as Louis's sister Constance was married to Raymond. If Louis decided to get involved on the count's side, Henry would be faced with an unwelcome dilemma: either breaking his feudal oath to Louis by military engagement, or withdrawing and abandoning his claim. While Henry did not have an ethical issue with breaking oaths, the consequences of breaking this one would be serious for Henry, for his family, and for the Vexin.

Noted for her great charm and determination, Eleanor quickly intervened and convinced Henry that it was now or never when it came to her ancestral right to Toulouse. Whatever misgivings Henry had, and they were no doubt slight to begin with, this was enough to overcome them. He had to defend Eleanor's honor and her rights; after all, as he was her husband, his honor and rights were also at stake. Before sending his armies in, Henry wanted to test the waters, so he invited Louis to a meeting at Tours. As they discussed the issue, Henry urged Louis to persuade Raymond to surrender and allow Eleanor to claim her right. Henry left Louis to ponder the proposition and then proceeded to organize a show of strength to frighten Raymond, forming an alliance with an enemy of Toulouse, the Count of Barcelona. But Raymond stood his ground. Gathering his forces, supplemented with Scottish and Welsh soldiers, Henry, with Thomas at his side, began his advance, making his way to lay siege at the citadel of Cahors in Toulouse territory. With the walls of the citadel in a bad state of repair, the citizens of Cahors just opened the gates and let Henry in; they had neither the means nor the interest to engage in a fight. With this success under his belt, Henry moved toward the city of Toulouse itself.

His king's partner in war, Thomas rode beside Henry. He had mustered an army of his own comprising seven hundred knights and, joining with the king's forces, he was ready for action. The army set up camp outside Toulouse. King Louis arrived to facilitate a parley between Henry and Raymond, doing his best to remain neutral in the whole affair. His brother-in-law, however, was not going to allow Louis the luxury of neutrality and, denouncing Henry as the aggressor, called on the French king to save him and his children, who were now in danger. Pushed to the wall, Louis chose family loyalty over his obligation to Henry and, gathering his own army, took up the defense of the city alongside Raymond.

The siege was laid and was soon deadlocked. Henry was in a bind. Foremost in his mind was the dynastic alliance; it seemed to be teetering. The city had natural features that made a siege difficult, and its citizens were ready to fight — they knew who the real ruler of Toulouse was, and it was not the English king by proxy of his wife. Louis had brought a small contingent and could be overcome quite easily, so an attack was possible but would lead to heavy losses in terms of soldiers. Henry turned to his advisors — his barons and his chancellor — for their opinions on whether he should attack or wait and see if Louis would withdraw.

Having considered the king's dilemma, the barons urged caution. They advised that he stay put and watch as there was too much to lose. Then the chancellor spoke. Thomas saw things differently — Henry should attack, he said. He had the means to take the city, and he should do so; every moment he waited, he was losing more of his advantage. Thomas accused the barons of cowardice. They just wanted to save their skins, he told Henry; they were deceiving him rather than advising him honestly. Henry had too much to lose by standing idly by; the knights would be suffocating in the summer heat, and should Louis bide his time and call reinforcements, the army would be useless in battle. Louis was, in fact, abusing his position as Henry's feudal lord, Thomas insisted. Indeed, he continued, in siding with Raymond, Louis had abdicated his suzerainty.

Henry listened, but disagreed with Thomas — he would follow the barons' advice. To his surprise, and to the horror of the barons, Thomas responded with defiance. He rejected the barons' advice again and urged Henry to ignore it as counsel doomed to failure and ignominy. A blazing row ensued, and Thomas pushed his position as he believed that his advice was militarily wiser and better served his king's cause. Furious, Henry ordered Thomas to be silent, and the chancellor obeyed, but Henry was taken aback at his friend's ferocity. Perhaps he noted a strength and passion in Thomas Becket that he had previously overlooked.[4]

Against Thomas's advice, Henry settled the army down to watch and wait, which they did until they saw, coming on the horizon, a large French contingent called by Louis to lift the siege. Henry was astounded — his barons had been wrong and Thomas right. Cursing his fate, Henry immediately lifted the siege and retreated with his army. He had lost his opportunity to take Toulouse. Fuming over the debacle, his barons' stupidity, and Thomas's unwelcome wisdom, Henry ordered the army to retaliate against the count and the French king by besieging and laying waste to castles and towns in the vicinity of Toulouse. Withdrawing from Cahors, he left Thomas in command of the citadel there and returned to Normandy. The chancellor would have to hold the citadel.

Thomas appealed to Henry for resources to pay the soldiers and get provisions. The king refused to grant them — the chancellor would have to find his own funds. In the end, the king offered to lend him money.[5] Henry had given Thomas a difficult task in order to punish him for his defiance, and, perhaps, for being correct in his assessment of the situation at Toulouse. Cahors was impossible to defend, which was why it was so easy to take in the first place; it would be impossible to keep. However, Thomas understood that as bad as his citadel was, it and the few garrisons around about the County of Quercy were all Henry had to show for his campaign, and they were meager. He would have to do something to ease the pain for his king.

As Henry's barons had also retreated — they had other things to do, it seems — Thomas was left alone, and that was perhaps a good thing. Cahors had to be secured. There were three heavily fortified castles not far from the citadel, and each posed a serious threat. Thomas gathered his troops and, donning armor himself, personally led his army in storming each of the castles in turn. The archdeacon was now a general, and he proved to be an extremely effective one. He had taken a huge risk, leading his troops into veritable ambushes, risking his life and the lives of his knights, but it was a risk that paid off. As he took each succeeding castle, some of his opponents fled across the River Garonne. Thomas was not prepared to let them go, so he went after them, even though he was not protected from the rear. It was utterly reckless, but it proved successful. With the ferocity of the warrior chancellor upon them, his opponents were overcome; realizing that they had no hope to win the fight, they surrendered. In victory, Thomas extracted from each of them an oath of homage to King Henry and returned triumphant to Cahors, now securely in Aquitaine's possession. When he had brought the entire County of Quercy under his command, Thomas returned to Normandy.

Henry greeted Thomas's news of victory with surprised delight and not a little puzzlement — he had never expected this of Thomas. However, he had more trouble to deal with, and it may have been a sign of Henry's renewed confidence in his chancellor, this time in the realm of warfare, that the king sent a message for him to come quickly to the Vexin as soon as Thomas was back in Normandy. Henry and Louis were at war in the region. Sensing Henry's weakness, Louis had invaded Normandy. In retaliation, Henry had invaded France, and now he needed Thomas, as a newly seasoned campaigner, to maintain control of the road between Paris and Orléans, which Henry had taken. This was a vital task, as the road divided the kingdom of France in two and allowed Henry to maintain a strategic advantage over Louis. Henry knew that he would not be able to keep France divided for long, but he wanted to take what he could before he was forced to retreat. Having been given 1,200 mercenaries to supplement his knights, Thomas engaged in a number of melees with the French army, again risking his life on a number of occasions, to ensure that the road remained in Henry's possession. In one encounter, he was involved in single combat with a knight. Knocking the knight from his horse, Thomas quickly subdued him and took the knight's charger as a prize.[6] It was an unlikely outcome, but the chancellor seemed to have a charmed life. As winter set in, both sides realized that they did not want to spend a long, miserable winter fighting, so a truce was quickly agreed to, and everyone went home to their fires.

As winter gave way to spring in 1160 and the truce expired, it was replaced by an agreed peace, and Thomas reverted from warrior to peacemaker. He led the negotiations for Henry and, given that he and Louis had a very cordial relationship, an agreement was quickly reached.[7] The terms would prove surprising for Henry, as Thomas was able to charm the French king into granting major concessions. Louis agreed to cede the County of Quercy to Henry if English troops were withdrawn from France. Then Louis did a most extraordinary thing: Disregarding the betrothal arrangement, he renounced the Vexin completely, with the exception of the town of Gisors and some strategic castles. These castles, however, would not remain in Louis's possession; rather, they would be put in trust under the command of the Knights Templar until young Henry and Margaret's wedding day, when they would be handed over to Henry as the final part of Margaret's dowry. Thomas had negotiated a peace that surpassed Henry's hopes, but it was not perfect: Henry wanted Gisors, too, and he began plotting how to get it.

On October 4, 1160, King Louis's second wife, Constance, died. Like Eleanor before her, she had given birth to two daughters but failed to give the French king a male heir. While four daughters are a blessing for any man, Louis did not want to entrust his kingdom to a woman — he was afraid that what had happened in England with Matilda's dispossession would repeat itself in France after his death. On November 13 of that year, Louis married for the third time, taking Adela, the daughter of the Count of Champagne, as his wife. Henry should have rejoiced in his feudal lord's marriage, but he did not, and it was not just Gisors that prevented him from joining in the celebrations: The new queen of France was the late King Stephen's niece, so Louis was looking over his shoulder at England as he was joined to her in marriage.

Adela was no shrinking violet. She was just as politically ambitious as her new husband, and though her claim to the English throne was a little flimsy, it was as much within her sights as within her husband's. For Henry, this marriage was not just a threat to his throne; it was the provocation he was looking for to justify taking action. Though canon law forbade marriage for those below the age of twelve, Henry had his young son Henry, who was five, married to Margaret, who was two, on November 2, 1160, at Neubourg, Normandy.[8] Upon the marriage, the Knights Templar had to honor their oath and renounce the castles in the Vexin to Henry. Furious at Henry's treachery, Louis struck out and invaded the Province of Touraine, and Henry, in response, entered France again, taking the strategic castle of Chaumont on the Loire River. The two kings were fighting again, and it was tit for tat. Thomas was not pleased to see the delicate peace he had negotiated now in pieces. It is doubtful that Henry sympathized with him; in reality, he was overjoyed. He finally had the Vexin — every field, every castle, and every town; the invasion was complete.

Following his marriage, young Henry was put into Thomas's care, as was the feudal custom.[9] Thomas was now responsible for the boy's education and formation. That Henry chose his chancellor for this honor was telling: Thomas was in favor.[10] With the heir to the throne entrusted to him, he now had the chance to be of tremendous influence on the future of England. There were already a number of young boys in the chancellor's household, sons of barons who were being taught by tutors while serving as pages. Young Henry would become a favorite of Thomas's, and it was not long before the young boy was looking up to him with utter admiration.

16
Thomas of Canterbury

The death of Pope Adrian IV in September 1159 plunged the Church into a crisis, one that would personally involve Henry, Louis, Theobald, and Thomas. In the conclave that followed, the Holy Roman emperor, Frederick Barbarossa, ordered the cardinals under his influence to vote for Cardinal Ottaviano di Monticelli. However, it was Cardinal Rolando di Siena who emerged as pope, taking the name Alexander III.[1] Rolando was a leading reformer within the College of Cardinals and was committed to the Gregorian Reforms. Furious, Barbarossa's cardinals elected Ottaviano anyway and in doing so, initiated a new schism in the Church. The strange practice of picking their pope now fell to the rulers of Europe. Henry's grandfather had claimed such a right in a schism that had taken place thirty years before. Though he was deeply opposed to the idea, Archbishop Theobald neither had the desire nor the energy to enter into a dispute with Henry II over the papacy. The archbishop knew what a schism within England would do; he would have to manage this crisis and the king very carefully.

Henry was actually unsure how to proceed, so, invoking his presumed authority over the bishops of England and Normandy, he forbade them from supporting either claimant until he had made up his mind; when he did, they would have to go with his decision. For six months, Henry mulled over the two candidates, and in that time, Alexander gradually asserted his claim. Theobald was in Alexander's camp and, through various meetings with Henry, quietly tried to woo the king to Alexander's side. Speaking of Alexander's virtue, competence, and learning, Theobald also pointed out that the majority of the French bishops had already acknowledged Alexander as pope and Ottaviano, who called himself Victor IV, as an antipope. Consulting with King Louis, Henry decided to wait another few months. However, all was not as it seemed. Henry was actually involved in secret negotiations with Alexander. In fact, he was trying to blackmail him: Henry would refuse to acknowledge Alexander as pope until he agreed to canonize King Edward the Confessor, thereby conferring sacred legitimacy on the throne of England, and also to approve the marriage between young Henry and Margaret of France even though it had fallen foul of canon law.[2]

Thomas was trying to keep aloof from Henry's underhanded scheme, though Theobald, when he got wind of it, blamed him for allowing the king to go ahead with this extortion of the successor of Saint Peter. If the chancellor had hoped to stay out of the row, he was quickly dragged right into the middle of it when two Norman bishops publicly condemned the king's behavior. Henry retaliated by ordering the bishops' homes destroyed, but Thomas managed to mitigate the damage to one of the houses, working on Henry to quell his rage and employing a little deception in delaying the orders.[3] In the meantime, Pope Alexander responded to Henry's demands — he agreed to grant permission for the marriage. Theobald was not pleased with Thomas's behavior in the whole matter; it was another to add to his list of disappointments.

By 1160, Theobald was quite ill and immobile: He now had to be carried about. As he knew death was coming, there were certain things he was determined to resolve. One of these issues concerned the income of the archdeacon of Canterbury. His brother Walter, when he was archdeacon, had introduced a levy on parishes of the archdiocese as a contribution to his salary; it was called the "second aids." The levy had proved to be quite lucrative, and when Thomas took over the office, this levy was still in place and was now helping fund the archdeacon-chancellor's lavish lifestyle. Theobald wanted to abolish the levy; it was unjust in his eyes, and given that Thomas had a good income from other benefices both as archdeacon and chancellor, he assumed it was not needed. The archbishop was wrong there. Thomas was living well beyond his means, and the levy was vital for easing his mounting debts.[4]

The archbishop wrote to Thomas, possibly in June 1160, indicating his intention to abolish the levy,[5] but the chancellor, who was in Normandy at the time, did not respond; he would later claim that he did not get the letter for a number of months.[6] Theobald's secretary John of Salisbury then contacted Thomas over his silence, rebuking him for ignoring the request of his archbishop, but Thomas was unmoved. The issue festered over a period of months, and Theobald then formally rebuked his archdeacon, calling him to obedience and summoning him to Canterbury. In this letter, Theobald reminded Thomas of all he had done for him.[7] The summons was not merely to rebuke his archdeacon; Theobald knew he was dying, and he wanted his protégé at his side for some of the time that was left to him.

Thomas was deaf to these appeals. Theobald then wrote to Henry and asked him to allow Thomas come to him, but to no avail. The archbishop finally decided to take an extreme measure: He threatened Thomas with excommunication for disobeying his bishop. However, he withdrew the threat when a royal messenger arrived to inform him that the king needed the chancellor and could not spare him. There was, it seems, a power struggle going on. Henry was most likely manipulating the situation to get proof from his chancellor that he was not divided between two masters.[8] Thomas may have been in a very difficult position. He had given his loyalty to Henry, and though he had tried to do what he could for the Church, he was primarily a royal servant; now that Henry had imposed his will upon him, he had to obey.

Theobald's health worsened, and he was confined to bed. John of Salisbury remained at his side, feeding him and tending him to the last. On April 18, 1161, this remarkable archbishop breathed his last. He died with a broken heart — the one he had loved as a son had abandoned him in his last days. While he left nothing to Thomas in his will, it is telling that though he was disappointed with his archdeacon, Theobald had named Thomas as the one who should succeed him. The archbishop probably suspected that Thomas was not entirely to blame and had not abandoned him willingly; and, ever the pragmatist, Theobald knew that only one man could have some sort of influence over Henry: his prodigal archdeacon.

Following the funeral rites, Theobald was buried in Canterbury Cathedral beside his predecessor Lanfranc. Despite his extraordinary life and work for the Church and his personal holiness, when the possibility of his canonization was raised, there was little interest; and though his body was found to be incorrupt following an exhumation in 1190, a cause did not advance very far.[9] He would remain plain Theobald of Bec, an archbishop very quickly overshadowed by his successor.

Speculation over who would succeed Theobald began as soon as he was resting in his tomb. For many, there could only be one candidate: the archdeacon-chancellor. Whispers at court and on the street gradually became more public, and even Henry was hearing suggestions as to who had the right credentials to become archbishop and primate. But the king held his peace; he had other things on his mind, and besides, the benefices at Canterbury would yield a nice income for him while he was pondering the question of a successor. Publicly, Henry said that the matter of bishops usually fell to the care of his chancellor, but Thomas suspected what was on Henry's mind and chose to remain silent himself — silent and, perhaps, fearful.

In the meantime, Henry was fighting with Louis again. The issue of the marriage and the Vexin had not gone away. Having taken to bed violently ill — he was hospitalized in a cell of the abbey of Fécamp outside Rouen in the summer of 1161 — Thomas had to host both kings at his bedside as he tried to negotiate a new truce.[10] Not even in his illness could he find a moment's peace from these quarreling monarchs. Once that squabble was resolved, Thomas remained in Normandy while Henry moved on to fighting rebellious barons in Aquitaine for the rest of that summer. As he was hacking the barons into submission, the king was also scheming, mulling over two possible plans. The first was to crown the young six-year-old Henry as junior king of England, allowing him to govern England while Henry senior remained on the continent building up his empire. This coronation would settle any succession issues that might lie ahead. The second plan concerned Theobald's successor to Canterbury. As many suspected, for Henry there could only be one candidate: Archdeacon-Chancellor Thomas — his friend, confidant, and faithful servant.

Henry's aim for the Church was to bring it into line under his authority, just as his grandfather Henry I had tried to do. Neither Henry accepted the reforms of Pope Saint Gregory VII, reforms aimed at pulling the Church free from secular control. As Canterbury was the primatial see, the king needed the man sitting on the ancient chair of Saint Augustine to be his man, willing to do his bidding and to ensure that the Church served the interests of the crown. Given that there would be a number of candidates who would be willing to do exactly that, Henry did not want to take any risks; he needed someone he could trust, someone he knew very well, someone who could carry out the obligations of the office efficiently. Thomas was the only credible candidate. Thomas was his devoted friend, and though they had disagreed, he always relented. Though the chancellor may well have wanted to go to his archbishop's deathbed, he had not gone; he had done what he was told and remained by the king's side. There was the issue of Toulouse: Thomas had shown a streak of independence and defiance there, but Henry was convinced that he had pulled him into line and that Thomas had been sufficiently chastened for his boldness. Besides, the chancellor's subsequent campaign in Quercy seemed to be a peace offering, a plea for forgiveness. Regarding the pope and any objections that he might raise, Alexander was struggling to overcome the antipope and was already indebted to Henry for his support; he might well turn a blind eye to a royal pawn in Canterbury, allowing Henry full control of the Church in England and, of course, of her benefices.

Henry persuaded himself that Thomas was the only man for Canterbury. He consulted the English bishops — if his imposition of the chancellor were to have a veneer of legitimacy, he needed the senior bishops

to support him in his choice. A group of them, including Roger de Pont
L'Évêque, archbishop of York, came to meet with the king in the spring
of 1162. It is also believed that Henry had a word with the cardinal and
papal legate in Normandy, Henry of Pisa, and he would later also claim
that he had consulted the pope and received his permission.[11] He was not
leaving anything to chance. There were others interested in the position
— the bishop of Hereford, Gilbert Foliot, for one;[12] he seemed to meet all
the necessary requirements of the office, and he was convinced that he
was not only the right man for the job but a far better candidate than the
chancellor. Henry realized such claims would have to be resisted; Thomas would have his unwavering support.

It did not take long for Henry to put his plan in place, and it was simple
enough: His man, Thomas, would be appointed archbishop. There was the
little matter of the election, which was traditionally held by the monks of
Canterbury, but that could easily be manipulated in the chancellor's favor.
The new archbishop would remain as chancellor and continue his work
for the kingdom while quietly implementing Henry's agenda of restoring
his perceived rights over the Church. Young Henry, his son, would govern
England, but Henry would appoint a regency council to govern in the boy's
name while he was still in his minority, and Thomas would be on that
council and have tremendous influence. In real terms, Henry knew Thomas would be governing England. That ought to be enough of a sweetener
to persuade him to accept. The plan was perfect. Conflict between Church
and state in England would be over, everyone would have a quiet life, and
Henry could get on with building his empire and doing a bit of hunting.
All Thomas would have to do was obey.[13]

Thomas was not so sure. As the rumors of his imminent appointment persisted, he grew more uneasy; indeed, he was horrified. For all
his bravado, Thomas knew himself well enough, and he was not the
stuff of which good archbishops were made. The office of the primate
deserved a more religious and saintly man; he was not suited. He was
always aware of Theobald's suffering for the Church and knew that as
Henry grew more comfortable on the throne of England, the next archbishop, if he was serious about protecting the Church's interests, might
well have much suffering to bear. Thomas prided himself on doing his

work well, and he had been obedient to the master he served at any given time, whether it was Osbert, Theobald, or Henry; but who was the master of the archbishop of Canterbury?[14]

Henry left the see of Canterbury vacant for almost a year. In February 1162, he summoned Thomas to meet him in Rouen. It was no doubt with dread that he walked into that meeting: He knew what was coming. Not given to ceremony, Henry informed Thomas that he was being sent back to England to be elected archbishop of Canterbury and that he was to crown young Henry as king. To ease the tension, Henry told him that he was relying on him; he needed a man he could trust. However, he had to go quickly. Thomas did indeed respond immediately. He said no. Henry quietly tried to persuade him. Thomas drew the king's attention to the fine clothes he was wearing — he was not a worthy candidate. He was too worldly, and a saintly man was needed for that holy see.[15]

The last thing the king wanted at Canterbury was a saintly man. Canterbury had had a number of them already, Anselm among them, and they had been nothing but trouble for kings. A worldly minion was perfect for his plans. Thomas continued to resist; in the end, Henry simply imposed his will and organized an "escort" to take Thomas to Canterbury and have him elected and ordained. To this end, he had a word with his leading barons; when they delivered Thomas to Canterbury, the king informed them, they were also to "advise" the monastic chapter as to whom it was to elect as archbishop; though it is almost certain that the royal chancellor was not favored by the monks.[16]

Meanwhile, the king had been making plans to have young Henry crowned. He had put contingency plans in place such that if there were no archbishop of Canterbury in time for the coronation, he would get another bishop to preside. The archbishop of York, Roger de Pont L'Évêque, was proposed — he managed to obtain papal bulls from Alexander to permit this.[17] The bishops of Canterbury province were objecting — only the primate had the right of coronation. Henry realized that this was not the time for a row with the Church, so he decided to downgrade his plans from a coronation to an investiture and an oath of fealty; Thomas as chancellor would preside and lead the barons and bishops in an act of homage.

The chancellor was duly dispatched with his "escort." At some point, he met with the papal legate, Henry of Pisa, at Falaise, and poured out his anguish over what was happening. Henry was a Cistercian raised to the cardinalate, so he was all too well aware of the burden of ecclesiastical office. In their conversation, the legate reminded Thomas of the sacred obligations that would be put on his shoulders, but told him that he was not to allow his scruples or his unworthiness to stand in the way of his accepting the office. The legate proved persuasive; Thomas finally relented and agreed to accept.[18] Continuing to England, he presided over the investiture of young Henry on May 23, 1162, which passed off without incident.[19]

The barons made their way to Canterbury with their captive, picking up some bishops on the way. Meeting with the monks of Christ Church Abbey, who had the right of election, they informed them of the nomination of the archdeacon and secured their agreement. Thomas was neither a monk nor a priest, so his election would be unusual given recent candidates. The monks raised this objection in the meeting, but the barons assured them it was not an issue; indeed, a more important issue they might need to consider was the king's favor or wrath. The monks decided that they were able to put their concerns to one side and elected Thomas unanimously.

On May 23, 1162, the Wednesday before Pentecost Sunday, a council was held at Westminster Abbey in London to confirm Thomas's election as archbishop of Canterbury and primate of England.[20] Young Henry represented his father. After prayers and speeches, the prior of Canterbury came forward to announce that under the inspiration of the Holy Spirit, the monks had elected Thomas of London, archdeacon of Canterbury, royal chancellor of the realm, to the sacred office of archbishop. Thomas may have been cringing, but his election was duly confirmed and applauded. However, not all were in agreement. Gilbert Foliot, bishop of Hereford, stood up to voice his objection. He deemed Thomas eminently unsuitable for the office; indeed, he was lowborn and worldly. Gilbert was intensely jealous; even if he were correct in regarding the whole appointment process as dubious, he would have had no objections if he had been the one in Thomas's shoes.[21] A number of those present shouted him down, and while he was forced to retreat, Gilbert muttered within earshot of many that the king had worked a miracle by transforming a warrior and a worldly man into an archbishop.[22] Though uttered in anger sarcastically, this statement would prove prophetic, though it was not Henry who effected the transformation. Gilbert was not alone in his hostility; there were others who had problems with Thomas's elevation, but unlike the bishop of Hereford, they chose to remain in the long grass for now.

Following the council, Thomas departed for Canterbury. Arriving at the gates of the cathedral city, he saw the streets thronged with people to welcome him, among them the young Henry. The monks, a number of abbots and barons, and fourteen bishops greeted him at the gates and led him into the city and to the cathedral. Though it was expected that he make the final part of the journey on his horse, Thomas dismounted and walked to the cathedral on foot as a simple pilgrim. The crowds may have been impressed, but perhaps the more cynical clergy turned their eyes to heaven with a sigh. If he heard about it, Henry might have smiled to himself. Thomas, as dramatic as ever, could do what he liked just as long as he did what he was told. Perhaps only God knew that Thomas's gesture was more than something to impress those around him.

On Saturday, June 2, Thomas was ordained priest at Canterbury Cathedral by his previous ally and protector, Walter, bishop of Rochester, Theobald's brother.[23] His episcopal consecration was due to take place the following day, but it was marred by a row over who would do it.[24] It was the customary privilege of the bishop of London to consecrate the archbishop of Canterbury, but the see of London was vacant. Hustling in for the honor were Roger de Pont L'Évêque, archbishop of York, and Walter, bishop of Rochester. Neither had a case, and so the honor fell to Henry of Winchester, the late King Stephen's brother.

The monks of Canterbury had chosen Trinity Sunday, June 3, 1162, for the consecration of their new archbishop. Crowds filled the cathedral from early morning. Vested as a simple priest, Thomas emerged and ascended the steps of the sanctuary. There, after a few moments of prayer, he came to the steps of the choir, where he renounced, and was released from, all obligations to the secular world (this included any debts he had incurred in his previous life). The consecration ceremony then took place. As the Book of the Gospels was laid upon his head, a verse was chosen at random to serve as a prophetic word. To the misfortune of poor Thomas, that verse was from the Lord's cursing of the fig tree in the Gospel of Saint Matthew: "'May no fruit ever come from you again!' And the fig tree withered at once" (Mt 21:19). Gilbert Foliot could be heard chuckling in his seat.[25] Ordained bishop, Thomas received the ring, miter, and crozier and was led to the throne, where he took his seat as archbishop and primate. Whether it was noticed or not, the Gregorian Reforms had been observed.[26] It was Bishop Henry of Winchester, not King Henry, who had invested him.

From his *cathedra*, the episcopal throne, Thomas may have looked down over the crowded nave and wondered how he had gotten this high office. For once in his life he had resisted promotion and honor; his ambition stopped short at the call to Canterbury, but here he was in an office he did not want and even feared. He was well aware that it was a political move, but did he consider that perhaps the providence of God had been at work? Thomas of London was now gone, having made way for Thomas of Canterbury, his new appellation. And what must he do now? So many expected so much of him, and among them were the ordinary, simple souls of England — the pious and the weak, many of whom had populated the streets over the last days to greet him and assure him of their prayers. That verse from the Book of the Gospels might have been a warning; if so, he needed to heed it. As a man of duty, Thomas knew that he would have to fulfill what was required of him. Perhaps he, like many others in England at that moment, wondered: Who is the master of the archbishop of Canterbury?

Part III

The Church's Servant

17

Of Scepters and Croziers

Thomas's reluctance to become archbishop of Canterbury may have been founded on another fear than that of unworthiness. He may have feared a clash with Henry over the implementation of the reforms of Pope Saint Gregory VII, more commonly known as the Gregorian Reforms. These reforms were among the prominent concerns of the day, and they were causing strife between the Church and monarchs all over Europe, leading to civil war in Germany and interminable power struggles between popes and emperors. These crises would have been well known to Thomas, Henry, and the other bishops of England, and no doubt many feared a repeat of them in England. As the reforms were the cause célèbre of the eleventh and twelfth centuries, the reformer's own life and struggles would become the paradigm for subsequent disputes, Thomas's and Henry's included.

The reformer, Saint Gregory VII, was born Hildebrand of Sovana in Tuscany, Italy, around 1015.[1] He had been a monk of Cluny when his former abbot was elected to the papacy as Leo IX in 1049.[2] This change in office for Leo brought a change in life for Hildebrand, too. Pope Leo appointed him deacon, papal administrator, and sometimes papal legate, and he would continue to serve subsequent pontiffs in these roles. Leo himself was an extraordinary reformer, pushing a radical moral and structural reform within the Church.[3] In his pontificate, Eamon Duffy notes, Leo reshaped the papacy from being an example of corruption to being the chief instrument for reform, a change his gifted deacon noted with approval.[4] Over the next number of years, Hildebrand rose to the rank of archdeacon and became a powerful and influential figure in the Church. Upon the death of Pope Alexander II in 1073, he was elected pope by acclamation, one of only seven popes in history to be elected in this manner.[5] From the beginning of his pontificate, he had his eye on reforms — and on one in particular: asserting the rights of the Church to choose and invest her own bishops and to depose them if the need arose.[6]

Up to this point, the Church was quite decentralized, and individual dioceses had a great deal of autonomy. Secular rulers, patterning their reigns on the fourth-century Roman emperor Constantine's self-appointed preeminence in the Church, saw themselves as particular patrons of the Church in their jurisdictions. From this, they developed the custom of rulers appointing their local bishops and, to varying degrees, governing the affairs of the Church. The more important the ruler, the greater role he played in governing the Church. Following on from Charlemagne, the Holy Roman emperors, based in what is now Germany, acted as quasi popes. Given the papacy's weak state and lack of direct governance outside Italy, the popes could do little to undermine this practice. Having appointed a bishop or abbot, secular rulers would, as a sign of their authority, invest the chosen candidate with the symbols of his office: miter, crozier, and ring. Other contentious issues included the rights of ownership over Church property; Church benefices, which rulers often claimed for themselves when a particular office was vacant; the roles of secular and Church courts when it came to dealing with clerics accused of crimes; and appeals to the pope in disputes. In essence, secular rulers' governance of the Church in these ways brought into question the autonomy and liberty of the Church. Pope Gregory VII was determined to bring this secular governance to an end: Caesar could have what was Caesar's, but not what belonged to God.

Over the course of his papacy, Gregory issued a number of decrees designed to pry secular rulers' fingers off the Church's liberties and functions. These decrees did not meet with universal acclaim. In 1075, he issued *Dictatus Papae*, in which he reiterated the nature of the papacy's power.[7] Among its decrees, the document stated that the Roman Church was founded solely by God and that papal power alone was universal. It decreed that the pope alone could depose, reinstate, or transfer bishops and that he may do so without the permission of a synod; it was the pope who made new laws, assembled new congregations, and established abbeys and canonries. Only the pope could call general synods, and should he pass a sentence, he was the only one who could retract it. As if these points were not controversial enough, Gregory also included among papal acts the power to depose an emperor. The last article of the decree would be even more provocative: The pope could absolve subjects from their fealty to wicked men. The crowned heads of Europe quickly realized that this article could be a thorn in the side for any monarch who found himself at war with the pope.

In a later papal bull, *Libertas Ecclesiae*, Gregory would push his reforms even further. Promulgated in 1079, this document detailed his view on the freedom of the Church and what must be put in place to protect it. In essence, it meant freedom from oppression by secular rulers, and he summarized this in three points that are ultimately drawn from *Dictatus Papae*. First, the Church must be free from interference by laypeople (read, secular rulers) in the election and investiture of bishops. Second, the whole Church was de facto and in every way necessary under the direct leadership of the pope. Third, the pope alone was the highest authority in all of Christendom. In an often-quoted passage, Gregory made it clear that he meant business and was prepared to fight for the Church's liberty: "We hold it to be far nobler to fight for a long time for the freedom of the Holy Church than to sink into a miserable and devilish servitude. For the wretched fight as limbs of the devil and are crushed down into miserable slavery to him. The members of Christ, on the other hand, fight to bring back those same wretches into Christian freedom."[8]

"*Libertas ecclesiae!*" — "The freedom of the Church!" — would become the slogan and cry of reformers all over Europe, and it was possible this document in particular would have confirmed Thomas in his ministry and in his stubborn stand for the liberty of the Church in England. The secular authorities did not react well to these decrees or to Gregory's progressive reforms, which sidelined their position and authority in favor of a stronger papacy. The Holy Roman emperor, Henry IV,[9] was not impressed, and his struggle with Gregory became the main field of conflict over the reforms.

Relations between pope and emperor were initially amicable. At the outset of Gregory's papal reign, Henry needed the pope's support as he tried to deal with a Saxon rebellion in his realm. However, as soon as he had defeated the Saxons in autumn of 1075, Henry moved to assert his rights in the north of Italy and, in doing so, appointed a cleric to the position of archbishop of Milan. Henry had taken an oath to support Gregory in his reforms; with this action, he broke that oath, and he received a swift and strong condemnation from Gregory. In response, Henry called a synod at Worms for January 1076 (also illegal under the Gregorian Reforms), and he had it pass a resolution declaring that Gregory, by his actions, had forfeited the papacy. The bishops at the council denounced Gregory, and Henry formally deposed him as pope, decreeing that a papal election must be held.[10]

As soon as he heard of the emperor's decrees, Gregory excommunicated him and absolved all his subjects from their allegiance to him, effectively deposing him.[11] This was a bold move, but it worked. Henry lost the support of the ordinary people, and Gregory grew in popularity. Local princes in the empire began to use the papal decree to their own advantage, and the Saxons reinstated their rebellion as various parties opposed to Henry within the empire grew in strength. When the elector princes called for a meeting of their council in Trebur for October 1076, Henry realized the situation had become critical. As they gathered to elect a new emperor, their failure to agree on a common candidate served as a reprieve for Henry, but it was temporary.[12] The electors urged Henry to make reparations to the pope and confirm his obedience; in the meantime, they sent an invitation to Pope Gregory requesting that he meet them in Augsburg to render his judgment on the conflict. Until the pope had delivered his verdict, the electors would regard the office of the Holy Roman Emperor as being vacant. [13]

The emperor realized that drastic action was necessary. He had to get to Gregory before Gregory got to Augsburg. He immediately sent an embassy to Rome with a request for absolution, but Gregory rejected it and started on his journey to Germany. Henry knew there was nothing else to do but travel to meet the pope on his way to the council.[14] In the extreme cold of winter, the emperor set out from his palace in Speyer toward the Alps with his wife, Bertha, and son Conrad. When the nobles of the Duchy of Swabia refused to open the alpine passes for him, he had to make his way around by Burgundy and cross the Alps at Mount Cenis, a perilous journey at the best of times. The members of the imperial family risked their lives crossing the dangerous passes, but it was worth it. When they came in sight of Canossa (in what is now northern Italy) on January 25, 1077, they learned that the pope was there. Gregory was staying as a guest in the castle of Matilda, the Margravine of Tuscany (often called *la Gran Contessa*), one of his most ardent supporters in his effort at reform.[15] As Henry arrived at the gates of the castle to request an audience with Gregory, the gates were closed in front of him by order of the pope himself.

With nothing else to lose, Henry turned penitent. Taking off his clothes and shoes, he donned a hair shirt and stood outside the castle gates barefoot in the snow, fasting. Gregory left him standing there for three days.[16] On January 28, the gates were opened, and Henry was admitted into the pope's presence. Falling down before Gregory, he begged absolution and thereby put the pope in a difficult political position. If he absolved Henry, Gregory would lose the advantage. With Henry restored, the council at Augsburg would be rendered ineffectual, if it decided to meet at all. He also knew Henry: He was well aware that the man on the floor in front of him might be penitent now for his own political reasons, but once absolved and back in Germany would resume his haughty position. But Gregory was a priest and a Christian — he was the pope, and he could not refuse absolution to one begging it. His religious nature and duty to his office overrode his political instincts and interests. After negotiations and pledges made by Henry, Gregory absolved him and readmitted him to full communion with the Church — he did not, however, rescind the deposition. Later that evening, he offered Mass and gave Communion to the prodigal.[17]

Henry hurried back to Germany absolved and, quite contrary to the pope's declaration, maintained that the deposition was also repealed. The elector princes knew the truth of it and were determined to proceed with an election, proposing another candidate, Rupert of Swabia, for the imperial throne. This led to civil war. At first taking a neutral position that did him little good in the eyes of the Germans, Gregory, after a long period of waiting, decided to support Rupert, and in 1080 excommunicated Henry again, reiterating the deposition.[18] The censure was harder to impose this time around, as Germany was divided into two camps, and Henry had the unwavering support of his princes even in the face of an excommunication. Henry called another council for Brixen in June of that year and once again deposed Gregory. This time, the thirty bishops present at the council proceeded to elect a "successor" to the deposed Gregory: Archbishop Guibert of Ravenna. Assuming the name Clement III, Guibert as antipope initiated a schism.[19]

Things would get worse for Gregory. Henry began to make his way to Rome. *La Gran Contessa*, Matilda of Tuscany, sent her troops to prevent the emperor's progress across the Apennines, but he diverted to take another route, down the east of Italy. The emperor's armies arrived in the Eternal City in 1084, forcing Gregory to flee to the Castel Sant'Angelo for refuge.[20] Once again, Henry was standing at castle gates, but this time as victor, demanding that Gregory surrender and personally crown him emperor. Gregory refused. Reiterating his request, Henry revealed the shallowness of his own loyalty: He offered to hand over the antipope Clement as a prisoner if Gregory would consent to crown him. Gregory insisted that Henry would have to appear before a council and do penance before he would consider the request. Henry appeared to agree, but his subsequent actions to prevent the forming of a council revealed that he was lying. Gregory managed to get some bishops together to form the council and, meeting with them, excommunicated Henry again.

Henry had withdrawn from the city at this stage, but when he heard of his excommunication, he returned with his armies on March 21, 1084, took possession of the papal palaces and basilicas, and forced Gregory back into the Castel Sant'Angelo. On March 24, Henry enthroned the antipope Clement in the Basilica of Saint John Lateran. In return, on March 31, the antipope crowned Henry as Holy Roman emperor in Saint Peter's Basilica. Despite this turn of events, all was not lost for Gregory. His ally, the Norman Duke of Apulia and Calabria, Robert Guiscard, was coming to his aid, and as soon as he arrived on the outskirts of Rome, Emperor Henry fled the city with his antipope Clement in tow. After the first thrill of liberation, things soured for Gregory; the riotous behavior of the Norman knights angered the people of Rome, and soon enough they blamed the pope and forced him out of the city. He found refuge in the Benedictine monastery of Monte Cassino before moving to the castle of Salerno on the coast. Gregory died the following year on May 25, lifting excommunications on all except Henry and Antipope Clement in the days before his death.[21]

A number of successes lay ahead for Henry and his antipope. Henry's part in the Investiture Controversy would continue through the pontificates of Victor III,[22] Urban II,[23] and Paschal II.[24] Guibert, also known as Clement III, would maintain his antipapacy through the reigns of Victor III and Urban II, occupying Rome or part of it until 1098, when he had to flee first to Albano and then to Civita Castellana in the wake of Paschal II's election. He died there the following year. Clement was succeeded by antipopes Theodoric (1100–1101), Adalbert (1101), and Sylvester IV (1105–1111); the schism finally came to an end when Sylvester submitted to Paschal II. The popes continued to press reform, using various revolts in Germany to gradually weaken Henry IV. On his death in 1106, Henry was succeeded by his son, Henry V, who was in favor of the papacy; he had rebelled against his father on this issue and had, in time, forced Henry Senior to renounce the line of antipopes. Though he himself would fall afoul of the papacy and even appoint his own antipope, the archbishop of Braga, Maurice Bourdin, as Gregory VIII (1118–1121), he eventually came to an agreement with Pope Callixtus II in 1122 with the formulation of the Concordat of Worms.[25]

This agreement brought the Investiture Controversy to an end for a time, but with compromises on both sides. The Church did not manage to implement all of Gregory's reforms, but the role of monarchs was curtailed. In the election of a bishop, the emperor would have the right to be present and resolve disputes that might arise. When the moment of investiture came following episcopal consecration, the emperor or his legate would not confer the crozier, ring, and miter; rather, he would confer a newly invented symbol, the scepter, to represent the worldly authority of the bishop that was derived from the emperor. However, given the way the agreement was constructed, the emperor could still get his own candidate into a particular diocese. In the years that followed, though secular rulers still had a hand in local ecclesiastical affairs, and some in the affairs of the universal Church, the prestige and power of the papacy began to grow; Gregory's suffering had not been in vain.

While Thomas, as he found himself elevated to the episcopacy, may have mused on these events and the struggle Pope Gregory had to endure, he was not unaware that as chancellor he had been the creature of Henry II in his attempt to control the Church and her benefices. And while Gregory and his conflict with Henry IV was far away from England and in the previous century, there was another uncomfortable conflict closer to home that informed Thomas's conscience and reminded him that as archbishop he was called to faithfully serve the Church and her interests. This was the dispute between his archiepiscopal predecessor, Anselm, and Henry's revered grandfather.

18

Anselm

The Investiture Controversy reached England during the reign of Henry I (1100–1135), a monarch for whom Pope Saint Gregory VII's reforms were deeply worrying. His dispute with the archbishop of Canterbury at the time, Saint Anselm (1093–1109), would become as famous as that between Emperor Henry IV and Gregory, and Anselm would have much suffering to endure, including exile. In time, a resolution would be found, though it would be temporary, as England discovered during Thomas's administration. Ironically, that initial resolution, uneasy as it was, provided a model for the solution found later at Worms in 1122.

When William the Conqueror invaded England in 1066 to push his claim to succeed King Edward the Confessor, he was glad of the pope's support. William had sent an embassy to Pope Alexander II to seek his blessing for the enterprise, and Alexander gladly conferred it, sending a banner of Saint George and a papal ring to William as symbols of his support, together with a letter to the clergy of England urging them to submit to the new monarch. Armed with these, William set out, defeating King Harold at the Battle of Hastings and founding a new dynasty to occupy the throne of England and unite it to the Duchy of Normandy.

Five years later, when the see of Canterbury fell vacant, Alexander appointed Lanfranc of Bec as archbishop and primate of England.[1] A trusted friend and former teacher of the pope, Lanfranc would also prove a friend to William, guiding the Church in England to accept the legitimacy of the new regime and appointing Normans to ecclesiastical offices in place of Saxons. However, the appointment would end up causing problems for Rome. Following the invasion, William began to move away from the pope, refusing to come to Rome and pay homage for his realm, while Lanfranc worked with him to maintain the independence of the English Church. This union between crown and Church flourished even as the reforms of Pope Saint Gregory VII were being implemented. While the Investiture Controversy raged in Europe, the bishops and abbots of England took little, if any, notice; they stood with the king, so nothing changed following the promulgation of *Dictatus Papae*. The situation would shift, however, when Lanfranc died in 1089 and the abbot of Bec, Anselm of Aosta, was elected to succeed him. Anselm's view of the Church was much more universal, and he was a convinced supporter of the Gregorian Reforms.

Anselm was neither Norman nor Saxon.[2] Born in Aosta in Upper Burgundy (now the north of Italy), he became a monk and was abbot of Bec when elected to the see of Canterbury in 1093, very much against his will. Anselm was an academic, and today the Church counts him among the Doctors of the Church for his writings. As abbot, he worked to make Bec one of the foremost seats of learning in Europe, and students came from all over the continent to study under him. He proved himself an attentive and loving father to those in his care, and it was this attribute, together with his eminence, that led the monks of Canterbury to seek him as the successor to the great Lanfranc. They were not alone. King William II of England (more commonly called William Rufus), the son of William the Conqueror, also pushed Anselm to accept the see. He had initially opposed Anselm and had even sworn before a sacred image of Jesus Crucified, the Holy Face of Lucca, that he would never allow Anselm to sit in Canterbury.[3] But a serious brush with death, which raised the prospect of possible imminent damnation, led to a change of heart, and William Rufus became one of Anselm's more strident champions, doing everything he could to make the abbot accept the office. [4]

Anselm considered the requests, informing William that he would accept if the king would submit to the Gregorian Reforms (returning Church lands, accepting Anselm's spiritual counsel, and accepting Pope Urban II as the true pope over the antipope Clement III). William was hesitant; he agreed to return Church lands, but not to the other reforms. After Anselm finally accepted the office, William reneged on his assurances and suspended preparations for the episcopal investiture. Under pressure, William returned some of Canterbury's lands, and plans went ahead for Anselm's consecration, which took place on December 4, 1093.[5]

As a metropolitan, Anselm had to receive the pallium from the pope. William Rufus refused Anselm permission to travel to Rome, as he claimed was his right. It was one of the tenets of the Gregorian Reforms that bishops could travel to Rome without their secular ruler's consent. But the issue at hand was not just one of authority. William Rufus had not yet decided whom to support — Pope Urban II or the antipope Clement — and as Anselm was making plans to go to Urban, this precipitated, in William Rufus's view, the royal decision. William Rufus called a council, held at Rockingham, Northamptonshire, in March 1095, to consider the matter. Anselm argued eloquently in favor of Urban, while reminding the king that one of the conditions of his accepting the office of Canterbury was the royal recognition of Urban as pope.[6] In the end, William Rufus refused to allow Anselm to go to Rome; he sent envoys to request the pallium from whichever pope was there. They found Urban in possession of the city, and the envoys returned to England with the pallium.

It was at this point that an issue of investiture arose. William Rufus intended to clothe Anselm in the pallium himself, but the archbishop refused — the king had no right to confer the pope's honor. In the midst of this row, trouble broke out in Wales and the north of England, and this chastened William Rufus; he and Anselm made peace and agreed to a compromise. At a ceremony in Canterbury Cathedral on June 10, 1095, the king's legate laid the pallium on the high altar, and Anselm then proceeded to the altar, alone and barefoot, to put the pallium on himself.[7] This precedent would, a number of years later, get Thomas out of a tight spot when his pallium arrived following his consecration.

Strife was never far away from Anselm and William Rufus. Things came to a head in 1097 when the king made accusations against the archbishop, causing Anselm to leave for Rome to present his case before Pope Urban.[8] The king again refused permission for Anselm to go, but the archbishop was determined and left England with the king's threat that he was never to return ringing in his ears. Anselm arrived in Lyon and sent word to the pope that he wished to resign his office. Urban refused to accept the resignation and told him to come to Rome immediately. Arriving in the city in April 1097, the archbishop was on hand to assist at a council with representatives of the Eastern Churches regarding the theology of the procession of the Holy Spirit.[9] When the time came for Anselm's case to be heard, the pope found in his favor and, given the seriousness of William Rufus's actions, he was ready to excommunicate the king. In the hope that his intercession might turn the king, Anselm pleaded with the pope not to do so, but to show mercy; Urban heeded the appeal and agreed.[10] News of Anselm's magnanimity reached England and enhanced his reputation among the people. The king, however, was not inclined to be magnanimous; he had already confiscated the archbishop's lands and income for his own use, and quite apart from holding his position in the argument, he was not prepared to relinquish them.

Anselm would never see William Rufus again. While he was once again staying in Lyon, he heard of the king's tragic death — in August 1100, William Rufus had been struck with a stray arrow while out hunting. Following hot on the heels of that sad news was another message: a summons from the new king, Henry I, William Rufus's younger brother. Anselm had to hurry back to England; his exile was over. But if the archbishop was hopeful of peace at last, he was mistaken. More trouble awaited him. The new king wanted his archbishop back so he could invest him anew in the episcopal regalia to assert his royal authority over the Church. There would be no Gregorian Reforms in Henrician England.[11]

Thus began the Investiture Controversy in England, and it reached its climax very quickly. Anselm refused to allow Henry to reinvest him with the regalia, as the new papal decrees forbade it.[12] Furious, the king sent to Rome, to the new pope, Paschal II, for an exemption.[13] Meanwhile, Anselm showed his goodwill by sorting out canonical difficulties to allow Henry to marry Matilda, daughter of King Malcolm III of Scotland, who had been living as a nun. Though she was not bound by vows, canonical barriers prevented her marriage to Henry. The archbishop also supported Henry in a dispute over the throne with his brother Robert. In September 1102, Anselm called a council in London to formally establish Gregorian Reforms in England.[14] Whatever about the reason for the council, Henry did not dispute Anselm's calling it — he had no problem with Anselm's submitting the Church in England to himself as archbishop of Canterbury, so long as Anselm submitted himself to Henry.

The response from Rome regarding a second investiture was not to Henry's liking: The pope said no. Henry immediately dispatched three bishops to submit a second request to the pope. In the meantime, Henry appointed bishops and invested them in opposition to Anselm, who in his turn refused to consecrate them.[15] When the episcopal appointees saw that Anselm wouldn't budge, they began to hand back their regalia to Henry, and those urged by the king to seek consecration from another bishop refused to do so. The three bishops returned from Rome with the pope's answer. The answer was the same as before: No. Anselm had, in the meantime, received a sealed letter from the pope confirming the initial decision not to allow Henry to invest him. While the three bishops, at Henry's prompting, it seems, claimed that the pope had orally agreed to the investiture, Anselm knew better. Apart from the evidence of the papal letter, he also had the report of friends in Rome who were quick to inform him that the pope had not given any oral assurance to the bishops, but was holding to his original decision. There was only one thing to be done: Anselm had to go to Rome himself and clarify things once and for all with Paschal. Unusually, Henry did not oppose him, but there was a condition: Anselm had to present the king's case to the pope. The archbishop agreed to do so, but objectively rather than persuasively, so the pope had all the facts.[16]

Anselm's second journey to Rome would also initiate his second exile. He left England in 1103 with an envoy from the king, arriving to find Pope Paschal irate at having to listen to yet another request from Henry. For the third time, the pope confirmed his decision to uphold the Gregorian Reforms and refused to grant an exemption to the English king. Furthermore, he excommunicated those bishops who had accepted investiture from Henry, and though he was close to it, the king narrowly avoided excommunication himself.[17] In response, Henry sent a letter to Anselm imposing exile on him. The archbishop proceeded to Lyon again but not to lie low. He would bide his time; in the interim, he concentrated on his writing, producing important philosophical and theological works.

Henry carried on as if nothing had happened, and in March 1105 Pope Paschal excommunicated those English bishops who had been invested by the king since the initial excommunication. He also excommunicated a number of the king's closest advisors while threatening the same for Henry. A month later, Anselm took up arms. Writing to Henry, he informed him that where the pope held back, he would not: He was now willing to excommunicate the king. Anselm sent the letter through the king's sister Adela to ensure that it was delivered into Henry's hands. Now mired in difficulties, Henry was afraid. An excommunication and the dissolution of his subjects' loyalty that came with it would be a disaster for him. He agreed to a meeting, and a compromise was reached in July 1105: Henry would renounce the claim to investiture, but only if clerics did homage for their lands.[18] Anselm told him that this compromise would require the pope's assent. In his submission to the pope, the archbishop recommended that the deal be approved, and Paschal consented, though both pope and archbishop agreed that this would be merely a temporary concession.

Anselm did not return directly to England, but remained in France for a time. He met with Henry at Bec in August 1106 and wrung further concessions out of him.[19] Henry returned all of Canterbury's assets and churches, even those seized under William Rufus that had never been returned, and promised that nothing more would be taken. As a gesture of goodwill, the king made a security payment to the archbishop and exempted bishops who had paid a controversial church tax from all tax for three years. The archbishop returned to England triumphant in early 1107 and soon after formalized the agreement with Henry in the Concordat of London.[20] In this agreement, Henry formally renounced his right to invest bishops and abbots but reserved the right to accept their homage for their lands, as was required of any secular vassal of the king. In essence, the concordat made a distinction between the secular and ecclesiastical powers of a bishop and clarified where loyalty and authority lay.

Anselm's final victory in this crisis was the subjection of the archbishopric of York to the primatial see of Canterbury. He persuaded Pope Paschal that when a new archbishop of York had been elected and consecrated, the pallium destined for the new archbishop was to be sent to Canterbury so that the new archbishop would first have to make his obedience to the primate before being invested. The incumbent at York, Archbishop Thomas,[21] was not pleased and refused to agree, thus initiating a dispute between the sees. This spat was resolved after Anselm's death when King Henry I and the bishops took the primate's side and ruled that York was subject to Canterbury.

Anselm died in peace on April 21, 1109, Spy Wednesday[22] that year, and was buried in Canterbury Cathedral. The holiness of his life, the heroism of his struggle, and his work for reform were cause for veneration. His writings would inspire scholars and assure his place among the Doctors of the Church, while the issue of his canonization would occupy Thomas during his time as archbishop. As for Henry II, it was Anselm's victory over Henry I that would occupy him; it was a terrible shadow over the royal dynasty and one that had to be exorcised for fear that the new archbishop should see it as a paradigm for his own administration. But as Henry and Thomas were to find to their cost, history was about to repeat itself.

19

Father

As archbishop of Canterbury, Thomas was the successor of Saint Augustine,[1] the Roman Benedictine monk sent by Pope Saint Gregory the Great in 595 to lead a team of missionaries to preach the Gospel in the south of England. Augustine founded the see of Canterbury, became its first bishop, and established what would become the primatial see for England. A number of holy men had occupied the chair of Augustine, fourteen of them canonized at the time of Thomas's accession. These included Saint Laurence and Saint Mellitus, Augustine's immediate successors and two of the original missionaries; Saint Deusdedit, the first native of England to hold the office; the reformer Saint Theodore of Tarsus; Saint Oda, the son of a Viking; the great Saint Dunstan; and Saint Alfege, who was martyred. Then there was holy Anselm, who would be canonized later but whose suffering and struggle against secular interference in the Church were still fresh in people's memory.

Though seen by some as a pawn of kings, the archbishopric of Canterbury had become one of the most notable in Western Europe, and having been occupied by many saints, it was considered by many to be a holy see. Because many dynamic and noteworthy men had sat on the chair of Augustine (though there were some unworthy ones, too), Thomas knew that the pope, the people, and perhaps even history expected that he would rise to the example of his holy predecessors. If that was not possible in sanctity, it was certainly possible in duty. And this was Thomas's bane: duty. For all his ambition and luxuriant lifestyle, he had a sense of duty. That sense of duty had torn him from Theobald's to Henry's side; he now suspected that it might tear him from Henry's cause and ambitions.

Like Theobald, he would have to travel around his archdiocese and even all over England on Church matters, and he would have to ensure that he was often present at court. But Thomas's new life as archbishop would be centered on the cathedral, officially the Cathedral Church of Christ (Christ Church), where the *cathedra*, the symbol of his office, stood in the sanctuary. In that cathedral, his monks chanted the Liturgy of the Hours several times a day. Thomas was not just an archbishop; he was now also abbot of that community, their father. That may seem unusual, but abbot-bishops had been the mainstay of many dioceses within the Church in England and many other dioceses throughout Europe for centuries. Though they had been manipulated into electing him, the monks of Christ Church Abbey now looked to him to lead them, as did the people and clergy of his archdiocese and the people and clergy of England.

Letters expressing congratulations and promises of obedience flowed into the archbishop's office. Bishop Arnulf of Lisieux sent another calming epistle assuring Thomas of his support and offering advice (the new archbishop may have made the wise decision to keep his distance from this unscrupulous minion of Henry's). But one of the first letters he received is believed to have been from the prior of Dover, Richard, a member of the Canterbury community of monks.[2] In his letter, Richard at first apologizes for not writing sooner, and then proceeds to write a letter full of affection and support for Thomas, now facing his new responsibilities. He advises the new archbishop to surround himself with good and faithful men to help him share these burdens; some scholars believe this letter to be an application for one of these posts within the new administration. While that may have been the case, Richard expresses genuine affection, and he would remain a friend to Thomas in his trials and eventually succeed him as archbishop in 1173. Richard warns that the responsibility the new archbishop now has summons him to vigilance. He is all too aware that Thomas is worn down by anxious care and arduous work, hence the need for reliable and faithful coworkers. Urging him to preserve and improve what is good in the church at Canterbury and to impose due order on what is awry, the prior reminds the new archbishop that he has been chosen to be father, pastor, and leader.

While this letter could be viewed simply as a pious exhortation coming from a man Thomas knew and liked from his years in Theobald's service, he may well have taken note of what Richard had to say and reflected upon it. There is little doubt that the prior's letter would have reinforced what Thomas had feared and now faced: the burden of the apostle. He was no longer a mere administrator, but a father and a shepherd of souls. Richard assures his new archbishop that he has confidence in him, that Thomas can and must rise to the challenge and be strong. Concluding his letter, the prior urges him to be constant; to stand erect, unbending and unbroken; to be strong in the Lord; and to conduct all his affairs in charity.

The office of archbishop, along with its great dignity and trappings of ecclesiastical grandeur, came with great responsibility. Though many before and after Thomas who have assumed the office may not have realized or lived the moral and spiritual responsibility, the new archbishop was all too aware that his true responsibility was not merely administrative. Thomas feared the office. His critics maintain that he feigned his objections to being appointed, but he knew what would be required of him: If he were to be as diligent in this office as he had been in the others he held, he would have to change.

Thomas's "conversion" is often situated at this moment in his life. However, it has to be borne in mind that dramatic conversions like Saint Paul's are rare. Conversion usually takes time; it is most often a gradual opening of the mind and the heart to God and to truth. This was the case with Thomas. There was no dramatic transformation in the first years of his life as archbishop, just gradual, small changes — though subsequent events would help reinforce those changes. For one thing, he was neither a bad man nor a rake, simply one whose affections lay with material things, honor, and ambition, but not to the total exclusion of the things of the spirit. The piety learned at his mother's knee was an ever-present reality and guided him to daily prayer, charity, and acts of penance. When he needed spiritual resources, he would always return to what she taught him.

One aspect of his life now assumed greater significance and importance: the Mass. In those first few days as priest and bishop, Thomas, who had often served the Mass as deacon, now entered into the sacred mysteries as a priest, and it seems that this experience marked him for the rest of his life. Cautious and careful in the offering of his first Mass, he maintained that reverence throughout his life. He was known for his recollection at the altar and for the great care he took in celebrating the Eucharist.[3] He did not celebrate Mass every day; refraining out of reverence, he did not want to allow familiarity to dilute the devotion and awe necessary for the Holy Sacrifice. When he did celebrate Mass, he prepared diligently, always reciting the prayers Saint Anselm had written to help priests prepare for the sacrifice. The external speculations of historians cannot probe the depths of Thomas's heart in his relationship with the Eucharistic Christ, but observing the change in his life provides the insight that becoming a priest made all the difference for him.

As a diligent administrator, Thomas would have easily taken on the administrative duties of archbishop. As archdeacon, he had been close enough to Theobald to observe and understand what he needed to do to run an archdiocese. His years as royal chancellor brought other skills and insights. However, there were other obligations. Every bishop is called to fulfill his office for the sake of the Church and, more immediately, for the sake of his flock. The duties of this office are threefold: to govern, to teach, and to sanctify.

The first of these is easily understood — the bishop should govern his diocese with care and diligence. For the most part, this is a practical office, the day-to-day administration of the territory and assets in his care for the sake of the Church and the people of his diocese. While this is an important duty, it is one a bishop can delegate to others; indeed, to others who may have greater gifts in the various areas of administration. A wise bishop will realize that this office is usually best served by supervising the work of his staff. This is what Theobald did: Employing the best clerks for his household, he allowed them to carry out the bulk of his administrative work. Thomas imitated this in his work as chancellor, and now he would do the same in his work as archbishop. The duty of governance also included canonical responsibilities. Now well versed in the law and in the Church's customs and practices, Thomas was equipped to fulfill these while delegating what he could to competent and diligent clerks.

Then there was the office of teaching. As a deacon, Thomas would have preached, but it was probably a rare occurrence; now, as archbishop, he would be expected to rise to the eloquence and depth of an official teacher of the Church. Thomas was quick to realize that he was not able to do this, given his poor education in philosophical and theological matters. He knew some theology, and his knowledge of canon law was superlative, but his understanding of the Scriptures and of the rich tradition of the Church's theological reflection was very poor. Living in an age of tremendous philosophical and theological debate, he may have found himself at the edge of despair at the thought of having to catch up. He could have adopted the manner of some who were raised to the episcopate and confined himself to pious platitudes, leaving the heavy lifting to those priests and deacons who might be better preachers. However, Thomas was a man of duty; if he was to fulfill his duty as teacher, he had to learn, and that would require great effort and even greater humility.

Shortly after he was consecrated, Thomas began serious theological studies. He engaged as tutor his secretary, Herbert of Bosham,[4] and so began a long and often arduous pilgrimage through the Scriptures, the works of the Fathers of the Church, and the writings of more contemporary theologians. He soon found that he had a taste for Scripture and began to devote as much time as he could to studying it. Before long, he was alluding to Scripture in his letters, and his deepening understanding of the Word of God equipped him not just for the pulpit, but also for his personal life. He developed a passion for books, and he would build up a substantial library.[5] His intellect awakened, he would find his leisure time moving from the country sports he loved to the books that became his new friends and advisors. Among the works in his library were commentaries on the Scriptures, the writings of the Fathers of the Church, philosophical works, books on canon and civil law, and devotional books that stirred his heart to prayer. The fruit of Thomas's study was his development as a great preacher and a true teacher of the Faith. As he grew in knowledge and confidence, his efforts at study and preaching moved beyond dutifully fulfilling what was required of him to satisfying a growing desire to teach the flock that had been entrusted to his care.

The third office of a bishop, to sanctify, is perhaps the most difficult to fulfill. This was to prove the great challenge to the new archbishop because he knew that to form people in holiness, he had to be holy himself. As he had said to King Henry, he was not holy — he was a pleasure-loving, lukewarm man too much immersed in the ways of the world. The same could be said of many bishops before and since, and elevation to become successors of the apostles did not change all of them. In Thomas's case, his sense of duty led him to fear the office, for he knew he would have to change at the most personal level of his being.

In the first years of his life as archbishop, Thomas began to take his spiritual life much more seriously. He had always prayed, but now his spiritual life grew more intense. He devoted more time to meditation and conversation with God; delving into the mysteries of Scripture provided him with much material for prayer. Each day, his monks would spend time in *lectio divina*, the prayerful reading and consideration of scriptural texts, and Thomas may have taken guidance in this. He had a chaplain, and this priest would have served him as a spiritual director as well as confessor. At some point, he began to observe night vigils — these would become a feature of his years of exile. As he grew in prayerfulness at Canterbury, he began spending certain nights in prayer either in the cathedral or in his private chapel. Thomas also intensified his penances, adopting the practice of taking "the discipline," a penitential physical scourging in atonement for his sins. Two of his monks would come to his room at various times to implement the penance. He would later supplement these penances by wearing a hair shirt. Thomas would struggle to allow his new life of piety reshape his personality and overcome his faults, as he had a strong personality and a strong will. In the end, it would take more than spiritual exercises to break him down, but that transformation lay in the future. His conversion would take time — indeed, it would take the rest of his life — but he laid firm foundations in the first months of his episcopate.

If he is to be what his order or diocese intends him to be, a priest must at some point pause and realize who he is now. The call to priesthood, and most certainly the appointment to the office of bishop, is ultimately a call to fatherhood. The pressures of parish life and the formality and caution of the office of bishop can cocoon a man from being struck by the radical nature of the office in which he shares. Though many priests and bishops may never realize it, the fact and the call remain. Confronted with this call, Thomas began to realize that he could not be just an administrator; he had to surrender and become a father. Like his conversion, this realization was gradual, but it was an insight that was clarified and strengthened in the heat of battle.

Thomas continued to wear his fine clothes and eat well. He loved his horses and hunting; now he had the estates of Canterbury to provide a forum for his country sports. Externally, he seemed the same; but it concealed a gradual change.[6] His enemies, growing in number, may well have found enough ammunition for future use in his perceived lavish lifestyle. His friend King Henry at first saw no change and blissfully looked forward to working with his new archbishop — or more correctly, to having his archbishop-chancellor work for him. Secretly, however, Thomas began to implement his decision to change, though it was a gradual process in the first years of his life as archbishop. Under his finery, he wore the habit of his Benedictine monks. He still served fine foods at his table and was as generous with his guests as he had always been, but he was eating less and gradually yielding to periods of fasting. Still lavish, the food was served on the finest plate with the choicest wines, but Thomas was creating a greater distance between it and him. Always known for his almsgiving, he now increased by a sizable degree what he gave to the poor.

Things were about to change dramatically in terms of Thomas's loyalty. As archbishop, Thomas knew that he was independent and auton-omous. Primate of the Church in England, he had no superior in the realm. He had answered the question many may have asked as the arch-deacon-chancellor rode to Canterbury: "Who is the master of the arch-bishop of Canterbury?" His answer was Christ. And between Christ and the archbishop was the Vicar of Christ, the pope — certainly not the Angevin.

The first sign of change came at the beginning of August 1162, about two months after his consecration, though it may have passed unnoticed. Upon his consecration, Thomas had to petition the pope to be invested with the pallium. It was usual that the new archbishop travel to Rome to meet the pope and receive the pallium personally from him; however, re-cent troubles with the Investiture Controversy had led some monarchs to refuse permission to their archbishops to go to Rome. For some reason known only to himself, and quite unusual given the close relationship that seemed to exist between them, Henry refused to allow Thomas to go to Rome.[7] Though annoyed, Thomas held his peace and in late June 1162 sent John of Salisbury and John of Canterbury to request the pallium for him. These two envoys were to have endless trouble on the mission. Pope Alexander III had been exiled from Rome by the Holy Roman emperor, Frederick Barbarossa, who was championing the legitimacy of his anti-pope, Victor IV. Alexander was supposed to be making his base in exile at Montpelier in Toulouse, but he was not there yet. The papal court was still making its way slowly through France. It took the two men six weeks to track Alexander down; when they did, the pope gladly conferred the pallium, and the envoys were on their way back to England by the begin-ning of August.

Henry's intention was to confer the pallium himself, as was the cus-tom of his grandfather, disputed as it was. However, he could not make the trip to Canterbury, so he sent a delegate to represent him. Thomas had no intention of being invested by the delegate — whether Henry knew it yet or not, his new archbishop was not going to resurrect this vestige of secular investiture. At a loss at Thomas's refusal, the delegate, taking the pallium from Thomas's envoys, dutifully followed their in-struction to lay it upon the high altar of the cathedral. On August 10, in a simple ceremony attended by his monks, some dignitaries, and the ordinary people of Canterbury, Thomas processed up to the altar barefoot; there, he carefully took up the pallium and, assisted by his monks, vested himself.[8] This was the moment when Thomas symbolically assumed his powers as metropolitan and primate; it would prove to be symbolic of many things.

Not long afterward, in the fall of 1162, as he immersed himself in his office and the challenges it brought, Thomas sent a letter to Henry, who was in Normandy. Four or five months into his episcopacy, due to the great burden of work now laid upon his shoulders and his onerous pastoral duties, Thomas was tendering his resignation as royal chancellor.[9] When Henry read the letter, he was apoplectic. Not only had Thomas renounced his duties to the crown and torn a hole through Henry's plans for a dual office, but Thomas had not consulted him as would have been necessary. Worse again, he did not even wait until Henry had returned to England. The new archbishop had suddenly asserted an independence and authority that the king had not allowed. Though his excuses concerned work and pastoral duties, Thomas's resignation was more about the noose around his neck than the pallium: He was cutting himself free of Henry's control. He probably realized that the king would not be pleased; would Henry now suspect that the new archbishop was going to be a maverick? Thomas may not have known for certain, but he knew his friend well enough to reckon that it might be dawning on Henry that he may have made a mistake. The king might have forgotten about the row at Toulouse; Thomas had not. The archbishop of Canterbury did indeed have a master that he would serve most dutifully, and it was not the king of England.

20
Zeal

Thomas's biographers Herbert of Bosham and John of Salisbury offer an account of the archbishop's daily routine when he was in Canterbury; it was regulated by the life of the monastery. His day began before two o'clock in the morning, when he rose with the monks to pray the night office of Nocturnes. For some reason, he decided to practice the Maundy Thursday[1] custom of giving alms after this office each day; thus, returning to his room after Nocturnes, he welcomed thirteen poor men under cover of darkness, washed their feet, and gave them alms. He then returned to bed for a short time. Rising again before dawn, he spent time in prayer and studying Scripture with his secretary-tutor Herbert of Bosham's assistance until the office of Matins at dawn. At eight o'clock, he prayed the office of Terce and then, on some days, he offered Mass. As noted above, he celebrated Mass with great devotion, rapidly but never carelessly, and he prepared for the Holy Sacrifice by praying devotions written by Saint Anselm.[2] Herbert, who it seems struggled with faith in the Eucharist, saw in Thomas a simple faith when it came to the Mass and Blessed Sacrament.[3] John of Salisbury associated Thomas's deep devotion with the gift of tears, commenting that the archbishop prayed alone until he was filled with the miracle of tears, and when he offered Mass, he was so caught up it was as if he beheld the passion of Christ before him in the flesh.[4] John may have been speaking metaphorically or out of devotion himself; it is not known whether Thomas actually had the gift of tears or had mystical experiences.

His workday began after Mass, when he would carry out various administrative duties, including his work as judge in the ecclesiastical court and meeting various people in audiences, until the office of None at 2:20, after which he retired for dinner. Some days, he took a short nap afterward, but he usually met with his tutor, scholars, invited guests, and members of his household to engage in religious conversation, discuss various matters of business, and seek advice on issues of concern to him. The office of Vespers was celebrated in the cathedral in the mid- to late afternoon, and he was usually present. Business, meetings, and private prayer occupied the rest of the day, until he retired to bed at nightfall.

As the letters of congratulations were coming in, Thomas was composing letters of his own, and one of the first was to his principal consecrator, Bishop Henry of Winchester.[5] This letter, while it began in effusive and fraternal terms, quickly modulated to a disguised rebuke and an ultimatum. Henry liked nice things, and he had taken a gold cross from the treasury of his cathedral for himself. In Thomas's eyes, this was theft — in the parlance of canon law, "alienating" from the Church that which was her property. At first encouraging Henry to stand up against his enemies and musing on how cunning those who walk the way of the serpent are, Thomas then accused the bishop of serious sin. His decision to remove the cross from the cathedral was ill considered. Ordering the bishop to obedience, he directed him to return the gold cross to the rightful ownership of the Church within forty days of receiving the letter. If he did not do so, Thomas demanded that he come to him within two months from that fortieth day to make satisfaction.

If Bishop Henry was shocked and displeased, others would join him in the coming months. The archbishop meant to continue what Theobald had started just before his death and tackle the problems his predecessor had been unable to deal with.[6] Surveying the lands and posses-sions of the archdiocese, which had been bought or gifted to the Church to allow the archdiocese to earn an income to meet its expenses, he saw that many of them had been seized by various barons or tenants who no longer paid their rents. The usurpation of Church property under Henry I and Stephen had encouraged this. In the fall of 1162, Thomas resumed Theobald's work, taking measures to recoup what was stolen and to re-view what was rented. With all the skill he had learned and used as chan-cellor, Thomas was relentless in his efforts. He claimed to have the king's permission, but as he put pressure on the barons, either Henry withdrew his permission or it was not as all-encompassing as Thomas presumed or claimed. Some usurpers relented, others held out, and Thomas had to resort to extreme measures, including ecclesiastical penalties, to force them to loosen their hold on the Church's assets. Again, some relented, grudgingly, but others dug in their heels and appealed to Henry for help.

One such case concerned the castle and estates of Saltwood in Kent, not far from Canterbury.[7] The castle had been acquired by Lanfranc, and Theobald had used it when he could. During the Anarchy, Henry of Essex, later constable of England under Henry II, illegally occupied it. When he fell into disgrace in 1157, he lost the castle, and Henry con-ferred it on Ranulf de Broc, officially an usher and marshal of the royal household and the one who organized Henry's extramarital trysts.[8] Ran-ulf was a rather unsavory character: uncouth, dangerous, and immoral, he cherished violence as the most "virtuous" means of getting what he wanted. He was also one of Henry's closest cronies. When Thomas re-quested the return of Saltwood, none of his arguments or his legal doc-umentation could persuade Ranulf to comply, and as for ecclesiastical censures, these meant nothing to a man who had no qualms about using force to get what he wanted. A long and bitter argument ensued, and while Ranulf uncharacteristically refrained from violence, he used his influence with Henry to resist the archbishop's pressure. In time, this dispute would have fatal consequences.

As he tried to oust occupying barons, Thomas was also reviewing rents.[9] While Theobald had been a fine archbishop, he had not negotiat-ed the best arrangements when it came to leasing lands. He had, in fact, been coerced in a number of cases, and being occupied with so many duties and the Anarchy, he had been unable to enforce his rights. Thomas was determined to set things right. Many of those renting Church lands were taking advantage, paying little and holding on to lands for too long, way beyond what had been agreed in the rental contracts. Examining these cases, Thomas revoked all these leases, and so began another battle. In their defense, some of the tenants claimed to hold the lands by hereditary right; Thomas dismissed this excuse and had a number of them evicted. While some of these appealed to the king, others took cases against him to the royal courts. When summoned, Thomas refused to attend or even plead, informing them that if any of them had a complaint against him, they had to take it to the archbishop's court at Canterbury. Thomas knew his law, and he was completely within his rights, though it could be said that his zeal might have been excessive and he would have been better served seasoning his actions with prudence.

One case would prove problematic: that of John FitzGilbert, often called John the Marshal. Thomas knew John well; they had both sat on the bench of the king's court. John was known to be a seasoned soldier and a tough man who was not afraid to fight for his rights on the battlefield or in the courts. As Thomas was examining the archdiocesan lands occupied by others, he noticed that some lands in Sussex had been "acquired" by John and incorporated into his estates. John may have believed they were his, but the archbishop did not, and he demanded that they be restored to the Church. Under pressure from Thomas, John went to the archbishop's court to defend his ownership. Asked to present proof that he had title to the land, the marshal could not, so Thomas threw out the petition. Not to be dismissed, John produced what he claimed was a Bible and swore on the book that he had been robbed. As later events would reveal, the book was not a Bible but a Mass book that John had intentionally chosen so he would not perjure himself in his oath.[10] Thomas prevailed over John, but the old soldier was not going to let the archbishop get the better of him — he decided to swallow the defeat for now and bide his time.

Thomas's actions, though legal and just, were earning him enemies. Henry was seething in Normandy as petition after petition arrived be-

fore him demanding, cautiously, that he restrain his archbishop and restore the archdiocese's lands to those who now claimed them. These petitioners were aware of the deep friendship between king and archbishop,
and they were not entirely sure that Henry was not giving his assent to
Thomas's actions. Henry seems to have been unsure as to what to do;
perhaps he needed to talk to Thomas and figure out what was going on,
and see whether they could hammer out a resolution. Either way, he decided to leave the petitions to one side for the moment and celebrate
Christmas 1162 in Normandy.

The weather was particularly bad that winter, so Henry was unable
to return to England until January 23, 1163, when he and Eleanor sailed
into the port of Southampton. Thomas and young Henry were waiting for
them, and as soon as the king arrived at his lodgings, he warmly embraced
his friend; it seemed to all that nothing had changed.[11] Over the coming
days, the two spent a lot of time together, often dismissing their attendants
and riding out into the country as they had often done when Thomas was
chancellor. The sight of king and archbishop so obviously close unnerved
the barons and other petitioners. John the Marshal was also present, and
he, too, had second thoughts. As the days wore on, it seems, many of the
disgruntled began to make themselves scarce. Over the next few months,
Thomas was often at court, and Henry came for various occasions to Canterbury, where he was received as warmly as ever.

Those with keener eyes, however, would have noticed a slight change.
Henry was not as effusive as he used to be, though he still engaged in
the external expression of affection for his friend. Whatever the two discussed in their time alone together, it took some days for one issue to be
raised: the office of the archdeacon of Canterbury. While Thomas had
renounced the chancellorship, he still held that office and, more importantly for Henry, its benefices. Thomas initially refused to relinquish the
office; but after much persuasion, he relented and vacated it, conferring
it on the king's new royal chancellor, the clerk Geoffrey Ridel, a man who
was, and would firmly remain, in Henry's camp.[12]

While tensions with Henry were growing, albeit unnoticed at this
point, and Thomas was engaged in battle with barons and tenants, he
sought to build bridges with others, one of whom was Gilbert Foliot, the

bishop of Hereford who had desired Canterbury for himself. Gilbert was still seething at Thomas's election, but the new archbishop wanted to bring him onside and found the means to do it: He would ensure that Gilbert would be elected to the see of London, the most senior suffragan diocese in the metropolitan Province of Canterbury. In this endeavor, Thomas had the king's full support. His efforts proved successful, and in a letter to Gilbert in March 1163, he notified him of his elevation, praising him as a fitting candidate for such an important see and stating that he would welcome the new bishop's assistance in the metropolitan province.[13]

Thomas's letter was an olive branch and written with genuine affection, but while Gilbert jumped at the offer, he did not share the same affection for his archbishop. Another letter from Thomas a month later,[14] just before Gilbert's installation in Saint Paul's Cathedral on April 28, 1163, is even more affectionate. One sentiment in the first letter may have raised alarm bells for the new bishop of London: Thomas mentioned "the duty to which the obligation of obedience draws you." Here the archbishop was subtly laying the groundwork for a request he would soon make — that Gilbert should profess his obedience to him as his metropolitan. Thomas may have been trying to build bridges, but he was all too aware of what was standing on the other side looking over at him.

In the meantime, Pope Alexander had called a council to be held in Tours in May 1163; Thomas and a number of English bishops were summoned to attend. The council was to deal with matters arising from the schism. By holding the council in Tours, which was in Henry's territory, Alexander was conferring a singular honor on the king, one probably designed to keep him onside as Frederick Barbarossa was trying to put pressure on England to accept his antipope, Victor, as the true pontiff. Thomas left England with eleven bishops and a sizable entourage. As he made his way to Tours, he was feted by the lords of the territories he entered, while many people came out to see this new archbishop who was creating a stir in the Church. The crowds were waiting to greet him as he approached Tours, among them a number of members of the papal court. Alexander himself stood to receive the new archbishop and warmly embraced him. But this was not only because he was Thomas Becket, archbishop of Canterbury, but probably because he was still believed to be King Henry's closest friend and confidant.[15] Unknown to Thomas, Alexander and Henry had been in correspondence, and Henry had agreed to support the pope against Barbarossa and his creature, Antipope Victor.

The council opened on May 19, 1163. Present were seventeen cardinals, 124 bishops, and 414 abbots. Thomas was seated on the pope's right, a place of honor given that he was the most senior of the prelates in the territory. The council would deal with some minor disputes; examine some issues surrounding Peter Lombard's *Sentences*; and take measures against the Cathars in the south of France, formally declaring them heretics.[16] The main business concerned the schism and Antipope Victor. As Bishop Arnulf of Lisieux, Henry's trusted counsellor in Normandy, stressed in his sermon at the opening ceremony, the theme of the council was unity: unity under the legitimate pontiff, Alexander III. The pope had already excommunicated Victor and Barbarossa the year before; but now at the council, he excommunicated the antipope's followers.

Thomas had business of his own for the pope, two matters: Anselm and Gilbert Foliot.[17] As Henry had sought the canonization of King Edward the Confessor to raise the prestige of the English monarchy and was granted it in 1161, Thomas sought the canonization of Archbishop Anselm as a means not only of recognizing Anselm's holiness but also of "canonizing" his position in the struggle with the secular powers in England. Thomas had asked John of Salisbury to write a biography of Anselm, what would now be considered a *positio*.[18] John had included accounts of various miracles that had been worked through Anselm's intercession as evidence of God's judgment on the man and his ministry. Alexander was aware that this request was not merely a matter of recognizing a saint. With one eye on how Henry might greet the canonization of the archbishop who triumphed over his grandfather, the pope told Thomas that he would defer the matter to allow further consideration. There were already a number of requests for canonizations at the council, so Alexander had an excuse to put Anselm to one side.[19] (Later, in June, Alexander would issue a bull[20] explaining that he did not consent to Thomas's request to canonize Archbishop Anselm because others present at Tours seeking canonization of their candidates might have been envious.) Instead, he asked Thomas to gather an assembly of bishops and abbots and other persons to examine the life and miracles of Anselm; whatever decision that assembly made, he would happily confirm. Thomas would establish the assembly, but its work was not completed before he went into exile.

The archbishop then brought up the matter of a profession of obedience from Gilbert Foliot, who was about to take up the office of bishop of London. Again, Alexander was all too aware that this request had an awkward political dimension. Gilbert was already being seen as a new ally of Henry's, and not wishing to provoke the king now, Alexander refused the request. Gilbert had already made a profession of obedience when he was elevated to Hereford, the pope insisted; another such profession was not required upon his translation to London.[21] The pope was technically correct, but that technicality got him out of a tight corner and kept Henry onside while creating difficulties for Thomas in his future struggle with Gilbert. The pope would issue a second bull in June confirming this decision.[22]

Thomas was defeated, yet he was still celebrated, and that eased the pain of Alexander's refusals. Meanwhile, Roger de Pont L'Évêque, archbishop of York, created a scene when he saw the seating plan. He demanded to be given precedence over Thomas because he had been consecrated before him, but in this matter, the pope sided with Thomas. As primate, he had precedence over the archbishop of York.[23] That may have gratified Thomas, but as he left Tours he may have pondered on all that had happened and realized that while the council appeared to have a been a success, in reality it was not. Someone else seemed to be pulling Alexander's strings, and he knew who it was: Henry. The pope seemed to be a man with a debt to pay; in his struggle to assert his claim to the papacy and exercise his office, he needed Henry, one of the most powerful monarchs in Europe, on his side. Thomas had also been made aware of his own shortcomings.[24] At one point, the pope had asked him to give an address, but as his Latin was not up to scratch, he had had to decline; that had been embarrassing. After all those subtle rejections, he may have doubted whether was he equipped or even ready for a fight. He may have wondered what lay ahead and how he would cope.

21
Alexander

As Thomas returned to England from Tours, he may have reflected on the pope and on where he stood. Alexander had been gracious to him, but this magnanimity had more to do with Henry than with the archbishop of Canterbury. The pope was fighting to prove the legitimacy of his election, and in his efforts to do so, he was lining up allies to support him. That his main enemy was not merely an antipope but the Holy Roman emperor made things even more difficult. In his coaxing the crowned heads of Europe to his cause, Alexander had to tread carefully, particularly when it came to matters that affected monarchs personally and to divisive issues concerning the Church in their realms. If a fight were to erupt between Thomas of Canterbury and Henry of England, where would the pope position himself?

Alexander was born Rolando di Siena, a member of an aristocratic family in the Republic of Siena, around 1105.[1] Destined for the Church, he studied law at Bologna and, after ordination, would initially dedicate himself to teaching and study, emerging as an acknowledged legal scholar and theologian. Committed to ecclesiastical renewal, he was a supporter of Pope Saint Gregory VII's reforms while being cautiously aware of the power of secular rulers over the Church. He had a particular animus against Frederick Barbarossa, whom he saw as desiring too much power over the Church. As he rose within the ranks of the hierarchy, Rolando was created cardinal by Pope Eugene III in October 1150, and in 1153 was appointed papal chancellor.

Well respected within the curia, Rolando supported the Church's developing a relationship with the Kingdom of Sicily in order to help balance power within Europe as Barbarossa grew in strength. When Pope Adrian IV agreed to negotiate a possible treaty with Sicily in 1156, Rolando led the embassy from the Holy See and successfully forged the Treaty of Benevento with King William I, much to Barbarossa's chagrin. A year later, Rolando further antagonized the emperor when in a speech he referred to the empire as a "benefice" of the pope to the emperor — in other words, a feudal servant. This pronouncement was met with howls of indignation from Barbarossa. Rolando, in his defense, maintained that he meant something else, but he knew that the term was ambiguous — he was in reality drawing a line in the sand, and the emperor knew it.[2]

Pope Adrian died on September 1, 1159, and a conclave was called for September 5; thirty-one cardinals assembled to elect a new successor to Saint Peter. Two days later, Rolando was elected pope by the majority, as required by law. Barbarossa, perhaps fearing that Rolando might be elected, had already instructed cardinals under his influence to elect Cardinal Ottaviano di Monticelli, a son of the noble Counts of Tusculum;[3] a minority of cardinals voted for him. Assuming the name Alexander III, Rolando was presented with the scarlet mantle, the traditional garb of popes at that time; but before he could put it on, Ottaviano came forward and forbade him from doing so. Ignoring the rebuke, the cardinals were going ahead with vesting Alexander when Ottaviano suddenly jumped on the new pope and tried to pull the mantle from him. After a tussle, Ottaviano was pushed back and Alexander vested. However, the minority cardinals were ready for every eventuality. Producing a mantle of their own, they vested Ottaviano, who then told the astonished college that he was Victor IV. One of the cardinals present later related that the mantle was put on in such a hurry that it was back to front, and Ottaviano's face was impeded by the hood.[4]

Disregarding his appearance, Monticelli dashed out of the chamber to present himself to the people, and the waiting officials, seeing him advance in the scarlet mantle, hailed him as pope. Right on cue, Barbarossa's armed men came out of nowhere, burst into Saint Peter's and acclaimed the new Pope Victor, forcing Alexander and the majority of the cardinals to flee.[5] Victor held the city of Rome for ten days before himself being forced to flee; Alexander could finally return. While he was validly elected, Alexander had little support. Barbarossa, of course, immediately announced his support for Victor. Had the emperor had been his only supporter, Victor could have been dealt with quickly, though it would have been difficult. It was the people of Rome who would initially prove problematic; seeing Victor's liberal ways and accessibility, while ignoring his love of luxury, the populace sided with him. Victor had himself crowned by the dean of the Sacred College of Cardinals, Imar of Tusculum, at the Abbey of Farfa, about thirty-seven miles northeast of Rome, on October 4. Alexander, forced to leave Rome himself not long after Victor, was crowned at the little village of Ninfa, southeast of Rome.[6] He would then make his way first to Sicily, to find refuge with King William, and afterward to exile in France.

Both popes sent emissaries to the royal courts of Europe for support. Victor would win most of them, most likely in deference to Barbarossa. Alexander could count on Sicily, Portugal, and Spain as allies; they recognized his election immediately. To push his antipope's cause, Barbarossa called for a council to meet in Pavia in northern Italy to decide which of the two candidates was the legitimate pope. Alexander refused to attend. He knew it would be a whitewash; and besides, according to the Gregorian Reforms, only he as pope had the authority to call councils. Even if he prevailed there, he would have ceded his authority to the emperor by attending the meeting. The council met on February 4, 1160; stuffed with Barbarossa's men, it acclaimed Victor as pope, as expected.[7] In response, Alexander excommunicated the emperor and a number of others, including Cardinal Imar, who had crowned Victor. To his credit, Imar repented shortly thereafter and submitted to Alexander; he died the following year.

By 1161, a number of monarchs had declared for Alexander — including those in Leon, Castile, Barcelona, Bohemia, and Hungary[8] — but France and England had yet to be won over. Theobald of Canterbury had been cautious, but he personally favored Alexander. By June 1160, he had persuaded the other bishops of England to acknowledge the pope; Henry was another matter. Louis of France had come over to Alexander's side, and now he and Theobald aimed to bring Henry along with them. Having exacted his price — the license for the marriage of the royal children, young Henry and Margaret of France, and the canonization of Edward the Confessor — Henry slipped into Alexander's camp.[9] As Alexander was then in France, he met with Henry and Louis at a spot on the Loire River, possibly Chouzy-sur-Loire; there, on September 23, 1162, both kings formally recognized Alexander as pope and were reconciled themselves following yet another row.[10] The council at Tours the following May would be as much about Coucy as it was about Church affairs.

It was obvious that Barbarossa was going to be a problem for some time. Indeed, he would champion Victor and two successor antipopes, Paschal III and Callixtus III, all three nothing more than imperial minions, until his defeat at the Battle of Legnano in 1176, after which he would formally renounce his position and finally recognize Alexander as pope in the Peace of Venice of 1177.[11] Alexander could not rest easy until then, but he could rely on Louis of France. While he was passionate and wild and needed to be reminded now and then of his duty as a Catholic monarch, Louis was loyal to the Holy See, and once he chose Alexander's camp, he never wavered. Henry was a different matter. The pope was well aware of the English king's fickleness and tendency to break oaths when it suited him. Alexander would have to measure what he said and did in order to keep the powerful Henry as an ally, and he probably hoped nothing serious would emerge to unsettle an arrangement that was already too fragile for his liking.

Aware of the pope's predicament, Thomas may well have wondered whether the pope could be trusted. Alexander found himself in an ironic position: As a supporter of the Gregorian Reforms and taking action against Barbarossa in this regard, was he now going to undermine the efforts of the new primate to solidify that same reform in England? Exiled from Italy thanks to imperial power there, Alexander was still committed to Church reform, and he was aiming do a great deal, even though his situation was not ideal. While as Pope Alexander III he was reliant on the kindness of kings and often given to evasion because of it, he was still Rolando of Siena, a man dedicated to the Church and her cause. Recent problems might have taught him the benefits of diplomacy and careful consideration of people and events, but he was not one to let go of his deeply held beliefs. He had firmly held on to that scarlet mantle when Monticelli tried to tear it from him, and now he had excommunicated an emperor to ensure that he would continue to wear it. How would he handle the king of England?

Had Thomas observed a certain determination in Alexander and taken heart, or was the pope's evasiveness disturbing him as he traveled back to England? For now, he would trust the pope; with the fight that he knew was coming, everyone would have to take a stand: Henry, Thomas, the bishops, and Alexander, too. The primate of England would indeed be a thorn in the side, but one that would reveal the integrity, ambitions, and diplomatic ability of many. Thomas of Canterbury and his "great matter" would push many a great personage to the wall.

22

Woodstock

For the next couple of months, trouble brewed quietly. Gilbert Foliot, bishop of London, had emerged as Henry's new trusted counsellor. The king now turned to him for spiritual support and appointed him as his official confessor.[1] Still smoldering with jealousy, Gilbert treasured his refusal to give obedience to Thomas. Meanwhile, the barons were still resisting the archbishop's efforts to take back Church property. One baron was particularly difficult to fight: Roger de Clare. He held Church lands in Tonbridge in Kent, and Thomas had had success in getting some back, but the case had gone to law at the common courts, where Roger was claiming the lands in chief of the king.[2]

For now, Henry was holding his peace. He may have been gratified by Pope Alexander's deference at Tours, but his focus was on restoring the civil and ecclesiastical status quo that had existed, as he saw it, under his grandfather, Henry I. Matters in Normandy dealt with, he had more time to devote to pushing his own reforms through in England; one of these was the restoration of an unpopular general land tax called the danegeld. To deal with this and other matters, he called a council to be held at his palace at Woodstock in July 1163.

Woodstock, outside Oxford, was the site of what had originally been a hunting lodge built by Henry I. Surrounded by a great walled estate, it was home not only to game, but also to lions, leopards, and other exotic creatures forming the royal menagerie. Henry II, with his love of hunting, was enhancing his grandfather's lodge, extending it into a palace that would, over time, play an important part in the history of England.[3] Those called to the council arrived at Woodstock on July 1. Among those present were Henry's brother William and various earls, barons, and royal officials. The princes of Wales and the king of Scotland, Malcolm IV, were also present; they were there not merely for a show of unity, but also to give homage to their feudal lord. Thomas led the delegation representing the bishops; with him were Gilbert Foliot of London and Robert de Chesney of Lincoln.[4]

Proceedings began peacefully enough, and various matters were dealt with. Henry then brought up the matter of the tax. The danegeld was originally a tax raised to gather funds to buy peace with or provide protection against the invading Danes; it literally meant "Danish tax." It later became a national tax to support the king's wars and appetites, confirming the universal experience of all subjects and citizens that once a tax is introduced for whatever the reason, it is rarely rescinded. Last collected in 1161–1162, it was very unpopular, and its method of collection inefficient as far as the king was concerned. While a respectable sum was collected, by the time tax collectors took their commission, the crown got very little; Henry intended to overhaul it. He proposed that a new tax would be levied on landowners, 2 shillings per 120 acres, not by increasing the tax burden, but by transforming an offering called "sheriff's aid" into a contribution to the crown. Sheriffs collected sheriff's aid each year to meet their legitimate administrative expenses. Under this new plan, sheriffs would still have to collect the tax, but would have to pay for their costs out of their own resources.

The new tax met with a muted response until Thomas stood up. He had imposed taxes when royal chancellor, some of them controversial, but now that he was archbishop, he was not inclined to support this innovation. Reminding Henry that stripping the sheriffs of a legitimate source of income was not just, he also pointed out that the aid was in fact a freewill offering from landowners to the sheriffs; it had nothing to do with the crown. Thomas had captured the mood of the gathering, and soon he was leading what was becoming fierce opposition to the proposal. He told the king that the Church would be more than happy to continue to pay the sheriff's aid as a voluntary stipend, but would withhold payment if it were transformed into this tax.

Furious, Henry swore back at Thomas, blaspheming: "By God's eyes," he retorted, "it shall be given as revenue and written down as such in the royal records." Thomas stood his ground and rebuked Henry: "By the eyes by which you swear, never while I am living will this money be given from my land!"[5] A row ensued, and as king and archbishop attacked each other, the assembled notables were dumbfounded. It was now obvious that there was indeed a rift between the two; the old friendship was strained at best. Thomas won the day. Henry realized that his archbishop was not alone in his objection to the tax. Most of the assembled courtiers also objected, as would most of England if he tried to impose it. He had to renounce the innovation or face a revolt.

Another matter also sparked a row between king and archbishop; this concerned a marriage. Henry was attempting to arrange a match between a young widow, Isabel de Warenne, a wealthy heiress, and William, Henry's younger brother, who was deeply in love with her. The king supported the romance because a marriage would bring with it estates in England and Normandy, which would fall under his influence. The marriage license had been agreed, but Thomas then stood to object to it. The young couple were too closely related; they fell within the prohibited degrees of marriage. While Henry tried to argue with his archbishop, Thomas was determined to win the day on this matter, too. In his time as chancellor, he had lost the case of Marie of Blois, who was now in an unhappy and invalid marriage to Matthew of Alsace; he was not going to have Henry trample on the Church's law on marriage again. Thomas prevailed again, as all the laws were in his favor, but his victory was a hollow one. He earned not only Henry's anger but also William's deep resentment, a hatred the prince would carry with him to his grave.

And Henry was not to be outdone. He would arrange another marriage for Isabel, this one to his illegitimate half-brother Hamelin of Anjou, for whom the prohibition did not legally apply, so the estates came under his direction anyway.[6]

However, the two men had shown their hands: Henry and Thomas were no longer close, and now everyone knew that there was a serious rift between them and that trouble lay ahead. This was not simply a matter of a king and an archbishop feuding — there had been many instances of that in recent history; what was about to play out was a very personal argument between two men who, until recently, had been living out of each other's pockets. Thomas was angry with Henry for his autocracy, his refusal to see sense; Henry was aggrieved at Thomas for what he perceived as ingratitude. Returning to Canterbury, Thomas would have been wise to make a mental note: He must ensure from then on that those working for him should give him undivided loyalty. If he was going to battle with Henry, he did not need royal moles in his household.

The two men would meet again in late July 1163, this time in London at an ecclesiastical gathering. Thomas had been engaged to preach a sermon, and he chose as his theme a verse from Saint Luke's Gospel describing an exchange between Jesus and his apostles just before they left the Upper Room for the Mount of Olives on the night of his arrest. The verse was this: "And they said, 'Look, Lord, here are two swords.' And he said to them, 'It is enough'" (Lk 22:38). Drawing from Saint Peter Damian's interpretation, theologians in Thomas's time understood the two swords to represent the cooperation of the Church and the secular ruler, the spiritual and temporal, in governance. Thomas spoke of both powers working together. Though he rarely paid attention to sermons, Henry was listening very carefully to this one. Thomas praised both "swords" — both powers — but he gave a greater precedence to the spiritual and to the Church. In accord with the Gregorian Reforms, he seemed to be exploring a Church that was independent from the state and from the power of the crown. Henry may have been getting restless in his seat, and not out of boredom.[7] Perhaps he was considering how much his former chancellor had changed since donning the archbishop's miter. Henry believed that the Church in England depended on him. It owned nothing without him and could do nothing without him, for he was the Lord's anointed. Was Thomas throwing down the gauntlet to challenge this belief? The answer came quickly as the controversial case of a priest, the *cause célèbre* of that summer of 1163, as Barlow calls it, that of Philip de Broi, the canon of Bedford, became a matter of contention between the two leaders.[8]

Philip de Broi had been accused of murdering a knight. As he was a cleric, he was brought to trial in an ecclesiastical court before the bishop of Lincoln, who had jurisdiction over the priest. The case was examined, and de Broi was acquitted. Initially, the family of the knight and the king himself accepted the verdict; however, a circuit judge, Simon FitzPeter, sought to have the case reexamined, this time in a civil court. Summoned to appear in that court and enter a plea, de Broi refused and, when chastised by the judge for this refusal, verbally abused him. FitzPeter decided to take the matter to the king; as Henry was getting an earful from the judge, his mind may have wandered to Thomas, the independence of the Church, and the unsettling situation, as he saw it, regarding civil and Church courts. He ordered a fresh trial, this time in the royal courts. When Thomas heard of it, he objected: De Broi was a cleric, and clerics could not be judged by laymen; they were to be tried in Church courts. Besides, Thomas insisted, the priest had already faced a legal process; it offended justice for him to be tried again for a crime of which he had been acquitted.[9]

Henry swallowed his pride. He would compromise and allow de Broi to be tried in a Church court, but he must also answer for insulting a judge. The offer was accepted, a committee of bishops was assembled to hear the case, and the priest was summoned. When it came time for him to plead, de Broi informed the court that he would not plead to the accusation of murder because he had already been acquitted by the ecclesiastical system. When asked to plead on the matter of insulting a royal judge, the priest refused again, saying it was beneath his dignity to engage in this quarrel since he was a great man from a great family. Thomas may well have been taken aback at the priest's arrogance, but it was the king's legal representatives who objected, demanding judgment. Given the priest's defiant response, there could be little doubt that he had insulted the judge. Though it may have irked him, Thomas had to agree with the king's party on this charge and passed sentence on the priest. He would be deprived of his Church income for two years — it would be given to the poor — and he was to go into exile for the two years. He would also have to receive a public flogging in the presence of the judge he defamed before leaving the country.[10]

The prospect of a priest being flogged for his insolence was not enough for Henry: He demanded the death penalty.[11] The judgment, he claimed, failed to respect his honor — since the insult had been aimed at a royal judge, it was also aimed at him, the monarch the judge represented. Turning to his new episcopal friend, Gilbert of London, who was on the bench of the Church court and had passed sentence with Thomas, Henry demanded that he take an oath swearing that he had given a true judgment and had not been lenient because de Broi was a cleric. Gilbert was shaking in his seat — his new friend, the king, had put him on the spot. As it turned out, none of the bishops had a problem taking such an oath since they had acted justly in this case, as they did in all the cases laid before them. To a man, all the bishops on the bench took the oath, and it was Henry who was now shaking with anger. Realizing there was nothing he could do, Henry had no option but to accept the judgment.[12]

Before the summer of 1163 was out, another matter arose to make things even worse between Henry and Thomas. The archbishop granted, as was customary, the income of a vacant church at Eynsford in Kent, a church within the Archdiocese of Canterbury, to a clerk, Lawrence by name. The Lord of Eynsford, William, a tenant-in-chief to the king, objected to the appointment, claiming that Thomas had no right to make it. Thomas informed William that he had every right, and when William expelled Lawrence's men, Thomas excommunicated him. William appealed to Henry. Under a decree issued by William the Conqueror, a tenant-in-chief to the king could not be censured by the Church without obtaining the king's consent. According to this decree, the archbishop had breached the law of the realm. Henry complained to the archbishop, quoting the law. Thomas informed the king that it was not up to him or any secular power to order the absolution or excommunication of anyone; that power lay alone with the Church.

Henry went into a sulk and refused to communicate directly with the archbishop. As his fellow bishops were not willing to support him in this matter, Thomas reluctantly lifted the excommunication not long after the council at Woodstock, hoping that Henry might see in this action some goodwill on his part.[13] The king, however, was not inclined to see any goodwill in Thomas at all. When informed of the archbishop's conciliation, the king, now at Windsor, revealed that there was no longer any love between them, saying, "Now I would not thank him for it."[14]

On July 22, judgment was given in the common courts on Thomas's case against Roger de Clare regarding the lands in Tonbridge in Kent; the archbishop lost.

23

The Council at Westminster

England's legal system was vexed at this time. Two legal systems sat uneasily side by side. Part of King Henry's frustration was that not only were there ecclesiastical courts rivaling his own, but up to a third of his subjects were formally classed as clerics and could not be tried in his courts. Another issue that bothered him was the perceived leniency of Church courts. Given that canon law was based on the Gospel, judgments were deemed too merciful, as in the case of Philip de Broi. Justifiably, Henry wanted to reform the legal system. It was a necessary reform — he would go on to gift England with a fine system of courts and jurisprudence. As he saw it — and he was not alone in this — the ecclesiastical courts seemed to be protecting criminal clerics from the full force of the law, reserving to themselves the right to try and punish clerics.[1]

According to Church law, clerics could be not tried by lay judges.

In a sense, this law followed the principle that they were to be judged by their peers, a principle that would be enshrined half a century later in the Magna Carta. When a man formally classed as a cleric (a bishop, priest, deacon, subdeacon, or any man who had received the tonsure) was accused of a crime, particularly a serious crime such as murder or rape, he could claim exemption from secular courts. Laymen accused of such crimes and found guilty were sentenced to death, but clerics found guilty in ecclesiastical courts received much lighter sentences, since the Church did not permit the imposition of the death sentence or any form of mutilation. Guilty clerics could be exiled, fined, defrocked, or sentenced to a variety of other punishments, including pilgrimage, which could be quite a dangerous affair then, or confinement in a monastery for a period of time or even for life. If a cleric was defrocked, he was then subject to the secular courts for any subsequent crimes he might commit, but not for the original crime. In the eyes of the king and his judges, such measures didn't seem like punishments at all. While Henry considered Church sentences lenient, they were founded on the "machinery of mercy" at the heart of the Christian faith; yet some could be heavy and imposed for life. In some of his cases, Thomas passed harsh sentences on those found guilty. Ironically, some of these defendants, if tried in the secular courts, would actually have received lighter sentences.

As Thomas reflected on a number of controversial cases that emerged to create disputes between king and archbishop, he came to see the issue of the courts as an issue of the Church's liberty. While Henry I had kept a firm hold on the ecclesiastical courts, under Stephen the Church had been able break free and further the development of her own jurisprudence and courts in England. For Henry II, the matter concerned his honor and the oath he took at his coronation to uphold justice: He was the primary judge in the kingdom, and no other could or should attempt to usurp that office. Thomas had no desire to do this, nor was his opposition based on the growing rift between the two. Rather, he saw it as his duty as archbishop to uphold the requirements of canon law; this was part of his obligation to govern. Despite the bad blood that existed between them, Thomas was supported in his position by Roger de Pont L'Évêque and Gilbert Foliot, as well as by the other bishops. This was not a personal matter between Thomas and Henry; it concerned the Church and her rights regarding her subjects — her clerics. It was frustrating for Henry that he could not drive a wedge between Thomas and his episcopal rivals.

As summer turned to fall in 1163, the king was nursing a number of grievances against the archbishop and the episcopal bench. Apart from the issue of the courts, he resented what he considered to be the Church's inordinate and irregular punishment of laypeople. Thomas had excommunicated his tenant-in-chief William of Eynsford without his consent; that any bishop could do likewise, or even impose a minor censure, was unacceptable. The issue, as Henry saw it, was the audacity of his bishops in handing down punishment to his subjects without his permission. After all, he was the one who appointed the bishops, and he was the one who provided them with an income in the sense that anyone who held land held it in deference to the crown. When a man was elevated to the episcopacy, he had to take an oath of fealty to the king with respect to the land he was inheriting. In this context, these bishops, as his subjects and appointees, owed their first loyalty to him.

As Henry reflected on the various events of the last year or so — Thomas's zealous campaign against his barons and tenants, the conflict in the courts, the rejection of the tax — he concluded that there was now a general disregard for the ancestral customs that had long governed the relationship between the royal and the ecclesiastical. The two were meant to work together under the guardianship of the king; that is how he understood it. But Henry was conveniently forgetting an important case with which he had been involved, one in which he himself had championed canon law as superior to secular law regarding a cleric.

The case concerned the death of the previous archbishop of York, William FitzHerbert. Osbert de Bayeux, archdeacon of York, had been accused of murdering him in 1154 by poisoning the wine used by the archbishop during Mass; Osbert had been a supporter of William's rival, Henry Murdac, for the archbishopric.[2] Charges had been brought against the archdeacon in 1154, before a royal council and King Stephen, but the king's death dissolved the council. Interestingly, when the archdeacon was accused in 1156, Theobald of Canterbury, to his disappointment, expected the secular courts to step in and try him according to civil law — Theobald wanted Osbert to answer for the murder before the Church courts. However, King Henry was not prepared to get involved in the case of the assassination of his rival king's candidate to the see of York. The king argued, with the support of his barons and civil lawyers, that as a cleric, Osbert should be tried in an ecclesiastical court because canon law took precedence. When it came to the larger issue he was now disputing, Henry may have wanted to forget this incident, but John of Salisbury had chronicled the whole affair, and Thomas knew all about it. If Henry wanted to argue against Thomas on the matter of the Church's authority over clergy, then he would find himself the chief witness for the Church's cause.[3]

In reality, Henry was looking for a fight — the issue was not just Church courts; it was Thomas, who had turned from being his friend and devoted servant to being his nemesis, in Henry's eyes pushing feigned liberties as a means to get back at him and revealing his utter ingratitude for all that he had done for him. The king did not consider Thomas's argument; he saw only deception and betrayal. Henry began to consult his advisors and gather evidence in order to take action against his former friend. The issue would be larger than control over courts or lands. It would concern the ancient rights of kings over the Church, rights that his grandfather had maintained, rights that Stephen had signed over during his chaotic reign. Henry II had declared at his coronation that he would restore the customs and power of the crown to what they had been in his grandfather's time. Now he would face down the Church and put her in her place — or more precisely, he would put a leash on Thomas and bring him to heel. With a great gathering of barons and clergy due to take place at Westminster in October for the solemn translation of the relics of the newly canonized Saint Edward the Confessor, Henry decided to use the occasion to hold a council and resolve the situation in his favor. He sent out his messengers to inform the bishops and summon them to the council. They received the news with anxiety, as most, if not all, of them realized that this meeting was not going to go well for them or their new primate.

The general body of the bishops and their legal advisors were quietly supportive of their archbishop. They understood that he was simply protecting the Church's rights, trying to restore what were Church assets and correct abuses that had gone unchecked for too long. However, they were also aware of the personal dimension to this developing feud and knew that if things got worse, Henry had the means and disposition to enforce his will by pure strength — perhaps even violence. They were anxious to keep the liberties King Stephen had granted them, but some of those liberties were novelties even if the Gregorian Reforms had confirmed them. There was no guarantee that they could keep them if their king was against them. There was also the matter of Thomas himself. Many of them did not have confidence in him. They regarded him as unsuitable, the king's candidate improperly inserted into the hierarchy, a lowborn clerk who might not be fit for the pressures of the office of primate. He also had enemies in Roger and Gilbert, and while they supported him in this matter, their backing would always be conditional.

On Sunday, October 13, 1163, the king, barons, and clergy of England gathered at Westminster Abbey for the solemn translation of the relics of Saint Edward.[4] The saintly king had originally been buried beside the high altar, a privilege granted not just because he was king but also because he had founded the abbey. A new shrine had been constructed on the same spot in the sanctuary. The body of the king had been exhumed, and an official *recognitio* — the formal identification of the remains — had taken place. The burial robes had been removed, and relics had been taken. Some would be sent to the pope, others distributed throughout the kingdom. Henry took for himself the saint's pilgrim ring. The body had been wrapped in fresh silk and then placed in a new wooden coffin, which was sealed in the presence of the king and other dignitaries. Henry himself and eight barons then carried the new saint's coffin in a great procession to the new shrine. Thomas was kept at a distance during the entire ceremony. Laurence of Durham, the abbot of Westminster Abbey and a favorite of Henry's, and his monks officiated at the liturgy.

At the conclusion of the ceremonies, the council began.[5] Henry stood to give the opening speech; Thomas braced himself. Henry was intent, it seemed, on neutralizing the sermon the archbishop had preached earlier in the summer and throwing down a gauntlet himself. King Edward had been raised to the altars, a testament to the sacred nature of the monarchy of England; as heir to Saint Edward and entrusted with the care of the Church, this new king would assert his rights. In his speech, Henry attacked the bishops for their lack of respect and then addressed the issue of ecclesiastical courts: "Criminous clerks," he said, would be punished by secular judges in the future.

Thomas remained silent as Henry threatened him and his brother bishops; when the king had finished, he stood up and left the room, calling the bishops after him to confer. In that conference, two opinions emerged among the hierarchy. The first, expressed by some rather fearful bishops, was that the Church could back down and permit clerics to be tried in civil courts. They argued, correctly, that canon law permitted priests convicted in ecclesiastical courts to be handed over to the civil courts for punishment. This was, of course, at the discretion of the individual bishop who had found a priest guilty of a crime so notorious that it endangered the community at large. Capitulation would placate Henry and bring the crisis to an end. This view was expressed by a minority of the bishops.

The majority, led by Roger de Pont L'Évêque and Gilbert Foliot, argued that Thomas was correct in his position: The Church must stand her ground and continue to try the cases of "criminous" clerics in her own courts. While some present were tempted to waver, Roger and Gilbert, to their credit, rallied support for Thomas and prevailed. Among the bishops was Thomas's old teacher from Paris, Robert of Melun. Thomas had worked to have him appointed to Hereford; he was present as bishop-elect and would be consecrated in December. Robert's thought two decades earlier had included ideas on resistance to tyrannical rulers; his presence was a comfort to Thomas, and he presumed his former teacher's support.

Returning to the council, Thomas stood to respond to the king's speech. Instead of arguing the king's point, the archbishop approached the issue from another direction, not so much in response to Henry but in response to the timid bishops' proposal. His point was one he and his advisors had been discussing in their evening meetings in Canterbury. His assistants and friends, Herbert of Bosham and John of Salisbury, had been doing research, and they had discussed the idea of double jeopardy — could a "criminous" cleric be tried for the same offense twice? To hand a cleric over to secular courts after he had been tried in the Church court would, in fact, be a case of double jeopardy. Thomas and his advisors in their reflections had drawn on Scripture and on the writings of the Church Fathers, most notably Saint Jerome, who said that if God, who is the judge of all, judges a soul once for a single fault, how then could human beings subject someone to two judgments for the same transgression?[6] While the jurisprudence of canon law had not considered this argument, Thomas and his advisors had wondered whether it could be used as a theological defense of their position.

Thomas argued this double jeopardy defense before Henry, and novel as it was, the king realized he was being pushed into a corner. A terrible vista now came into view, not only for the king but also for the fearful bishops. Based on this argument, the loophole allowed in canon law was not permissible. The transfer at the discretion of a bishop of convicted clerics from the ecclesiastical court to the civil court for punishment was not an option, even in exceptional situations, since it seemed to be prohibited. For once invigorated, the fearful bishops stood behind Thomas. With his usual eloquence and charm, Thomas reassured the king that they, the bishops of England, sought to heed his will in all things as long as it was not against the will of God and the dignity of his Church. If the king's will were against God's, though they loved him, they could not dare assent to it.

Henry was in a bind. His attack had backfired, and a loophole he could have used was now closed to him. But he had another plan up his sleeve. Taking a charter from the reign of his grandfather and waving it about, he asked the bishops if they would obey the ancestral customs and give their allegiance to him. Now it was the bishops who were put on the spot. They knew what he was up to. An affirmative response would imperil the liberties of the Church, while a negative response would amount to an act of treason. But Thomas was no fool. He gathered his bishops around him to confer — he had the solution, and they agreed to it. Facing Henry again, Thomas, as respectful as ever, responded, "Yes, in every way, saving our order."[7]

The king was dumbfounded. The response was designed as a check-mate. The bishops could wriggle their way out of obedience if they claimed that whatever was demanded of them was contrary to canon law or their position as churchmen. It was essentially a *no* — a very cleverly disguised *no*, but a *no* nonetheless. It was utter defiance. No doubt knowing that bishops are essentially weak men, Henry approached each individually and demanded an answer from them. All but one responded with Thomas's formula. The one who didn't was Bishop Hilary of Chichester, who was already embroiled in the dispute with the king over Battle Abbey; he had lost the will to fight. He simply said, "Yes, in every way, in all good faith." Not even that response placated the king.[8]

Henry launched into a vicious attack on the bishops, but aimed it specifically at Thomas. He accused the archbishop of conspiracy against him, saying that poison lurked in the phrase "saving our order." It was pure sophistry, Henry raged. Thomas was not to be outdone. He reminded the king that each bishop had taken an oath of fealty to him when elevated to the episcopacy, and that inherent in that oath was their recognition of the ancestral customs. Indeed, Thomas reminded him, the oath included the very phrase to which the king was now objecting. But Henry was not listening; he had descended into one of his sulks and just kept repeating his demand that they all conform to his will. Thomas stopped talking; he was getting nowhere. Looking Henry straight in the face, he refused to comply.

The king stormed out of the chamber and left Westminster the next morning, leaving business and legal matters still to be concluded. Before he left, he ordered Thomas to return all the castles and estates that he had held from the crown and to send young Henry back to him. Thomas was no longer to be trusted with the heir to the throne.[9] His tutorship was finished; the friendship was over; Thomas was persona non grata. The bishops were in confusion, having no idea what was going to happen now. It surely seemed that strife lay ahead. Thomas was distraught and angry. He rebuked Hilary of Chichester for his cowardice in failing to hold the line with the bishops and the Church.

Thomas returned to Canterbury for the worst part of this saga: telling eight-year-old Henry that he had to leave and return to his father. The child would have to leave a safe and stable environment at a vulnerable age to find a place for himself in what was a chaotic court with a willful father and a dysfunctional family. Time would reveal the toll this would take on Prince Henry in his short life. If anything made Thomas regret what had happened at Westminster, it was perhaps little Henry's parting glance.

24

A Very Public Quarrel

Thomas had left Westminster with a memento of his dispute with the king — a relic, and a symbolic one at that: a piece of stone associated with the bishop Saint Wulfstan. Before the ceremonies of the translation of the Confessor's relics had begun, he had asked the abbot of Westminster for it, and his request had been granted. The stone was from the original tomb of Saint Edward, and it had been the centerpiece in a miracle worked by the saintly king.[1]

Wulfstan had been the bishop of Worcester, serving from his consecration in 1062 to his death in 1095. As bishop, he was a great reformer, a man devoted to the poor who was noted for his opposition to the slave trade. He had witnessed the invasion of William the Conqueror. As the new king of England began to replace the land's Anglo-Saxon officials with Normans, the bishops were included in the purge. At first, Wulfstan was asked politely to vacate his see, but he refused. As William applied pressure, Wulfstan sought refuge in the prayers of King Edward, coming to his tomb and begging him to help. Offering his crozier, he prayed to the Confessor, telling the saintly king that as the king had given the crozier to him, now he was returning it to Edward; he then pierced the stone of the tomb with the crozier, which was miraculously held in place. No one could release the crozier from the stone; but when William finally relented and allowed Wulfstan to remain in his see, the holy bishop simply slipped it out from the stone as from soft butter. Now in Thomas's possession, that stone may have been a poor consolation, but it represented hope for him. Perhaps after some reflection, Henry might think better of his decisions at Westminster.

Later in October, brooding over what had happened at Westminster, Henry summoned Thomas to a meeting at a spot on the River Nene, outside Northampton. When the archbishop arrived, the king was waiting for him. Perhaps sensing a tension between the two men, their horses were giddy; failing to settle their steeds, king and archbishop had to dismount, change horses, and stand at a distance from their entourages.[2] The conversation was passionate and difficult.[3] Thomas was rebuked for his ingratitude — did he not raise the archbishop from the humble and the poor? Thomas replied that he was grateful for all the favors he had received, but not just from the king — also from God, who was lord to them both. I must obey God more than men, he asserted.[4] Henry did not want to hear pious platitudes. Rounding on the archbishop, he asked him if he were not just the son of one of his villeins,[5] a lowly subject. Offended, Thomas reminded Henry that Saint Peter did not have royal ancestors, to which Henry responded: Did not Saint Peter die for his Lord? Thomas was just as quick: "I will die for my Lord when the time comes."[6] Henry was quick to respond: Thomas relied too much on the manner of his ascent. Thomas responded that he had confidence and trusted in God.[7] The conversation modulated between row and quiet words carefully pronounced. Thomas assured Henry that he would obey and honor him, but reiterated what he and his brother bishops had said at Westminster: that they were ready to please and honor him, saving their honor as bishops. Henry eventually lost his temper, told Thomas that the matter would be dropped, and rode off.

Henry would now employ new tactics to force Thomas to acquiesce. The row was no longer a matter of another king and archbishop in dispute; it was personal now, and Henry was determined to prevail. He concluded that Thomas's elevation to Canterbury and the primacy had made him arrogant. The man had to be broken. The first tactic the king could employ was to bring the bishops onside. He could cajole or threaten them, even exploit their ambitions, as with Gilbert Foliot, who was still smarting having lost Canterbury, as he saw it. As Henry had the measure of his former friend, Thomas, he was also wise enough to know the fears and ambitions of the bishops. Henry turned to his faithful supporter Bishop Arnulf of Lisieux to advise him on how to approach the bishops.[8]

One possible ally for Henry in this plan was the archbishop of York, Roger de Pont L'Évêque. Though his relationship with Thomas was not good, there was always the chance he would stand with his brother archbishop should the king launch a direct attack. However, as Arnulf and Henry knew, Roger was ambitious, and there was always the dispute over precedence between York and Canterbury that Roger had adopted as his own; here was material for manipulation. Roger had his eye on the position of papal legate. Thomas was a rival candidate for this office, so it would be in Roger's interest for the archbishop of Canterbury to be taken out of the equation; he just needed to be persuaded that he and Henry had common ground and should work together.

Henry and his advisors got to work on the bishops, and their efforts proved successful. Next, it was necessary to win the pope to the king's cause. Once again, the ever-faithful Arnulf was entrusted with the mission. Pope Alexander III was now settled in Sens, in north central France, under the protection of King Louis. Assembling a diplomatic team, Arnulf set off for Sens toward the end of 1163 to meet with the pope. He was charged with obtaining two decisions from Alexander: first, papal recognition and approval of the ancestral customs; and second, the conferral of the office of papal legate on Roger, making him Thomas's superior in England. Arnulf would travel three times to the pope between late 1163 and 1164 trying to persuade him to take Henry's side in the dispute.

What Henry did not know was that Thomas had had the same idea and that as Arnulf was prostrating himself in desperate appeal before the pope, John of Canterbury, now bishop of Poitiers, and clerks Henry of Houghton and Hervey of London were making the case for Thomas in secret meetings with Alexander. These meetings had to be secret because, technically, Thomas's appeal to the pope was an act of treason.[9] In the meantime, flush with anticipated success, Roger de Pont L'Évêque was now having his cross carried before him whenever he came down to Thomas's ecclesiastical province, a symbolic act of precedence.[10] Thomas was quick to deal with that outrage, charging his delegates to seek an immediate prohibition from the pope. Alexander was happy to comply with this request; he rebuked Roger, who was furious with the reprimand.

Alexander had enough trouble to deal with without a budding catastrophe in England. He may have turned his eyes to heaven, and not merely as a gesture of prayer, when Bishop Arnulf appeared before him as Thomas's delegates were waiting for him behind the arras. That he was caught between a rock and hard place was all too obvious. He needed Henry's support in the ongoing battle with Barbarossa and his antipope. Sens was a place of exile — he had to get back to Rome. However, he was not prepared to deliver an archbishop into the hands of a king who was developing all the characteristics of a tyrant. Regardless of who the archbishop was, a decision in the king's favor might spell disaster for the Church in England and establish a dangerous precedent universally. Thomas may have been seen by the pope as a liability at this stage — perhaps some regarded him as a troublemaker — but Alexander realized that he could be of some use to him. For one thing, Thomas had the ear of King Louis, who himself might find some advantage in supporting the archbishop in his very public quarrel with his king.

As the pope weighed what to do, not long after the encounter with the king at the river's edge, Hilary of Chichester came knocking at Thomas's door.[11] Hilary's pleading with Thomas to agree to the ancestral customs revealed that Hilary was now Henry's sop. When Thomas stuck to his position, Hilary verbally attacked and threatened him. The conversation teetered on the edge of a discussion of Henry's becoming a tyrant, and while Hilary defended the king, Thomas conveyed to him the benefit of his experience: The king would extract whatever he wanted from Hilary or anyone else, but no one could force him to stick to his own promises. The encounter ended awkwardly, but Thomas now knew that Henry had probably won most, if not all, of the bishops to his side. He realized he needed to prepare for every eventuality. Calling his clerks to him, he sent some of them as envoys to Henry of France, archbishop of Reims and the brother of King Louis, and to Yves, Count of Soissons, to ask if they would be prepared to give him refuge if he had to go into exile. The clerks returned with positive responses: Both the archbishop and the count were willing to offer him sanctuary. Hearing of the archbishop's predicament, King Louis himself sent a secret message offering him his protection and refuge if he needed it.[12]

In the meantime, by October 1163, the pope had come to a decision: He would defer a verdict and play for time. Alexander was not prepared to make a pronouncement that would offend the king. He wrote to Thomas and asked him to stay quietly in Canterbury; he was not to travel about the country.[13] He had heard the archbishop's case and acknowledged that Thomas was a true defender of the Church, but now was the time for prudence, to stay quiet. This advice, the pope told him, was to ensure that the archbishop would not be compelled to renounce the rights and dignities of the Church and to lower the risk of his falling victim to any "misfortune." Thomas was not pleased. Unknown to him, the pope had also written to Gilbert Foliot, urging him to use his influence with Henry to find some resolution to the dispute before things got worse.

In December 1163, Alexander sent envoys to England to negotiate peace between Thomas and Henry. Leading them was the Cistercian abbot Philip of l'Aumône, a prominent churchman in France who had served as prior in Clairvaux under Saint Bernard.[14] Philip called on Henry first, and in their discussions, the king quietly said that all he wanted was an assurance from the archbishop that he would assent to the ancestral customs. Indeed, Henry reassured Philip, he did not even want an oath; a simple verbal assent would do. Believing the king to be conciliatory and with the hope of reconciliation within his grasp, Philip arrived in Canterbury to discuss the matter with Thomas. Philip had with him a number of letters from cardinals begging him to make peace with Henry, and he pleaded with Thomas to agree to the king's request: a simple verbal assent without the incendiary "saving our order." Philip was accompanied by Robert of Melun. Thomas perhaps looked at his former teacher, whom he was about to consecrate bishop, and wondered where he stood and why he had departed from the position he had held at university on how to deal with tyrants. Philip advised Thomas that this simple assent would avert a major crisis for the Church. Thomas accepted the advice and relented.

Without delay, Philip put Thomas on a horse, and the delegation left Canterbury for Woodstock to meet with Henry. The archbishop may well have been tearing himself apart within, but now was the time to swallow his pride and drink a major draft of humility. Henry was waiting for them and received them with studied graciousness. Standing before him in the chamber where the two had clashed before, Thomas gave an emotional speech begging Henry to destroy and abrogate forever the abuses of tyrants and to seek to be like the saintly kings of old. Henry was likely squirming — he did not like sermons, and here was his nemesis expounding on the virtues of holy kingship. Thomas then got to the point: He promised, without any reservations, that he would observe all the customs of the realm (whatever they were, he may have said to himself) and, remembering Hilary of Chichester's weaselly addendum, adopted it himself, adding "in all good faith" to his promise to obey the king in what was right.[15]

Henry was appeased, Philip and his envoys were relieved, and Thomas was drowning in humiliation. But the matter was not over. Henry might have assured Philip that a simple assent was all he required, but he had no intention of accepting that assent alone. Thomas had defied him in public; now he had to make his assent in public in order to restore the king's honor. Henry decided to call a council to meet in a month's time, in late January 1164, at his palace at Clarendon, near Salisbury. There, before all the bishops, earls, and barons — indeed, before the representatives of all the people of England — Thomas would promise his obedience to Henry. The king then brought the meeting to an end and left Woodstock to join the queen and his family for Christmas. That year, the royal family would gather in Berkhamsted, at one of the castles Henry had taken from Thomas after the council at Westminster.[16]

The papal envoys returned to Sens. If they had a bad feeling about what was about to unfold, they were correct; Henry had played them for fools. Thomas returned to Canterbury. He ordained Robert of Melun bishop on December 22;[17] it may have been a difficult thing to do, given what he may have seen as his former teacher's betrayal. A quiet Christmas followed as Thomas licked his wounds and reflected on what had happened and what might lie ahead in the new year. The time had come to make concrete arrangements for exile. John of Salisbury was charged with an expedition to the continent to recruit allies, prepare an escape route, and arrange safe refuge. Thomas might well have to throw himself upon the mercy of the French. Disguised as a wandering scholar, John slipped out of England.[18]

25
The Clarendon Affair

If Thomas had hoped to keep his plans for exile a secret from Henry, he was not entirely successful. Although the king may not have suspected that Thomas was getting ready to flee, a silly mistake alerted him to what might be happening. Thomas had asked John to have a quiet word with Queen Eleanor before he left for France to see if she could intervene or at least grant him a license to leave England legally. But while there were growing tensions in the marriage, Eleanor was still loyal to Henry; she refused both requests and complained to the king.[1] In retaliation, Henry seized John's revenues, leaving him in a state of destitution as he crossed the English Channel. John's parting message to Thomas was a plea to settle the dispute, as a life of poverty did not appeal to him. Little did he know that there was worse in store for all of them.[2]

Henry wasted no time in making preparations for the council. He had sent Arnulf of Lisieux back to the pope in Rome to test the waters; the word was that Alexander was coming around to his side. This put Henry in a buoyant mood, and he was sure that the council in his favorite residence, the hunting lodge at Clarendon in Wiltshire, would see the end of the quarrel and the end of Thomas Becket.

January 25, 1164, was the day fixed for the council to begin.[3] For a couple of weeks beforehand, bishops, earls, barons, and magnates began making their way to the lodge; the number at the gathering would be significant. The council was planned to last a few days, so royal servants were busy preparing rooms and devising menus for what promised to be a major event in the life of the kingdom — or at least Henry thought so. He was gratified to see that most of the earls and barons were turning up; he also noticed that with the exception of three bishops, excused on health or other satisfactory grounds, the entire hierarchy of England was present, a rather sedate Thomas leading them. As he entered into the gathering, Thomas noticed among the nobles his former friend and mentor, Richer de L'Aigle, perhaps no longer an ally; there is no record of how the two interacted over those days, if they did at all. Among the members of the royal family present was young Henry. Still smarting at having had to leave Canterbury, he was struggling to understand why his father and his mentor were at loggerheads. Young Henry jointly presided over the council.[4]

Henry opened proceedings and, without ceremony, called on Thomas to show himself before the entire assembly, demanding that he promise to obey the ancestral customs of the realm in all good faith and to obey the king in all that was right, as he had done privately just a month before. Henry's imperious attitude and haste put Thomas on his guard. The king was up to something; he suspected a trap. Whether this dawned on Thomas before his arrival or just at that moment is unknown, but the archbishop should have realized that it was odd for Henry to call such a large and distinguished gathering just to hear him utter one sentence of obedience — that could have been done at any royal event. Thomas's attention quickly turned from the waiting king to his brother bishops; whatever Henry had up his sleeve, they had to be prepared.

Without answering the king, Thomas turned to the bishops. He was well aware that many of them were now against him, but if they remained in the grasp of the king, it would not be good for any of them, never mind the Church in England. He asked their advice, but they barely spoke to him. As disgruntled as some of them were, as a college they did not want to change the response they had given at Westminster, and if Thomas wanted them to submit to Henry now, he was the one who had to explain himself. In reality, they were terrified of the king, and yet they did not want to advise Thomas to give in. Henry was getting impatient; the bishops were conferring too long for his liking. Thomas tried to discuss the matter with them, but many were suspicious. Some felt he had exposed them to danger with the escalation of the dispute. Eventually, Henry had enough. With no answer to his demand appearing to come any time soon, he summoned his knights to round up the bishops and lock them up in a room together. Confinement might just force them to stop their incessant debate and comply.

For two days, Thomas and the bishops argued in their makeshift prison cell. Gilbert Foliot, despite the king's wooing, had taken to heart the pope's request that he try to influence Henry in favor of the Church and was encouraging the others to stand firm and not give in — to stand with Thomas. All but two of the bishops were eventually persuaded. Bishops Jocelin of Salisbury and William of Norwich held out and were trying to convince Thomas to relent — Henry had grudges against both of them, and if the bishops continued to defy him, they would be the first to suffer. Thomas, realizing that both men were speaking out of terror, spoke gently to them, encouraging them not to be afraid. He would stand steadfast, and so must they.

The king was getting tired of the impasse. In desperation, he sent two of his knights, together with henchmen, to threaten them. Castration was mentioned, but the knights also employed a softer approach: They assured the bishops that they respected them, but that unless they satisfied the king, they would carry out an "unprecedented danger," meaning assassination, with their own hands. Swords were drawn, and one knight stood right at Thomas's face to browbeat him. Serenely, Thomas replied that it would not be unprecedented for him to die for the laws of the Church; indeed, many saints had taught this by their words and example. God's will be done, he said.[5]

Seeing their resolution and Thomas's courage, the knights withdrew. Henry decided on another approach — he sent two Knights Templar to negotiate with the bishops.[6] Renowned for their heroic work in the Holy Land, the Knights Templar had established houses in England and owned vast estates that earned an income to support their work in Jerusalem. Henry was patron of the English branch of the Knights — hence their willingness to rally to his cause. Among the knights, as noted by Roger of Pontigny, was the Grand Prior or Master of the Templars in England, Richard de Hastings.[7] The knights reassured the bishops that the king had no deceit in mind; there was no fraud planned, so their refusal to disavow the formula that so irritated him was unreasonable. The bishops were not inclined to believe that. In an attempt to win them, the knights said they would stake their eternal salvation on Henry's honesty. That may have raised more than a few eyebrows and should have convinced the bishops that these knights were no more to be trusted than the king. However, the knights managed to move the bishops, and with the real threat of slaughter hanging over them, Thomas had to relent. He told his brothers that he would give the king the assent he sought.

Gathered again in the great hall, Thomas stood before Henry and, as at Woodstock in December, he bowed before the king and said, "Now that I have hope, thanks to your prudence and kindness, I readily agree, in all good faith, to observe the customs of the realm."[8] Some may have breathed a sigh of relief, but that would have been premature. If Thomas had suspected a trap, he was right. Henry, delighted with the assent, now ordered all the bishops to follow Thomas's humble compliance and each declare individually their own assent. They had no choice and to a man reluctantly followed the lead of their primate according to the formula he had just pronounced.

Henry was not finished yet. To the astonishment of the bishops, he immediately ordered his clerks to go out of the room to compile a document, a record of all the laws and customs that prevailed in his grandfather Henry's time. When it was complete and met Henry's approval, the bishops, to a man, were to sign it in the presence of the representatives of the kingdom. Henry had lied. He had lied to the pope, to the papal envoys, to Thomas, and to the bishops. He never intended to be satisfied with a simple verbal assent, not even in the gathering of the great and the good. He had intended all along to put everything in writing for posterity. Henry wished to push the knife in deeper; his vendetta against his archbishop was by no means over. That the clerks returned very quickly with a charter was proof enough to Thomas that this had all been planned. If the document had not been written long before the meeting, at least a template had already been prepared.

The king ordered the document to be read aloud, and though he did not look at it, he told the bishops that what they were about to hear were the ancestral customs of his realm to which they had assented. As the clerk read the document, Thomas's face blanched, and there were gasps from some of the other bishops, while others sat rigidly trying to keep a tight rein on their anger. Some of the items were customs already known and observed, though perhaps resented; but the document also included new "customs," inventions that were creatively constructed to have an air of authenticity but that were nothing more than innovations added to attack and subdue the Church.

The document read as follows:[9]

In the year 1164 from the Incarnation of our Lord, in the fourth year of the papacy of Alexander, in the tenth year of the most illustrious king of the English, Henry II, in the presence of that same king, this memorandum or inquest was made of some part of the customs and liberties. and dignities of his predecessors, viz., of king Henry his grandfather and others, which ought to be observed and kept in the kingdom. And on account of the dissensions and discords which had arisen between the clergy and the Justices of the lord king, and the barons of the kingdom concerning the customs and dignities, this inquest was made in the presence of the archbishops and bishops, and clergy and counts, and barons and chiefs of the kingdom. And these customs, recognized by the archbishops and bishops and counts and barons and by the nobler ones and elders of the kingdom, Thomas Archbishop of Canterbury, and Roger archbishop of York, and Gilbert bishop of London, and Henry bishop of Winchester, and Nigel bishop of Ely, and William bishop of Norwich, and Robert bishop of Lincoln, and Hilary bishop of Chichester, and Jocelin bishop of Salisbury, and Richard bishop of Chester, and Bartholemew bishop of Exeter and Robert bishop of Hereford, and David bishop of Mans, and Roger elect of Worcester, did grant; and, upon the Word of Truth did orally firmly promise to keep and observe, under the lord king and under his heirs, in good faith and without evil wile,-in the presence of the following: Robert count of Leicester, Reginald count of Cornwall, Conan count of Bretagne, John count of Eu, Roger count of Clare, count Geoffrey of Mandeville, Hugo count of Chester, William count of Arundel, count Patrick, William count of Ferrara, Richard de Lucy, Reginald de St. Walelio, Roger Bigot, Reginald de Warren, Richer de Aquila, William de Braiose, Richard de Camville, Nigel de Mowbray, Simon de Bello Campo, Humphrey de Bohen, Matthew de Hereford, Walter de Medway, Manassa Biseth -steward, William Malet, William de Curcy, Robert de Dunstanville, Jocelin de Balliol, William de Lanvale, William de Caisnet, Geoffrey de Vere, William de Hastings, Hugo de Moreville, Alan de Neville, Simon son of Peter William Malduit-chamberlain, John Malduit, John Marshall, Peter de Mare, and many other chiefs and nobles of the kingdom, clergy as well as laity.

A certain part, moreover, of the customs and dignities of the kingdom which were examined into, is contained in the present writing. Of which part these are the paragraphs;

Here begin the customs which are called ancestral.

1. If a controversy concerning advowson* and presentation of churches arise between laymen, or between laymen and clerks, or between clerks, it shall be treated of and terminated in the court of the lord king.

2. Churches of the fee of the lord king cannot, unto all time, be given without his assent and concession.

---

*This term refers to the patronage of an ecclesiastical office or benefice.

3. Clerks charged and accused of anything, being summoned by the Justice of the king, shall come into his court, about to respond there for what it seems to the king's court that he should respond there; and in the ecclesiastical court for what it seems he should respond there; so that the Justice of the king shall send to the court of the holy Church to see in what manner the affair will there be carried on. And if the clerk shall be convicted, or shall confess, the Church ought not to protect him further.[10]

4. It is not lawful for archbishops, bishops, and persons of the kingdom to go out of the kingdom without the permission of the lord king. And if it please the king and they go out, they shall give assurance that neither in going, nor in making a stay, nor in returning, will they seek the hurt or harm of king or kingdom.

5. The excommunicated shall not give a pledge as a permanency, nor take an oath, but only a pledge and surety of presenting themselves before the tribunal of the Church, that they may be absolved.[11]

6. Laymen ought not to be accused unless through reliable and legal accusers and witnesses in the presence of the bishop, in such wise that the archdeacon does not lose his right, nor any thing which he ought to have from it. And if those who are inculpated are such that no one wishes or dares to accuse them, the sheriff, being requested by the bishop, shall cause twelve lawful men of the neighborhood or town to swear in the presence of the bishop that they will make manifest the truth in this matter, according to their conscience.[12]

7. No tenant-in-chief of the king, and no one of his de-

mesne servitors, shall be excommunicated, nor shall the lands of any one of them be placed under an interdict, unless first the lord king, if he be in the land, or his Justice, if he be without the kingdom, be asked to do justice concerning him: and in such way that what shall pertain to the king's court shall there be terminated; and with regard to that which concerns the ecclesiastical court, he shall be sent thither in order that it may there be treated of.[13]

8. Concerning appeals, if they shall arise, from the archdeacon they shall proceed to the bishop, from the bishop to the archbishop. And if the archbishop shall fail to render justice, they must come finally to the lord king, in order that by his command the controversy may be terminated in the court of the archbishop, so that it shall not proceed further without the consent of the lord king.[14]

9. If a quarrel arise between a clerk and a layman or between a layman and a clerk concerning any holding which the clerk wishes to attach to the Church property but the layman to a lay fee: by the inquest of twelve lawful men, through the judgment of the chief Justice of the king, it shall be determined, in the presence of the Justice himself, whether the tenement belongs to the Church property, or to the lay fee. And if it be recognized as belonging to the Church property, the case shall be pleaded in the ecclesiastical court; but if to the lay fee, unless both are holders from the same bishop or baron, the case shall be pleaded in the king's court. But if both vouch to warranty for that fee before the same bishop or baron, the case shall be pleaded in his court; in such way that, on account of the inquest made, he who was first in possession shall not lose his possession, until, through

the pleading, the case shall have been proven.[15]

10. Whoever shall belong to the city or castle or fortress or demesne manor of the lord king, if he be summoned by the archdeacon or bishop for any offense for which he ought to respond to them, and he be unwilling to answer their summonses, it is perfectly right to place him under the interdict; but he ought not to be excommunicated until the chief servitor of the lord king of that town shall be asked to compel him by law to answer the summonses. And if the servitor of the king be negligent in this matter, he himself shall be at the mercy of the lord king, and the bishop may thenceforth visit the man who was accused with ecclesiastical justice.[16]

11. Archbishops, bishops, and all persons of the kingdom who are tenants-in-chief to the king have their possessions of the lord king as a barony, and answer for them to the Justices and servitors of the king, and follow and perform all the customs and duties as regards the king; and, like other barons, they ought to be present with the barons at the judgments of the court of the lord king, unless it comes to a judgment to loss of life or limb.[17]

12. When an archbishopric is vacant, or a bishopric, or an abbey, or a priory of the demesne of the king, it ought to be in his hand; and he ought to receive all the revenues and incomes from it, as demesne ones. And, when it comes to providing for the Church, the lord king should summon the more important persons of the Church, and, in the lord king's own chapel, the election ought to take place with the assent of the lord king and with the counsel of the persons of the kingdom whom he had called for this purpose. And there, before he is

consecrated, the person elected shall do homage and fealty to the lord king as to his liege lord, for his life and
his members and his earthly honors, saving his order.[18]

13. If any of the nobles of the kingdom shall have dispossessed an archbishop or bishop or archdeacon, the lord
king should compel them personally or through their
families to do justice. And if by chance any one shall
have dispossessed the lord king of his right, the archbishops and bishops and archdeacons ought to compel
him to render satisfaction to the lord king.

14. A church or cemetery shall not, contrary to the king's
justice, detain the chattels of those who are under penalty of forfeiture to the king, for they (the chattels) are
the king's, whether they are found within the churches
or without them.

15. Pleas concerning debts which are due through the
giving of a bond, or without the giving of a bond, shall
be in the jurisdiction of the king.[19]

16. The sons of rustics may not be ordained without the
consent of the lord on whose land they are known to
have been born.[20]

Moreover, a record of the aforesaid royal customs and dignities has been made by the foresaid archbishops and bishops,
and counts and barons, and nobles and elders of the kingdom,
at Clarendon on the fourth day before the Purification of the
blessed Mary the perpetual Virgin; the lord Henry being there
present with his father the lord king.

There are, moreover, many other and great customs and dignities of the holy mother Church, and of the lord king, and of
the barons of the kingdom, which are not contained in this writ.

And may they be preserved to the holy Church, and to the lord king, and to his heirs, and to the barons of the kingdom, and may they be inviolably observed forever.[21]

All these customs, both ancient and newly minted, were now terrifyingly codified. Henry had forged laws out of individual situations and used every loophole in canon law to give power and favor to the king. Given its fine legal craftsmanship, it was obvious that this document had been a long time in gestation. At the heart of it was Henry's bugbear, in article three: Clerics would be tried and sentenced in civil courts, then sent on to the ecclesiastical courts to be tried and, if convicted, defrocked — dismissed from the clerical state — in the presence of a royal officer, and then sent back to the civil courts to be punished as laymen, under the full rigor of the secular penitential system. Indeed, the whole document neutered the Church in many areas of her life, undoing any of the Gregorian Reforms that had been introduced and subjecting the bishops to the king even regarding their relationship with the pope.

Once the clerk had finished reading the document, Henry turned to Thomas and invited him to affix his archiepiscopal seal to the document as the formal means of his assent and submission. Though he may not have shown it, Thomas was most likely panicking. No doubt, foremost in his mind were his brother bishops, who were furious; many of them may well have thought that he had betrayed him. His enemies within the episcopate, Roger de Pont L'Évêque and Gilbert Foliot, had stood behind him; were they now convinced that they had been right all along and that Thomas was untrustworthy and unfit for office? He needed to talk to them, receive their advice, and decide what they must do now.

Standing up, he addressed Henry. Pleading his youth and inexperience in such matters, he said he needed to take advice before proceeding. Henry may have smiled to himself; this was, he hoped, the last request of a condemned man. Henry would give him the reprieve he requested, but only for now. He knew an awkward night lay ahead for Thomas and the bishops; it might be worth letting them stew in desperation. Noting that the hour was late, Henry consented to an adjournment and went to his chambers satisfied.

26
The Darkest Hour

Whatever sleep he may have had that night did not help Thomas. He and the bishops engaged in a fiery debate for a number of hours, but they failed to reach a solution to the problem that now faced them. It was all Thomas's fault, they said. Putting their seals to that document would do no more damage than had been done — their individual verbal assents had sealed their fates — but they still balked at the idea of having to impress their personal seals on what they regarded as a perfidious text.

As soon as the council assembled the next morning, Henry again demanded that Thomas fix his seal on what would be known as the Constitutions of Clarendon; there would be no further discussion. Thomas was now over the shock, the rebellious side of his personality kicked in, and he gave vent to his fury: "By God Almighty," he cried, "as I am living, I will never set my seal on this!"[1] He had been misled by the king, by the Templars, perhaps even by the pope, whose soothing representatives had broken him down. Henry had made a fool of him. Despite his rage and indignation, he was also afraid: He had been compromised, and there seemed to be no way out. He knew full well that as primate, he had led his bishops and the Church into slavery to a tyrant. If he consented, he would offer the Church to vassalage; but if he refused, he would perjure himself. His discussions with the bishops had yielded no answer and had only enraged them further. He would have to make a decision, and the only one that seemed possible was a unilateral submission that would land them all in serious trouble; Thomas was on his own.

For some reason, Henry decided to make the decision easier for the archbishop, or, most likely, found an even more evenhanded way to gain his acceptance. Perhaps he was acting on advice from some of the compliant bishops, but it is more likely that he knew his former friend well enough to reckon that Thomas, having been pushed into a corner, might well jump back at him, refuse to put his seal on the document, walk out, and continue the fight in exile, as had previous archbishops in their battles with English kings. Henry was aware that the crown did not always come out well in those conflicts. He suggested that instead of the archbishop's seal being affixed to the Constitutions, a chirograph could be drawn up and divided between them. That should make the medicine a little easier to swallow. A chirograph was a legal document that did not require signing; rather, after preparation, it was carefully torn in as many equal parts as there were parties to the agreement enshrined in the document, and a part was given to each party. The result would resemble a jigsaw puzzle — each part fitted neatly with the others and was revealed not to be a forgery. Physically taking a piece of the chirograph was taken in law to signify acceptance of the agreement.

After the chirograph containing all the articles of the Constitutions was prepared, Henry had it torn in three — one part for him, one for Roger as archbishop of York, and one for Thomas. The king stepped forward himself and handed one part to Thomas, who almost automatically took it from him. That insignificant movement of his hand — an act of betrayal — would be a source of regret for the rest of his life. He would later claim that his receiving this document did not signify his consent; indeed, as he held the parchment in his hand, he told Henry, that he accepted neither as consent nor approval, but as a precaution and a defense of the Church so by this evidence he and the bishops would know what was to be done against them.[2] That was merely self-delusion; he knew full well that he could not merely take the document for informational purposes. Hoodwinked as he may have been, in taking it from the king's hand, he had legally assented to the Constitutions.

In the moments that followed, the full extent of what had happened dawned on Thomas and the bishops. Henry had forced through his will. The Church in England had, through his sleight of hand, been reduced to a royal vassal, and the archbishop of Canterbury had allowed it. It was true that Henry had lied. He had deceived the pope and his envoys; he had either deceived or bribed the Templars, who had staked their salvation on the king's honesty — if God were to take them at their word, this squalid affair might see them damned. Though they supported him, Henry's earls and barons could not deny that there had been gross dishonesty involved in this transaction, that the king had used his power and mischievous means to roast the bishops. When she heard of it, even the king's mother, the Empress Matilda, expressed dissatisfaction with what her son had done and the manner in which he had done it.[3] She believed Henry's personal hatred of Thomas had led him to mismanage the whole situation. Though he had triumphed over the bishops and Thomas, this affair at Clarendon did Henry's reputation little good; indeed, it earned him condemnation from many, including the pope.

Herbert of Bosham records in his biography of the archbishop that as the entourage rode back to Canterbury, Thomas was silent, "unusually disquieted and gloomy." He spoke to no one, keeping to himself, distracted. As he seemed to be sinking deeper and deeper into melancholy, his servants became alarmed and tried to engage him in conversation, asking him why he was uncharacteristically sad, why he had withdrawn from them and was not talking to them as he usually did. Thomas eventually replied, "No wonder I seem like this when the Church in England which my predecessors, as the world knows, governed with such prudence in the midst so many dangers, should by my sins be delivered into slavery."[4]

Thomas had no illusions; he had betrayed the Church. As he made his way back to Canterbury sunk in depression, he pondered over the many conflicts the Church in England had endured, how her bishops and priests had fought bravely and triumphed. Some, he remembered, gave their lives in defense of the Church. But now her primate had taken "the lady who stands before me," as he called the Church, and made her fit for slavery. He told Herbert that he wanted to die, that it was no wonder the Church should be reduced to this, seeing as her archbishop had never been fit for this office. Unlike his predecessors who had risen from the Church, he said, he was raised from the royal court rather than from a holy place like the cloister, not from the school of the Savior but from the guards of Caesar.[5]

For the rest of the journey, Thomas pondered over his ambitions and his life of leisure and realized that each of these condemned him. The man who had taken the office of primate to be a shepherd, a pastor of souls, had been proud and vain — a keeper of hawks, a patron of actors, a follower of hounds. "I do not know who has set me as guardian of the vines," he told Herbert, "I who did not watch over myself, but rather neglected myself."[6] His life, he said, was certainly far removed from the well-being of the Church, and now he saw what his unworthiness had done. Indeed, he mused, he was worthy only to be abandoned by God and removed from "the holy seat" that he now occupied. Before long, Thomas began to cry bitterly. Unable to continue speaking, he fell back into silence.

Herbert, in his account, tells of how he tried to encourage Thomas by drawing on the Scriptures to comfort him, reminding him of Saint Peter, King David, and Saint Paul, reassuring him that if he had fallen, with God's support he could rise up stronger. The exhortation seems to have soothed Thomas, and for a while, he was a little reinvigorated.[7] Just after Herbert delivered his consolation, one of the bishops came up to the archbishop; it may well have been Hilary of Chichester, since Herbert identifies him as the bishop who caused the phrase "saving our order" to be dropped. This bishop also tried to console Thomas, by reassuring him that he had done the right thing. Thomas turned to the bishop and rebuked him: "Get behind me, Satan!" he said and moved on away from the company to complete the journey alone.[8]

Along the road to Canterbury, unknown to Thomas, his clerks had been reassessing their future, and a number of them were considering leaving his service. Some were murmuring against him. One of the most faithful of the clerks, Alexander Llewellyn, the archbishop's crossbearer, who would stay by Thomas's side throughout his exile, voiced his opinion, commenting, "What virtue is left to a man who has betrayed his conscience and his reputation?"[9] Thomas was asking himself that same question. Though he was angry with Bishop Hilary, he knew he had no one to blame but himself.

When Thomas arrived back at his residence, he retired to his room. He divested himself of his finery and put on sackcloth, the traditional garb of penance; he would never wear bright clothes again, assuming from this moment on dark and somber attire. He put ashes on his head and began a severe fast, which he would maintain for some time. He took the discipline and embraced other penances, but in a more radical way than before: Now was the time for reparation, and he was not going to spare himself. The most difficult penance of all was his suspending himself from offering Mass.[10] He regarded his sin as so serious that to celebrate Mass would be a desecration. Thomas then sat to write a letter to the pope confessing his sin and asking pardon. David Knowles notes in his biography that, in the six months that followed, Thomas was active in his diocese and took no notice of the "objectionable" clauses in the Constitutions.[11]

Pious tradition locates Thomas's conversion at the time of his elevation as archbishop of Canterbury; however, as noted previously, it is more likely that it was a gradual turning away from his worldly ways. The weeks and months following the council at Clarendon were influential in that process, as a major change took place in his life; it seems his conversion was not only consolidated, but also deepened. His intense self-reflection and radical asceticism at this time led to a greater determination to finally dispense with many of his worldly ways and take greater control over his appetites. The darkness that descended on his soul proved fruitful. It made him outwardly stronger — the coming months would see a much more contentious archbishop emerge. Some of his contemporaries and secular historians would see what they considered to be a greater arrogance and recklessness, and while recklessness may factor into some of the encounters that lay ahead, one must be careful not to ascribe arrogance as the only motivation in his actions. One can only speculate about the internal life of his soul, but it is obvious that Thomas's spiritual life deepened at this time; and as he had already established a faithful regime of daily prayer and study, that must surely have assumed a greater prominence in supporting him and guiding him in what he needed to do.

Having worn the archbishop down and forced agreement out of him, Henry was not content to let matters lie. He wanted Pope Alexander to confirm the Constitutions of Clarendon, not only to establish the ancestral customs on a firm basis but, regarding his former friend, to push the knife in a little further. As he agonized, Thomas found that he had no choice but to join Henry and Roger de Pont L'Évêque in sending an appeal to the pope seeking recognition.[12] Perhaps some relief might lie ahead should the pope respond negatively. In addition to the formal letter of request, Thomas sent his personal letter of penance to Alexander at Sens and waited for the response.[13]

Thomas did not have long to wait; while his letter of penance remained unanswered, Alexander wrote to him concerning the Constitutions in a letter dated February 23, 1164.[14] The Church, he told Thomas, must not suffer any diminution, but must be preserved in its original state through the archbishop's endeavor and care. With this in view, the pope then urged him — indeed, directed and ordered him — that if at any time Henry required from him anything hostile to the liberty of the Church in England, then Thomas should not attempt to do it, nor should he promise to do it, not even in a novel way. Furthermore, Alexander wrote, if Thomas were already bound to anything like this by the king, then he should not in any way observe that promise, but rather "take care to revoke it" and strive to make his peace with God and the Church "in respect of that unlawful promise."

Burdened by guilt as he was, Thomas was much relieved to read Alexander's letter. With the pope's dismissing the promise made to Henry and urging him to revoke it, he was now free of the commitment he had given the king. The pope himself had acknowledged that it was unlawful, so neither king nor conscience could convict him as he renounced it. He would now wait and see how things developed. While Alexander may have been annoyed with Thomas, he was certainly not pleased with Henry, with the Constitutions, or indeed with the manner in which Henry had bound the bishops to observe his so-called ancestral customs. When Henry's messengers arrived at Sens to present his own appeal, the pope was firm with them, calling the customs obnoxious, as they infringed upon the liberty of the Church. Alexander was now safe in France, but he did not want to isolate Henry — the shadow of Barbarossa was too close for comfort, and he did not want to push the English king into the emperor's camp. He would have to take great care. But while he was not going to antagonize Henry, neither was he going to allow him to ride roughshod over the Church or over the archbishop of Canterbury. Alexander was getting ready to play the long game, and he would have to do so with great prudence.

The pope hinted to the messengers that he might tolerate some of the customs, and in time he did so, though most of them he condemned. However, perhaps as a means of compensation, and keeping the king onside, in February 1164 he granted Henry's request to appoint Roger de Pont L'Évêque, the archbishop of York, as papal legate, but imposed limits on the new legate's powers and rights so as not to give him precedence over Thomas in the Province of Canterbury.[15] When Roger received the decree of appointment and saw the limitations, he was furious — he had the title, but little to go with it. As he made the appointment, Alexander wrote to Thomas to reassure him: "Do not let the grant of the legation cause your spirit to falter or give itself up to despair."[16] He had no intention of making either Thomas or Canterbury subject to another, Alexander promised. He asked Thomas to inform him if Henry tried to use the legation against him; if Henry did, Alexander would declare Thomas and the archdiocese and city of Canterbury exempt from the legate's jurisdiction.

Around the same time he informed Thomas of Roger's appointment as legate, around April 1, 1164, Alexander finally wrote a letter in response to Thomas's letter of penance.[17] He focused on Thomas's abstention from offering Mass, warning him that it might be a source of scandal. He counseled Thomas to differentiate between actions committed with free will and those carried out under ignorance. He believed that Thomas had acted under ignorance and compulsion, and directed him to go to confession to any priest and receive absolution. On his part, Alexander willingly absolved him of what he had done and, by virtue of his apostolic authority, released him from any sin. He then advised and commanded him not to abstain from celebrating Mass on account of this matter. Alexander wrote that he held Thomas in great esteem and affection, though he recognized the difficulties he had caused. He promised him that he would do all that was possible to increase the archbishop's honor and his standing in Henry's eyes. Above all, the pope assured him, he would aim to make certain that the rights and dignities of the Church were preserved.

Thomas and Henry would meet again at least once in the months following the gathering at Clarendon, at the ceremony of dedication of the church of Reading Abbey on April 19, 1164.[18] The abbey had a particular importance for the royal family, as it was the burial place of Henry I and of the infant prince William, Henry and Eleanor's firstborn; Henry II would prove to be a lavish benefactor to the abbey and its monks.[19] It also preserved a relic of the apostle Saint James — his hand, which Henry's mother had brought back from her time in Germany. Given the abbey's relationship with her family, she had made a gift of the relic to the monks. In 1157 Barbarossa asked Henry to return the relic to Germany, but Henry ignored the request.[20] Other members of the hierarchy were also present at the abbey on that day, including King Stephen's brother, Bishop Henry of Winchester. Nothing of note seems to have occurred at the ceremonies and the meetings that surrounded it, though for Thomas at least, it was most likely an awkward affair.

Perhaps emboldened by the pope's words on the situation, Thomas decided to seek reconciliation with Henry. Over the next few months, he made two attempts to meet with the king; each time, the gates of the royal residence were closed in his face. Henry's brother William had died on January 30, not long after the council at Clarendon, reportedly of a broken heart from being unable to marry Isabel de Warenne. This became another reason for Henry to despise his former friend. Meanwhile, the king's envoys to the pope were not having an easy time and were sending back stories of how Thomas was frustrating their efforts to bring Alexander onside and how his friends were slandering the king in Europe. None of this was true, but that did not matter to Henry; the archbishop was now a hated enemy about whom nothing good could be said. Thomas tried other means to effect reconciliation. In a July letter to King Louis,[21] he appealed to him to intercede on his behalf, requesting that Louis, while engaged with Henry in discussions about peace, speak to him about reconciliation as well. Thomas went further: He asked the French king to "reprove" Henry for ever having believed anything false about one "who has served him so well and so faithfully, and who has always loved him with sincere affection."

John of Salisbury had met with success in forming alliances in France, and it seemed as if exile might be the best prospect for Thomas. John had kept the archbishop informed of what was happening, and he advised him that he did not see how anything positive could be achieved regarding reconciliation and asserting the Church's liberties while Henry was in his present mood. He counseled Thomas to contact the abbot of the Cistercian Abbey of Pontigny, near Sens, in order to establish a relationship. If exile was coming, then this place would be ideal. Indeed, John said, he himself had chosen Pontigny as his own place of exile.[22]

Thomas decided to take John's advice. One day at the beginning of August 1164, very early in the morning, he rode out of his manor in Stowting in Kent with a small group of companions, including Herbert of Bosham, and quietly made his way to the coast. At Romney, he hired a ship to take them across the channel. Aboard and out at sea, it seemed things would progress according to plan, until the sailors, realizing who was on board and that no license had been granted for him to leave England, staged a mutiny — they feared reprisals from the king. Thomas and his companions ended up back in Romney. A second attempt to flee also failed, and the little group had no choice but to return to Canterbury.[23]

When he arrived back at his palace, Thomas found the place deserted — the clerks had fled. An uneasy night followed. Aware that news of his flight was by now public knowledge, Thomas expected retribution from Henry. It was not long in coming — the king's men arrived in the morning to confiscate his goods.[24] Believing that he had been successful in his flight, the men were taken aback when Thomas came down to meet them; he managed to send them off empty-handed. Henry was beside himself with anger, but he maintained his wits. He realized that he now had to tread carefully — he knew that an ill-judged response could force the archbishop to appeal to Alexander, who, it seemed, might impose an interdict on England. Important developments — the recent death of Antipope Victor and Barbarossa's poor health — had given Alexander the opportunity to increase his authority. Henry could not now be sure that if he tugged the pope's strings, he would get a favorable reaction. Indeed, he may well have uttered a sigh of relief on hearing that Thomas's efforts to flee had failed. Otherwise, the archbishop could be standing before the pope. The promulgation of a formal papal censure would increase his woes by creating an unwelcome tension between king and people. Henry was fearful of a papal rebuke; he would have to choose another means of decapitating this troublesome archbishop, metaphorically speaking — one that could see him rid of Thomas, but yet in favor with the pope.

Not long after his return to Canterbury, in the early fall, Thomas received, to his surprise, a summons from Henry to come to Woodstock. He had tried to gain an audience with the king since the end of August, but he had had the gates of Woodstock closed in his face.[25] He was suspicious, but he obeyed. Arriving at the palace, he was surprised again to receive a warm welcome. For the next few days, Henry treated Thomas with all the former graciousness and generosity he had bestowed on him in the days of their friendship. Indeed, the king made extraordinary efforts to be polite and respectful. He referred to Thomas's attempted flight in a jocular way; though he added, with a hint of sarcasm, "So, my lord, you wish to leave my kingdom. I suppose it is not large enough to hold both of us."[26] Thomas was not fooled; he knew Henry too well to think that the king could simply put all the trouble between them to one side. Henry was, without doubt, plotting.

As Henry poured the ale for his archbishop, his eyes were on John the Marshal (the old soldier whose claim on Church land Thomas had successfully opposed), who was now slinking around the royal court. Both intent on revenge, Henry and John found in each other's grievances, which would be the glue to form an alliance that could serve both their interests.

27

Crisis at Northampton

On cue, John the Marshal entered an appeal to the king's court against Thomas. In his request, he sought to recover the lands he had lost in his case before the archbishop's court in 1162. In the submission he lodged with the court, John cited the king's ancestral customs, as defined in the Constitutions of Clarendon, which made the property rights of senior clergy subject to review in the king's courts. Given that he had a dispute regarding such lands, it would fall to the civil court to resolve it. A summons was issued for Thomas to appear before the court on September 14, 1164.[1]

Thomas was no fool; he knew exactly what John was up to. Instead of appearing himself, he sent a delegation to represent him with evidence proving John's wrongdoing in the matter, together with proof of his insufficient pleading before the archbishop's court. As it happened — or as he arranged — Henry himself was sitting as judge that day, and when Thomas's representatives laid out their case, he roared at them and asked where the archbishop was. Why had he refused to answer the summons?

Throwing Thomas's representatives out of the court, Henry told them that the archbishop had insulted the king by refusing to attend and by refusing to give an acceptable excuse. For this, he cried, Thomas would be punished. He granted John the Marshal a new writ, and decreed that the archbishop would be brought to trial at a council set for October 6 in Northampton, in the east midlands of England. There, Henry informed the representatives, Thomas would respond to John's appeal.

The king, of course, had other plans. He had bided his time, seeking an excuse to prosecute Thomas, and now he had one. But he would need more accusations and misdeeds if he were going to crucify the archbishop. While the court was meeting and the king was tearing strips off Thomas's representatives, royal officials were already engaged in a thorough audit of the records from Thomas's time as chancellor. Every decision, every penny spent, every letter would be scrutinized to reveal mismanagement, embezzlement, and even treason, if it could be found. The outcome was already decided; Henry just had to find enough material, ambiguous or otherwise, to bring the archbishop to the edge of the cliff so he could push him over. The council at Northampton would be a show trial, with Henry directing the entire affair. He sent summonses to all the barons and bishops to attend so that they would witness, and indeed confirm, the condemnation of the archbishop of Canterbury. Thomas was aware that if he did not answer the summons personally, Henry would most likely charge him with high treason. He may have wondered why one case among so many disputing titles to land was causing Henry such angst.

Thomas and his retinue arrived at the king's castle in Northampton on Tuesday, October 6, 1164, as directed. Barons and bishops were also arriving in great numbers. His clerks were uneasy; the sight of what seemed to be a very organized affair filled them with dread. Thomas sent some servants ahead to prepare the rooms that would have been set aside for him, but when they arrived, they were told the rooms were occupied by a group of squires who would not move. When Thomas arrived and was informed of the impasse, he asked to see the king to sort out the problem, but he was told the king was not there — he was out hunting. He had no other choice but to find temporary accommodation. Inquiries yielded an invitation from the prior of the nearby Cluniac Priory of Saint Andrew. The priory had plenty of room, so Thomas and his retinue could settle themselves there for the night.[2]

Rising early the next morning, Thomas offered Mass, and after breakfast left for the castle with his retinue.[3] When he arrived, he was told that Henry was at Mass. When the king emerged from his chapel, Thomas went forward to give the customary kiss, but Henry pushed him away. Chastened, Thomas stood back and spoke very formally, informing the king about the squires who were occupying the rooms assigned to him. Henry agreed to have them expelled, but when the archbishop's servants went to take possession of the rooms, the squires were still in situ and refused to move. As further negotiations failed, and Henry did nothing to enforce his agreement, the servants went back to Saint Andrew's and asked if the archbishop and his retinue could continue to stay there. The prior agreed. Meanwhile, Thomas, still in audience with the king, requested a license to go to Sens to consult with Pope Alexander. Henry not only refused but shouted at him, declaring that Thomas would answer to him first for the injury he had done to John the Marshal. With this, the audience was over, and Thomas withdrew. John the Marshal had not yet arrived at the castle, so proceedings were postponed until the following day, Thursday. The archbishop returned to Saint Andrew's.

The next day, there was still no sign of John the Marshal; it was said that he was detained by the king's business. He would never turn up; he was now surplus to requirement. The trial began on Thursday; by then, all the important barons had arrived, and Henry wanted to get on with the show. First, Thomas was charged with contempt of court and disobedience to the king, as he had no acceptable excuse for his failure to attend court in September. To the charges, Thomas simply replied that he was not legally bound to explain his actions to a royal court. This sent a shiver of fear around the room. It was obvious that the archbishop was not going to go down easily. Some thought him arrogant — one should not speak to the king in such a way, it was said. Henry agreed with that sentiment. He decreed that Thomas had disobeyed him and then called for judgment to be passed on the archbishop.

Those present, barons and bishops, decided that Thomas was indeed guilty of contempt of the crown, and that the punishment would be forfeit of all his movable assets at the king's mercy. Thomas was shocked by the swift operation of this court. The sentence had to be formally delivered, and given that the barons and bishops formed the council with the king in this trial, the king could call on any of them to pass sentence for him. He looked to them and asked for a volunteer. The fearful barons and bishops huddled together to choose one of their number to pronounce the sentence, but none of them would do it. Contemptuous of Thomas as many of them were, no one wanted to deliver what they knew to be a questionable censure of the primate of England. The barons tried to argue their way out of it by claiming that such a duty fell to the clergy, since Thomas was a churchman. The bishops argued that this was a civil affair and did not involve them, so it had to be a civilian. Losing patience, Henry eventually ordered Bishop Henry of Winchester to pronounce the sentence, which he did under duress.

Thomas was now essentially destitute — his material goods were for the most part gone, to be seized by the king. He may have reflected on this later. In his early life, he had sought to amass wealth and honor; he had lived a luxurious lifestyle and had fine clothes and good animals for his hunting. Now, in a moment, it was all gone. Ironically, or perhaps providentially, Henry of Winchester, who passed sentence, was the one who had consecrated him bishop. Perhaps Thomas found it fitting that the man who had ordained him a successor of the apostles should be the one used to bring him to the poverty that had marked the lives of the apostles in their service of the Gospel, as indeed it had marked the life of Christ himself.

Henry moved on to the next accusation: the case of John the Marshal. He demanded that Thomas address the issue of the appeal. Again, Thomas quite simply responded that he had no case to answer. John the Marshal had no evidence to prove his right; in fact, the evidence was there to disprove it. Indeed, he added, John had resorted to deception: He claimed to have sworn on the Bible, but in reality he had used a Mass book so as to avoid perjuring himself. The law required that oaths be taken either on the Bible or on a saint's relic. John had intentionally avoided using either — and for good reason, a reason that was clear to all. Thomas may have noted that John's absence was revealing. It was obvious that he feared having to take his oath again, this time on the Bible. Besides, Thomas went on, if John was able to appeal to a higher authority in claiming land by using unlawful oaths and not even turning up in court to explain himself, a dangerous precedent would be established by which any member of the baronetage could lose his lands to tenants. A ripple of consternation ran through the assembly of barons as they realized that the archbishop not only had a point, but was entirely correct. They were moving into dangerous waters concerning their feudal rights. Henry could sense the change among his barons and realized that it was time to drop John the Marshal, as he was defeated on this issue. It was time to get to the heart of the drama.

Henry now called on Thomas to provide an account of his administration as chancellor, asking the archbishop specific questions about particular financial matters. Henry's clerks had carried out meticulous work, carefully examining the transactions of Thomas's chancellorship, and they had come up with some discrepancies, as Henry would have interpreted them. Thomas was at a loss. This line of questioning seemed to come out of nowhere, and it was so specific he could not answer any of the questions without examining the individual issues and preparing himself for interrogation. The archbishop suddenly realized what the king was up to. Taking the conflict out of the realm of Church liberties, which was the real issue, and making it seem objective when it was highly subjective and personal, Henry was moving in for the kill on matters that Thomas would find it almost impossible to answer without looking over his accounts and papers.

Thomas responded that he could not answer these charges because he did not have the documentation he needed to engage with the specific issues. That said, he would have known there was probably insufficient documentation to defend himself, not because he was guilty, but because of the rather loose system of accounting that existed at the time. In most institutions, courts and households included, paperwork was kept to a minimum, and transactions were not filed in detail. In terms of royal taxation, which was Thomas's responsibility, the modus operandi was simple: Henry knew what was to come to him, and it was collected and passed on. There was an understanding that if a larger amount was collected, Thomas, or any chancellor, could keep the surplus to pay his staff and run his household. There was also a fee that was applied to cover expenses that were incurred when working on behalf of the king, and this fee was deducted from the king's amount. Each year, Thomas met with Henry to go through the accounts, and Henry would have approved them. This meeting would have been casual, not only because Henry trusted Thomas but also because the king was not inclined to waste time on paperwork and would have wanted this meeting to be as short as possible. There would have been no formal documents approving the accounts, no files with reams of receipts, just the usual casual management of a medieval monarchy where the king wanted what was due to him and got it.

Henry was not prepared to listen to Thomas's plea; he continued to address individual issues. The then chancellor, the king insisted, had spent more of the royal finances than he should have and was now in serious debt to the crown. Indeed, the king insisted, he had not authorized such expenditure. It was now becoming clear that Henry was accusing Thomas of not only financial mismanagement but embezzlement. Thomas reminded the king that he had been summoned to answer charges regarding John the Marshal, not his chancellorship, and asserted that it was unfair for him to be interrogated on these matters without time to prepare a defense. Furthermore, he told Henry, following his appointment as archbishop, he had been formally freed at the consecration ceremony from all outstanding debts according to custom and right. Surely the king was aware of that. Henry insisted that he had not freed Thomas from his debts, and now the archbishop had to answer for these irregularities. Realizing that it was futile to try to defend himself, Thomas relented and said that he would not allow money to get in the way of reconciliation; he agreed to reimburse whatever was owed to the crown. Though he now had nothing, there were some who would grant him sureties to help him pay, and he would reimburse them over time from his income at Canterbury. Some of the bishops also agreed to help him.

As night had fallen, the king dismissed the defendant, as he now was, and the gathered assembly; the trial would continue the next day.

Thomas was exhausted and returned wearily to the priory. The atmosphere in the castle had become oppressive. Everyone was on tenterhooks, especially the bishops. Henry was proving his mastery over the archbishop, and they feared he might turn on them when he had finished with Thomas. Their own financial situations were not ideal, and many of them were in debt to the king. Thomas had a quiet night. No one came to see him, which he may have expected; no one wanted to be seen associating with him, lest they fall with him. Having prayed and dined, he went to bed wondering what would happen the next morning. It was obvious Henry had a plan, and the outcome was already decided: he, Thomas of Canterbury, would fall.

At the council the next morning, Henry turned to the campaign for Toulouse. During that campaign, the king explained, Thomas had borrowed five hundred marks from him to add to another five hundred marks he had borrowed from a Jewish moneylender. The money owed to the king had never been repaid. Again, Thomas protested that he had not been given notice of this charge; and again, Henry rejected his plea. He tried to answer in a general way — that money due to the king had been written off, he insisted. Henry denied this and asked for proof there and then that it had been written off. Thomas could not produce it, so the king demanded sureties to meet the debt. Without thinking, Thomas agreed, saying his assets would meet the debt, but Henry reminded him that he had none — he was broke. If he did not provide sureties immediately, Henry informed him, he would be imprisoned. Thankfully, in turning to some of those present, he was able to find such sureties. Thomas had some friends in the council, and he may have hoped that when all this was over he would be able to repay these sureties by future income from the archbishopric and personal benefices.

Henry was prepared for the possibility that the archbishop would find help to meet his debts. He next asked Thomas to provide an account for all the other revenues that he had dealt with in his years as chancellor. There were serious shortfalls, the king insisted, and these must be accounted for and reimbursed through fresh sureties. The amount of money concerned here would have been vast. Without doubt, Thomas now realized that Henry had figures already prepared to present as debts;

whether they were correct or not was another matter. Henry had set a trap, and the archbishop had fallen into it. He now faced bankruptcy, life imprisonment, perhaps even the confiscation of Canterbury's lands and assets, and with it the financial autonomy and security of the primatial see.

Remaining calm — though he may have been overwhelmed and no doubt furious with Henry, he tried not to show it — Thomas asked the king for time to look at the issue and to take counsel. The king decided to grant it. The court adjourned for the night.

28

The Archbishop
Goes to War

The bishops arrived at Saint Andrew's Priory early on Saturday morning to begin deliberations with Thomas. Henry would await the results of the consultation before reconvening the court. Bishop Henry of Winchester chaired the discussion, and he suggested that two thousand marks be offered to Henry in settlement of any debt that might be owed; a mark was worth two or three pounds, so it was a substantial sum of money. The bishops agreed, and Bishop Henry returned to the castle to negotiate with the king. He was sent back with his tail between his legs — the king had bawled a refusal at him. A contingent of knights returned with him to surround the priory, locking up the bishops to force a speedy and realistic response out of them.

Thomas's enemies then spoke. Gilbert Foliot told him that a catastrophe was coming: He was going to fall, and he would pull the Church down with him. It was time for him to resign, he advised, and to make humble obeisance before the king. That might restore Thomas to good, or at least tolerable, relations with the king and avert a disaster for the Church. No doubt, the archbishop and others among the hierarchy noted that Gilbert, now the king's favorite, would succeed to Canterbury if it were rendered vacant as result of this crisis. Henry's other creature, Hilary of Chichester, agreed with Gilbert, and his address to the assembly won over other bishops who now saw no other option. Henry of Winchester did not agree. He said that if the archbishop primate of England, who had the care of souls, resigned at the threat of a secular prince, then the whole Church would be forever subject to the will of the king. Hilary disagreed; turning on Thomas, he rebuked him, informing him that the king had made up his mind that there was no place for both the king and Thomas Becket in England, so the archbishop had to go. It would be best, Hilary continued, to leave everything to the king's mercy; otherwise, he might become violent. Bishop Henry of Winchester urged Thomas not to give in. He knew a tyrant when he saw one, and the Angevin was a tyrant. It would be a mistake to put his trust in Henry's mercy.

The bishops debated all day. As there was nothing to bring them back to court, Saturday passed into Sunday and the Sabbath rest. The court would not meet until Monday. For Thomas, that Sunday was not so much a day of rest as one of turmoil. After Mass, he met with his clerks to discuss all that had happened. They were becoming extremely worried for him as they saw the burden of the last few days taking its toll. It came as no surprise to them when, that night, Thomas fell ill with a flareup of his colitis. He was violently sick, shaking with the cold and in terrible pain such that he was unable to leave his bed on Monday morning. When the king was informed of this, he accused the archbishop of faking the illness. With tensions high, a rumor was circulating that Henry had insisted that if Thomas did not yield, he would have him executed or, at the very least, thrown into prison to rot and die.

Thomas's condition improved over Monday, and on Tuesday morning he was judged fit enough to ride to the castle. As he was preparing to leave, some bishops arrived at his chamber. They told him that they had received news that Henry was intending to put him on trial for treason that very day. They urged him to resign and surrender unconditionally to the king. Calling all the bishops to the priory chapel, Thomas informed them of his decision: He was not going to resign. Having prayed and reflected on the matter, he was going to stand his ground. In all of this trouble, he told them, what had hurt him most was not the attack of the world but the failure of his brother bishops to stand with him. They had abandoned him. In an extraordinary move, invoking his supremacy, he then bound the bishops in obedience to him as their primate, prohibiting them from taking any further part in judgment of him. He formally announced that he was appealing to the pope regarding these issues. If anyone should lay violent hands on him, he informed them, in obedience to him they had to excommunicate those responsible. He himself would not abandon the flock, he told them; he was ready for the fight. Gilbert Foliot tried to object. Under the customs as reiterated by the Constitutions of Clarendon, he insisted, appeals to the pope were forbidden without royal consent. Thomas ignored him and brought the meeting to an end. The bishops left for the castle with a feeling of dread hanging over them. Two stayed with Thomas to provide counsel: Henry of Winchester and Jocelin of Salisbury.

Thomas then went to offer Mass. He chose to celebrate a votive Mass in honor of Saint Stephen the Protomartyr.[1] News would later reach Henry that Thomas had done this; the king saw it as another slight against him. Thomas's contemporary biographers note that the introit for that Mass included the passage from Psalm 119 that reads: "Even though princes sit plotting against me, your servant will meditate on your statutes" (Ps 119:23). He may have meditated on this verse and also on the fact that it was Tuesday, October 13, a year to the day from the translation of Saint Edward the Confessor's relics. Though Henry had wanted to use Saint Edward to push the exaltation of his own status as king of England, the saintly king had been a very different kind of king, a very different kind of man. Fortified by the Eucharist, Thomas took off his vestments, but retained the pallium over his clothes. He placed a host in a pyx and put it in his pocket. Whatever was going to happen, he would have the Blessed Sacrament with him — perhaps even for a hasty viaticum. He set off for the castle on horseback with his retinue.

Arriving in the courtyard, Thomas dismounted. His crossbearer, Alexander Llewellyn, also dismounted from his horse and took up the cross to carry it in front of the archbishop as was required. Thomas took the cross from him and, carrying it as if it were a weapon, entered the castle. Henry had been watching his arrival from a window in the castle, and when he saw the archbishop march in with such confidence holding his own cross, he was furious. He was also afraid. When Gilbert Foliot saw Thomas coming with the cross, he called him a fool and tried to take it from him. Thomas resisted and pushed Gilbert out of his way. "You hold the cross in your hands," Gilbert shouted, "if the king were to take his sword, then we would see a king well arrayed and an archbishop well arrayed!" meaning both being armed for conflict. "If it was possible," Thomas shot back at him, "I would always hold it in my hands. But now I know what I am doing, preserving the peace of God and of my own person and of the English Church. Say what you wish," Thomas continued, "if you were in my place you would feel otherwise. If the lord king, as you say, was to take his sword now, that, of course, would not be a sign of peace."[2]

He then took a seat in a small room beside the great hall to await the beginning of the proceedings.

The court was called to order, but unusually, the bishops were directed to see the king in his chamber. Filing out fearfully, they left Thomas seated alone in the room. He could hear an argument upstairs; it seemed Henry was not having it all his own way. The king was attempting to get the bishops behind him in his condemnation of the archbishop. He had decided that the financial route was the way to go, though he wanted to resurrect the issue of conflicting courts again. The bishops, now bound under obedience to their primate, were resisting. As time went on, it became clear that Henry was not going to meet Thomas face-to-face, and Thomas knew why: The king was afraid of being excommunicated. The archbishop's close advisors had been recommending excommunication as a course of action to deal with Henry, but Thomas had not assented to it — not yet, anyway. In the meantime, Henry sent some of his barons to meet Thomas. They asked if he could produce the documentation to support his argument against the king on the accusations of financial mismanagement and embezzlement. Furthermore, they informed him that as he had made an illegal appeal to the pope, he would now have to answer for that, too.

Remaining seated as the barons stood, Thomas addressed them formally. He told them that while he was bound to his king in fealty, as a priest he was bound to oaths of justice and equity; the trial he was now enduring was, in fact, an abuse of the system of justice. He had been summoned only to answer charges in the case of John the Marshal, not these new charges of fiscal mismanagement. He had been freed of all debt by the king himself on his elevation to the episcopate at the ceremony of his nomination in Westminster Abbey in 1162. Henry might deny it, he said, but it was a fact known by all the barons and bishops who were at Westminster and witnessed it. As for his appeal to the pope and the prohibition he had placed on the bishops, he continued, though the barons might complain about it, the matter was now with the pope; he maintained that no one had the right to judge him while the appeal was being examined by the pontiff. "I still appeal," he said, "and so place my person and the church at Canterbury under the protection of God and the lord pope."[3]

The die was cast. While some of the barons accused Thomas of blasphemy, others were silent; they knew they had been outmaneuvered. They returned to report to Henry. The row now escalated as some barons called for Thomas to be executed, castrated, or thrown into prison. Henry was trying to work out what to do now that the stakes were higher. He wanted to keep the bishops on his side — he needed them to be part of the condemnation of Thomas for the sake of legitimacy. He was also aware that if this dispute became the pope's business, a rational, objective examination of the trial would reveal his cunning and the basic injustice of the whole affair. Before all of Europe, he would be condemned by the pontiff, and perhaps also excommunicated. There was also another development of which the king was not aware: For many in England, Thomas was now emerging as a hero, while Henry was beginning to be seen, in some quarters, as a tyrant. If Thomas or even the pope were to excommunicate Henry and absolve his subjects from their loyalty to him, that could prove politically problematic at the very least.

Meanwhile, the bishops were fighting among themselves. Some

wanted to stand with Henry; others were loyal, in some part, to Thomas. A delegation of bishops went down to their primate to ask him to lift the prohibition upon them and withdraw the appeal to the pope in the hope that a solution could be found among those gathered. It was perhaps a mistake that Roger de Pont L'Évêque led the delegation. In direct contravention of the pope's order, Roger had been walking around the castle with his cross being borne before him in a gesture of episcopal precedence even though the castle was within the Province of Canterbury. Now, as he approached Thomas, the archbishop took up his own cross and challenged him. The two archbishops stood facing each other, as if about to come to blows with their crosses. Hilary of Chichester then accused Thomas of being the cause of all this trouble, having led them one way at Clarendon and then turning in another direction. Staring Hilary in the eye, Thomas told him that no one was bound to keep an oath that should not have been taken; an unlawful oath was not binding.

The bishops had little success for their efforts; Thomas would not budge. In the end, they placated Henry, telling him that they could lodge an appeal with the pope against Thomas's appeal if he would excuse them from sitting in judgment on their archbishop. By this time, Henry had had enough. He wanted to pull Thomas down, not create a civil war with the bishops, so he relented on the issue of who would pass judgment. Gathering all the barons and summoning his knights and sheriffs, he had them formulate the judgment and sentence. As expected, they found Thomas guilty of all charges, and it is believed they sentenced him to life imprisonment.

The king charged the barons and knights to impose the judgment and sentence on Thomas and then sat back in his chair. The chamber was cleared, and Henry was left alone. Robert de Beaumont, Earl of Leicester, was the one chosen to deliver the sentence. As he and the other barons entered the room where the archbishop was waiting alone, Thomas refused to stand; he remained seated, immovable and holding his cross. As Robert began to pronounce the sentence, what he was doing suddenly become apparent to him, and he was nervous. But before he had time to impose the sentence, Thomas interrupted him. Standing to his full height and raising his cross in the air, he exclaimed that it was not for the earl to judge his archbishop.

Robert was dumbfounded, and mayhem ensued. Some barons, infuriated by what they saw as the archbishop's arrogance and insult to the king, called him a traitor, while others shouted "Perjurer!" at him. As the uproar increased, Bishop Hilary of Chichester tried to take charge and settle things down so the sentence could be imposed, but to no avail. In the midst of the chaos, Thomas began to walk toward the door, and as invectives were been thrown at him from all sides, he made it to the great hall. While he managed to retain his grace, at one point he stumbled, and it raised a chorus of mocking howls from some. In what may have seemed a miracle, no one prevented him leaving the castle. Suddenly aware of the providence of it all, Thomas quickly mounted his horse. Pulling his secretary, Herbert of Bosham, up behind him on his mount, he reared his horse and charged toward the gates; some of his clerks quickly mounted their horses and followed him. On reaching the gate of the outer part of the castle, they discovered it locked and the porter missing. A hasty search yielded the keys, and the gate was soon open. Thomas and his retinue fled the castle and made for the priory. Furiously urging his horse forward, Thomas clung to his cross with one hand while Herbert frantically clung to his archbishop from behind. As they fled, Thomas may have heard the cheers of the ordinary folk of the castle. Unlike those of the barons and sheriffs, these were cheers of admiration.[4] In the eyes and hearts of the simple people of England, the haughty chancellor-turned-archbishop was now a champion, the one who had faced down the tyrant.

29
Exile

Thomas arrived back at the priory in time for Vespers and, always conscientious in his prayers, prayed the Divine Office with his clerks. Given the events of the last few days and the gradual disintegration of his health, he was weary; following the infusion of adrenaline that saw him out of the castle and riding across the fields, he was exhausted. After prayer, he went to the refectory, where his clerks were dining, and as he sat to eat, a number of them came over one by one to ask him to discharge them from his employment, as did his knights. Thomas released them, though as he did so, Herbert made snide remarks about loyalty and friendship.[1] The archbishop was all too well aware of the human desire to avoid trouble and conflict and of what fear could do. Though he was risking his life in defense of the Church, he had no right to ask anyone else to do the same, much less the powerless, who were very vulnerable before the might of kings. As news of Thomas's fate reached Canterbury, the young boys who were being educated in his household also left.[2]

Finishing his meal, Thomas sent a message to the king requesting safe conduct back to Canterbury. A reply was sent by return: His request was refused. He had safe conduct in Northampton, but if he should try to return home, he was subject to whatever trouble might occur on the road — rumors had begun to circulate that there could be violence.[3] Thomas had little doubt that the king had already deployed knights to arrest him as soon as he left Northampton. Realizing that the time for exile had come, Thomas took Herbert and his three most trusted servants aside and told them that they would leave that night under cover of darkness. He instructed Herbert to travel to Canterbury to get as much money as he could and as many other valuables as it was possible to carry and then to travel on to the continent, to Saint-Omer in Flanders, where they would rendezvous.[4]

As Herbert slipped away in secret, Thomas informed his retinue and the prior that he wanted to spend the night in the chapel in prayer. The monks set up a bed for him behind the altar and observed him supposedly asleep as they gathered for their night offices. Just before daybreak, Thomas donned a lay brother's habit and, with his three clerks, quietly rode out of the priory in the last darkness of the night.[5] They knew one of the gates of the town to be unguarded, so they left Northampton by it and made their way down the country toward the south coast. To avoid the king's knights and spies, they took a convoluted route, heading first north toward Lincoln, and then around to the south. Calling himself "Brother Christian," Thomas would travel mostly by night, hiding out at one stage for a period of days with Gilbertine monks in the Fens.[6]

On the morning of the archbishop's flight, Bishop Henry of Winchester arrived at Saint Andrew's Priory to see how he was. By this time, Thomas's absence had been discovered by his chamberlain, and it was he who informed the bishop that the archbishop was doing rather well, seeing as he had left last night in a hurry and no one knew where he was. Bishop Henry may have smiled to himself. When King Henry was told, he did not smile, but grimaced. "We have not finished with this one yet,"[7] he chided. As he boarded a boat at Sandwich Bay in Kent as light was breaking on November 2, All Souls' Day,[8] Thomas likely agreed that the matter was not over. It was only starting.

Piled into a little skiff with nothing but the clothes on their backs and whatever articles they could carry on their persons, Thomas and his companions crossed the English Channel to land, in the afternoon, at the beach at Oye, east of Calais, in the County of Flanders. Thomas was ill; the crossing had been rough, and the strain of the flight and the subsequent circuitous journey had caught up to him. Disembarking, he struggled to find his balance on the stony beach and collapsed. One of the clerks managed to find a packhorse; they sat the archbishop on the animal, and the party slowly made their way to the town of Gravelines, about five miles distant, arriving after dark. Finding accommodation at an inn, they settled into their room and then went down to eat a simple dinner in the public room.[9]

Thomas's flight was now common knowledge. Given his height and obvious elegance, he attracted attention despite his weakness and pitiful state and, though disguised, unknowingly betrayed his identity to those in the inn who were listening intently to his fine French and educated accent. Leaving early the next morning, the little group took the southern road for Saint-Omer and their meeting with Herbert. Despite Thomas's attempts to hide his identity, a series of encounters along the road led to some recognizing him. These unwelcome events made the party even more fearful. Though they were no longer in Henry's territory, they were in Flanders, where the ruler was a relative and ally of the English king. Count Philip, King Henry's cousin, remembering the archbishop's efforts to prevent his brother Matthew of Alsace's marriage to Marie of Blois, might be very happy to hand the fugitive back to Henry. The little company had to be careful and swift.

Despite the secrecy of their journey, Thomas was able to glean information on developments in England. His flight was now known and had been condemned by the king and his allies. Henry had dispatched a delegation bound for Sens to meet with Pope Alexander and seek Thomas's suspension. Ironically, Henry's envoys had crossed the channel the same day Thomas had. He later learned that Gilbert Foliot was leading the delegation — likely no surprise to Thomas — accompanied by Roger de Pont L'Évêque and Hilary of Chichester; they were all Henry's men now for varying reasons. The Earl of Arundel was accompanying the bishops, along with the usual retinue to ensure that they got to Sens as quickly as possible.[10]

Thomas and his company made for the Abbey of Notre Dame at Clairmarais outside Saint-Omer, the agreed meeting point with Herbert. The abbey had been founded by Saint Bernard himself in 1140, and its community was known for its solid faith. Herbert had already arrived, and while he had a tale of woe to tell — he had not been able to get much at Canterbury, only one hundred marks and a few silver items — his frustrations vanished when he saw the archbishop. Thomas was deathly ill. Gaunt, haggard, and now stooped, he was a shadow of the man he had left in Northampton just a few weeks before. Thomas was delighted to see Herbert, and the two sat to exchange news. Herbert told him that Henry's delegation was staying in Saint-Omer itself, just a few miles away. Immediately fearful, Thomas had to decide how to ensure their safety. There was an old hermitage, said to have been once occupied by Saint Bertin, at Eldemenstre; surrounded by marshes, it was secluded and secure. They could lodge there in secret until the delegation had left Saint-Omer.[11] The other exiles agreed to the plan, and they and the weary archbishop made their way by rowboat to the hermitage.

Henry's delegation left Saint-Omer a couple of days later. When it was confirmed that they had gone, Thomas and his companions left the hermitage for the Abbey of Saint Bertin. Founded in the seventh century, the abbey was home to Benedictine monks. Since its foundation, it had risen to become one of the most important abbeys in Europe, its library noted for its vast collection of works. The abbot was Godescal, a man who had kept up to date with all that was happening in England and who regarded Thomas as a hero. When the archbishop arrived, he was greeted with a warm welcome by abbot and monks and offered hospitality but also, most importantly, refuge for as long as he needed it.[12] Safe within a Benedictine community like that of his own monks at Canterbury, Thomas took time to rest and pray.

But even in the environs of the monastery, peace seemed to elude the archbishop. He had not been long at Saint Bertin's when one of his vassals,[13] Richard de Lucy, on his way back from a pilgrimage to Santiago de Compostela, arrived at the abbey. Having heard of Thomas's fate, Richard, who was chief justiciar of England, had come to convince him to submit to Henry. Richard couched his petition in terms of friendship. When Thomas refused and tempers flared, the justiciar swore that from then on, he would be Thomas's enemy. Reminded that he was the archbishop's vassal, Richard spat back that he withdrew his homage, to which Thomas replied, "It wasn't meant as a loan."[14] Richard stormed off. Other visitors to Saint Bertin's were more welcome. A number of Thomas's clerks arrived in the days after their archbishop — not all had abandoned him, and these faithful ones had willingly sealed their fate to their archbishop's. His ever-faithful and ardent crossbearer, Alexander Llewellyn, was among them, as were his personal chaplains, Robert of Merton and Richard of Salisbury. They had had a difficult time getting out of England, and once it was discovered that they were standing by the archbishop, they would most likely lose everything they had in England and Normandy. These were now the company of exiles, poor men who would rely on the charity and discretion of others. Milo II, the bishop of Thérouanne, an Englishman by birth, also visited the abbey to offer his friendship and support.[15] While Thomas now knew who his enemies were, he was also discovering new friends, people who were prepared to take risks to help him.

The matter foremost in the minds of those at the abbey was how to get the archbishop safely out of Flanders and into France and under the protection of King Louis. Count Philip of Flanders was bound by the requirement of his loyalty to Henry not to harbor fugitives; Thomas could easily be arrested and sent back to Henry.[16] The abbots of Saint Bertin's and Clairmarais decided to visit the count and personally request safe conduct for him. While Philip did not directly refuse — he did not seem to be intent on seeking immediate revenge for his brother's marital difficulties — his equivocation alarmed the abbots, and they concluded as they left his presence that Thomas had to be smuggled out of Flanders as quickly as possible. As soon as they returned to the abbey, preparations were made quickly, and Abbot Godescal himself took charge of the flight. When darkness fell, Thomas mounted a horse supplied by Bishop Milo and, led by the abbot, traveled down to the border of the county, crossing into France just south of the town of Cambrai. Arriving at the town of Soissons a few days later, he found refuge for a brief respite.

From there, he sent Herbert on another mission, this time to spy on Henry's delegation. Proving he had an aptitude for espionage, the clerk was soon relaying important information back to Thomas and the exiles.[17]

The king's delegation had made its way to King Louis's court, then sojourning at Compiègne, before turning south to Sens to meet with the pope. In their audience with Louis, Henry's envoys asked him not to give asylum to Thomas, whom they referred to as the "former archbishop." The treaty that he and Henry had signed, the envoys reminded him, envisaged that neither of them could give succor to the enemies of the other. Louis was noncommittal — he was playing for time. The envoys asked him to write to the pope in support of Henry's cause and their mission. Louis agreed to write a letter, but as soon as the delegation departed for Sens, he wrote a letter to Pope Alexander on Thomas's behalf. The next day, Herbert arrived and told Louis the whole story from the archbishop's viewpoint. Louis granted the company of exiles safe conduct to Sens to meet with the pope, and after seeing Herbert off to continue his espionage, himself left for Soissons to see the archbishop.[18]

Thomas may not have been expecting Louis, but when he heard the king had arrived, he was delighted. Coming out to greet the king, he knelt before him; the king was shocked to see the state of the archbishop. Louis had a tremendous regard for Thomas; the two had formed a deep respect for each other ever since the marriage negotiations in 1158. He promised Thomas goodwill and financial aid and informed him that he and the other exiles had safe conduct for their journey to the pope in Sens. Louis, however, was a careful man. He did not want to offend Henry too much, so his assistance would have to be limited and surreptitious.

Thomas now looked toward Sens. He would have to make his way there as soon as possible in order to appeal to the pope and seek his aid. Herbert's messages were keeping him up to date on the progress of Henry's delegation: They were already at Sens making their arguments before Pope Alexander, but with moderate success. Whatever had come over them, the various envoys were making grammatical mistakes in Latin and were being assiduously corrected by curial officials mid-speech. When they descended to making uncharitable and unworthy remarks about the archbishop, Alexander himself was quick to intervene and rebuke them. As the envoys praised Henry's magnanimity toward the Church and the pope, Alexander replied to each invocation of acclaim — with perhaps a tinge of sarcasm — "We are glad that the king is so good. May God make him even better."[19]

The envoys then tried to bribe Alexander. Henry was requesting that the pope order Thomas back to England and appoint legates with the power to hear and judge the appeals made at Northampton, but in such a way that the judgments could not be challenged. If the pope granted that request, then Henry would increase the Peter's Pence contribution from England.[20] Meanwhile, some of the envoys were also secretly bribing cardinals in the hope that they would sway the pope in Henry's favor. While Alexander was not as free as he had been a few months before — Barbarossa had recovered from his illness and had had another antipope, Paschal III, elected — he was not inclined to allow Henry to manipulate legates for his own purposes, as the pope was sure he would. In the meantime, Herbert had arrived at the papal court and was speaking to Alexander behind the scenes. The pope played for time, suggesting to the envoys that he could not make a decision until Thomas had come to defend himself. Seeing that they were not going to get anywhere, and under orders from Henry not to conduct the archbishop's case in the papal curia lest the pope rule on it, the delegation packed up and began the journey back to England.

As the delegation left Sens headed north, it came face-to-face with a large group of about three hundred horsemen heading south. The envoys' initial investigation revealed that it was Thomas and his entourage on the way to Sens.[21] They were disturbed by the size and nature of the entourage; it seemed that the archbishop had powerful allies on his side, and this was worrying. Carefully avoiding the archbishop, the delegation continued on its way but made the decision to send a spy, Guy Rufus, Dean of Waltham, back to Sens to observe and report on the proceedings.

Thomas arrived in Sens toward the end of November 1164. When news of his approach reached the papal curia, most of the cardinals rode out to greet him and accompany him for the last few miles of the journey. As he entered the papal residence, Alexander stood to welcome him and embraced him warmly. An initial conversation between pope and archbishop was followed by a debate over which of Thomas's companions would be chosen to present his case. Thomas felt he was not able to do the presentation — he may have lost his nerve, or perhaps he was too tired. However — as everyone acknowledged — realistically, only the archbishop could do it, so he relented. He would present his case before the pope and cardinals the next morning, but in a private audience, not in public as he had hoped. Retiring to the quarters reserved for him, Thomas spent the evening working on his speech.

The next morning, Thomas came before the pope and cardinals.[22] His speech is extant in a number of versions, with minor differences.[23] He began by informing Alexander that he had fled to his presence at great risk so that Alexander, as pope, the "most holy father," might consider the cause of his persecution. He explained that he had lamented the gradual destruction of the Church in England and its rights "dispersed to the avarice of princes." Binding himself to God, he had sought to resist this disintegration, but had fallen victim to the "accusations and malicious charges" of these princes, and these charges were the pretext for his prosecution. He preferred to be expelled, he explained, than to allow this to happen. If these wrongs were not enough, he continued, he was then dragged before the king and tried as a layman while being deprived of a defense. The bishops who should have supported him were prepared to censure him according to the will of the courtiers, so he "gasped out an appeal" to the pope. He was happy to render to Caesar what was Caesar's, he said, but though the king should be obeyed in "many things," "he must not be obeyed in those things which cause him not to be king."

He then addressed the bishops' conduct. While he was not surprised at the behavior of the laymen, he was surprised at the behavior of his brother bishops. They abandoned him, little knowing that they were conspiring to bring about their own destruction; so full of hatred, they were in reality annihilating themselves in order to destroy him. They had dared to condemn him when he made this appeal to their pontiff. These bishops, he insisted, were neglecting their spiritual duties in order to tend to temporal matters, and all the time losing in both. Ignoring the king's excesses, which led to their slavery, they had urged Thomas not to provoke the king. Musing on their behavior, he asked, "And when is constancy more needful than during persecution?" "How will they win, if they always lie down?" he wondered. Surely, he argued, "they must resist at some point?"

Directly appealing to Alexander, Thomas asked him to look kindly on his "fight and persecution." He said that it was on the pope's account that he was being assailed. "Act with the firmness of your office," Thomas pleaded. "Restrain those by whose instigation the accusation in this action was sprung on us." Ending his speech, he referred again to the king, but in a more magnanimous manner: "Nothing of this should be imputed to the lord king," he stressed, "for he is the servant of this conspiracy rather than its author." This was not, perhaps, mere generous charity on Thomas's part, but an acknowledgment that there was another force at work in all this. John of Salisbury had cautioned Thomas not to directly impugn the king; it would be better to blame "the untamed beasts of the court."[24]

Thomas then presented the pope with a copy of the Constitutions of Clarendon, calling them the evil laws that had led to his exile. Spreading it out before Alexander, he went through each of the articles and so-called ancestral customs. [25] Commenting on each as they were explained to him, Alexander referred to many of them as obnoxious, reminding the archbishop that he was not bound to the promise he had made under duress; indeed, he was absolved from adherence to these customs. Poring over the document, the pope and cardinals understood better Thomas's ordeal, and some were reduced to tears. Those cardinals who had opposed him now revised their opinion and assured him of their support. It was agreed that the Church had a problem, and that she must come to the aid of England and her primate.

Thomas left the pope and cardinals to reflect on what they had heard; it was time to retire for rest and a good night's sleep. The next morning, the audience resumed, again in private. Making another speech, Thomas admitted his faults. The troubles of the English Church, he confessed, were due to his flaws, his inexperience, and his inability. He had accepted the office unwillingly, but it was the will of man and not the will of God that saw him elevated. However, despite this, he was not willing to abandon the Church in England to the willfulness of the king by resigning his office when it was demanded by his brother bishops — it would have been "an evil precedent." Instead, he had come to the pope.

Given all that had happened up to now, what followed was not widely expected. Thomas continued to speak, condemning himself. He recognized that his appointment was far from canonical and, fearing things could get considerably worse, had decided there could be only one course of action. The gathered cardinals and clerks may well have held their breath. To the dismay of his clerks, Thomas removed the episcopal ring from his finger, placed it in Alexander's hands, and said, "Into your hands, Father, I resign the archiepiscopate of Canterbury."[26]

Part IV

Servant of Christ

30
Pontigny

Pope Alexander withdrew to his private quarters carrying Thomas's ring in his hand. He had to confer with his advisors. Some of the cardinals urged him to accept the resignation. Thomas could be given another office befitting his status in the Church, and his removal from England would allow reconciliation with Henry and the chance to fix things. An experienced man in Canterbury could turn things around, they suggested.[1] Alexander listened to the advice and then went to take his own counsel. Some historians say he took three days to come to a decision, one suggesting that Thomas was left stewing after what was no more than a theatrical gesture.[2] This opinion of the resignation emerges out of a view that he was arrogant enough to gamble his office and the Church in England to triumph over Henry. This view fails to take into account the fact that Thomas knew that Alexander was no longer in a strong position: Alexander now needed Henry more than he had a few months before. The pope might easily have seen Thomas's resignation as an opportunity to grasp quickly. Thomas may have meant what he said and rejoiced more in his naked finger than some would give him credit for.

Alexander made up his mind and called Thomas to him. He praised him for his zeal and his stand in adversity;[3] it was obvious the archbishop had a clear conscience. Returning the ring to him, the pope refused his offer of resignation. However, Thomas was not to return to England until the dispute was settled. Instead, he was to go to the Cistercian Abbey of Pontigny with a few of his friends as companions. Like his holy predecessor Anselm, Thomas might need to prepare himself for a long exile. In the abbey, he would have to live without the trappings of comfort. It would be penitential, but there would be time for prayer and reflection. Alexander would make arrangements with the abbot; until then Thomas would remain at Sens for Christmas.

At the end of December, the abbot of Pontigny, Guérin of Galardun, arrived in Sens in response to the pope's summons. He agreed to accept Thomas and his companions, but it would have to be a small household, as space in the abbey was limited. The archbishop and his chosen few packed their belongings and, in the midst of winter, made their way to Pontigny, which was thirty-three miles from Sens and twelve miles from Auxerre, in the middle of a wilderness in the Duchy of Burgundy.[4]

The Abbey of the Assumption of Our Lady at Pontigny had been founded in 1114, the second daughter house of the Cistercian motherhouse at Cîteaux. A canon of the cathedral of Auxerre, Hildebert, had approached one of the founders of the Cistercians, Saint Stephen Harding, requesting that a monastery of the new Cistercian rule be established on a site he had obtained for the purpose. Saint Stephen sent Blessed Hugh of Mâcon, a relative of Saint Bernard, with twelve monks to Pontigny, where they carved an abbey and a life of devotion out of the wilderness. Pontigny quickly became renowned for the holiness of its monks and attracted so many vocations that it soon began to found daughter houses, establishing twenty-two in all. Various buildings, austere in their design and with little comfort in mind, were added to the original house, and work began on the abbey church in 1140. Built to accommodate more than a hundred monks, the church was an extraordinarily beautiful building: lofty, austere, and architecturally brilliant. Most of it was complete by the time Thomas and his party arrived there in December 1164, and it was the heart of the monks' spiritual and liturgical life. Apart from being a school of holiness, Pontigny was also developing a reputation as a house of refuge. Exiles from other disputes found peace and quiet in the cloisters and entered into the daily work of the community. It was no surprise, then, that Alexander should choose it for Thomas and his exiles. John of Salisbury had recommended it, and the pope may have been aware of the initial contact between the archbishop's representatives and the abbot.

As they approached the abbey, Herbert of Bosham's heart sank.[5] It was utterly isolated. The area was densely wooded and, it seemed, far from civilization. Things looked even worse when they were conducted to their accommodations: Thomas's household would be split up among the small buildings of the abbey, "little rooms in Noah's Ark," as Herbert described it.[6] Cistercians liked solitude; for them, being far from the world was a means of their interceding for it. However, it seemed to Herbert that in this place they were not only far from the world but even far from one another. Alexander had chosen wisely: Here, Thomas would also be far from Henry.

Whatever austerities they would have to face in this isolated citadel, Thomas and his companions were warmly greeted by the abbot and his community. Though there would be hardship, the monks immediately made the archbishop part of their community, an honored guest who would receive much kindness and generosity. It took about a week for rooms to be organized, and then most of the exiles adjusted themselves to abbey life and customs. Herbert would never settle. While the diet was basic, the abbot did what he could to vary it for Thomas — it must have been difficult for him to readjust from a fine and delicate diet to one that was much more primitive and hard on his stomach, which was not in good shape at the best of times.[7]

However much Herbert complained, and he complained a lot, Thomas approached the situation very differently — he seemed to welcome it. He may have seen Pontigny as a place where he could atone for his sin at Clarendon; indeed, the crucible where he could progress further in his conversion.[8] He had advanced in those dark months after the council; now he could advance even further in the time allotted to him in this place of prayer and penance. Perhaps it was not just the will of the pope but the will of God that the war-weary archbishop should be sent to such a venerable school of holiness.

The abbot offered to modify the lifestyle for him, but Thomas refused. Always directed by duty, he would enter wholeheartedly into the life of the monks, and this would endear him even more to the community. He ate what was given with gratitude and without complaint; he joined them for prayer and spiritual exercises; he embraced their penances and shared in the joys and trials of the monks. He wore the monastic habit and, beneath it, a hair shirt.[9] He offered Mass, chanted the Office in choir, and regularly gave himself to night vigils in the abbey church. He often ordered his chaplain, Robert of Merton, to scourge him with the discipline, and some mornings he would go down to one of the local streams known for its cold waters and immerse himself as an act of penance. In the first months of his sojourn, Thomas inflicted harsh penances on himself in reparation for his sins. These were the acts not of an arrogant man, but of a repentant one; as Dom David Knowles remarks, regarding these penances, we "may be allowed to respect his sincerity and high courage."[10]

Though his spirit was willing, Thomas's body was weak, and before long he fell seriously ill and had to be confined to bed. The exiles and the monks alike feared for his life.[11] Succumbing to infections and ulcers, he fell into a fever and became delirious. In moments of bewilderment, he relived his pleading before the pope and cried out in distress. Herbert and his other servants nursed him through the crisis, and gradually he regained his health. Following his recovery, the abbot and Herbert had choice words for him: The archbishop's abstinence and penances had been the source of his illness and could have claimed his life. He would have to be more prudent. He was advised to resume his usual diet and to take more rest. If he wanted to do penance and to use this time at Pontigny wisely and for the good of the Church, then he might be better engaged in more reading and study.

Thomas was forced to agree. He took good meals and plenty of rest and, in obedience to the abbot and his companions, turned to books — to theology, to canon law, and, most joyfully, to the study of Scripture.

He also found a way to occupy Herbert and moderate his complaining: He asked his secretary to prepare a complete edition of Peter Lombard's *Great Gloss* on the psalms and Saint Paul's letters. Thomas would commission other books during his time at Pontigny, borrowing money to pay for them. Wandering through the abbey's library and scriptorium, he marveled at the fine manuscripts, spending time reading them and digesting their arguments while having some copied for his personal library.[12] This devotion to study was not just to fulfill his obedience to the abbot or for his personal education, but also to equip him to deal more effectively with Henry, as Anselm equipped himself six decades earlier in Lyon to face Henry I. Thomas also understood, again from his predecessor's experience, that he could still govern the Church in England from his monastic exile. Both Saint Anselm and Theobald had continued their work both for Canterbury and England, in so as far as they could, during their exiles. The prayerful isolation of Pontigny gave Thomas time and space to think, plot, and write, and though his physical absence from his see presented difficulties, he was determined to overcome them as far as he could to ensure that no one forgot that he was still archbishop and primate.

While the archbishop was adjusting to the peaceful life in Pontigny, Henry was not so peaceful in England. Thomas's exile had consequences for his family and the families of his companions. Henry was determined to strike against the archbishop, and if Thomas was now out of his reach, his possessions and family were not. Two days after Christmas 1164, with festive charity out of the way, the king ordered the confiscation of all of Thomas's possessions and the forfeiture of the benefices of the archbishopric of Canterbury.[13] All the churches of Thomas's clerks and their revenues were also seized. Members of his family were equally deprived of their property and assets and then deported; men, women, and children fled to the continent, and with them members of his fellow exiles' families, suffering similar deprivations.[14] With no income, these new exiles were reduced to destitution. Thomas's sisters Agnes and Rose and their children were arrested in London and imprisoned overnight before being brought to a ship bound for the continent and unceremoniously pushed onboard. His youngest sister, Mary, by then a nun in Barking, may have been allowed to stay, though it is not beyond the bounds of possibility that she, too, was exiled from her monastery and sent abroad. Ranulf de Broc, the squatter at Saltwood, played a pivotal role in seizing Thomas's properties and arresting and exiling his relatives.[15]

It is believed that as many as four hundred were exiled.[16] Some tried to make their way to Thomas at Pontigny, and the abbot tried to accommodate as many as he could. Others had to fall upon the mercy of various religious houses in France. Convents took in the women and children, while the men tried to find work to support themselves and their scattered families. King Louis himself took an interest in caring for the exiles — no doubt he was making a point about Henry's view of justice. As a man concerned about his faith, the French king was no stranger to charity. Even Henry's own mother, Matilda, reached out to help exiles, financially supporting a number of them.[17] Meanwhile, Henry revealed the extent of his charity by decreeing that no support should be given to Thomas Becket, not even prayer.

While Henry was persecuting Thomas's family, the archbishop was appealing to a member of the king's family: his mother, the Empress Matilda. In a letter written soon after his arrival at Pontigny,[18] he asked her to "urge [her son] very diligently to take care of the Church's peace." Though he was writing to the king's mother, he did not hold back, telling her directly that "it was broadcast from East to West that he [Henry] is afflicting the churches of his realm beyond endurance and demanding from them unheard of and unaccustomed things, which, if former kings sought them, they ought not to have sought them." Switching to a more diplomatic tone, Thomas noted that while Henry himself might not abuse the powers he sought, those coming after him might; he must have written this with his tongue firmly in his cheek. He asked the empress to help her son remember how God had exalted him even beyond his parents' great nobility and dominions. Pointing out the dangers to his soul, to the realm, and to the Church, he urged Matilda to call Henry back to the right path. He assured her that he was praying for the king and for her. Thomas's letter was a masterpiece of supplication, and Matilda would respond in kind, urging Henry to listen to the pope and accept reconciliation.

In early 1165, Thomas received a long letter from Bishop Arnulf of Lisieux,[19] still an ally of Henry, predictably urging Thomas to settle his dispute with Henry but referring to Henry's approach to the French king on the matter. This alerted Thomas to the king's attempts to persuade Louis to withdraw his support from Thomas. Sailing to the continent in February, Henry met with his cousin Philip, Count of Flanders, to win him to his cause and then proceeded to work on Louis. Henry's plan was to pull Louis from Pope Alexander and then, using the threat of the Emperor Barbarossa and his new antipope, force the pope to sacrifice Thomas in order to keep Henry and England onside. In his letter, Arnulf explained to Thomas that Henry was coming around and that now was the time to seek reconciliation. Arnulf was not being truthful. If the king's actions were any indication of the state of his mind, he was not softening regarding the dispute; on the contrary, he was preparing to dabble in the mess that was European politics in order to capture his prey.

While Thomas was not persuaded by Arnulf, he was exploring the possibility of another initiative for peace. Turning to one of his secretaries, Master Ernulf, he asked him to organize a meeting between himself, Henry, and Louis. Ernulf was able to persuade Louis, who in turn conferred with Pope Alexander, and the two agreed that a meeting should be arranged. When informed of the proposal, Henry also seemed to be agreeable. The Cistercian Abbey of Le Val-Notre-Dame, near Pontoise, was chosen as the venue, and the meeting was set for April 1165.[20] Pontoise is just outside Paris, so the location was convenient for all involved and safe for Thomas. Informed of the arrangements, he made preparations to leave Pontigny for the meeting. The pope himself headed for Paris with members of his curia, no doubt hoping that some light might penetrate the darkness of the dispute. Preparations were made at the abbey to receive the pope, kings, and archbishop, but when Henry heard that the pope would be present, he decided not to go. He feared that if Alexander were present and chose to issue another condemnation of the Constitutions, that meeting could descend into a stalemate and, in frustration, the pope could go as far as to excommunicate him on the spot.

The other participants greeted the news of Henry's decision with disfavor, but the main participants did not want to abandon the effort, so a new plan was put in place. While the pope remained in Paris and Thomas at the Abbey of Le Val-Notre-Dame, Louis made his way to Gisors, where he met Henry, who was on his way to Rouen to meet up with Philip of Flanders.[21] Whatever the two kings discussed, it yielded nothing. Despite Henry's efforts to demonize his former friend, Louis was not convinced by the arguments against the archbishop. Henry had to recalibrate his plans: He decided to reach out directly to Barbarossa. If Louis and Alexander could not be torn away from Thomas, then it might be worth creating trouble for them with the emperor.

Henry had already tested the waters with the emperor early in 1165. Sending a letter to Barbarossa's chancellor, Rainald of Dassel, archbishop-elect of Cologne, at the beginning of the year, he complained about Alexander and said he felt tempted to renounce him for supporting Thomas and condemning the ancestral customs. The imperial chancellor was all too willing to listen, and when he arrived in Normandy to meet with Henry, dynastic alliances came up in their conversation.[22] Under discussion was the possibility of arranging a marriage between Henry's eldest daughter, Matilda, who was nine, and the emperor's cousin, Henry the Lion, Duke of Savoy and Bavaria, who was thirty-six and divorced from his first wife, Clementia of Zähringen. To further cement the alliance, another marriage was also suggested: between Henry's second daughter, Eleanor, who was three, and Barbarossa's son Frederick, who was just a year old.[23] In May, Henry sent envoys to the Council of Würzburg held on May 23, 1165, a gathering the emperor had called to formally recognize the antipope Paschal III as supreme pontiff. There, on Henry's behalf, his envoys confirmed on oath his agreement to the marriage plans. They also took a more decisive step: With the other delegates to the council, the English envoys swore an oath renouncing Alexander and recognizing Paschal as pope — also, it was presumed, on the king's behalf.[24]

When the Empress Matilda heard of Henry's budding alliance with Barbarossa, she was quick to rebuke him and refused to receive the emperor's ambassadors when they arrived to pay their respects.[25] Chiding Henry, she told him that they were schismatics and that he would be better served concentrating on finding a solution to his disagreement with the archbishop. Henry ignored her, but only for a while. Opposition to his plans was growing and beginning to make him think again. Word had spread that his envoys had taken the oath of Würzburg on their king's behalf, and the news was not being received kindly in England, at the papal court in Sens, or among his allies. In an attempt to backtrack, being an oath-breaker himself, Henry told one of the envoys, John of Oxford, to swear that he had done nothing against the Church and the honor of Pope Alexander; John duly did so. However, when Henry's new ally Barbarossa heard this, he was quick to respond. In a letter to the people of his realms, he insisted that the envoys did indeed take the oath — Henry was lying. Thomas, when he heard of this, was quick to condemn John of Oxford, accusing him of perjury in a letter to the Archbishop of Mainz in November 1166.[26]

Around this time, there were new developments in Rome that would give Henry further cause for concern. Tired of chaos and instability, the Romans decided to take action against Antipope Paschal. Sending a formal request to Alexander, who was still in Sens, they begged him to come and claim his see. Barbarossa was rampaging across Italy, and supplies to the city were becoming scarce. Never prepared to starve for the sake of a papacy, the Romans pragmatically changed sides. When Alexander received the request, he was overjoyed and immediately made plans to leave for Rome. He would travel to the south of France and take a boat down the Mediterranean, avoiding the Genoese and Pisan navies, allies of Barbarossa, to disembark at the port of Ostia outside Rome. Thomas decided to accompany the pope for part of the journey, as far as Bourges, and used the opportunity to discuss his situation. Alexander once again assured him that he was exonerated from the sentences imposed on him at Northampton.

Thomas expected more support from the pope, but it was not forthcoming. Later in his journey, Alexander wrote a letter to Gilbert Foliot, instructing him to urge Henry to stop his attacks on the Church. As he neared his destination, news reached the pope of the increasing fluidity of this dangerous game of kings and emperors, and he grew fearful. Writing from Clermont, he counseled Thomas to be prudent, to stay quiet and do everything he could to recover the favor of the king.[27] The archbishop may have wondered why the sudden change in the pope; it was due to finances. As Henry held on to the Peter's Pence contributions from England, Alexander was beginning to feel the pinch, as the papal treasury was badly in need of funds to meet growing costs. A more benign approach to the dispute, the pope reckoned, might convince Henry to release England's contributions. It was perhaps for this reason, or out of fear that the archbishop might get desperate in his solitude, that Alexander went further than counseling prudence — he removed Thomas's power to impose excommunication until Easter of the following year.

Returning to his life in Pontigny, Thomas was perhaps glad of the isolation and serenity of the abbey. He would soldier on, praying, studying, writing letters, and governing his archdiocese from afar. Alexander triumphantly entered Rome on November 23, 1165, as the people of the city welcomed him back and hoped for better days. Moving into the papal apartments in the Lateran Palace, he may have wished for a quiet period so that he might enjoy his pontificate, preside over the liturgical life of his diocese, and perhaps dabble in minor politics. But such luxuries were not for medieval pontiffs surrounded by squabbling monarchs and political and ecclesiastical disputes of every shade, the woes of the archbishop of Canterbury being one. Gilbert Foliot responded by letter to the pope's request, passing on Henry's replies to his concerns. The king was not aware, he claimed, that Barbarossa was excommunicated. However, while he would not impede bishops visiting the pope, appeals to Rome would be limited in accordance with the ancestral customs. And as for the archbishop, Henry insisted, he had left England of his own accord — he was the architect of his own misfortunes. For now, Gilbert assured the pope, he would get the funds from Peter's Pence; they would be sent on to him soon.

Alexander may have raised an eyebrow as he read Henry's responses, but at least the money was coming. With Thomas unable to censure anyone until Easter 1166, the pope could let the matter sit for the time being. As news emerged that Henry was at war with the Welsh princes again and that he was facing serious defeats, there was a hope that his arrogance might take a beating. In the midst of his battles, it was unpleasant for Henry to learn that the Welsh king and the Church in Wales had written to Thomas pledging obedience to him and supporting his cause. As if that were not bad enough, Henry soon heard that Adela, the new queen of France, had given birth to a son. King Louis's succession crisis was resolved, and the dynastic marriage of his daughter to young Henry was now effectively neutralized. The year 1165 was not ending well for the English king; perhaps he hoped that 1166 might be better. It might finally bring peace; if not, things could get a whole lot worse.

31

Vézelay

In March 1166, with the English king on the continent, King Louis tried once again to persuade him to meet with Thomas and seek reconciliation. Henry refused. Louis then suggested that he meet with some of Thomas's clerks who had had their incomes confiscated. Perhaps they could be reconciled in some way so as to enable them to rise out of their destitution. Henry agreed to this; he would meet the clerks after Easter at Angers, on the Loire River.[1]

Easter Sunday fell on April 24 that year; and with it, Alexander's suspension of Thomas's powers of censure lapsed. As he celebrated the various liturgies of the Resurrection of the Lord, the archbishop was contemplating what action to take. His clerks were to meet with Henry at Angers later that week: His long-suffering friend John of Salisbury, who had been living in Paris; Herbert; and another, Philip of Calne, had been granted an audience with Henry. Thomas decided to wait and see how their encounter with the king went before making a decision on how to proceed. The king had granted the clerks safe passage to and from the meetings, but King Louis led the little delegation with Thomas among them, though Henry would refuse to meet with him.

Meeting the clerks was the extent of what Henry was prepared to do.[2] John, living in a state of penury and desperate to meet whatever demands the king would impose, intended to appeal to his honor while remaining true to the archbishop. In his audience with the king, he discovered this was not possible. Henry demanded that he swear an oath to observe the ancestral customs as written down in the Constitutions and renounce his loyalty to the fugitive archbishop; John could not do it. Though he had struggled with his allegiance to Thomas at times — he could not take to a life of poverty as the archbishop could — when pushed into a corner, he would not abandon his friend.

Henry's meeting with Herbert was a much fierier affair. Like John, Herbert was asked to swear to observe the Constitutions and renounce Thomas and, like John, he refused. While John was philosophical and stoic, Herbert was sarcastic. When Henry turned nasty, Herbert gave as good as he got. A row ensued, and as Herbert cared little that he was arguing with his king and as Henry's servants were cringing in fear, the king himself was eventually reduced to silence. Like his master, this clerk had the measure of the Angevin and was not afraid to put him in his place. Sensing that his servants' fear had turned to silent admiration for the clerk, Henry realized it was time to dismiss him and send him back to his exile and to poverty.

Philip of Calne fared much better than the other two. He was not as involved in the dispute as were the others, so when Henry told him that his goods in England were confiscated, he gasped, "Dear God, why should the good king want to take something from me?"[3] This response must have disarmed the king: In an act of mercy, he told Philip that he would restore his goods to him and sent him away without even asking him to take the oath. When Philip reported this to the others, John became very sour and wondered why Henry could not be gracious with him. Herbert did not comment, as he did not expect consistency from this king. He and John were too close to the archbishop to have had a fair hearing.

Thomas and his clerks returned to their places of exile: Thomas,

Herbert, and Philip to Pontigny, but John to Reims, to the Abbey of Saint Rémi. There he would immerse himself in his books and write the works that have since made him notable. It seems that at this point, he was beginning to see that the battle between Thomas and Henry was not merely a personal one, or even a political one, but a cosmic one. His archbishop was in conflict with one who had given himself over to evil.

Not long after Thomas returned to Pontigny, he received a letter from the pope. Alexander had had a change of heart: The letter reversed what he had decreed in the last months of 1165.[4] Not only did he reiterate that the suspension was lifted, but he also informed Thomas that he should go ahead and do whatever he needed to do — the pope would confirm his actions, even any excommunications that he imposed. Alexander wrote, "We direct and command your fraternity by letters apostolic not to defer exercising ecclesiastical justice when you consider it opportune. ... By God's will we shall confirm and ratify whatever you shall reasonably do in the matter." However, the pope did impose a limit: He did not give the archbishop a particular mandate over the king. Coupled with this letter came another, dated April 8, 1166, confirming Thomas in the primacy; this letter was signed not only by the pope but also by his senior cardinals.[5]

The time had come to deal with Henry and those who had usurped the lands of Canterbury. Thomas wrote to the king in April.[6] In this letter, he cautioned Henry, asking him to listen to him with a serene mind and heed the admonition he was about to deliver. While he faced many difficulties, Thomas assured Henry, he would rather suffer at the hands of man than at the hand of God, so he would not be silent. He pleaded with him to free the Church: "In your land, the daughter of Syon, bride of the Great King is being held captive, oppressed by many, ill-used ... by those who should honor her rather than abuse her." God is patient, he reminded him, but he is also a severe avenger and will come with a strong army to free his spouse from "oppression and servitude." If Henry listened to him, Thomas assured him, God would be kind to him; but should he resist, then the sword would never leave his house until the Most High was avenged. He then urged Henry to meet with him "to have a friendly conversation."

When the letter arrived at court, the recipient was none too pleased; indeed, he was incensed and abused the messenger who delivered it — Urban, the Cistercian abbot of Cercamp. The abbot was to provide supplementary information to the king and report back to Thomas; it proved to be a rather unpleasant task. Having felt the full force of Henry's abuse, the poor abbot returned to Pontigny severely chastened and poured out his woes to the archbishop.[7] Thomas was not going to let matters be; he was prepared to write again. Bearers of these subsequent letters to Henry fared as badly as Abbot Urban.[8] In the meantime, Henry met his council in Le Mans to ask advice on how to silence the archbishop. No one had any ideas. For their confusion and fear, the king branded them traitors. His anger increased when news reached him that Pope Alexander had appointed Thomas papal legate for England with jurisdiction over the entire country with the exception of the Archdiocese of York and its archbishop, Roger de Pont L'Évêque — this was not unusual given that Theobald's legatine jurisdiction had also excluded York. Thomas's powers had increased; not only could he excommunicate, now he could also impose interdicts. The pope was arming his archbishop to the full, and that archbishop was preparing for battle.

For all his indignation, Henry realized he was in trouble. He had exhausted his means of vengeance on Thomas, and now, with the pope more powerful in Rome, he had few cards left to play. Thomas understood that he, too, had to be careful — this was not the time for imprudent gestures. He had to use his weapons carefully and effectively. First, he needed to inform the Empress Matilda that the time for talking had passed. She had done what she could to plead the archbishop's cause. Now she deserved to know that her son was about to fall under the censure of the Church. Thomas also wrote a second letter to Henry in late May, again calling him to repentance and urging him to restore the Church's freedom and her assets. This letter was warmer than the last, written in the context of the friendship that had once united them.[9] He opened this letter with a heartfelt greeting taken from Saint Paul's First Letter to the Thessalonians: "We endeavored the more eagerly and with great desire to see you face to face" (1 Thes 2:17). While the aim of the communication was to admonish the king, it was affectionate. Thomas told him he must chasten him because Henry was his king and was king over others, who deserved a good king. The archbishop must also admonish him because he regarded Henry as his spiritual son; Thomas was concerned for his welfare and salvation. The letter ended with a warning that if Henry did not repent, he would suffer "divine severity and vengeance."

Thomas then turned to write a pastoral letter to the bishops of the Canterbury province, his suffragans.[10] This piece of writing is a powerful reflection on the nature of the episcopacy, drawing on Scripture to explore the duties of the successors of the apostles. Thomas wanted his brother bishops to know the meaning of their titles, to ponder carefully and follow faithfully "the footsteps of him who was made a priest forever by God, meaning that they follow Jesus." His scriptural and theological exegesis soon gave way to the real purpose of the letter: an admonition to the bishops to now do what their office demanded. They must fulfill their duty to protect and fight for the Church now that she was under attack. He told them that the authority of the Holy See was being challenged, that those who needed to seek the pope's advice were prevented from doing so — they could not even visit him. This intolerable situation, he chided, must be dealt with.

Invoking his power as their metropolitan, but also as legate with the authority of the Roman Church, Thomas then bound the bishops in obedience by apostolic authority and "in peril of your orders" to excommunicate those who laid violent hands on clerks in the service of the Church. The same was to be done by the bishops in their neighboring dioceses. Furthermore, they were to impose a sentence of anathema on those who obstructed appellants or penitents seeking to come to the pope or to himself. This censure was to be applied not only to those who sought to obstruct but also to those royal officials who compelled others to do so. "Take care for yourselves and your churches," Thomas urged them, "lest, if you neglect this injury to the Roman Church any longer, you will rightly be seen to have conspired with the unholy against her."

Thomas left no wiggle room in this letter; the bishops had their instructions and their warning, and if they failed to heed them, their metropolitan was prepared to take action against them. Ending the letter with a direct note to Gilbert Foliot, his chief suffragan as bishop of London who was now acting as if he were primate of England, he warned him: "We issue this mandate, and we command by the virtue of obedience, at the risk of your order, and by apostolic authority, that with all speed and diligence you show this letter to our brethren, the fellow-bishops of our province, and have what is contained in it strictly observed."

At the end of May, Thomas and some of his clerks left Pontigny to undertake a pilgrimage to Soissons, 120 miles to the north of Pontigny, before making their way 35 miles south of Pontigny to Vézelay, where the great abbey held the relics of Saint Mary Magdalene.[11] There was method in Thomas's madness; he had carefully planned a particular spiritual program for a serious reason. The Shrine of Our Lady of Soissons was renowned for a relic believed to be the Blessed Virgin's shoe or slipper. In 1128, when the city was ravaged by the plague, victims had come to the shrine to invoke the Mother of God, and she was said to have appeared to them and healed their affliction. Thomas had always been devoted to Our Lady; his mother had instilled in his heart a deep and childlike devotion, and he never lost it. In moments of trial and difficulty, he turned to the Mother of God and asked her help. Joining pilgrims in Soissons, he spent three days in prayer and penance, asking Our Lady's advice on what he was planning to do.

Soissons had two other shrines that pilgrims visited as part of their spiritual exercises. One was to Saint Gregory the Great, the pope whom the English considered their particular papal saint because he sent Saint Augustine to England as an apostle to proclaim the Christian faith. As a successor of Saint Augustine, Thomas felt a special affinity with Saint Gregory, and now he turned to him for help in the great matter he was considering. The second shrine was the tomb of Saint Drausinus.[12] In the seventh century, when this local saint was bishop of Soissons, he had had to deal with a tyrant. Local piety held that those who spent the night at the saint's tomb would be made invincible, so he was invoked by those preparing to go into battle. As he commended his troubles to Saint Drausinus, Thomas settled down for a night at the tomb alongside other pious souls who sought the saint's help in their troubles.

Leaving Soissons on June 3, Thomas made his way to Vézelay. As he traveled, he heard that Henry had fallen seriously ill.[13] The Benedictine Abbey of Saint Mary Magdalene at Vézelay was one of France's great shrines. Founded in the eighth century, it became a place of pilgrimage in 1050 when relics of Saint Mary Magdalene were translated there from her tomb in Saint-Maximin in Provence. The shrine's popularity grew over the years, and as the crowds of pilgrims increased, a new church had to be constructed to accommodate them; it was completed and dedicated in 1104. The abbey had been the venue for a number of important events over the years. Saint Bernard had preached the Second Crusade there, and now Thomas was about to make history there, too: the formal excommunication of those oppressing the Church in England.

That he chose the Shrine of Saint Mary Magdalene as the location where he would carry out his censure was no coincidence. Saint Mary Magdalene is venerated in the Church as the apostle to the apostles because Jesus chose her to announce the Resurrection. She had been rebuked by their disbelief, but later vindicated when the Risen Christ came into their midst and revealed himself. Thomas could identify with that. He, too, had suffered the rebuke of the successors of the apostles as he tried to proclaim the truth in their midst; now he too put his trust in the Risen Christ. Perhaps he found companionship in the figure of Saint Mary Magdalene for another reason. In her encounter with Jesus outside the tomb on that Easter Sunday, she had tried to cling to him, to the old life and ways, but Christ had urged her, "Do not hold me" (Jn 20:17). Now her life had to change, everything had to change — now the Gospel had to be proclaimed. Thomas would have understood that: To carry out the mission God had given him, he too had had to change.

Thomas arrived in Vézelay just before the Solemnity of Pentecost, which was celebrated on June 12 that year. As archbishop and papal legate to England, he was invited to offer High Mass in the church for the solemnity and to preach the sermon. Clad in the red vestments symbolizing the fire of the Holy Spirit and attended by a large liturgical retinue, Thomas processed to the high altar of the abbey and offered the Mass of Pentecost. A large crowd gathered in the church for the celebration, and many were intrigued to see the famous archbishop of Canterbury, who was being spoken of all over Europe as a hero of the Faith. [14]

As Thomas delivered the sermon, he stood at his full height and appeared awesome in the pulpit; Herbert would later testify that it seemed as if he were filled with a fire — he seemed to be "a man possessed" by the Holy Spirit. In his sermon, Thomas gave the pilgrims an account of all that had happened in England in recent years and of the oppression the Church there was now facing. He denounced the king and rebuked him for his failure to respond to his communications and reprimands. Then, to the surprise of his clerks, he condemned Henry's "ancestral customs," describing them as perversities. He had not told his clerks that he was going to do this for fear they would try to dissuade him. It came as an even greater shock to them when, from the pulpit, he began pronouncing the excommunication of all those who were enforcing, or even defending, the so-called ancestral customs. He also decreed that the bishops of England were now absolved from any obligation to obey these customs.

The archbishop was just getting started. As the congregation listened in astonished silence, he named Henry's envoys to the imperial council at Würzburg, John of Oxford and Richard of Ilchester, and pronounced them excommunicated for taking the oath of the schismatic Germans. John had also taken the office of Dean of Salisbury without Thomas's consent, so his censure was also in punishment for that. He then excommunicated Richard de Lucy and Jocelin de Bailleul[15] for promoting royal tyranny and drawing up the Constitutions of Clarendon. For their usurpation of Church property, he excommunicated Ranulf de Broc and his henchmen Hugh de Saint Clair and Thomas FitzBernard. If Thomas also wished to excommunicate Henry, he could not, in obedience to the limit imposed by Alexander; the king was spared for now. John of Salisbury, who suspected Henry might come under censure, had also cautioned against it. Aware of Henry's illness, Thomas may well have felt some pity for the king — if the illness that had struck him down claimed his life, Thomas might risk his damnation by excommunicating him. He may also have hoped that the illness might bring Henry to his senses. In his final censure, Thomas suspended Jocelin, bishop of Salisbury, for allowing the appointment of John of Oxford. His sermon ended with a final warning to Henry to repent and a public declaration that if he did not, Thomas would excommunicate him.

When he returned to his lodgings, Thomas had his secretaries write a series of letters, all dated June 12, 1166, informing those who had been excommunicated of their censure, while notifying various bishops, including the pope, of his decrees. He also composed a letter to the bishops of his province rebuking them for not acting on his last pastoral letter. He explained to them that he had deferred, for now, excommunicating the king to allow him come to his senses. He then ordered them to act on these censures and publish the pastoral letter.

He also wrote another letter to Henry, this one stronger and more threatening than the last.[16] He asked him if he wanted to be a good and Catholic king. If so, then he must remember he was a son of the Church and not its director. Launching into a litany of examples, Thomas exposed how Henry sought to control and oppress, rather than serve God. He then spoke of a kind of separation of Church and secular kingship — God appointed the priests, not the powers of the world, to govern the Church. Their appointment was to be made by the Church and not by the world. "Christian kings," he told him, "should submit their judgments to ecclesiastical prelates, not set their judgments above them." He warned Henry that kings had been excommunicated, giving examples while urging him to repent. If he did not desist from his actions, God would "come in the staff of his fury." In a veiled way, he informed Henry that he would excommunicate him if he did not relent. The archbishop ended his letter asking his former friend to remember his last day: He would die, he reminded him, so he needed to repent "in true humility and speedy penance."

The excommunications at Vézelay caused uproar in England.[17] The bishops were now compromised and placed in a difficult position; in desperation, they dashed off a series of letters to the pope asking him to lift the censures. For Ranulf de Broc, a brute of a man whose currency was violence and who cared for neither God nor man, the excommunication meant nothing except that he was now intent on repaying the archbishop for disgracing him in public. Even Queen Eleanor was infuriated: Jocelin de Bailleul was now in her service, so she regarded his excommunication as an offense against her person. From then on, she was Thomas's sworn enemy, not that she had ever been a great friend before this.[18]

Despite the frantic appeals of the English bishops, and though he was losing his grasp on Rome as Barbarossa was on the march again to return his antipope to Rome, Alexander was true to his word: He confirmed and ratified the excommunications.[19] Henry, now recovering from his illness, was not prepared to repent or even to suffer Thomas's latest attack. Putting pressure on the bishops, he called a council to meet in London in June 1166 in which he urged them to appeal the excommunications.[20] He charged Roger de Pont L'Évêque, Gilbert Foliot, and the excommunicated John of Oxford to go to Rome and appeal to Alexander to revoke his ratification. If Alexander refused, Henry told them, and if he would not depose Thomas and recognize the ancestral customs, then Henry would renounce Alexander and give his allegiance to the antipope. With Barbarossa in Alexander's backyard, Henry hoped this ultimatum would force Alexander to comply.

32

The Legates

As Thomas returned to Pontigny, he may have wondered how Henry would respond: Would he finally come around and seek reconciliation? Knowing the king as well as he did, he must have doubted it. As long as Henry had some semblance of power, he would not back down on anything unless it was in his interest; and for now at least, finding common ground with his archbishop was most likely against his interests as he saw them. As his bishops were rallying to Rome in the following months with their appeals against the censures, Henry had another trick up his sleeve — he would oust Thomas from Pontigny and render him homeless. If the archbishop were forced to drift around France as a pariah, he surmised, it might break him down. The king began to put pressure on the English and Norman Cistercians. Writing to the General Council of the Cistercians at the motherhouse at Cîteaux in September 1166, Henry complained that the monks at Pontigny had offered sanctuary to a traitor. He promised the council that if Thomas were not expelled from Pontigny, then he would expel all Cistercians from his realms and seize their property. Indeed, if Cistercians assisted Thomas in any way, he would do so.[1]

Gilbert, the grand abbot of Cîteaux and an Englishman, arrived at Pontigny with an entourage of bishops and abbots to inform Thomas of Henry's threat. While he was adamant in his refusal to be driven out, Thomas was concerned for the monks at Pontigny who had opened their home to the exiles and for the Cistercian Order, for which he had a great regard.[2] Though it was fall and winter was coming, he decided that it would be best to leave the abbey to spare the abbot and monks. On November 11, Thomas left his oasis of peace. Abbot Guérin and the monks were in tears as they bid him farewell; doubtless the same could not be said for Herbert, who had never settled and had found the austerities and isolation hard to take. Herbert now appealed to Thomas for them to find an urban setting, but Thomas disagreed — it would be better for them to stay in a monastery or another place of solitude. When the other clerks backed Herbert's suggestion, Thomas relented.[3] He sent Herbert to King Louis to inform him that they were being forced to leave their refuge and asked him for help. The French king was willing to help and successfully interceded with the abbot of the Abbey of Saint Columba, outside Sens, to provide accommodation for the exiles. Saint Columba's was much more to Herbert's liking — it was just outside the city and situated in pleasant countryside. Indeed, Herbert was so happy with the sweetness of Sens after the austerity of Pontigny, he wrote a panegyric of "la douce France" in his biography of the archbishop.[4] Meanwhile, not wishing to be a burden on the community, Thomas wondered how they would pay for their accommodation; King Louis assured him that he would cover all expenses.

The Abbey of Saint Columba was home to a Benedictine community and dedicated to a third-century virgin martyr whose tomb was preserved in the abbey church. Suffering under the Emperor Aurelian, Columba was beheaded near a fountain and her body left unburied for some time, until a man who was healed of blindness through her intercession interred her. A chapel was built over her grave, and later the abbey. A new church had just been built, and Pope Alexander had dedicated it on April 26, 1164, during his own exile in Sens. The exiles received a warm welcome by the abbot and monks of the abbey, and while Thomas was gratified and grateful, he was low in spirits. The night before he had left Pontigny, he had had a disturbing dream in which he saw himself put to death by four knights. He was also aware by now that the censures pronounced at Vézelay were being successfully challenged and contained by Henry and the bishops in England.

As at Pontigny, Thomas entered fully into the life of the monastery, joining the monks for the Divine Office, offering Mass, spending a great deal of time in personal prayer, and resuming his penances. He was eating less and had lost a lot of weight; he was now gaunt and, having been wearing a beard for some time, had deteriorated greatly in appearance. While outwardly he seemed to be living well, sleeping with fine linens on his bed and taking good wine at his table, he was hiding a severe ascetic program of penance and reparation. His wine was diluted — his stomach ailment was as bad as ever, so he needed something to settle it, and now a little wine seemed to help. He was wearing rough and uncomfortable clothing. His chaplain continued to scourge him with the discipline frequently, and the night vigils continued as before. Relating the extremity of these penances, one biographer was led to believe that Thomas had killed any carnal desires that he may have still had to that point.[5] But now he was always cold; he found it difficult to get warm. He ate ginger and cloves to try to help revive him, but his health was in serious decline.

His greatest cross at this time, apart from the political and emotional effects of his dispute with Henry, was the endless denunciations being made against him. He was accused of being arrogant and stubborn and regarded as a traitor both to his king and to the Church — a man immersed in folly who was prepared to destroy everyone and anyone so he could claim victory. He had been in correspondence with Gilbert Foliot over a number of months, and this added to his suffering. The bishop of London was attacking him for the excommunications, sparing nothing to expose what he saw as Thomas's faults in this whole affair. Gilbert took every opportunity to denounce him and remind him how completely unfit he was for the office of archbishop of Canterbury. Thomas had defended himself and had made his own accusations against Gilbert, but in his heart he seemed to believe that his nemesis was probably correct in part — hence his need for penance. For the sake of the Church, however, he could not give in to Henry; whatever pride he had, his physical penances were the means of atoning for his faults. His penances and continual prayer were also the means by which he implored God to allow him to prevail over the king for the sake of the Church — Thomas still had far to go in his spiritual journey. In the end, it was not his victory over Henry that would give the Church the hope of preserving her liberties; rather, it was his apparent defeat beneath the blow of a sword that would achieve it. Thomas had yet to understand that.

Another cross awaited him. Pope Alexander's position was worsening, and this would have consequences for Thomas. Barbarossa had invaded Italy again and was making his way toward Rome. The pope was also in serious financial difficulty. When Henry's delegation arrived before the pope in late 1166, the pontiff realized that he might need to offer some gesture to maintain good relations. In his meeting with the pope, John of Oxford laid out the king's objections. Recognizing that he had to give the king something as a token of goodwill and in hope of reconciliation, Alexander decided to lift John's excommunication and suspend Thomas's power to impose further censures.[6] When Thomas heard this, he was downcast — the pope was wavering again. In a letter to the archbishop, written in December 1166, Alexander tried to be conciliatory.[7] He promised to do what he could to get Henry to meet with him, but until he could achieve that, Thomas had to be patient and be prudent. If Henry persisted in his obstinacy, then Alexander would restore Thomas's disciplinary powers. In the meantime, the pope had decided to appoint two envoys to act as mediators to help achieve reconciliation. He wrote to the bishops of England in the spring of 1167 to inform them that he was appointing two legates a latere[8] with plenitude of power to mediate between King Henry and Archbishop Thomas. In the meantime, the pope decreed, any of those under the censure of excommunication, if in danger of death, could be absolved by a suitable priest on the condition that the excommunicated person swore that, if he recovered, he would submit to a papal decision.

By February 1167, two prelates had been chosen. Alexander had allowed Henry to choose one, and he had decided on William of Pavia.

William was in royal favor because he had granted the license for young Henry's marriage to Louis VII's daughter. William was a Cistercian, a monk of the Abbey of Clairvaux, who rose to become the archdeacon of Pavia. His star continued to rise when he was first made cardinal deacon and then elevated to the higher rank of cardinal priest. Thomas knew him, having met him at Sens during his discussions with the pope, and he would have known that he was favorable to Henry. Alexander chose the second legate, Otto of Brescia, cardinal deacon of Saint Nicholas in Carcere Tulliano. It was meant to be a more impartial choice, but the fact that Henry was happy with the pope's candidate was seen as an ill omen for Thomas's supporters. When King Louis heard who the legates were, he was not impressed either; in fact, he was antagonistic toward them.[9]

William and Otto left Rome in May 1167, but their journey to France would take five months, as many delays lay ahead. For one thing, they almost came face-to-face with Barbarossa's army and had to make various diversions to avoid it. William also had to carry out a mission in Sicily to scuttle support for the antipope, and he did this en route to Normandy. As the legates inched their way toward Thomas and Henry, Barbarossa arrived at the gates of Rome, making things worse for the pope. On July 22, the emperor's armies entered the Eternal City, forcing Alexander to flee south — he would take up residence in the city of Benevento and continue to govern the Church from there. With his antipope in tow, the emperor made his way to Saint Peter's Basilica and enthroned him as "Pope" Paschal III. In exile once more, Alexander realized that his bargaining power with Henry was much diminished and sent word to the legates that they were not to be distracted from their mission, which was to effect reconciliation, but were also to keep Henry out of the emperor's camp.

In the weeks that followed, the pope found that his position was not as bad as he thought: Rome's sultry summer was inflicting miseries on Barbarossa and his troops. Surrounded by swamps, Rome was a cesspit of malaria, and during that particularly wet and hot summer, the mosquitoes were in fine fettle and finding German blood very much to their taste. Many of the emperor's troops were struck down with malaria and other ailments. A large number died, and Barbarossa's hold on the city weakened. Making things worse for the emperor, the Romans were none too hospitable — they had already expelled the antipope some time before, and they were not pleased that he had turned up again. The emperor, his loyalty governed by pragmatism, realized that a tactical retreat was in order if he wished to save his army; the antipope could fend for himself. Leaving Rome in August, he made his way north, only to face blockades by Lombard tribes intent on revenge, and had to fight his way to safe refuge in Pavia. Alexander was thrilled. However, when he attempted to return to Rome, he discovered that the antipope remained in charge; even though the people of the city were not pleased with his presence, Paschal had enough support and armed men around him to hold Saint Peter's Basilica and the Lateran Palace. Alexander would remain in Benevento until February 1170, even though Rome was free. The penultimate Barbarossan antipope, Giovanni, abbot of Struma, self-styled Callixtus, would make peace and relinquish his claim in August 1178. Nevertheless, Alexander was in a much stronger position; sending a message to the legates William and Otto, he extended their remit. They were to strive to make peace between Henry and Louis, who were arguing again. The dispute over the archbishop of Canterbury had strained the relationship between the two kings, and that had to be healed. In a gesture to Thomas, the pope informed the legates that they were not to go to England, even if Henry insisted, and he forbade them from consecrating any English bishops.

The legates finally arrived at their destination, Caen, in early November. Henry wanted a show of strength from the hierarchy for the legates' benefit, to reveal the extent of the opposition to the archbishop, so he called some of the bishops of England and Normandy to the conference.[10] Meeting with Henry, the legates found him unruly and angry, grumbling even more than usual about Thomas's supposed treason; things were not looking good. The conference got off to a bad start when the king's clerks found discrepancies between Alexander's letters to Henry and the legates' letters of credential. It seemed, Henry said, that the legates did not have the power to force Thomas to accept their judgment, and this led to a heated argument. Henry and his advisors eventually agreed to accept the legates as judges in the case; it remained to be seen whether Thomas would accept them. When the ancestral customs came up for discussion, the king insisted that they were not novelties. Protracted negotiations followed, but it seemed to the legates at the end of it that they had managed, or at least they thought they had managed, to force a concession out of Henry, as he appeared to renounce his prohibition of appeals to the pope and his requirement that clerks had to appear before royal courts. It seems Henry, in his complaints about Thomas, also suggested that the archbishop was a source of discord between him and King Louis.

In the end, the legates' conference with Henry achieved little; they just hoped they had kept the door open for further negotiations. They were sure they would have more luck with the archbishop. As Henry had refused to grant Thomas safe passage into Normandy, the legates arranged to meet him at a site in France near the border with Normandy, between Gisors and Trie. They met him on November 18, but before they could get down to discussing reconciliation, the archbishop bombarded them with complaints, including his difficulty in getting horses and the problems he faced at having to gather his clerks, who at this stage were scattered all over France.[11] Once they had offered some assurance that these difficulties would be dealt with, the legates were able to discuss Henry's grievances with him, asking Thomas how he thought he could respond to them. Peace, they told him, could be achieved only if he remembered all that Henry had done for him, and if he in turn behaved with humility and moderation. Would he, they asked, be prepared to agree to this? After speaking with his clerks, Thomas said that he would only humiliate himself before the king as long as the honor of God and the liberty of the Church could be safeguarded, his good name could be preserved, and the possessions of the Church and his men could be returned.

The legates then tried to bring Thomas to a practical discussion of how he would demonstrate this humility. They asked him whether he would agree to the ancestral customs — that some sort of compromise be put in place whereby the king would quietly implement them, and Thomas would turn a blind eye and pretend not to notice. Thomas refused. They were evil customs, he said, and silence implies consent. He would prefer to die in exile, even die in defense of justice, than make peace on such terms. He reminded them that Pope Alexander had condemned these customs himself — how then could they be trying to get him to give his assent to them? After he had established that the legates' letters of credentials revealed that they actually had no power of judgment over him, as far as Thomas was concerned, there was no use continuing the conference. He told William and Otto that he could not give them any more answers until the confiscated lands and assets of Canterbury were returned. Thomas was not just being difficult — he was asserting his rights under canon law, which decreed that such discussions could not take place while one party held the possessions of the other as a bargaining chip. When these were restored, Thomas told the legates, he would be happy to proceed in accordance with the pope's instructions.

William and Otto knew they were not going to get anywhere with Thomas. They had to return to Henry; but before doing so, they sought an audience with King Louis. They had no luck there either; Louis was firmly on Thomas's side insofar as he could be.[12] The legates had hoped to find some evidence in their meeting with him to suggest that, in the royal disputes, Thomas might have incited trouble between the two kings, as Henry had claimed. The archbishop had always denied it, and now not only did Louis deny it, but he took an oath to confirm his denial. Indeed, Louis told them, Thomas had always advised him to preserve peace with Henry. This was not what the legates wanted to hear. Returning to Henry, who was now in Argentan, the legates updated him on their progress, or lack of it. Annoyed with the legates' apparent impotence, he declared that Thomas had made fools of them but that he, Henry, had been victorious: He had been proven correct in all he said about the archbishop. He then stormed out of the room. As the audience was over, the legates went to find horses to get back to their lodgings, but quickly discovered there were none. Their mounts were gone, and they were stranded. After some time, they were able to borrow horses, but upon reaching their lodgings, they found themselves under an unofficial house arrest for a number of days. When they tried to contact the king, they discovered that Henry had disappeared; he had gone hunting and was avoiding any contact with them.[13]

On November 29, a delegation of bishops led by Roger de Pont L'Évêque, Gilbert Foliot, and Hilary of Chichester arrived to meet with the legates. Gilbert attacked the legates for their naivete in their encounter with Thomas and their utter failure to deal with him. He informed them that Henry was going to renew the prosecution of fiscal mismanagement against the archbishop and demand the restitution for his embezzlement that Henry had claimed was owed to him at the Council of Northampton. Henry finally met the legates again on December 5, the day they were permitted to leave for Italy. He begged them to suspend Thomas or, better still, depose him and send him somewhere else. Suddenly, to the astonishment of the gathered assembly, Henry began to weep; it was a display to convince the legates that he was, in fact, the wronged party. William of Pavia was soft enough to join the king in shedding tears, but Otto could barely hold back his laughter.[14] Though the amateur dramatics did not convince Otto, the king managed to persuade the two men to absolve the excommunications imposed by Thomas at Vézelay. The legates left to meet Thomas again. In their conference with him on December 14, they presented the appeals of the bishops, but Thomas rejected them. He was also angry at their absolving the excommunications; calling it a scandal, he informed the legates that he considered the absolutions to be invalid.

In the end, the legates departed for Italy defeated. It now seemed that the only one who might be able to make any progress was Alexander. Though these two cardinals had been considered favorable to Henry, their view of him had changed. Otto wrote to the pope to tell him that he was shocked by the king's attitude and had decided that he would have nothing more to do with the attempts to censure Thomas. As for the pope, he was inundated again with complaints from every side.[15] The legates considered themselves scapegoats, and everyone else was disappointed, angry, and, it seemed, even more entrenched in their positions. Louis of France was outraged at his treatment by William and Otto, and his nobles also lodged complaints about the offense to their king. Henry told the pope that the legates had acted in a very irregular manner — they had attempted to deprive him of his rights over the Church and clergy of England, he insisted. And as for Thomas, he was aggrieved at the pope for his failure to defend him as he was trying to defend the Church. Alexander realized that the legates had made the situation a hundred times worse.

33
The Two Kings

As the year 1168 dawned, Emperor Frederick Barbarossa was in serious trouble; this would bode well for Pope Alexander, but not
for Henry of England. While Henry was occupied with uprisings in the
County of Poitou on the continent — the local barons were resisting
changes to administration and customs — Barbarossa was still struggling with the Lombards in the north of Italy. In the spring he had been
forced to flee north to Savoy disguised as a servant. As Barbarossa pondered renouncing his antipope and finally accepting Alexander in the
hope of finding a way out of his troubles, the antipope Paschal III found
himself in dire straits in Rome. The antipope's troubles would only end
with his death on September 20, 1168, but the Church's troubles would
continue, as Paschal was replaced by another antipope, Callixtus III, who
discovered he had even less support than his predecessor.

Barbarossa did not contemplate recanting for long; though weakened, he resolved to fight on. Henry, on the other hand, was feeling the
brunt of the emperor's beleaguered situation. As another of Henry's em-

bassies arrived at Benevento in early 1168 seeking to have Thomas deposed, Alexander was able to resist their demands. Henry then tried to bribe his way into the pope's affections, but that did not work either. At their wits' end, his ambassadors resorted to extreme threat: They told the pope that if he did not depose the archbishop, Henry would convert to Islam and make all England Muslim.[1] While the pope was deaf to this intimidation too, he informed them that he would maintain for now the suspension of Thomas's powers to censure.

Thomas, by various means, letters included, was also putting pressure on the pope, reacting strongly to Henry's continued attempts to have him deposed. Alexander wrote to him in January 1168, again advising him to be patient and not to make peace with Henry at the expense of the Church.[2] Thomas may well have balked at this advice — he was in exile for doing just what the pope advised. Alexander also suggested that he should go as far as he could, saving his honor as a bishop and mindful of the liberty of the Church, to humble himself before the king and do whatever he must do to recover his friendship and grace. Easier said than done, the archbishop may have said to himself.

Life for the exiles at Saint Columba's was pleasant enough: Thomas and his companions participated in the spiritual life of the community, and Thomas maintained his life of prayer, penance, and study. Financially, things were tight. Louis had paid their expenses, but since John Cumin, archdeacon of Bath and a supporter of Henry, had convinced him to reduce his contributions, the exiles were in need of funds to make up the loss.[3] Thomas was forced to find ways to raise money to pay their way at the abbey and to fund his cause, which was proving quite expensive. John of Salisbury went questing on his behalf, and this helped, but it also gave rise to criticism that Thomas was sending out the begging bowl to maintain a lavish lifestyle. While he was not in the lap of luxury, Thomas had never had to budget — up until then, he had always had what he needed to meet his needs and those of his guests — but by 1168 he was in serious debt, and funds were spent as soon as they arrived.

Another attempt at reconciliation was arranged for May 1168.[4] The pope appointed a number of monastic leaders to engage with the feuding parties. Alexander had initially selected the bishop of Belley, Saint

Anthelm,[5] and the prior of the motherhouse of the Carthusian Order; however, he revised this decision and instead chose Simon, prior of the Carthusian house of Mont-Dieu near Sedan in the Ardennes, and Bernard de la Coudre, prior of Grandmont in La Marche. The house from which Bernard hailed was within Henry's jurisdiction, and the king was known to respect his order.[6] These delegates were charged with delivering a letter of admonition to Henry urging reconciliation with Thomas. Should he fail to do so before Ash Wednesday of the following year, 1169, which fell on March 5, then the suspension on the archbishop would be lifted; Thomas would be free to impose sanctions again.[7]

Things did not go as planned. Henry was on the road with his army, so the monks took some time to find him, and with Thomas in Sens, there was a lot of traveling with little progress. To make matters more complicated, Henry and Louis were fighting again — the French king, thinking that the English king was on his last legs, had entered into a confederacy with Henry's enemies in the hopes of dismantling the Angevin Empire. Henry had retaliated. The war that followed caused enough trouble of its own; but ironically, it would lead to another hope of reconciliation and the first meeting between king and archbishop in four years. By the beginning of 1169, Louis decided he had had enough of fighting and agreed to meet with Henry to resolve their dispute. In light of this coming reconciliation, the pope's delegates saw an opportunity and urged Thomas to attend so there could be another opportunity to resolve the crisis. The two kings agreed to meet at Montmirail, a neutral venue halfway between Le Mans and Chartres, on January 6, 1169, the Epiphany.

When Thomas was informed of the plan and summoned to Montmirail, he realized that this could indeed be his last chance for reconciliation. By now, the dispute had taken its toll. Though only forty-eight, he looked much older. Frighteningly gaunt and weak, he was suffering bouts of depression and feelings of growing isolation. It seemed his only refuge was prayer, and he found solace in devotion and in the liturgical life of the abbey. But his spirit was still robust, and when he needed it, he discovered the strength required to continue fighting for the sake of the Church in England. Given his faith, he knew this strength came from God's grace. Even though king, pope, and bishops seemed to have abandoned him, Christ had not. There is a tradition that Christ actually appeared to Thomas to sustain him during his exile. Whether this happened or not cannot be established for certain, but there is no doubt that Thomas was aware that Jesus was with him, and he kept the vision of the suffering Christ before him in his daily recollection and in moments of trial.

Thomas made his way to Montmirail and, upon arrival, discovered a huge gathering of troops and royal officials from the Anglo-Norman and French courts.[8] A number of ecclesiastical figures were there to ensure that this crucial meeting between Thomas and Henry brought an end to the dispute. To his surprise, he also saw imperial officials: Barbarossa too, it seems, had a stake in the discussions between Henry and Louis. The emperor did not favor an outright reconciliation, at least not one that would affect his alliance with Henry; rather, he wanted to support Henry and put pressure on Louis to make concessions.

As he usually did, Henry would rise to the occasion in the negotiations, employing the theatrical skills he had demonstrated to William and Otto, to the latter's amusement. Presenting himself as a most reasonable man, a man pleading with his liege lord Louis, he sought peace. What Louis thought of the display is not known, but Henry milked what he thought was the French king's gullibility and added that if he found reconciliation with the archbishop, he would take the cross and go on Crusade. As a man who had been on pilgrimage to Jerusalem, and for whom the Crusade was an important service to Christ and the Church, Louis was swayed and agreed to reconciliation.

The two kings established a new treaty, once again confirmed in the dynastic alliance already effected — the marriage of their children young Henry and Princess Margaret. Henry agreed that the young couple would inherit all his dominions. Henry's younger son Richard, later known as Richard the Lionheart, would be married to Louis's daughter Alys, and they would inherit the Duchy of Aquitaine. Richard's younger brother, Geoffrey, would have Brittany, but he would have to offer feudal homage to Louis. Henry would also renew his feudal homage as Duke of Normandy. On Louis's part, he would recognize Brittany as Henry's and stop sending aid to the rebel barons there. Pleased with the outcome, Henry promised Louis that he would arrange for the coronation of young Henry and Margaret.[9]

Thomas was now waiting to play his part in the drama. As he heard of the reconciliation between the two kings, he was no longer sure whether he could rely on Louis to defend him — the newly forged royal friendship was too fresh and precious to allow a fissure for the sake of the archbishop. Papal officials held a conference with him; they advised him to follow the pope's command to do all he could to effect reconciliation, to humble himself as much as possible to please Henry. Henry was in a state of constant anxiety when it came to the archbishop, they reminded him, and he was highly sensitive for his honor on this matter. Thomas would have to throw himself on the king's mercy, but of course he could not sacrifice the Church to do it. It may have seemed to the poor archbishop that they wanted him to square the circle, but he realized he had to swallow his pride again and do what was required. The advisors told him that he should agree verbally to observe the ancestral customs. This whole affair was not just about Thomas of Canterbury, they insisted — this was about peace in Christendom. If he made a mistake now, the result would be a disaster for the Church.

They broke him down. Tired and ill, Thomas could not resist the arguments or indeed the prestige of these papal officials. While he consented, he had a sense of something evil at work. He had resisted Henry because this king sought to bring the Church under his control, to govern it as if he were Christ's vicar in England; the ancestral customs were only a part of that. The real issue was the perverted will of the king. And yet, though they all knew it, these papal envoys, men of the Church, were prepared — for political expediency and a superficial, unsteady peace — to turn a blind eye. As he mulled over what he had endured these last years and what he was now being urged to do, he may have wondered what was going on. Were these churchmen, who had been bickering away at him for the last few hours, asking him to sell the Church in England into slavery, into the unreasonable will of a tyrannical king? It seemed to Thomas that the answer was yes.

After the two kings had celebrated their reconciliation, the royal officials called for the archbishop of Canterbury to come before them.

Thomas was escorted to where Henry and Louis sat. There was a large audience gathered to witness the meeting: bishops, barons, and royal and Church officials. His own companions, his fellow exiles, also looked on, no doubt worried but hoping that this awful drama would be over soon so that they could get back to normal life, whatever that might be. Facing his former friend after so many years, Thomas likely noticed a change in him. Now thirty-five, Henry was a man immersed in power, transformed by his battles and victories, a man used to getting his own way. He was as turbulent as ever and, little did Thomas know, the king's marriage was not good, burdened as it was by the king's now frequent infidelities.

The king himself would certainly have noticed a change in Thomas: The elegant chancellor had become an old man, with the marks of suffering on his face and body, and he seemed to have diminished in height.[10] Though he was weakened and obviously in poor health, there was still a light in Thomas's eyes, which the king may have interpreted as defiance. Henry was not a man given to pity, as many had discovered through personal experience — including Bishop Arnulf of Lisieux, who had tried to advise Thomas. There was no chance of turning his heart, no reason to expect him to be magnanimous. Neither was he a man to forgive and forget what he saw as betrayal. When one transgressed against this king of England, nothing less than utter obeisance would satisfy the hope for reconciliation, and even then there could never be hope of renewing old friendship. Thomas just had to fall on his sword and give in; that was the only hope for peace.

Thomas, as instructed, fell to his knees and waited. The king had the prerogative to speak first. Perhaps delighting in the moment, Henry waited a moment before speaking. All he wanted, he said, was a simple verbal assent to the ancestral customs; that would be enough. He looked to the archbishop — now he was allowed to speak. Thomas stood. Having memorized the response the papal officials had told him to deliver, he began to recite it faithfully and humbly. Throwing himself upon the mercy of the king, he assured him that he had indeed found fault with himself in this matter and that the afflictions that he had suffered were the fruit of his own failings.

All was going well, and the papal officials were pleased — the archbishop had taken the bitter medicine in good part and was doing exactly as he had been advised. It seemed as if the dispute was about to come to an end. As Herbert of Bosham recorded later in his biography, Thomas, having said what was required, finished the speech by offering the pledge that was demanded of him, saying, "Therefore my lord, on all that is between you and me, today I submit my cause to your clemency and judgment in the presence of our lord king of France, the bishops, nobles and others present here." He would observe the ancestral customs to win peace and favor and do all he could in accord with Henry's will ... "saving God's honor."[11]

34

Ad Honorem Dei

If there was a stunned silence, it did not last long; the gasps from the gathered onlookers were quickly drowned out by Henry's roar. The king launched into a torrent of abuse, calling Thomas a traitor, a proud and vain man. He mocked the archbishop for trying to drag the honor of God into the dispute. "I will never accept these words," he cried, "or it will appear that the archbishop wishes God's honor preserved and not I — though I really want it preserved more than he does!"[1] Henry then reiterated his accusations against Thomas, now adding a claim that when Thomas was chancellor he had received oaths of honor and fealty from the king's men — an act of dishonor to his king.[2] Thomas remained silent. He had finally learned that it was a waste of time trying to interject and respond to Henry when he was like this; he would wait until the king had burned himself out. When he had, Thomas quietly and serenely responded to the accusations.

As chancellor, he reminded Henry, he had done a great many things for the honor of his king. He had been faithful and rendered the service that was required of him in that office. Henry should not be attacking him now; indeed, he should be thanking him for his dutifulness. Pointing to King Louis, Thomas said that this king of France and all those present, indeed the whole world, knew how much he had done to serve the king's honor; that Henry should use that service as a reproach against him was shameful and indecent.

Henry knew deep down that Thomas was right. How could he have forgotten his then-chancellor's abandonment of his spiritual father, Archbishop Theobald, in his last days because of his sense of duty to his new master? But Henry was selective in his recollections. He refused to listen to the archbishop and turned to Louis to denounce him: "My lord, take note, if you please, how foolishly, how arrogantly, this man deserted his church," he said. He did not expel him from England, he protested to Louis; rather, Thomas voluntarily took flight in the middle of the night. "But now," Henry continued, "he is suggesting to you that he is pursuing the cause of the Church and is suffering for the sake of justice, and in this way he has deceived many." Henry assured Louis that he wanted the archbishop to return to preside over the Church in full liberty as did his saintly predecessors.[3]

At the mention of the saintly predecessors, Louis, a devout man, seemed to be won over to Henry's cause, just as Henry intended. The English king was not merely expressing his exasperation. He wanted to drive a wedge between Thomas and his most powerful and generous ally. Louis, for his part, was not just weighing up the accusations against Thomas. He knew full well that Henry had no intention of allowing the Church to preserve her liberties if they affected his power — he, too, was acquainted with the Constitutions of Clarendon — but there was now the question of the dynastic alliance. Louis turned to Thomas and sighed, "Lord Archbishop, do you want to be more than a saint?"[4]

While Henry was pleased with this rebuke from Thomas's most ardent supporter, the archbishop was not upset or disturbed. With an extraordinary serenity and respectful confidence, he responded. He did indeed want to return and watch over the Church in his care with its liberties, as did his holy predecessors, but he refused to accept the ancestral customs that were, in fact, to the detriment of the Church's liberty. As

Henry had mentioned the saintly fathers of the Church in England, he well knew that these customs were contrary to the precepts of those holy men. As for his flight from England, Thomas was justified in leaving, even in secret in the middle of the night, and he was ready to give a full account as to why he had to flee.

It was at this point that the papal envoys interrupted and pulled Thomas out of the debate. The archbishop was treading on dangerous ground; if he continued, he would expose Henry as a ruthless tyrant and that would end any hope of peace. In desperation, they tried to persuade Thomas to recant. Exchanges like this did nothing to further the cause of reconciliation — they just made things worse. "Give glory to the king," they insisted, urging him to suppress the phrase that offended Henry and cautioning him to be silent, to subject himself absolutely to the king's will and judgment. There was now an opportunity for peace, they said, and it must be taken. Everyone else had agreed to peace, they reminded him, everyone but him and his men, they chided.[5] Thomas was bombarded on all sides: the papal envoys, the secular officials — English, Norman, and French. Members of religious orders who were present had a word with him and advised the same course of action. All he had to do, they urged, was remove the phrase "saving God's honor"; if he did, he would receive the honor of the king and the honor of all present.

It seemed to be a case of *Thoma contra mundum* — Thomas against the world, but he would stand against their advice. It was not fitting for him, as a priest and archbishop, to submit himself in any way to the judgment of a worldly man, particularly when the cause of the Church's liberty was at stake. The phrase that he had included should not have offended the king, Thomas implied, not if the king did not want to usurp what was God's. It was dark by the time the envoys gave up arguing with Thomas; he was not to be moved. Henry cursed the papal envoys for their trouble; they had failed in their mission to talk the archbishop around, to deliver his head on a platter.

As it was dark and cold, Henry and Louis mounted their horses and rode off, Henry denouncing Thomas as he rode. The crowds also scattered, and Thomas was left standing alone in the field; even his clerks were keeping their distance.[6] He pulled his cloak around him to stave off the bitter cold. There was nothing to do now but return to Sens, if they would let him in. Thomas and his clerks traveled back to Sens in the company of the French king and his entourage. Not once did Louis come near him, nor did he provide any food for the exiles. It was thanks to the archbishop of Sens and the bishop of Poitiers that Thomas and his companions were able to eat on the three-day journey home. These English exiles were a sorry company: poor, hungry, and now friendless, relying, it seemed, on the kindness of prelates motivated by the requirement of Christian charity not to let the hungry starve.

As his party returned to the abbey, Thomas spoke with the clerks. The time may have come, he said, for them to make alternative arrangements should they be expelled from Saint Columba's. Thomas feared that Louis would withdraw his support and financial assistance. The clerks suggested that the best thing to do would be to seek refuge further south in Provence, out of the realms of both kings. Thomas agreed. Apart from being out of reach, the warmer climate might help his health; here, it seemed as if the cold had penetrated right into his bones.

The abbot and monks of Saint Columba's did not expel them. When Thomas and his companions returned, they were welcomed with the same hospitality as before. Going to his chamber, Thomas began to compose a letter to Alexander to explain everything that had happened.[7] He decided to send some of his clerks to the pope to give him a full account, but in this covering letter he reiterated what he had said to Henry. "It is a thing unheard of amongst us from the beginning of time," he told the pope, "that any bishop should be compelled to bind himself to a secular prince, beyond the maintenance of those things contained in the formula of fealty." To do so, Thomas wrote, "will set a dangerous example for other princes not only in our own time but in our successors' times, if he should obtain a further obligation from us." If he was to give in to Henry, then "the authority of the Apostolic See would either disappear from England or be reduced to a minimum." The Church at Canterbury had always resisted this. As he pondered the advice of the papal envoys, he noted that Henry had found and retained many supporters among the papal court.

After he had finished his letter to the pope that same night, he wrote others to some curial officials. There was another letter he had to write, one more difficult to compose than that to the pope: one to Henry.[8] It was a short letter in which he merely repeated his promise "to observe the customs which our predecessors had observed to yours." He conceded to observe these, he continued, as far as he could, saving his order, and if he knew of anything else that he should promise more clearly, then he would do so. However, seeing as Henry was not pleased with this, he asked the king to remember the service he had rendered him. "I am bound by oath," he wrote, "to preserve your life, limbs, and all earthly honor, and I am prepared to do whatever I can do for you, according to God, as for my dearest lord." Henry received this letter, but he never responded to it. In a letter to the archbishop of Sens, the king complained that Thomas was completely to blame for the dispute — as he was the cause, he had to offer a solution; as he had caused the damage, he would have to provide the remedy.

The meeting at Montmirail was an important development in the dispute. Thomas's response to Henry's demand transformed the whole affair from a personal feud and a struggle for the Church's liberty within the Kingdom of England to a matter concerning the honor of God. While it may be suggested that Thomas was deploying a lawyer's trick to fulfill the requirement of the pope and his advisors while still refusing to budge — that was how Henry saw it — it cannot be dismissed that Thomas himself had come to see the matter in a new light. In changing from "saving my order" to "saving God's honor," he shifted the emphasis from himself and his office to the One who created both the man and the office. He also pushed Henry into an unenviable position: He might consider himself superior to his bishops and even the Church in his land, but did he consider himself superior to God, whose Church it was? In his letter to the king, he reiterated his loyalty and his intention to fulfill the oath he had taken, but without depriving God of his precedence. In essence, Thomas was saying, in his own way, what another would say more than 350 years later — he was indeed the king's servant, but he was God's first.[9]

In the days following their return from Montmirail, the exiles discussed their future. In the course of one of these conversations, Thomas suddenly laughed, to the surprise of the others. He then explained why: He was the cause of their misfortunes, but when he was gone there would be no one to persecute them. "Be strong and do not be frightened," he told them. In response, they told him they were not upset for themselves, but for him, as he was the one who had been abandoned by friends. "We commit our care to God," he replied.[10]

Soon after this, just after Thomas spoke, according to Alan of Tewkesbury,[11] a messenger from King Louis arrived at the abbey and asked to see the archbishop. The king was summoning him to court, he told Thomas. Thomas was surprised, while some of his clerks were fearful. He was being summoned, one said, to be expelled from the realm. Thomas urged the clerk not to start prophesying doom, as he went to prepare to leave at once — albeit with some trepidation.[12]

When he and his companions arrived at Louis's residence, they were immediately conducted into the king's chamber. Louis was sitting in his chair with a sorrowful expression on his face. He did not rise to greet the archbishop as he usually did, and this sent a ripple of anxiety though the clerks — perhaps their colleague was a prophet after all. There was an awkward silence as Louis put his head in his hands. After a few moments, to everyone's astonishment, Louis burst into tears. Rising up from his seat, he threw himself down at Thomas's feet. Recovering from his surprise, Thomas bent down and lifted the king up; tears were streaming down Louis's face. "Truly, my father, lord of Canterbury," he sobbed, "you alone saw it. We were all blind, we who, contrary to God, advised you in your cause, or rather God's, to forgo God's honor to obey man. I repent, father, gravely I repent. Forgive me, I pray, and absolve me from this fault." Louis then promised to lay himself and his kingdom open to God and to Thomas; he would not fail him again. As Louis requested it, Thomas gave him absolution and a blessing and then sat to hear what had led to Louis's distress and change of heart.[13]

Henry, thinking that Louis was no longer a threat, had broken his promises. Throwing his commitments to the winds, he had turned to take vengeance on the rebellious barons in Brittany who had allied themselves with the king of France. He had then stormed Aquitaine, not only attacking the sovereignty of his wife, Eleanor, but also subjecting those he had taken prisoner there to the most dreadful of conditions in their imprisonment and leaving them to starve to death in chains. In a snub to Louis, he had had great trenches dug along the border of the once disputed Vexin to secure it from the French. As one injury followed another, Louis realized that it was Henry who was treacherous, not Thomas, and that he had been fooled into condemning a holy man who was suffering at the hands of a tyrant. It was now obvious, Louis explained, that the papal advisors and even the pope himself had also been misled.

Thomas may well have been gratified, but mostly he was relieved. Not only had he regained his most powerful supporter and ensured that his fellow exiles would not go hungry, but Henry's malice had once again been exposed. Despite his efforts, Louis's peace treaty with Henry was in tatters. Now he was wiser and back on Thomas's side; indeed, more entrenched than ever, so Montmirail may have had its advantages. Perhaps the pope and his cardinals might come to see the truth about the English king, and he could finally win them to his cause. Thomas had not forgotten the assurance from Alexander that if Henry did not make peace by the beginning of Lent, then Thomas's disciplinary powers would be restored and he could impose any censure he deemed necessary. As that deadline approached, Henry had behaved as unscrupulously as ever, and the whole world was aware of it now. Thomas had to deliberate about what must be done: Was it time to excommunicate the king of England? And would the pope confirm it?

35
Patience and Impatience

Though Alexander must have been disappointed with the outcome of the conference at Montmirail, he was determined to get Thomas and Henry back into negotiations. Conscious that his suspension of Thomas's disciplinary powers was coming to an end, he knew that having assured the archbishop that he could do what needed to be done, he would have to confirm whatever censures he imposed. The pope did not want to find himself in a situation where he would have to either confirm the excommunication of a king, making that king an enemy, or absolve it and increase Henry's sense of dominance over the Church and her pope. While he was still in exile in Benevento, Alexander was in a stronger position than he had been. He was now allied with the Lombards, who were championing local independence in the north of Italy against Barbarossa, who was now under extreme pressure. The pope's strength and influence were growing. An antipope still held Rome, but he was not living there — Callixtus III, formerly Giovanni, the abbot of Struma, had taken up residence in Viterbo, where it was safer. Alexander also noticed that Barbarossa did not seem to give Callixtus the same support he had given to Victor and Paschal.

The pope instructed his envoys to arrange another meeting between king and archbishop; he would arm them with another ultimatum to deploy, should it be needed. Henry and Louis had agreed to meet on February 7, 1169, to discuss the breach of the most recent peace agreement between them; it was to be held at Saint-Léger-en-Yvelines in the Vexin.[1] As with the last peace conference at Montmirail, Thomas's case was put on the agenda. The same papal delegates arrived again, now chastened by their last encounter with Thomas and wiser to Henry's penchant for treachery. Among those appointed by Alexander to facilitate these negotiations between king and archbishop were William, the archbishop of Sens, and two English priests, members of the Victorine Order: Richard, prior of Saint Victor's in Paris, and Richard of Warwick.

Whatever hopes the envoys may have nurtured, they came to nothing. Henry was as slippery as ever, continuing to demand that Thomas consent to the ancestral customs, with the archbishop agreeing to do so, but still with the proviso that the king found so offensive: "saving God's honor." Henry insisted it was an insult, a snide accusation that suggested he would intentionally act in opposition to God. Henry also continued to insist that he had not driven Thomas into exile. After much time was spent in what they realized was circular argumentation that was producing more heat than light, the papal envoys turned to the ultimatum. They announced that if Henry did not agree to peace with the archbishop, restore his land and property to him, and return the income of the other exiles, then Pope Alexander would impose ecclesiastical censures on the king and on England.

Henry might have been shaken, but he was canny enough to realize that he needed to buy time. He informed the envoys that he had to consult the bishops. The envoys had had enough of Henry's tricks and refused to agree; they wanted a written answer from him then and there. But Henry was not about to give up. He tried another avenue: He would submit himself to the judgment of the prior of Grandmont, Bernard de la Coudre, and call the bishops to a conference on the matter.[2] The envoys, for some reason, seem to have agreed to this and left the conference.

Before they left, they advised Thomas to be patient and not to respond with any hostile action, but for now to cooperate with the process as it unfolded. Thomas reluctantly agreed, but his patience was wearing thin. In the end, nothing came of this effort at resolution. Henry proposed another meeting for Tours on February 22, but that conference never materialized. Thomas was growing frustrated, and sensing this, the envoys continued to advise him not to impose any sentences, even when his suspension lapsed on March 5, 1169.[3]

Thomas was not the only one who was frustrated; Alexander had reached the end of his patience. The king's envoys had been coming and going to the papal court at Benevento with one request after another, one solution after another, but in the end they all amounted to one thing: Henry's refusal to compromise. He wanted full control of the Church or the deposition of the archbishop. Once informed at the end of February that nothing more could be done, the pope realized that now was the time to take sides; and given that Thomas had cooperated with every effort and Henry was the problem, it was the English king who received the papal rebuke. In a letter dated February 28, Alexander finally refused all of Henry's requests, but he was still not prepared to abandon negotiations. There would be a new mission, he said, but this might be the last. A new set of envoys would be chosen for that mission, and they would facilitate negotiations in the early summer of 1169. As he made arrangements for this effort, Alexander was well aware that Ash Wednesday, when Thomas's power to censure would be restored, was not far away.

Thomas would not be informed of this new mission until he received a letter from the pope in May. In this letter, Alexander requested that he not impose any censures before this new set of meetings.[4] Relying on the letters he had received when Alexander put the suspension in place and unaware of this later request, Thomas believed his powers were restored when Ash Wednesday arrived. However, he decided to wait before doing anything. Spending Lent in prayer at Saint Columba's, he pondered what he would do, whom he would need to censure, and the reasons for doing so. He was not going to use his power for vengeance but rather as it was intended to be used — for medicinal reasons, to justly punish those who deserved it. He chose Palm Sunday, April 13, 1169, as the day for his formal pronouncement of censure, but he would not make it in Sens; once again, he would make a pilgrimage beforehand to ask heavenly advice — this time to the venerable Abbey of Clairvaux, where Saint Bernard had lived.

Just before the beginning of Holy Week 1169, Thomas left Sens for Clairvaux, arriving as planned in time for the celebration of Palm Sunday. He was not the only pilgrim coming to the abbey. As at Vézelay, numerous pilgrims gathered to celebrate the sacred feast in what was now regarded as a holy place. Though Bernard had not yet been canonized — Alexander would canonize him in 1174 — his memory was alive in the minds and hearts of the people, as was that of his friend, the saintly Irish archbishop Malachy,[5] who shared the same tomb as Bernard in the abbey church. Pilgrims were already making their way to this tomb seeking favors and help in their trials.

Thomas joined the clergy for the Palm Sunday procession and the Mass. When the ceremonies were over, he ascended the pulpit as he had at Vézelay. Invoking his authority as archbishop and papal legate, he formally pronounced the censure of excommunication on a number of figures.[6] He first excommunicated Gilbert Foliot, bishop of London and his senior suffragan bishop in the Province of Canterbury. Gilbert earned this censure for his behavior in the controversy and for leading the appeal to have the Vézelay sentences dismissed. Next, he excommunicated Bishop Jocelin of Salisbury for appointing John of Oxford to a deanery in defiance of papal prohibition. Thomas then excommunicated seven men who had seized the Canterbury estates: Ranulf de Broc and his nephew Robert; Thomas FitzBernard; Hugh of Saint Clair; Nigel de Sackville, who was keeper of the royal seal; and two other minor figures — Letard, a clerk of Northfleet, and Richard de Hastings, a clerk censured for seizing Thomas's church at Monkton.[7]

Later, writing to inform those excommunicated, Thomas announced that he would add to their number on the feast of the Ascension if action were not taken to restore stolen Church property. On Ascension Day, May 29 , having heard nothing to this effect, he excommunicated sixteen more individuals, including Richard de Lucy; Richard Ilchester; Geoffrey Ridel, the archdeacon of Canterbury and Henry's royal chancellor;

and Geoffrey's brother Robert, the deputy archdeacon. He also suspended Geoffrey and Robert from their offices. Also excommunicated were clerics from other dioceses within the Canterbury province: John Cumin, archdeacon of Bath, and Guy Rufus, dean of Waltham. Noticeably absent from both lists was John of Oxford, for fear that Alexander would rebuff that censure.[8]

News of the excommunications came to England gradually because Henry, hearing of them, was trying to prevent formal notification of any decrees, which would put them into effect. As Thomas expected, the censures were met with indignation, but also with caution. Now that Pope Alexander was no longer in fear of the emperor and it was generally known that Henry had pushed him beyond endurance, those sanctioned and their supporters could no longer be confident that the pope would hear, never mind grant, an appeal. As notice of the sanctions gradually got through to England in May and Thomas's letters were received, and thereby formally promulgated, the bishops could not avoid heeding them, regardless of what they thought of Thomas. He was their primate and papal legate — these excommunications were valid and licit. No one dared disobey him lest he, too, incur papal censure. Gilbert Foliot, however, attempted to resist, claiming that London was superior to Canterbury and that Thomas's decrees had no jurisdiction over him. In this, Gilbert was simply deluded, and everyone knew it.

Thomas wrote to Alexander requesting papal confirmation of the excommunications, but to his surprise received the pope's delayed letter asking him to hold back on censures for the time being.[9] News of the excommunications came to the pope in early June, and he was not impressed. In a letter, dated June 19, he reprimanded Thomas and asked him to suspend the excommunications for now.[10] Before long, he was dealing with appeals from Henry to have the censures overturned, and he also discovered that Henry was conspiring with the king of Sicily and some of the Italian city-states to foment unrest as a threat to the papacy. There was to be another conference, Alexander told Thomas. He had to continue to work with mediators and seek peace. If this last attempt at reconciliation failed, then that would be the end of the road for Henry. If he wondered whether Alexander meant what he said and how long that particular road was, Thomas could have been forgiven; for now, the road seemed endless. With each successive set of meetings, it was becoming clearer that Henry did not respond to civil discourse as a means of finding a solution to this dispute. Indeed, perhaps unknown to Thomas, Henry was now making advances to Louis, through the bishop of Sées and others, to have the archbishop expelled from France. He was also urging Gilbert Foliot to resist and fight his censure.

Alexander chose two of his curial officials to facilitate this new round of talks: Vivian, archdeacon of Orvieto, who worked as an advocate in the curia; and Gratian of Pisa, a subdeacon, papal notary, and nephew of the late Pope Eugene III. These men were heavyweights, well used to tough negotiations, and prominent canon lawyers. Gratian was also an old friend of John of Salisbury. When Herbert heard that Gratian had been appointed, he was delighted. Quite apart from his distinction, learning, and ability, Gratian was considered gracious and might be inclined to Thomas's plight. He was also honest and above reproach: He would be immune to Henry's attempts to bribe him. Thomas may have been hopeful given the intermediaries' abilities, but there was always Henry to blight that hope.

Vivian and Gratian arrived in France around the middle of July 1169.[11] Following an initial meeting with John of Salisbury at the Abbey of Vézelay, they met Thomas at Saint Columba's toward the end of the month. Thomas retold his side of the story; they took careful note of his position and why he maintained it. The mediators then went in search of Henry. He was difficult to find as he was winding his way through his dominions. However, when they tracked him down, they held a number of conferences with him at various places between August 15 and September 2: Argentan, August 15 and 16; Domfront, August 23 and 24; Bayeux, August 31; and Bur-le-Roi, September 1 and 2.[12] At the meeting in Argentan, for once, Henry was not obsessing about the archbishop. His priority at this point in time was Brittany, where he was anxious for battle and victory. The dispute with Thomas was merely an irritant at this stage, and he was now inclined to get it sorted. He was agreeable with Vivian and Gratian, but he was also evasive. Aiming to appear as open and conciliatory as possible to win the two officials over, he spun excuses, twisted his words, and lied through his teeth. The mediators were no fools, but they realized they had to keep speaking, even if it was almost impossible to nail the king down on anything.

By the end of August, the mediators were taking the talks in a more serious direction. Henry may have been getting alarmed and assumed a very different approach from his agreeable tone in previous meetings. At Domford, where he was hunting with his son, young Henry, in his meeting with the mediators, he lay down a precondition to talks: Thomas's excommunications had to be lifted without those sanctioned having to take the customary oath to accept the archbishop's judgment. Far from wilting, Vivian and Gratian refused to accept this diktat. A row ensued, one that would last for the whole day. By evening, Henry had had enough and wanted to withdraw; deciding to employ a familiar tactic, he threatened the mediators. Complaining about how Alexander was not interested in hearing his side of the story, he swore, "By God's eyes, I mean to do something about it!"[13]

If Henry thought the mediators would allow him to storm out of the room with that denunciation dripping from his lips, he was wrong. Gratian immediately stood up to him, revealing the man behind the diplomatic mask. "Do not threaten us, my lord," he said quietly. "We come from a court that is accustomed to command emperors and kings."[14] Cool and calm, Gratian looked Henry in the eye, and the king suddenly realized he was not top dog in these talks. These men came with the power of a pontiff who could unseat him, and it seemed they were now prepared to do so. Henry apologized and sat down to resume the discussions. After a time, they went for a walk on the estates to talk things over more informally, but the discussion became heated again, Henry threatening them and they rejecting his demands. In the end, Henry stormed off, swearing that he would never listen to anyone who wanted him to make peace with Thomas.

While Henry was throwing caution to the wind, his Norman bishops were fearful. As he was engaged with the mediators, Henry had summoned them, and a number of abbots, to seek their advice and support.[15] The bishops knew the power Vivian and Gratian possessed, and they could see that an interdict might not be far off. Present at the later meetings with the mediators, they approached Henry and begged him to concede, warning him that if he continued to treat the mediators with contempt by making demands they were not prepared to meet, he could lead his dominions into serious trouble.

At the meeting at Bur-le-Roi on September 1, the bishops themselves spoke with Vivian and Gratian and asked them to grant the absolution of the clerks. Concerned that this last effort at reconciliation would fail, they agreed to offer Henry a compromise: They would absolve those excommunicated if these individuals came to them in person and did penance. Henry seemed to be content with that and agreed to be reconciled with Thomas. However, he added, there were those who could not come to the continent, so one of the envoys or a clerk must sail to England to absolve them there. Henry was never happy; he always had to seek more and get his way. The mediators refused to agree, and Henry flew into another tantrum, telling them to do what they liked — he did not consider these excommunications valid anyway: "I don't rate you and your excommunications," he yelled, "and doubt if they are worth an egg!" And he stormed out.[16]

Henry did not get the chance to make a dramatic escape. His bishops surrounded him just as he mounted his horse, and they told him that he had spoken badly to the mediators. Henry was forced to dismount and listen to his bishops. They suggested they write to the pope, but as the bishops busied themselves writing letters, it became very clear to them that the mandate the mediators possessed rendered these efforts fruitless. Speaking with Henry they once again made him aware that these mediators could create a lot of trouble for him. He conceded that they could put an interdict on his realms, but he was powerful, too — he had conquered fortified castles. A few clerks should be no problem to deal with.[17] The bishops quickly reminded him that he was not dealing with clerks, but with the pope — these two men had the power of the keys with them. It seems this affected a change in Henry. Calling the mediators to his chambers, he agreed to the original compromise. True to their word, Vivian and Gratian met several of those under Thomas's sentence and absolved them.

Henry may have heeded his bishops' advice, but he was not finished. After the mediators had lifted the sentences of those condemned at Clairvaux, a copy of the formal agreement was delivered to them. To their horror, they discovered that Henry had added a qualifier to it: He would agree to the peace terms "saving the dignity of my realm." He still wanted Thomas to bow to the ancestral customs. Meeting again with the king, Gratian rejected the text of the document and denounced him as a trickster. As far as the mediators were concerned, the talks and the agreement were null and void; but Henry, in turn, rejected that nullification and immediately dispatched envoys to Italy with a copy of the disputed document to seek ratification and agreement from the pope.

Thomas was receiving updates on how the negotiations were going, and they were proceeding as he would have expected. When he heard that Henry's envoys had been sent to Alexander, he sent his own to warn the pope. This king was not going to compromise, he informed Alexander; Henry would remain inflexible until he got his way. His own patience now spent, Thomas decided not to wait for a response from Alexander. Given Henry's subterfuge, he saw the mediators' absolutions as being abused; in response, he reinstated the excommunications. But this was not enough — the time had come for more serious action. Thomas announced that he was now considering imposing a general interdict on England. This censure would suspend the administration of all the sacraments with the exception of infant baptism and last rites to the dying. In response, Henry issued his own decree declaring that if an interdict were imposed, he was ready to formally break from communion with the pope and lead his realms into schism. He would also confiscate the assets and lands of anyone in England known to be Thomas's supporter. Every man over fifteen years, he ruled, would have to take an oath to obey all of the king's prohibitions, and anyone carrying papal decrees or letters to or from the curia would be hanged. To show he was serious, Henry closed England's ports and directed sheriffs to begin imposing the oath on his subjects.[18]

When he heard the king's response, Thomas was horrified — he was deeply concerned for the priests and people who had remained faithful to him. He may now have been aware that many in England were on his side. One of those who finally took his side, but only regarding this extreme reaction from the king, was Roger de Pont L'Évêque. To Thomas's surprise, Roger denounced the king's decree — this was going too far, he said. The king was not happy simply to impose outward conformity, Roger insisted; now he wanted to police the minds and thoughts of his people and punish them for what he thought went on in their minds. Complaining to the papal curia, Thomas went even further and claimed that Henry wanted to change the law of God, to take God's place, creating a church of his own that he would control under a compliant archbishop.

By now, Thomas was utterly worn out. His dispute had reached epic proportions and had involved not only the pope and distinguished envoys and mediators but also several crowned heads in Europe. The "Becket Controversy" had become a source of division, and few remained neutral. Henry had shown his hand too many times for his intentions to be ignored or his tyranny dismissed. Thomas was now prepared to take drastic action; Henry had to be dealt with. It was also dawning on him that a price might have to be paid to bring peace and protect the Church's liberties. It is not known when Thomas came to see what that price was and that he was the one who would have to pay it, but in his prayer, in those silent night vigils at Saint Columba's, he must surely have struggled to say yes.

36

Montmartre

Frustrated with Henry's chicanery, the envoy Gratian left France and made his way back to Italy; he would not engage with the king any longer. The other envoy, Vivian, may not have been as wise as his colleague, and before he had finalized his plans to leave, Henry asked to see him. Perhaps, the king suggested, it might be possible to arrange yet another peace conference. Vivian was impressed with the king's seeming hopes for a resolution, and he agreed; one last effort might finally bring this dispute to an end.[1] But Henry was not interested in peace; he had his eye on his dynastic agreement with Louis, and there was the matter of a coronation. At the back of the king's mind was the knowledge that only the archbishop of Canterbury could anoint and crown young Henry and his wife, Margaret. A coronation was vital if he wanted to settle any future succession issues and keep the French king happy. Vivian got to work on organizing the peace conference.

Thomas was informed that he had to make his way to Paris for fresh negotiations. The conference was due to take place in the middle of November 1169.[2] Once again, the archbishop took to the road. When he arrived in the city, he was told that lodgings had been prepared for him with the Knights Templar. A program for the negotiations had already been finalized: Henry and Louis would meet at the Abbey of Saint Denis to the north of the city on November 16; Thomas would go to Montmartre, to the Chapel of the Holy Martyrs there, where he would take his part in the negotiations from a distance. He may well have smirked when he heard this. Saint Denis, the bishop of Paris, had been beheaded with his companions on that mountain in the third century and, according to legend, the martyred bishop stood up and carried his head to the spot where the abbey now stood; it had been built over his tomb. Was Henry intending to decapitate another bishop there now? The plan was for mediators to go back and forth between the chapel and the abbey furthering the progress of the talks or, as Thomas may have mused, symbolically carrying his head back and forth to Henry to appease him.

King Louis led the negotiations; Thomas and Henry would not meet for now. To start the discussion, Henry, to everyone's surprise, agreed, if in noticeably vague terms, to renounce all evil customs that would enslave the Church and to restore the exiles' property. As a smiling Louis arrived and informed Thomas of this, the archbishop was a little taken aback; was it possible that Henry was now prepared to back down? Perhaps it was providence that arranged this conference after all. Willing to meet Henry halfway, Thomas agreed to accede to the king and to offer the homage that was required.

Henry seemed satisfied with this, and constructive negotiations began to flesh out this preliminary undertaking from both sides. Henry asked the negotiators to have Thomas draw up a list of the property and assets that had been confiscated so they could be returned. While Thomas was happy to comply with this, he said that having been in exile so long, he was not sure what had been taken. He suggested that they could agree that what had belonged to Canterbury under Theobald should be established as the inventory and that anything in the possession of others should be returned. While this seemed innocent enough, Thomas was actually trying to settle his score against John the Marshal and Ranulf de Broc. Seized with confidence, he said, rashly, that if these were not returned he would rather stay in exile.

Surprisingly, Henry remained calm and agreeable. However, things became difficult when the matter of reparations came under discussion. Henry agreed to pay them in lieu of the exiles' lost income over the years. A broad but not inexact figure of twenty thousand marks was submitted to Henry, an extraordinary amount of money at the time; however, Thomas conceded, they would be prepared to accept half of that sum as a goodwill gesture. Henry would indeed be glad to accept a goodwill gesture, but the figure he had in mind was one thousand marks, about two thousand to three thousand pounds. This amount was not acceptable to Thomas, and an impasse emerged as both sides refused to budge. Louis decided to intervene; he persuaded Thomas not to let this effort fail because of money, as there were greater things at stake. Thomas agreed and relented. Before the day was out, it seemed that peace had been won.

With the agreement in place and prudence dictating that final speeches were best avoided, a ceremony of reconciliation was arranged. As was custom and practice, such agreements were sealed with the "kiss of peace," a sign of reconciliation and fraternal love. It was also the usual symbolic greeting that was exchanged between the king and archbishop. Thomas asked that the reconciliation be effected by this symbol before the gathered mediators. This was a request that everyone expected, and Louis was happy to inform Henry that the dispute would formally end with the exercise of this tradition. To Louis's dismay, Henry refused, saying that he had made a promise to himself that he would never again give the archbishop the kiss of peace, even if they were reconciled, and he did not intend to break that promise. Given Henry's attitude toward oaths and promises, his insistence on keeping this one was ironic, if he had made it at all — perhaps it was merely an excuse. Thomas was surprised when Louis came with the news. Pope Alexander had once told him never to seek a pledge of peace from the king if they ever resolved their dispute; the kiss of peace would be enough. Thomas had agreed, but now Henry was refusing to give even that.[3]

The archbishop was in a bind. Should he go ahead, agree to reconciliation without the kiss of peace, and return to Canterbury, ultimately putting his trust in a king who had not made any formal or symbolic gesture of peace? He was not inclined to do so. Louis himself had his own concerns, and told Thomas that he could not advise him or the exiles to return home. It was obvious that Henry could not be trusted, and they would be foolish to do so. He was not alone in coming to this conclusion. Other nobles present agreed with Louis and advised that he should not return until Henry acquiesced to give the kiss of peace. Thomas accepted this advice. He sent news to Henry that he could not consent to abandoning the kiss of peace; he urged him to reconsider.

Meanwhile, Vivian was in discussion with Henry, trying to persuade him to relent and concede to the gesture — they had all come so far that they could not lapse now. Thomas had agreed to sacrifice the bulk of the reparations that were due to him in justice in order to make peace; surely Henry could swallow his pride, too. But the king continued to refuse: He could not break such a solemn oath, he said; indeed, he would not. In the end, Vivian left, loudly complaining that Henry broke oaths and spoke falsely, that he should be hateful in the sight of God and man. He also suspected that he had been used by the king. The failure of this conference, he said, lay with Henry alone. As darkness had fallen, Henry left with Louis for his accommodation. Totally oblivious to the fact that he was the cause of the failure, he blamed Thomas for his arrogance and cursed him as he rode to his lodgings.

Thomas and the clerks spent the night at their lodgings outside Paris, but that night peace would elude him as some of his clerks, who had come to the conclusion that the dispute was now about Thomas seeking the concession on the kiss of peace rather than God's honor, remonstrated with him. It was the archbishop's duty, they insisted, to accept the king's terms so they could return to England and he could assume his duties and responsibilities again. Remaining silent, Thomas thought over what they had said. When he spoke, he rejected their conclusion; the pope had told him that he was to obtain the kiss of peace. However, if they wished, they could send an embassy to Alexander, relate all that had happened at the conference, and seek his advice.[4] Thomas and the exiles returned to Sens the next day. As it seemed as if no end was in sight, Thomas realized that he must take further direct action; Henry was not going to change. What had led the king to seek this latest conference, he did not know, but he knew Henry too well now to think he had good intentions — the king was up to something. Thomas was now ready to impose the interdict on England. But he was also prepared to go further: Perhaps the time had come to excommunicate Henry. If he was pondering over all that had happened as he made his way back to Saint Columba's, Thomas may have thought he would surely have the pope's support for such sanctions.

Thomas was correct. When Pope Alexander heard of the failure, he was as angry as the archbishop. He also concluded that it was time for him to take direct action. Sending bishop-legates to Henry, the pope informed him that if he did not ratify the agreement with the archbishop on Montmartre with the kiss of peace, then not only would Thomas impose an interdict on England, but the pope would impose an interdict on all of Henry's realms. While he was prepared to have Thomas kneel before the king of England as long as the liberty of the Church was maintained and the danger to the exiles was averted, the status quo was now unacceptable, and Alexander would no longer stand idly by.

Emboldened by the pope, Thomas wasted no time. In the days following his return to Sens, he confirmed his excommunications again and excommunicated five other allies of the king, including John of Oxford, whom he had spared at Clairvaux in deference to Alexander.[5] He then wrote to Henry informing him that if he did not restore peace to the Church by February 2, 1170, then he would impose an interdict on all of England and excommunicate him.[6] By the end of 1169, not prepared to submit, Henry resorted to subterfuge again, appealing to Alexander and giving him the impression that he was willing to submit the entire dispute to the pope's judgment.[7] In his Christian charity, the pope postponed the interdict in the hope that another effort at reconciliation might be possible.

Realizing that his relationship with Frederick Barbarossa was broken beyond repair, Henry understood that his most important continental ally now was King Louis of France. As Louis was an avid supporter of the archbishop of Canterbury, Henry realized that he had to make another concerted effort to pull the two apart, and the most effective means of achieving this was to exploit the dynastic arrangement they had made.

While Louis's succession crisis had been resolved with the birth of Prince Philip, he still had two daughters whose futures and status had to be secured. Both were either married or engaged to Henry's sons, but more had to be done to keep Louis bound to the English royal house. The coronation of young Henry and his wife, Margaret of France, would achieve that. Henry had tried to have young Henry crowned in Theobald's time, but the dispute that ensued saw only his investiture, and a crown could not be put on his head; he wore a simple corona, a small crown. If he was to be properly enthroned as junior king, he had to be anointed and crowned. Only the archbishop of Canterbury could do this by right, and as Thomas was in exile and the dispute was as bad as ever, Henry would have to make alternative arrangements. This could prove controversial, perhaps even destructive.

Henry understood he had to be careful when it came to making arrangements for his son's coronation, so as a diversionary tactic he intimated that he was going to take the cross and go on Crusade. Louis was organizing another journey to the Holy Land for 1171, and Henry let it be known that he intended to join him to fight for the liberty of the holy places.[8] When Thomas and the exiles heard this, they may have greeted it with disbelief, perhaps wondering why Henry was insisting on this campaign to the east, a perilous task. Thomas was too busy with his own affairs to worry about the pious inclinations of his nemesis, so maybe he did not suspect that Henry's plan was a subterfuge to hide the fact that he was laying the groundwork for their final conflict.

37

The Crown Affair

Henry was planning to return to England from Normandy in early 1170. Moving his entire court from the continent, he was furthering his plans to have his son crowned. Time was of the essence. He knew that an interdict and his own excommunication might not be far off, so he had to have the ritual over and done with before he was censured. He also realized that he would not face a response from Thomas alone, as Pope Alexander would be quick to condemn the action as well. He had few episcopal allies in England; most of the bishops of England would refuse to cooperate. Only the archbishop of Canterbury had the right, by ecclesiastical law, to crown and anoint kings, and though many of the bishops were unofficially in dispute with Thomas, none of them would usurp this ancient right. Despite this, Henry did have the support of the archbishop of York, Roger de Pont L'Évêque, and the ever-faithful Gilbert Foliot of London, whose eyes were always focused on the chair of Saint Augustine. It was the king's plan to have Roger anoint and crown young Henry and his wife, Margaret, with Gilbert assisting.[1]

Gilbert was still excommunicated; if he was to assist at the coronation, he had first to be absolved. Henry was already making appeals to Alexander to have the new sentences rescinded by papal decree, but Gilbert thought he might have more success if he made his way to the pope and pleaded in person. He figured that he could get back to England in time for the coronation ceremony. Leaving England, Gilbert began the journey down through France. As things turned out, he did not need to travel to Benevento. Meeting the king's envoys on the way back from their papal audience, he discovered that they were in possession of papal absolutions of the excommunications of a number of the king's allies, including Gilbert himself and Bishop Jocelin of Salisbury. In a touching scene, Bishop Jocelin's own son, Reginald, had personally begged the pope to absolve his father.[2] Preoccupied with his struggle with Barbarossa, Alexander was finally making inroads and preparing to move closer to Rome. Why he agreed to the absolutions without considering the wider consequences of his actions is unknown; it may have been a moment of weakness or of charity.

Henry arrived back in England on March 3, 1170. While he made the crossing safely, horrendous weather led to a number of his attending ships' being shipwrecked, and a number of people are said to have drowned.[3] He called his barons to attend a council to be held at Windsor Castle at Easter to discuss the arrangements for the coronation. When he learned that the pope had lifted the censures, Henry was elated; everything was going according to plan. He fixed June 14 as the date for the ceremony to take place, according to ancient tradition, at Westminster Abbey. He sent a message to fifteen-year-old young Henry, then on the continent, to return to England with his wife. At some point, Thomas learned of the king's plans, and he was furious.

No sooner had Henry's envoys left the pope than it began to dawn on Alexander that he had made a dreadful mistake. He immediately issued decrees rescinding the absolutions, but it was too late. When Thomas heard that the pope had lifted the censures, he was incensed and set himself to compose one of his most angry letters, in which he rebuked the pope for his actions.[4] Attacking the pope's advisors, he reminded Alexander that Henry could not be mollified by mildness or favors — the only way to deal with him was severity, and it fell to the one holding the office of Peter to do so. Referring to Alexander's predicaments, he reminded him that "Peter's zeal has not been exiled from the Apostolic See"; as pope, he must deal with the one who "disdains Divine and apostolic authority" so that he may see "that here is a prophet in Israel." Henry, Thomas wrote, "is an enemy of the Church and the fomenter of schism, he should be punished and destroyed." Quoting the old saying to beware of Greeks bearing gifts, he pointed out that the king of England was "a species of Greek," promising the pope satisfaction but, in reality, only increasing damage to the Church and prolonging Thomas's exile.

Next, Thomas turned to attack Gilbert Foliot. He was a man who impeded the Church's peace, he snarled, and thanks to Alexander's absolution, Gilbert and Archbishop Roger of York would now go forward to crown young Henry in defiance of the pope's own prohibition. He then wrote to Alexander, begging him to grant the petitions aimed at dealing with the unfolding crisis that he was sending with his emissary. Thomas ended his letter in a more fraternal and loving tone: "You should know that, whatever they [his enemies] may do, neither death nor life nor the present nor the future, by God's grace, shall separate us from your love, obedience and service." However, his final remark was a veiled reproach in itself: "May your name be blessed forever, and may the Church for which you will have to render an account, be swiftly and effectively comforted."

Alexander would indeed send a decree prohibiting the coronation if it were not to be carried out by Thomas; but Henry, expecting such a response, put measures in place, including closing the ports, to ensure that the decree was not allowed into England and therefore not officially promulgated. Expecting such restrictions, Thomas had his own plan to get the decree into England, and he was not prepared to allow just any messenger to take it. He had a royal ally to help him: Marie of Blois, the nun forced into marriage with Matthew of Alsace. She had finally escaped the marriage, and it had just been annulled on the grounds of lack of consent on her part. She had not forgotten that Thomas as chancellor had battled Henry to prevent the marriage. Now that he needed a safe pair of hands to deliver the papal decree to England, she was more than willing to volunteer. She set out for Westminster under an assumed name and easily slipped through Henry's embargo.

On Sunday, June 14, 1170, crowds gathered outside Westminster Abbey to witness the coronation of young Henry. Though it had been organized in haste, no expense was spared. Barons and most of the bishops of England gathered for the ceremony, which Roger de Pont L'Évêque would carry out with great gusto, assisted by Gilbert Foliot and Jocelin of Salisbury. At some point before the ceremony began, Marie of Blois managed to get to both Roger and Gilbert as they were preparing themselves for the rituals, formally presenting them with the papal decree and informing them that they could not proceed by order of the pope. Both were flustered, and though the decree was now officially promulgated and the bishops under the ban, they cast the documents away and went ahead. Marie slipped away and, making for the coast, took a boat back to the continent to the Abbey of Saint Austrebert at Montreuil to return to the consecrated life.[5]

Young Henry was anointed and crowned according to the ceremony composed by Saint Dunstan,[6] the one still used today for coronations in England.[7] However, he alone was crowned; in the rush to get him to the throne, his wife, Margaret of France, had been forgotten and left behind. As her husband was placed on the throne of England, she was stranded and fuming in Caen in Normandy. King Louis was not impressed either. Once again, as he saw it, Henry senior had reneged on a promise. In response, he sent troops to the border with the Vexin, poised for action. The coronation over, Henry was finally happy. Unless disaster struck, any future succession crisis had been averted. Returning to Normandy, he decreed that young Henry would now govern England, with Richard de Lucy to assist him.

When he arrived back on the continent, ten days after the coronation, Henry found a formal delegation of papal legates waiting for him: Archbishop William of Sens, an ally of Thomas's, together with Bishops Rotrou of Rouen and Bernard of Nevers. They were fully armed with papal decrees and extraordinary powers to force Henry to agree to the peace negotiated at Montmartre.[8] Alexander would not take any more nonsense from the king of England. Presenting Henry with the decrees, the legates drew his attention to a paragraph in which he was warned that if he did not agree to the peace within forty days, then the pope would formally excommunicate him. The legates' task was wider than this. With immediate effect, they imposed a general interdict on the king's continental realms, including Aquitaine, which was technically his wife's. Thomas had been about to issue his own interdict, but he never imposed it; Alexander was now doing it for him. Perhaps rebuking a pope could sometimes get a pontiff to throw fear and politics to one side and do the right thing.

Though he had been expecting censure, Henry reassessed his situation and was forced to concede. While in theory, it may have seemed possible to resist an interdict, it proved very different in reality. It meant that, with the exception of baptism and last rites, no sacraments could be celebrated; for a people who cherished their faith and expected the ministry of their priests, an interdict could be intolerable, and perhaps also the king who was to blame for it. Confiding in King Louis, who was not inclined to act as counselor for his brother king at this point, Henry said he was prepared to negotiate again. Over the next couple of weeks, with the legates as intermediaries, it was agreed that Henry and Thomas would meet at a castle at Fréteval, on the frontier between France and Normandy, on July 20, to discuss peace terms. Henry and the legates would first negotiate; Thomas would arrive two days later to receive the king's peace. The day of his arrival, interestingly, would be the feast of Saint Mary Magdalene, at whose shrine in Vézelay he had promulgated his first censures.

Tensions were growing between Henry and Louis over Margaret's being cast aside and left behind as her husband was crowned. Henry needed to deal with this before he could proceed to negotiations. Arriving at Fréteval, the two kings hammered out an agreement that would see Margaret crowned at a later date.[9] Louis sent word for his army at the Vexin to stand down and return to base. As they took a walk afterward, Henry made an offensive remark about Thomas, calling him a thief. In a subtle rebuke, Louis mused how happy he would be to have Thomas as his archbishop. If Henry finally conceded and granted peace, Louis advised, then he would have honor before God. The English king was not inclined to think so, and when the two monarchs returned to the castle, they engaged in a heated discussion on the matter.

Thomas was being prepared for his meeting with Henry. Under advice, he had agreed to modify his demands, and it was now decided that he would not request the kiss of peace, but rather agree to the settlement without it. Hearing of this modification, Henry was happy to accept it, and he swore an oath that though he refused the kiss, he was not preparing a trap for the archbishop. The stage was set. His part of the drama now over, Louis left, and Henry made his way to an arranged rendezvous point outside Fréteval to meet with the archbishop. It had been decided that the reconciliation would take place in the open air rather than in the confines of a castle, which could be construed as being coercive to either party.[10]

As the two approached each other in a clearing in the woods, Henry removed his hat and greeted Thomas. This gesture of respect surprised Thomas. As they spoke, the king was pleasant and gentle, and he invited the archbishop to come away with him to a distant part of the meadow where they could converse by themselves. Thomas's companions may have been suspicious, but as the two rode off on their horses together and began to talk, the clerks' qualms changed to astonishment: King and archbishop seemed to be talking and engaging with each other in the way they used to when they were friends. Thomas's body relaxed; the two seemed totally at ease and comfortable with each other. In fact, the two were speaking as if the years of dispute and exile had never happened. Henry did not mention the ancestral customs, but spoke about reconciliation and his desire for peace and the good of the Church. Thomas was completely disarmed. As they continued to speak, Henry agreed to restore the lands and assets of the Church and the exiles and said that perhaps, in time, he could bring himself to resume the kiss of peace. Thomas was just as conciliatory and began to wonder whether Henry had been as bad as he thought he had.

However, while Henry was proving virtuous, Thomas slipped. He brought up the issue of the coronation, and it was a mistake.[11] For all his progress under suffering, Thomas still had a flaw: He lacked a humility that would have advised caution and even cunning. He told Henry that he could not overlook Roger de Pont L'Évêque's violation of the rights of the archbishop of Canterbury; the king would have to make amends. While Henry drew breath to hold his patience, Thomas continued to complain, giving him a history lesson on the privileges of the church of Canterbury. To defend himself, the king cited a grant issued by the pope a long time before the dispute, before Thomas was appointed to Canterbury, allowing for the coronation. Though caught off guard, Thomas rejected the grant's validity. He then personalized the issue and reminded Henry of his dislike for Roger and his once having said that he would prefer young Henry to be beheaded than crowned by Roger. It was a step too far, and Thomas realized it as soon as the remark was out of his mouth. He quickly apologized. He did not mean to insult young Henry; he desired the young man's success.

Henry was stung. He reminded Thomas of the love young Henry had for him, saying that if he loved the boy, then he would do all that was necessary for him. Thomas agreed. But things had changed. While he remained polite, Henry seems to have turned cold, though Thomas did not initially notice it. He said that he knew the archbishop would indeed avenge himself on the bishops who had betrayed him, and he promised that he himself would also pay back those who betrayed him and the archbishop. Thomas did not pick up on the subtlety that others did when they heard this — was Henry including Thomas in those he would punish for betraying him? Oblivious to the change, Thomas dismounted and knelt at Henry's feet in a gesture of obeisance; as he remounted his horse, Henry held the stirrup for him.[12]

Returning to their entourages, Henry and Thomas parted on what the archbishop believed to be good terms, the peace restored. The king's officials were left to complete the negotiations with Thomas's party, and while it was going well, the archbishop again gave in to a foolishness born of arrogance: He insisted that every inch of Canterbury lands be restored before he set foot back in England.[13] He was too confident, and his demand smacked of distrust, the very thing Alexander had warned him against, given that Henry was hypersensitive on such issues. When the king came by to see how things were progressing, Thomas was argumentative, perhaps through tiredness, and this annoyed the king. When

Henry suggested that Thomas move back to his former lodgings at the Norman court until the plans for his return to England had been finalized, the archbishop refused — he wanted to return to Saint Columba's and then visit King Louis to thank him for his hospitality.

Progress slowed further when it was suggested that Thomas reconcile himself with those he had censured in a gesture to mirror Henry's magnanimity toward the exiles. He refused — their offense was different, he insisted, and different measures were required to resolve his dispute with them. This raised the ire of some of those censured who were present, and they started shouting and arguing. Henry had to assume the role of peacemaker. Taking Thomas aside, he advised him to ignore the insults being hurled at him and then asked for his blessing before leaving for Fréteval Castle.

Thomas may have gasped in astonishment. It seemed as if the dispute was over; he and Henry were reconciled. Gathering their belongings and mounting their horses, the exiles made their way back to Saint Columba's for what they thought was the last time, to make preparations for their return to England. There had been no mention of ancestral customs; lands and assets would be restored; and the sight of king and archbishop on their horses conversing as when they were friends seemed to convince the exiles that the end to the dispute had finally come. Perhaps some of them were unnerved by Thomas's foolhardiness and feared it might turn Henry against them again. Little did they know that as he rode back to Fréteval, Henry was pleased, not with the reconciliation — as far as he was concerned that did not happen — but with his observing to the full what the pope required of him to prevent the interdict.[14] This matter was not finished yet, and Thomas's behavior was proof to the king that he was not worthy of reconciliation. Only one would rise as victor from this dispute, and as far as Henry was concerned, it would not be Becket.

38

Return

Thomas's foolishness did not end at Fréteval. As soon as he returned to Saint Columba's, instead of leaving things lie for the time being, he wrote to Alexander requesting the ratification for his excommunication of those involved in the coronation. Around the same time, Henry fell seriously ill with fever, and it seemed that he was dying. Making his will, he divided his realms between his sons, leaving young Henry the greater part and giving Richard the prize of Aquitaine. While rumors claimed that he had died, Henry began to recover, so that by the end of September 1170, he was fit enough to make a pilgrimage to the Shrine of Our Lady at Rocamadour.[1] He also moved to address the issue of the reconciliation, directing his officials to begin obstructing any attempts to return the Canterbury lands to the archbishop.

As Thomas's clerks advanced their plans to return to England, they were growing suspicious. Documents relating to the return of property and assets were arriving, but in them they noticed a phrase, "saving the honor of my realm," that seemed to establish a limit as to what Henry

354 *Servant of Christ*

was prepared to settle.[2] Thomas may have been growing uneasy himself, but he continued to make plans to return to England, spending a little time with Louis to thank him for his support. Pope Alexander was also growing suspicious. The meeting had been very successful — almost too successful. Had Henry experienced a Damascene conversion? Though he believed in miracles and the power of God's grace, the pope was inclined to be skeptical, as were many at the papal court.

Leaving Saint Columba's in early October, Thomas and his companions were to make their way to Tours to meet up with Henry's court on October 12 for a brief sojourn. It may have been with a sense of trepidation that they crossed the border from France into Henry's realm, where they no longer enjoyed the protection of the French king — they were now at the mercy of their former nemesis. When they arrived at Tours, they found the reception to be quite frosty, and Henry treated Thomas with contempt. Taking up lodgings, Thomas was left alone with his exiles. The king did not visit; indeed, it seemed as if Henry were keeping his distance. When they did meet to talk, the two men ended up quarreling over how long it would take for the restoration of property to make any progress.[3] Then one morning, Thomas awoke to discover that the court had moved on without telling him. Packing up, he and the exiles went in hot pursuit of the king, eventually finding him halfway to the town of Amboise.

The atmosphere had thawed somewhat by the time the court arrived at Chaumont-sur-Loire. Henry was in a better mood, and he and Thomas spent some very pleasant hours together in conversation. There the two agreed on plans for the archbishop's return to England. First, the exiles would return to Sens to finalize their departure, and then they would make their way to Rouen, where Henry hoped to meet them and accompany them across the channel to England. All agreed, they parted in good spirits, the king wishing Thomas well and saying he was looking forward to seeing him again soon, either in Rouen or in England. In their final conversation, Henry asked Thomas why he had not done what Henry wanted; if he had, Henry would have put everything into his hands. Thomas immediately thought of the devil's temptation of Jesus in the desert. He then had a premonition. Disoriented, he told Henry that he had a sense that he would never see him again in this life. Henry was shocked and offended — it appeared that Thomas was accusing him of treachery. "You consider me a traitor?" he chided. Thomas protested, "Far from it, my lord," he said.[4] The two parted, Thomas to Sens and Henry to Chinon, southwest of Tours.

Herbert of Bosham and John of Salisbury were the first to return to England, in the middle of November, to begin preparing for Thomas's return. They found that the ordinary people were celebrating the prospect of the homecoming of the archbishop, who was now regarded as a hero. They discovered even greater excitement in Canterbury. Thomas was now deeply venerated there, and this may have given the two men pause. The man originally considered Henry's pawn was now hailed as the one who stood against the tyranny of the king, the advocate for the poor. But the two were growing uneasy, for while the people loved Thomas, there was little love for him among the ruling class. Strangely, those they considered dangerous enemies were also looking forward to his arrival; this was disturbing.[5] They also noticed that not all monks at Christ Church were enamored at the thought of their archbishop's return.

As they tried to sort out the financial problems Henry had caused by his confiscation of the Canterbury estates and benefices, Herbert and John discovered that monies that, thanks to the agreement between Thomas and the king, should have been forthcoming from the estates were not — they were earmarked for the king. They soon uncovered another shocking development: Henry had signed a document, addressed to young Henry, ordering that only the lands and benefices that Thomas and the exiles had held three months prior to their leaving England were to be restored.[6] This fell far short of what was agreed. Henry was keeping for himself and his allies those estates and benefices that were the subject of the original dispute. For example, according to this decree, Saltwood Castle and its estates would remain in the possession of Ranulf de Broc.

There were other problems, too. Rumors were circulating that the king intended to force Thomas to take an oath to observe the ancestral customs before he would be allowed reenter England.[7] It was also becoming obvious that some of the bishops had organized a campaign to prevent his return, no doubt in response to fears that Thomas would censure them. Leading this campaign were the usual suspects: Roger de Pont L'Évêque, Gilbert Foliot, and Jocelin of Salisbury; they may have been the ones who were trying to persuade Henry to force Thomas to take the oath. Herbert and John were deeply concerned and began to wonder whether any of them should return at all. John wrote and shared his concerns with Thomas. In his own letter to the archbishop, Herbert went a step further: He advised him not to come back — not yet, anyway. It was too dangerous. He had a particular concern about Ranulf de Broc and his cronies. They seemed to have turned Canterbury into wild country, and even the southern coast was now hazardous as the de Brocs had resorted to piracy in anticipation of the archbishop's return. It seemed that they were planning to capture and confiscate Thomas's belongings as they were brought back across the English Channel.

Thomas took note of what his secretaries were saying, but he was now immersed in a spirit of charity, which led him to conclude that he would have to be generous in order to make this peace with Henry work. He may also have been hopeful of swaying the king away from the advice of his enemies. Perhaps they could rekindle their relationship of old, and he could bring the king onside. But he could not completely escape reality. He knew Henry too well, and this charitable approach to the matter was a gamble. In a letter, Thomas shared his thoughts with the pope: He had to be moderate for now; he had to give the king some space and allow him remain true to his agreement and assurances.[8] He understood that Henry wanted his unconditional surrender, but inflaming the situation would make things worse; there might be another way to win him over. Thomas was growing in charity, but also in wisdom and prudence. He was aware that he was taking a risk — this approach could fail, but he knew how to respond if it did.

Toward the end of October, Thomas wrote to Henry revealing his concerns about his return, mentioning in particular the actions of Ranulf de Broc.[9] He began the letter reminding the king that he had entered into their agreement with pure intentions and sincere affection, being assured by the king's own words and pledges that everything would be restored to him and the exiles; however, the promised restitution had now been held up by Ranulf. This situation, he gently chided Henry, did not just cause damage to the Church, but also to the king's salvation and honor. Ranulf, Thomas told him, was rampaging through the Church's property, occupying Saltwood Castle, and taking the archbishop's provisions into his own stores. He feared that when he returned to England he would not long rejoice in the king's peace. Indeed, he suggested, Ranulf might well take away his life. The Church in Canterbury, he asserted, was being persecuted; it was perishing through the hatred aimed at its archbishop, and Ranulf and his associates were the persecutors. In an extraordinary passage, Thomas reassured Henry that he would return but avowed that he was ready to die, ready to suffer a thousand deaths and every torment as long as God's grace sustained him. He would die to prevent the destruction of the Church in her affliction, unless the king in his piety took measures to prevent it and offered comfort to the Church. But, he ended his letter, whatever happened to him, he would continue to hold the king and his family in his affections, praying God's blessing upon them.

Thomas also wrote again to the pope requesting ratification of the excommunication he wished to impose upon Roger de Pont L'Évêque, Gilbert Foliot, and Jocelin of Salisbury for their part in presiding over the coronation of young Henry.[10] Alexander responded in early November agreeing to the censures and ratifying them. Alexander went a step further: He informed Thomas that, with the exception of Henry, Queen Eleanor, and their children, Thomas could impose censures, even excommunications, at will, and they could be considered already confirmed by the pope. He also confirmed Thomas as papal legate to England with jurisdiction over every diocese and bishop with the exception of Roger de Pont L'Évêque and his Archdiocese of York. The pope also imposed interdicts on Henry's continental realms. As he finalized his preparations, Thomas was emboldened: Now, finally, Alexander was with him.

Others, however, had their concerns. King Louis was not at all comfortable with Thomas returning to England without having received the kiss of peace from Henry. Thomas was aware of Louis's fears and had agreed that he was taking a risk in returning, as the agreement seemed to be crumbling: "We are going to England to play at heads," he said. Louis advised him to stay in France: "As long as I am alive," he told the archbishop, "you shall not lack wine and food and French abundance."

Thomas was grateful. In all his troubles, with the exception of one disagreement, the French king had been loyal and generous. "Let God's will be done," he responded.[11]

Around the middle of November, Thomas and the remaining exiles bade a sad but grateful farewell to the abbot and monks of Saint Columba's, who had provided generous hospitality for almost four years. Turning toward Rouen for his meeting with Henry, he was apprehensive. He was leaving safe refuge for the unknown. Whether through reason or revelation, he suspected he was returning to his death, embarking upon his final pilgrimage. He was accompanied on the journey by a cavalry and a group of his creditors, who were to be repaid by monies Henry was to provide at their meeting.

Henry did not turn up at Rouen.[12] When the exiles arrived at their meeting point, it was John of Oxford who was waiting for them. Handing Thomas a letter from the king, he said Henry was dealing with an uprising in Auvergne; he was to accompany the archbishop instead. Thomas was not impressed; not only was it an insult that his guardian back to England was his foe, but it also was perhaps a sign that he was indeed to be handed over to his enemies for the sake of the Church. When he asked about the funds Henry was to bring with him, John told them that the king had sent none, so Thomas had to settle his debts from his own resources, which were by now quite meager. After staying a few days in Rouen, Thomas and his party, led by John of Oxford, left on November 24 and made their way to the coast. The company called upon friends and allies along the way to Wissant, outside Calais, where they waited for good weather and a boat to ferry them across the channel.

As they were waiting, Thomas and some of his exiles decided to take a walk along the beach to get some air and exercise. Across the channel, he could see the English shore and its white cliffs beckoning. The silence of the moment was broken by an English accent: A cleric, Milo, the dean of Boulogne, was suddenly standing in front of him; he had sailed up the coast to meet the archbishop. Thomas greeted him graciously and joked, asking the dean if he were looking for a ride to England. Milo was quite grave. He had come with a warning from the Count of Boulogne: Thomas was not to cross the channel. There were too many enemies conspiring against him, and it was most likely that as soon as he set foot in England, he would be accosted and thrown into prison. Thomas was not unaware of that. He responded, telling the dean that he was returning to his people and to the church of Canterbury. Even if he did not get to them alive, he would be buried at Canterbury. He asked Milo and the count for their prayers.[13]

On the other side of the channel, Roger, Gilbert, and Jocelin, having learned of their excommunication by the pope, had made their way to Dover and were planning to cross to the continent to meet with Henry. They sought to fill some vacant dioceses with their own men before Thomas could exercise his right to do so. Though the bishops knew about their censures, the decrees of excommunication had not been officially served; when Thomas heard of the bishops' mission, he had his servant Osbern dispatched immediately across the channel to find the bishops and formally serve them with the censures. The young man was fit for the task. Arriving at Dover, he managed to find the three bishops in the Church of Saint Peter at the port. Thrusting the decrees into their hands, thereby effecting their suspension, he fled the scene before the three had time to react.[14]

Thomas boarded ship on December 1 and set sail for England, arriving at the port of Sandwich.[15] As his ship came into harbor, Thomas's archiepiscopal cross was raised onto the prow. A crowd of poor people was waiting for him; acclaiming him, they knelt for Thomas's blessing.[16] However, also waiting for him on the quayside was Ranulf de Broc with a gang of his ruffians, armed to the teeth. As he stepped ashore, the archbishop was greeted with threats and accusations. Ranulf swore that no good would come to the archbishop if he did not lift the excommunications there and then. Keeping his temper, Thomas quietly informed him that he had no power to lift the censure on the archbishop of York; only the pope could do so. However, he said, he would be happy to lift the excommunications of Gilbert and Jocelin if they came, sought pardon, and swore their submission to the pope's final judgment. Though furious, Ranulf could do nothing. Thomas walked off into the crowds who had seen him arrive and, gathering around him, they welcomed him back.

Thomas and his companions may have spent the night at Sandwich.[17]

When it came time to leave, he mounted a warhorse and began the journey to Canterbury. An entourage formed around him, so progress was
slow. Along the twelve-mile route, more crowds came out to welcome
him, and festive celebrations were held at every town and village along
the way. The people cheered him, hailing him as a liberator as church
bells rang and solemn processions took place to welcome him into the
various parishes. But it was not only the ordinary people who came out
to greet him; formal delegations of local commissioners, defying the
king's orders, came out to officially welcome their lord archbishop primate and heroic shepherd of the people back to his see. Herbert, taking
it all in, would later compare it to the Lord's entry into Jerusalem on
Palm Sunday; like Jesus' route, Thomas's route was covered with cloaks
and garments as the people laid them down in front of the archbishop's
horse.[18]

When he arrived at the gates of the city of Canterbury, the great bells
of the cathedral began to peal. The gates and streets were decorated as
for a solemn feast day, and throngs of denizens lined the streets. As he
made his way to the cathedral, Thomas may well have been overcome:
He knew what lay ahead, but his people had no idea. Their joy would not
last, he thought to himself. They acclaimed him as a hero, their defender,
but these very titles could cost him his life. He was guest of honor at a
great banquet that had been arranged to formally welcome him back;
afterward, he was escorted to his cathedral. After six years in exile, he
entered the sanctuary to take his place on the *cathedra*, and his monks
came forward to offer him homage. Though many of them were overjoyed at his return, not all of them were.

The acting prior of the monastery, Odo, was not happy to see Thomas. While the archbishop was away, the prior of the monastery, Wilbert,
had died in 1167; Odo had been chosen to replace him temporarily.
However, the manner of his election was not ideal or according to the
law. His friendship with Ranulf de Broc, who was by then in charge of
Canterbury, may have been a factor in his elevation.[19] As he had not
been confirmed in his office, and Thomas most likely considered him
an unworthy candidate, his days as prior were probably numbered.
There was no love lost between the two men, and Odo's seeming close

relationship with the de Brocs would not have inspired generosity in the archbishop. Yet for all these irregularities, Odo had proven himself to be a capable man, and he was loved by the monks and local people. He was also admired by the king, though in Thomas's eyes that might not have been a good thing.

For Thomas, however, there were more important things to deal with. That evening, gathering with his monks in the chapterhouse, he preached a sermon in which he reminded them that we have no abiding city; rather, we have to seek the one that is to be found in the life to come. In the midst of their euphoria, Thomas had to prepare them: Dreadful days lay ahead.

39
Christmas

Whether Thomas slept easy that first night back in his old bed is not known. But early the next morning,[1] Henry's officers and negotiators arrived, seeking an audience with him. When they entered the archbishop's hall, they greeted him with the demand that he lift the excommunications on the bishops.[2] These censures, they maintained, were contrary to the ancestral customs. Thomas took note of the context of their appeal — the dreaded ancestral customs. He refused, reiterating what he had said to Ranulf the day before. Lengthy discussions ensued, and it was reported that two of the bishops, Gilbert and Jocelin, were prepared to agree to the conditions but that an intervention by Roger de Pont L'Évêque prevented them. Neither of these bishops had come to call on the archbishop themselves; the clerks considered this ominous. Before the officials left, Thomas suggested that a conditional absolution might be forthcoming for Gilbert and Jocelin, but he would first consult with Bishop Henry of Winchester and other faithful bishops on the matter. At that moment, Bishops Roger, Gilbert, and Jocelin were, in fact, bound for the continent. Before they boarded their ship, they sent a message via Geoffrey Ridel and Richard of Ilchester to Henry the young king, informing him that Thomas was now plotting to have him deposed and advising him that he should take action against the archbishop.

Young Henry had never lost his affection for Thomas. A teenager now, he was governing England on behalf of his father, and this not only gave him a sense of importance but seemed to persuade him that his father did, indeed, love him, even if he had not shown any signs of it previously. While he would not normally be inclined to doubt Thomas, who had been more of a father to him than Henry, young Henry was still his father's son and just as inclined to irrationality as his father; he was, after all, the child of a dysfunctional family. Given the nature of their father-son relationship, young Henry held Thomas in esteem; however, a number of factors caused him concern. He had heard of the welcome Thomas had received by the ordinary people of England, and knowing how strong and proud the archbishop could be, he wondered whether he might take advantage of his popularity to seize power. Hostility still existed between the archbishop and his father, and given that his father was not the popular young king he had once been, there was no guarantee that Thomas would not be successful. Such considerations may have convinced young Henry that the warning from the bishops could be correct. Once the bishops had poured poison into his ear, he was not inclined to give Thomas the benefit of the doubt; it seemed to him that this dispute was not over at all, and that the archbishop was now trying to alienate the people of England from their liege lord. When a gift of three fine horses from Thomas arrived at the court for young Henry, it was obvious the archbishop would seek an audience and aim to be reconciled with his former charge. This threw the boy into a quandary: Should he receive the archbishop or not?[3]

Thomas spent a week at Canterbury getting settled in. His vast library, which had just escaped Ranulf de Broc's pirate ships, was being put in place in his residence. His wine had not made it — it was being stockpiled in the cellars of the de Brocs and their allies, as were his other possessions. Once he was settled, he had duties to perform: to call on the junior king at Woodstock and be formally reconciled with him, and to seek counsel with Bishop Henry of Winchester regarding the excommunications and other matters.

Thomas set out again on December 7 or 8 to make his way to Woodstock by way of Winchester. He also decided to conduct a visitation of some parishes in his archdiocese. His first port of call, however, was London. He had arranged to stay, with Bishop Henry of Winchester's permission, at Winchester House in Southwark, on the south side of the River Thames. Thomas was received graciously. Before he even entered the city, crowds came out to greet him. The Augustinian canons of Southwark Priory led a procession in his honor, singing the *Te Deum* in thanksgiving for his safe return and his triumph over tyranny. Once again, bells pealed from churches, and the crowds acclaimed him. Londoners loved a rebel, and here was their native son who had defied the king, returning to claim his rightful place among them. In the midst of the jubilation, a disturbed woman identified as Matilda, a lady who was considered a nuisance among the clergy and officials of the city, shouted out to him, reminiscent of the soothsayer's warning to Julius Caesar:[4] "Archbishop, beware of the knife!" Those around her tried to silence her — she was ruining the celebration — but her anguished cry echoed out over the acclamations. She was ignored.[5]

The following morning, as he prepared to continue on his journey to Woodstock, messengers from young Henry arrived at Winchester House. The junior king did not wish to see the archbishop;[6] Thomas was ordered to turn back to Canterbury and was not permitted to visit any other cities or towns. Thomas was surprised. He asked the messengers whether the young king was refusing peace and reconciliation with him. They said he was not, and when he tried to question them further, they said that they were there to deliver a message and not to discuss it. When he asked them to take a message back to young Henry, they refused to take it: "You have plenty of clerks for that purpose," they told him. When he asked them to at least help his clerks in getting to Woodstock, some of the knights accompanying the messengers responded by rebuking a man attending Thomas for "consorting with an enemy of the king." Then the messengers left.[7]

Thomas was baffled; he decided to send a message to young Henry seeking clarification, entrusting it to the abbot of the Abbey of Saint Albans. Hearing that the junior king had moved on to Windsor, he sent the abbot there. The abbot's mission proved eventful but unfruitful. Young Henry's attendants tried to prevent him from seeing the young monarch or even passing the message to him, leaving the abbot distressed and frustrated. While he failed in that mission, a chance event led the abbot to locate some of Thomas's missing wine. He would return to Canterbury with a sorry tale and a cartload of wine.

Thomas was trying to keep up to date with what was happening at court. To this end, he sent a spy to Reginald, Earl of Cornwall and uncle of King Henry senior, who was a supporter. The earl was quite ill, and he had been regretting how the dispute had turned out. He had supported Thomas, but now he feared that the archbishop would drag the kingdom and all of his supporters down into eternal ignominy, perhaps even sending them all to hell. Thomas's spy, William of Canterbury, had little success in his mission. The earl's doctor had recognized him and tried to force William to take an oath of secrecy regarding all that he saw unfold; William was told to leave as soon as it was dark. But there was a message for the archbishop from the earl: Thomas and his closest associates were in grave danger. They would need to take great care; if they were found, they would be killed. They should flee the kingdom to safety. When William informed Thomas and John of Salisbury of this warning, the secretary broke down in utter distress. Thomas turned to ease the man's fears. Touching his own neck with his hand in two places, he said to his companions, "Here, here, is where the knaves will get me." It seems that Thomas had received some form of revelation regarding his fate.[8]

Thomas did not heed young Henry's order immediately. Instead of returning to Canterbury posthaste, he visited some deaneries before making his way to his manor at Harrow, to use it as a base as he visited a number of parishes and administered the Sacrament of Confirmation; he also managed to visit London again. He still intended to go to Winchester, but prudence dictated that he postpone his visit to Bishop Henry, for it was being reported to young Henry that the archbishop was wandering around the country in defiance of the royal prohibition. Around December 17, Thomas left Harrow to return to Canterbury. On the way back, he received what he saw as a confirmation of what was to come. As he was passing through the parish of Chiddingstone, the curate came out to greet him. Giving the archbishop relics of the martyrs Saints Lawrence and Vincent, deacons, and Saint Cecilia, the curate told him that he had had a dream in which Saint Lawrence urged him to give these relics to the archbishop. Saint Lawrence had told the curate to refer, as a sign of the authenticity of his vision, to an incident in which Thomas had discovered one day that his hair shirt had split. As the split hair shirt was known only to the archbishop and to heaven, the curate's knowledge of the incident confirmed to Thomas the veracity of the curate's vision. Thomas accepted the relics and asked the curate to remain silent on the matter. On discovering that the priest was poor, Thomas promised him a better benefice, a promise that was honored.[9] The relics of the martyrs seemed to confirm what he now believed lay ahead.

As he approached the city of Canterbury, Thomas saw a great commotion around the city gates and walls. Ranulf de Broc and his thugs had invaded the city from their base in the occupied castle at Saltwood. The gates were guarded by de Broc's men, who had also taken up strategic positions around the city walls. Groups of them had made incursions into the city and were invading and robbing shops and terrorizing the townspeople. For now, there was little Thomas could do — a strong reaction with the few men he had could make matters worse. Making his way to the archiepiscopal palace, he would bide his time over the next few days. For the most part, the de Brocs were targeting him and his suppliers, so he was the one suffering most from this attack, and he dealt with it as best he could.

Thomas spent the days before Christmas quietly carrying out his episcopal duties and preparing for the solemnities to come. On December 20, he ordained a number of priests and conferred orders on some of the monks and clerks. He had come to realize that he had to reconcile with some of the monks in the community, and while initially refusing admission to orders for those who had arrived into the community when he was in exile, in a spirit of charity and conciliation he relented, receiving them with great emotion. This gesture proved apt and prudent; as Christmas approached, peace was restored to the community.

On December 21, Thomas celebrated his fiftieth birthday, doubtless a moment for reflection. He was not the same Thomas who had grown up in London, nor the one who had lived fast and fancy free in Paris, nor even the one who worked with Osbert or Theobald. The years of exile had left their mark. He was still a man of great nobility, but now he bore a different kind of eminence. He was still taller than many, but now he was stooped and gaunt; physically, he was a shadow of the handsome young man who had charmed his way to success. The monks had been astonished at the sight of him on his return. He had left them a vigorous man, strong even if burdened by trials and tribulations; he returned an old man, bent over with the weight of the cross. Perhaps, they feared, he might not have long to live; perhaps the sufferings he had endured would claim him as he tried to settle back into a life of peace. But there was little peace in Canterbury. Ranulf and his men were continuing their mischief, creating havoc in the city. One incident had been so bad that Thomas had threatened to excommunicate some of them if they did not desist, but they ignored him.

The three bishops, Roger, Gilbert, and Jocelin, having reached Normandy, made their way to the court of King Henry senior at Bayeux, arriving on December 21. Henry was in a good mood, but it soured when the bishops entered and told their tale of woe. Weaving a story that was more a patchwork of lies than anything resembling the truth, they told the king that Thomas's censure on them was nothing more than a strike at the legitimacy and validity of his son's coronation. If there was one issue that would catch Henry's attention and set him off, it was any attempt to frustrate his plans for the succession. The archbishop was planning sedition, they told him, and soon he would lead a revolt against him and have the ordinary people of England depose their rightful king. Indeed, the bishops informed him, Thomas was already wandering around the kingdom at the head of a strong force of armed men.[10]

Henry was no fool. He may well have known that this was a fantasy conjured up by angry and resentful men who wanted to be rid of their primate, but he decided to accept what they were saying as true. It served a purpose. Roger de Pont L'Évêque advised him to take counsel with his barons and knights; they alone could help him decide. To rub salt in the wound, Gilbert Foliot then said, "My lord, while Thomas lives, you will neither have peace nor quiet, nor see good days."[11] Such a shocking statement from a bishop did not seem to raise eyebrows, but it may have planted a seed in the minds of some who were present, later easing the consciences of four of the king's knights, who could remind themselves that the bishop of London had suggested that only the assassination of the archbishop of Canterbury would bring an acceptable resolution to this long and painful dispute.

On Christmas Eve, Henry senior met with some bishops and his barons and knights at his court at Bur-le-Roi to discuss what was to be done with the archbishop. The proceedings seemed more like a trial than a consultation, as the old accusations were made against Thomas and, in absentia, he was condemned.[12] The three bishops egged Henry on, as if he needed it. He denounced Thomas as an evil man and a dangerous enemy, for despite the peace negotiations at Fréteval, the archbishop wanted to deprive the young king of his crown. This was treason. Bishop Arnulf of Lisieux entered the fray and explained that not only had Thomas undermined the kingdom by his actions, but he had also damaged the Church by his carelessness and irresponsible zeal. He had failed as a pastor, the bishop informed the assembly, and he had failed in charity in not permitting those he threatened with censure to defend themselves or even repent before excommunication was imposed. The barons then gave their view of the archbishop; one after another, they condemned him, one even suggesting that he must be hanged from the gallows. Henry was inclined to agree; he decided to send knights to arrest Thomas. However, perhaps caught up in his usual rage, Henry turned on his barons and knights: It was time to chastise them for their failures. His words would prove fatal.

Henry complained that there was a man who had eaten his bread who now defied him. A man, he added, who for all he had received from the king, was contemptuous toward him and brought shame upon the royal family. Now this man went trampling about the kingdom, and there was no one to avenge the king. This one man, Henry spat, was a lowborn clerk who came pushing his way into the court mounted on a lame pack mare. This man — and Henry stared at the assembled men

— was turning out the proper heir and sitting in triumph while they just stood watching, not one of them willing to take a stand for their king, to avenge him of the wrongs that he had suffered. These words stirred the fury of four knights to an act of vengeance. There is no evidence that Henry ever uttered the infamous line "Will no one rid me of this turbulent priest?" This could be a later invention, though the sentiment and complaint were factual.[13]

Reginald FitzUrse, William de Tracy, Richard de Brito, and Hugh de Morville were standing at the back of the assembly. These minor courtiers — household knights, but also landowners in the south of England — were stung by Henry's words. Three of them knew Thomas: Reginald, William, and Hugh had sworn homage to the archbishop, saving their allegiance to the king. They had come together for some reason and may well have been plotting something before the king's words stirred them to action. They spent the next day or two pondering over those words and discussed what they could do to save the king's honor and relieve him of this ungrateful servant.[14]

Thomas offered both the Christmas night Mass and Mass on Christmas morning in his cathedral before large crowds.[15] The cathedral liturgy was sumptuous, as befitting the great solemnity of the Nativity, and Thomas likely cherished those hours of prayer with his people. After the High Mass in the morning, he ascended the pulpit to deliver his Christmas sermon. The people were keen to hear what he had to say, as he had proven himself to be a powerful preacher. The theme of the sermon was the Christmas proclamation of the angels over the cave of the Nativity in Bethlehem: "Glory to God in the highest, and on earth peace among men with whom he is pleased!" (Lk 2:14). He told the gathered crowd that he had returned to them, but now the "time of his dissolution was at hand." He spoke to them about the saints of the church at Canterbury, among them Saint Alfege, the martyred archbishop. There would soon be another archbishop martyr for Canterbury, he told them: himself. The people were shocked, and many began to cry. A murmur broke out among them as they wondered what was about to happen and why the archbishop was making such an awful prediction.

Thomas then addressed the situation in Canterbury and beyond.

The city and the lands of Canterbury were occupied and subject to un-lawful acts, he told them, by those who were not men with whom God is pleased. There were those conspiring and working against the Church in defiance of her laws and her people, and there were bishops who fa-cilitated that. Herbert of Bosham noted in his biography that Thomas seemed like a prophet, a prophet animal who had the face of a man and the face of a lion;[16] he was on fire with zeal. Thomas then pronounced excommunication on Ranulf de Broc and his kinsman Robert de Broc, who had laughed in Thomas's face when Thomas rebuked him for his unlawful harassing of the people and the city. He excommunicated those who still held on to Canterbury lands and reiterated his censure on the three bishops and other clerics who had resisted his authority and the rights of the Church.[17]

When the ceremonies were over, exhausted as he was, Thomas joined his clerks and monks for dinner. Though it was Friday, it was Christmas Day, so he relaxed his penitential observance, and Herbert noted that he ate well and was in good spirits. Having observed the offices of the solemnity with the monks in choir, he retired to his rooms for the night. The next day, the feast of Saint Stephen, he offered Mass in the cathedral with his clerks, after which he took Herbert and his faithful crossbearer, Alexander Llewellyn, to one side and entrusted them with a mission. They were to leave that day for France and the court of King Louis. They were to inform him that the peace at Fréteval had failed. The two men were hesitant to go and, in tears, begged him to let them stay. He was only sending them away, they said, so they would not be assassinated with him. Thomas urged them to go and gave them a tearful final bless-ing. Reluctantly, they obeyed.[18] Perhaps Herbert looked back at Thomas as he left the chamber to commit to memory this last image of the man he had served so faithfully; he knew he would never see him again.

Thomas had another task to complete: a letter to Bishop William of Norwich,[19] who had been an ardent defender of Thomas's cause during his years of exile. Thomas acknowledged with gratitude the fervent prayers William had offered, raising his hands to God for him. Recog-nizing with gratitude the graces and blessings these prayers had brought him, he assured the prelate of their effect, "changing our tempest into a gentle breeze, and calming the motion of the waves." Expressing a great desire to see the old bishop again, Thomas hoped that such a meeting would strengthen him in his weakness, for God had set this good bishop "as an immoveable column in his house" during these difficult times. It was the last letter Thomas ever wrote. William responded quickly and with just as much affection. Sure that he himself, now in extreme old age, would die before meeting Thomas, William ended his own letter with a simple valediction: "Farewell forever."[20]

40

Alfege

Thomas's sermon at the Christmas Day Mass was noteworthy for revealing something that was occupying him spiritually: his coming martyrdom, which had been on the wind as he crossed the English Channel. But while martyrdom is an honor for a Catholic, it is also frightening. Facing down a king was one thing; facing the brutal force of a fatal blow was another. Thanks to his conversion, Thomas was aware of the imperfections of his early life, his love of comfort, his misdeeds as chancellor. While he believed in God's mercy, he may have wondered whether his principled stand for the liberties of the Church and the suffering he took on with that stand were enough to erase the effects of his sins, or whether he was guilty of pride.

In this context, while Thomas had no doubt been pondering the struggles of his predecessor Saint Anselm, the life and death of another of his predecessors, Saint Alfege, was also the subject of his meditations. This Anglo-Saxon saint had lived a life very different from Thomas's, but its ascetic aspects may well have appealed to him following his own conversion. As he faced the reality of his own impending death, per-haps Alfege's life and martyrdom resonated at a deeper level with him: As archbishop, how does one prepare to die, and to die well, for the sake of the flock?

Saint Alfege, or Ælfheah as he was known in the Anglo-Saxon, was archbishop of Canterbury from 1006 until his death in 1012. In 1070, at the instigation of the then archbishop, Lanfranc, one of the monks of Canterbury, Osbern, wrote an account of Alfege's life and martyrdom to aid the petition to have Canterbury's first martyr, as Thomas would call him, canonized. When Lanfranc arrived in Canterbury, he found a num-ber of "saints" interred in the cathedral, Saints Dunstan and Alfege among them. One of his main tasks was to restore the cathedral and regularize its liturgical life. While these "saints" were venerated locally, there was no proper documentation of their lives and miracles, and they had not been officially canonized. In what some saw as a hasty action, Lanfranc suspended the cults of Dunstan and Alfege in order to carry out a proper process of regularizing their positions within the Church. As a Norman with a regard for order and precision, he was not comfortable with the Saxon manner of proclaiming saints, not even the synod at Winchester in 1029, which had ordered the observance of Dunstan's feast.[1]

Dunstan, in fact, posed few problems. When it came to Alfege, how-ever, Lanfranc had his doubts as to whether he was a martyr or not, given that he was killed as a result of his refusal to allow himself to be ran-somed. A conversation with Anselm eased his concerns, and Lanfranc decided to proceed with a Cause. In writing the life of Alfege, Osbern put great emphasis on the martyrdom, drawing upon details already men-tioned in the *Anglo-Saxon Chronicle* but adding a great deal due to his reliance on an already existing scheme for hagiographies.

Little is known of Alfege's early life. Osbern indicates that he came from an illustrious family, and some have identified Weston in Somerset as the place of his birth, sometime around 953. He became a monk of Deerhurst monastery near Gloucester, receiving the habit at an early age. From there he went to Bath, where he embraced the hermetic life, build-ing a little hut and shutting himself in to pray and practice penance. But peace and quiet were to elude the hermit, as people came to hear about the holy monk at Bath and sought him out for his prayers and advice. Recognizing in this the will of God, Alfege guided souls from his hermitage, and some of these were inspired to gather around him and form a little community of monks. By the early 980s, Alfege was acknowledged to be the abbot of Bath Abbey, having joined the community from his hermitage. During his administration, he introduced the Rule of Saint Benedict to govern the life of the monks.

In 984, upon the death of Æthelwold, bishop of Winchester, Alfege was elected to succeed him, thanks to the influence of the then archbishop of Canterbury, Saint Dunstan. Alfege proved a great bishop, building up the faith of the people, carrying out important works in the cathedral, and restoring and constructing parish churches. He promoted Æthelwold's Cause for canonization and the cult of another bishop of Winchester, Saint Swithin. He was soon renowned not only for his good governance and concern for his people — most notably, the poor — but also for his holiness of life. He continued to live an ascetic life, so much so that he lost a great deal of weight. Osbern notes in his work that Alfege was so thin that he when he raised his hands at the elevation of the host at Mass, daylight could be seen through them.[2]

In November 1005, the see of Canterbury became vacant following the death of Ælfric, another archbishop destined to be venerated as a saint. Alfege was elected archbishop to succeed Ælfric and, though he resisted initially, was installed at the age of fifty-two. Soon after, he left for Rome to receive the pallium from Pope John XVII; but on his way, he was assaulted and robbed and so arrived penniless into the Eternal City. While in Rome, he had a vision in which he witnessed the death of the man who succeeded him as bishop of Winchester. The vision turned out to be correct, and when news of this vision became known, it would increase his reputation among the English.

Returning to Canterbury, Alfege threw himself into his pastoral duties, showing a particular concern for catechesis and the orthodox teachings of the Church. He was devout in offering the Mass and presiding over the other liturgical ceremonies of the cathedral and archdiocese. He continued to foster a particular love for the poor and encouraged acts of charity among his flock. He also called a number of synods to promote evangelical measures and battle certain errors that were circulating among the faithful. In 1008, he called a council to meet at Enham and there passed various disciplinary measures.

At this time, England was being ravaged by attacks from the Danes. Usually called Vikings, these pirates from Scandinavia made their living by pillaging coastal towns and monasteries, leaving wholesale death and destruction in their wake. In his biography, Osbern makes note of two of these Danish leaders, Swan and Thyrkill,[3] who were responsible for horrendous atrocities in England. Swan had been violent and plunderous enough, but when Thyrkill succeeded him as leader, the attacks escalated. The English king Æthelred, known as "the Unready," had been rather weak in the defense of his realm. Alfege was deeply concerned for the victims of these raids, so in the midst of the crisis, he sought out the leaders of the Danes to negotiate peace.

Alfege met with the Danes. He would not only try to get them to abandon their raids, but also attempt to convert them to the Faith. As he succeeded in winning freedom for those kidnapped by the raiders, paying a ransom for them, he also made some conversions. This effort at evangelization was not welcome by all the Danes; a number of them not only resisted, but also plotted to capture and ransom him, as they could demand a considerable sum for him given his status. These Danes were not alone in formulating this plot; an Englishman, the king's prefect Edric, joined forces with them to avenge his brother, whom he believed King Æthelred was responsible for killing. Edric and the raiders made a pact to act together to kill the king to satisfy Edric and to kill the archbishop to satisfy the Danes.[4]

Some of Alfege's friends heard rumors of the pact and urged him to flee, but he refused. On September 8, 1011, the combined forces of the Danes and Edric's men laid siege to Canterbury; the siege would see twenty days of horror and atrocity. The city eventually fell. Many of its citizens were slaughtered, their possessions pillaged, and the archbishop, who had been active in the defense of the city and his people, was captured. As they left, the Danes set fire to the cathedral, which burned to the ground.[5]

Alfege would remain in captivity for seven months, and Osbern chronicles his patience and kindness toward his captors. In one incident, when a serious illness befell the kidnappers, Alfege blessed bread and gave it to them to eat; those who ate it were healed.[6] While the healing was accepted, little mercy was shown to the archbishop. Word was sent to the king that a ransom would be required for the archbishop to be set free. Alfege, however, made it known that he did not want a ransom to be paid — such monies should be used for the relief of the poor. Osbern relates how, at one point in his captivity, the devil tempted Alfege and set him free, but the old archbishop was not going to flee the cross, and an angel led him back to his prison.

The kidnappers' fury grew, and they finally concluded that they were not going to get anything for this old man and that they would be better off just killing him. On April 19, 1012, the Saturday in the octave of Easter, the archbishop was brought to a gathering of Danes at Greenwich, east of London, on the south bank of the River Thames. In a drunken rage, they fell upon him, striking him on the head with the edge of an axe and with stones. After beating him, they hacked him to death. Suddenly fearful of the consequences of killing a holy man, they decided to throw his body into the river to conceal the deed.[7]

Meanwhile, Alfege's converts arrived; distressed at what had happened, they challenged the killers, asking for the body to be given a proper burial. The killers disputed Alfege's holiness; if these new Christians wanted the body, then the dead archbishop would have to provide a sign. An oar was dipped in the archbishop's blood — if it sprouted into a tree during the night, the killers insisted, then the converts could have the body; otherwise, it would be cast into the river. At dawn, the oar, still dripping in blood, was revealed to have grown into a tree in full bloom. This converted Alfege's killers, who joined with the other converts to bring the body to Saint Paul's Cathedral, where it was interred; it was later translated to Canterbury. Alfege's Cause, promoted by Lanfranc and bolstered by Osbern's biography, was successful: He was canonized in 1078 by Pope Gregory VII.

Alfege's successor, now preparing for martyrdom himself, may have noted that Saint Anselm said of Alfege's martyrdom, "He who dies for justice, dies for Christ."[8] Thomas's premonition of his own death — the two blows to his neck — seemed to echo Alfege's death; it is not known whether he spoke symbolically about his death imitating that of his predecessor or whether he understood that this was how he, too, would die.

On December 26, as Herbert of Bosham and Alexander Llewellyn were making their way to France in obedience to Thomas's orders, the knights FitzUrse, de Tracy, de Brito, and de Morville quietly left the royal court at Bur-le-Roi and headed at top speed to England. They had agreed to separate on the journey so as not to raise suspicions and thus left the continent from different ports, having arranged to meet at Saltwood Castle, where they knew they could rely on Ranulf de Broc to assist them.

Reginald FitzUrse was the self-appointed leader of the four. According to historians, he was a natural bully. His last name meant "son of the bear," which was appropriate given his personality. From landed gentry in Somerset, he had inherited his father's estates upon his death in 1168 and had been a devoted follower of King Henry II since his youth, serving as a knight attendant. Richard de Brito was also from Somerset and a neighbor of FitzUrse. While having a share in his family's estates, he had been in service to Henry's brother, William, Count of Poitou, until the count's death in 1164. He had his own score to settle with Thomas. After the archbishop refused to grant the dispensation to allow William to marry his cousin, it was said that the count died of a broken heart; de Brito sought vengeance for the count's death. Hugh de Morville had been in the service of the king since 1158. He was not only a knight attendant but also Lord of Westmorland. William de Tracy, originally William de Sudeley, was a relative of the king. His maternal grandfather, also William de Tracy, was the illegitimate son of King Henry I, and had therefore been granted a barony, which the young William inherited from his mother; he assumed her surname upon receiving his inheritance.

The four reached Saltwood Castle on the afternoon of December 28. Ranulf was not there when they arrived — he had heard of their coming and had gone to meet them, and they missed each other on the road. His wife received the knights and made them comfortable as they awaited Ranulf's return. When he arrived, Ranulf was very happy to welcome them. Given the warm reception they received, it is not beyond the bounds of possibility that Ranulf was already acquainted with their plan, and he may have been involved in the plot himself. Spending the night at the castle, they formulated a plan of action. The next morning, the four, with Ranulf, mustered a small army of knights and armed men and left for Canterbury.[9]

Entering the city quietly, the knights and a small detachment of men made their way through the precincts of the cathedral to the archbishop's palace. As the knights dismounted in the courtyard, the rest of their men scattered and went about the city trying to raise a mob from among the men of the city. Using the name of the king, they ordered the citizens to take their weapons and come to the palace. The people were fearful and refused to respond. Failing to persuade or threaten them, Ranulf ordered the citizens back to their homes — he was imposing a curfew. If anyone ventured out, he told them, they would be dealt with. Ranulf placed his men at strategic points around the archbishop's palace and had the gates closed and guarded: There would be no chance for anyone to escape or attempt a rescue.

The four knights took off their swords, leaving them leaning against a mulberry tree in the courtyard of the palace; then, throwing cloaks over their chain mail, they entered the building.[10] By now, it was the middle of the afternoon, and dinner had just finished. The palace servants were occupied in the great hall, clearing dishes and taking leftover food to the kitchens. The knights entered the hall crying out, "King's men, king's men!" startling the servants, but they did not see the archbishop; Thomas had retired to his chamber for a rest. Calling out for the archbishop, they demanded to see him. Impatient and fueled with adrenaline, the knights were rough with the servants. The quick-witted steward of the household, William FitzNeal — who had been firmly in Henry's camp during the dispute and had proven himself unfaithful to Thomas and untrustworthy — welcomed the men and, learning that they had come from the king, offered them hospitality and refreshments. The knights refused refreshments — they just wanted to see the archbishop. The aim of this meeting, they said, was to force Thomas to lift the excommunications and give a pledge of good behavior. After that had been achieved, they would ensure that he submitted to be taken away for trial and imprisonment, or whatever the king deemed necessary. William gladly told them to follow him, and he led them to Thomas's private chambers.

The steward informed Thomas of the knights' arrival and their demands to see him. He was in his inner chamber, his bedroom, with some of his closest advisors, as was usual at this time during his daily routine in Canterbury. In an outer chamber, other members of his household were carrying out various tasks. Thomas had spent most of the day in devotion. He had risen early and offered Mass. After thanksgiving, he had made a little pilgrimage to the various altars in the cathedral, spending time in prayer with the saints to whom they were dedicated. This was a spiritual exercise he regularly practiced when in Canterbury.[11] Next, he had gone to confession to his chaplain, Robert of Merton, and he is known to have taken the discipline three times during the day. At two o'clock, he had had dinner in the refectory — pheasant was on the menu — and afterward, retired to his chambers to meet with his advisors. The knights had arrived at about three o'clock.

Thomas waited for some moments before directing the servants to let the four in. He continued to speak with his advisors, but saw the knights enter out of the corner of his eye. Initially unsure of what to do, the knights sat down and waited. They found Thomas sitting on his bed; he seemed quite relaxed, speaking freely with his clerks. When he was ready, Thomas turned to them. They were barons as well as knights, so custom dictated that the archbishop should have stood to receive them as they should have stood to greet him; but Thomas remained seated and looked straight at them. Greeting them, he mentioned only de Morville by name, and this was noted by the others. Reginald FitzUrse took it upon himself to address the archbishop; the others found themselves lost for words, an affliction that never troubled FitzUrse, who had been saving up what he wanted to say to Thomas Becket for some time. "God help you," he announced. "We have brought you a message from the king."

41

Vespers

Thomas flushed red at FitzUrse's insult and arrogance, but held his temper. FitzUrse asked whether he wanted the conversation to take place in public or in private. Thomas said it did not matter, but when his clerks got up to leave, he told them to stay. John of Salisbury whispered to the archbishop that it would be best in private, but Thomas disagreed: What was about to happen had to take place in the presence of witnesses. These things should not be uttered in private nor in the chamber, but in public. It was providential that they stayed: The knights would later admit that, given how the confrontation went, they would probably have beaten the archbishop to death then and there with the cross that stood by his chair if they had been left alone with him. The clerks stayed and committed to memory what occurred that December afternoon. Among them was Edward Grim, who would later write it all down; his account of the martyrdom would be the most detailed and accurate, providing the basis for future biographies, including this one.[1] Three other future biographers also witnessed the events: John of Salisbury, William of Canterbury, and William FitzStephen.

FitzUrse launched into a tirade of accusations against Thomas. When the king had made peace with him, he said, he had sent him back to Canterbury with the dispute settled, as was the archbishop's request. However, he continued, instead of being grateful and gracious, Thomas had insulted the king, broken the peace, and excommunicated those who had crowned the young king. "You arrogantly labor in evil against your lord," FitzUrse accused. He then charged the archbishop with wanting to take the crown from the king's son — everybody now knew that Thomas had labored to contrive against his king. These knights, Thomas was told, had come to take him to the king to answer charges: "For this purpose, we have been sent," FitzUrse said. The knights were claiming to be official delegates, which they were not. This claim would cause endless trouble for King Henry later.

Thomas immediately defended himself. It was never his wish, he insisted, to take the crown away from young Henry; he would wish that he had three crowns. Indeed, he would help him conquer the rest of the world in accordance with reason and fairness. This accusation against him was unjust; it was unfair for the king to be angry with him. His men usually accompanied him on his travels, he conceded, but as he had often been deprived of them in the past, now it was their comfort to be close to their archbishop. If he had offended the king, he was more than willing to seek forgiveness, but why should the king forbid him to enter the cities, towns, and villages of England? As for the sentences, Thomas explained, they were imposed by the pope. The knights rejected this: "They were suspended by you," they shouted, "and you must absolve them!" Thomas agreed that he had had a part in the imposition of the censures, but now the matter had gone to a higher court — as the censures were now papal, only the pope could lift the excommunications. Those under censure would have to go to him. Furious with this response, the knights informed him that he and his men must leave the kingdom. "This is the king's command," they lied. There would be no peace in England, they said, until Thomas Becket and his ilk were gone; it was they who had violated the agreed peace.

"Cease your threats and calm your quarrel," Thomas retorted. "I trust in the king of heaven who suffered on the cross for his own. For from this day," he promised, "there will be no sea between me and my church." The king had granted him safe conduct at Fréteval; he had not come back to flee again. He continued, "He who seeks me will find me here."[2] As for the king, Thomas responded, he should not be making demands; he had thrown enough insults at him and his people without adding any further threats. The king has ordered this, FitzUrse and the knights insisted, and they intended to make good on that command. "You should have bowed to the royal majesty," they chided, instead; they said, Thomas had followed the decree of his own furious passion, casting the servants and ministers out of the Church. "I will strike anyone, whoever it is, who presumes to violate the agency of the Holy Roman See or the laws of Christ's Church and does not make satisfaction," Thomas responded, "nor will I refrain from correcting the offender with ecclesiastical censure."

The knights jumped to their feet in rage. Standing before him and leaning down to stare at him in the face, they threatened: "We caution you, you have spoken with risk to your head!" "Have you come to kill me?" Thomas asked. "I have entrusted my cause to the Judge of all things; I am not moved by your threats, nor are your swords more open to strike than my soul is for martyrdom." They could stare at him as much as they wanted, he continued, but he would not run away. "Seek those who will fly from you," he said. "As for me, you will find me foot to foot in the battle of the Lord."

The knights realized that they were not going to get any further. There was already a commotion in the outer chamber as clerks and servants, pushing up against the door, were panicking in reaction to the argument. FitzUrse called out to them, telling them that if they were loyal servants of the king, now was the time to abandon the archbishop. No one moved. Furious, the knights stormed out of the room, FitzUrse yelling back, commanding the clerks and monks in the king's name to seize and hold Thomas so he could not flee and escape before the king's justice was exacted on his body. Thomas got up and followed them. Standing by the door and touching the back of his neck, he called out to them, "Here, here you will find me." The knights had to push their way out of the palace as clerks and servants unwittingly hindered their retreat. Grabbing some clerks and taking them with them, the knights cried out, "To arms, to arms. King's men, king's men!" They dragged the doorkeeper away from his post to prevent him admitting anyone from outside; they aimed to trap the archbishop and prevent a rescue.

Returning to sit on his bed, Thomas began to console his clerks and servants, who were by now deeply distressed. Some of them insisted that the knights were drunk — it was the drink talking, nothing would come of this row. Others reminded the archbishop that he was under the king's peace, that he was safe. Another reminded them all that it was Christmas, the season of peace and mercy. John of Salisbury, on the other hand, was very worried. He asked if perhaps a milder approach to these men might have been better; Thomas should have taken their advice on this matter. This suggestion would later fuel speculation that if the archbishop had cooperated with the knights and gone with them, blood would not have been shed. This remains one of the accusations against Thomas to this day.

"You are doing what you always do," John chided him. "You act and speak just as you think best, without asking anyone's advice." Thomas asked him what he would have him do. "Call a meeting of your council," John said. "Those knights want nothing more than a good reason to kill you." Thomas reminded him that he had listened to his advisors and pondered their advice, but with what was about to happen with these men, he knew well enough what he ought to do. "We all have to die," Thomas reminded him, "we must not deviate from justice for fear of death. I am more ready to meet death for justice's sake and for the Church of God than they are to inflict it on me." John was terrified to hear this. "We are sinners, the rest of us," he blurted out, "and not ready to die! I cannot think of anyone except you who is asking for death at this moment." Thomas replied quietly, "God's will be done."[3]

The four knights went out into the courtyard. They had arranged a signal with some of the others to come into the palace yard. Returning to the mulberry tree, they took off their cloaks and threw them over the branches. Taking up their swords and axes and tramping over to the porch of the archbishop's hall, they attempted to reenter the building. The clerks had been quick; as soon as the knights had left, two of them,

Osbert and Algar, had slammed the door shut and bolted it, constructing a makeshift barricade against it. Despite their efforts, the knights failed to pry the door open and were forced to find an alternative entrance. Robert de Broc, one of the group, had been occupying the archbishop's palace during the years of exile, so he was able to guide them into the palace by another route. Going through the orchard, they made their way to an outside stair that was being repaired. The workmen had left their ladder, and the knights purloined it to gain access to a window into the archbishop's hall. With their axes, they broke open the window and climbed in. Pulling down the makeshift barricade, they unlocked the door and admitted their men.[4]

Alerted by the noise of the breach, clerks and servants tried to flee the building, making for the cloister. There they found the knights' men herding away people who were coming to the cathedral for Vespers. Some clerks ran to the archbishop and informed him that the knights were in the palace, advising him to flee to the cathedral and take sanctuary there.[5] Thomas reassured them that they were not to be afraid — sometimes monks are too timid, he said; they must not be so easily intimidated. At the moment the bell for Vespers rang, the clerks intensified their pleading. Thomas continued to refuse; he would remain in his chamber, and whatever was about to happen would take place there with no danger to the monastic community. They continued to insist that he take refuge in the cathedral; he would be safe there, they said, and it would not be right for the archbishop to be absent from Vespers. "You have here a truly holy martyr, and dear to God — Alfege; divine mercy will provide you with another; you won't have to wait."[6]

Seeing an opportunity to save him, some of the monks took hold of him and dragged him away toward the cathedral. Thomas tried to resist, but they managed to get him out of his chamber and down into the cloister. By now, the clerks could see that the palace and cathedral were surrounded. The shorter route to the cathedral would have been through the west door, but that was too dangerous now — the knights' men were harassing the people there. Taking the longer route around the cloister, they made for the north door. Pulling himself away from the clerks, Thomas straightened himself up and called for his crossbearer —

Alexander was on his mission to King Louis, so another clerk, Henry of Auxerre, was fulfilling the office temporarily. Thomas decided that he would not resist any longer — everything was now in God's hands. With his cross going before him, he would enter the cathedral from the cloister into the north transept. However, as the clerks were trying to hurry him along, he lagged behind them to make sure that all of them were safe and none left behind should the knights appear after them. Some of Thomas's biographers note a strange occurrence at this time, an event they have come to regard as the "Miracle of the Lock." As the clerks were leading the archbishop to the cathedral, they discovered that the door into the north transept was locked, and they could not find the key. Because the court was thronged with armed men, there was no alternative route. One of the clerks ran at the door in order to force it open, but as he approached it, the door opened as if of itself. In the panic of the moment, little notice was paid to this unusual occurrence — the priority was to get the archbishop to sanctuary and safety — but later it was remembered and recorded.[7]

Once they had the archbishop inside the cathedral, the terrified clerks locked the door, but Thomas rebuked them: "It is not fitting to make the house of prayer, the church of Christ, into a fortress which, even though it is not shut, it serves to protect." Though they initially protested, they reluctantly unlocked the door. "We will triumph over the enemy," Thomas promised, "not by fighting but by suffering; we come to suffer, not to resist."[8] The cathedral had a congregation present for Vespers. Some had come having heard the commotion and thinking they would be safe inside. The monks in the choir had been trying to begin to chant the Office; but disturbed by the din, they were straining to see what was happening. When they saw the archbishop enter, some ran to him to see whether he was harmed — the uproar outside was growing, and they were starting to fear for his life. Thomas assured them that he was fine and directed them to go back to the choir for prayer; he would join them. Perhaps some may have urged him to hide — the cathedral had plenty of nooks and crannies, and the crypt and roof would also have provided protection. If such a suggestion were made, Thomas did not address it.

The monks returned to the choir, and Thomas began to ascend the steps after them. At that moment, FitzUrse and his companions threw open the door from the cloister, their swords drawn. "Where is Thomas Becket, the traitor to the king and the kingdom?" FitzUrse roared. Thomas turned and looked at them, but no one responded. "Where is the archbishop?" he asked again.

Thomas stepped back down toward him. "Here I am," he said, "not a traitor to the king, but a priest. What do you want?" The knights stopped in their tracks. Thomas took a stand by the east wall of the transept, at a pillar between an altar dedicated to Our Lady and another dedicated to Saint Benedict. Edward Grim, now holding the archbishop's cross, stood beside him. FitzUrse demanded absolution for those excommunicated. Again, Thomas refused. "Behold, I am ready to suffer in the name of him who redeemed me with his blood," he said. "Far be it that I will flee or depart from righteousness for the sake of your swords."[9]

"Absolve and restore to communion those you have excommunicated, and return to office those you suspended," FitzUrse demanded again. Thomas responded, "Satisfaction has not been made, I will not absolve them." Brandishing their swords, the knights threatened him once again: "You will die, then, and get what you deserve!" "I am ready to die for my Lord, that in my blood the Church may attain liberty and peace," Thomas responded, "and I forbid that you in any way, in the name of Almighty God, to harm my men, cleric or layman."[10] Thomas then put his arm around the pillar to hold himself firm.

The knights rushed at him; hoping to get him outside and kill him there, they grabbed him roughly and tried to pull him away from the pillar. John of Salisbury and two other clerks ran for their lives, while three remained with Thomas: his chaplain Robert of Merton, Edward Grim, and William FitzStephen. Thomas was not easily hauled away; the knights tried to heave him onto the shoulders of William de Tracy, but the archbishop resisted, throwing his arms around the pillar. Edward Grim put his arms around Thomas to help steady him and stave off the knights. Unable to pry him away, FitzUrse came up with his sword to threaten him, flipping off the archbishop's cap: "Flee, you are a dead man," he shouted.

Thomas was quick to respond, telling Reginald not to touch him and reminding him that, by law, he was his sworn vassal — he owed the archbishop fealty and obedience. He and his accomplices were acting like fools, Thomas chided. FitzUrse wielded his sword against Thomas's bare head. "I have no fealty or allegiance to you against fidelity to my lord the king," he spat out. As FitzUrse grabbed Thomas's cloak to pull him away, the others also declared that they were loyal only to the king.

Thomas is believed to have exclaimed, "Get your hand off me, Reginald, you pimp," alluding, it seems, to FitzUrse's unofficial duty with Ranulf de Broc to seek out female company for Henry senior. Thomas pushed FitzUrse away, knocking him over. "I will not leave this church," he said. "If you wish to kill me, you must kill me here." Thomas had resisted to this point. Martyrdom must not be seized — it is thrust upon the Christian disciple. However, now that he knew it was inevitable, to resist it would seem like an act of pride and a refusal to lay down his life, so he let go of the pillar. He bent his head in prayer, joining his hands; he then lifted them up in the gesture of priestly supplication.

"Strike, strike!" FitzUrse cried as Thomas covered his eyes and prayed, commending himself and the Church to God and Mary and the saints who protected and defended the cathedral, in particular Saint Denis and Saint Alfege.[11] William de Tracy's sword came crashing down on Thomas's head but slipped off and cut right into his shoulder. Edward Grim jumped forward to prevent a second blow and received the full force of the sword on his arm, which was almost severed; he fell back in agony.[12] Blood was pouring down Thomas's face; he put his hand to head and, seeing the blood on it, prayed, "Into your hands, O Lord, I commend my spirit."[13] He fell to his knees, stretching his hands out in prayer. De Tracy hit him again; Thomas fell over, right in front of the altar of Saint Benedict. Dazed and in agony, he was still praying, barely able to speak. The clerks, still trying to fight off the knights, heard him say, "For the name of Jesus and the protection of the Church I am ready to embrace death."[14] These were his last words.

In utter fury, Richard de Brito slashed at Thomas's skull. The blow was so forceful that the top of the archbishop's skull was cut right off and his brains exposed; the sword, striking the paving stones and scattering sparks everywhere, was split in two with the force. "Take that!" he shouted at Thomas, "For love of my lord William, the king's brother."[15]

Of the four, Hugh de Morville had been standing back and did not inflict a blow on the archbishop; he had been charged with making sure no one could intervene to save Thomas. But there was another who had his own revenge to take: a clerk called Hugh of Horsea, a man known for his corruption. Coming up to the lifeless body of the archbishop, he put his foot on Thomas's neck and, with his sword dug deep into the skull, tore out the brains, and scattered them across the cathedral floor. "Let's go from here, knights," he sneered, "this one will not rise again."[16] It was four thirty in the afternoon of the fifth day of Christmas.

The knights fled the cathedral and went back into the palace shouting, "*Reaus*! Royal knights! King's men, king's men!"[17] Entering Thomas's chamber, they ransacked it, taking gold and silver vessels. Then, coming out of the courtyard, they mounted their horses to make for Saltwood Castle. Ranulf de Broc was not to be hurried. As the knights left, he and his men got to work and looted the palace, taking as much as they could load onto their carts, and raiding the stables to take whatever horses were there. When they had satiated their greed, they left the city for Saltwood, where they would divide the spoils and sit down to a hearty dinner.

A terrified silence permeated the cathedral after the murder. The monks and townspeople were frozen in shock — they had witnessed the entirety of the martyrdom. More people from the city were beginning to crowd into the cathedral in response to the commotion. When they saw the body of the archbishop, many began to wail. Edward Grim lay on the floor near the corpse, his arm hanging from him. The monks knew that they needed to tend to Thomas's body, but they were afraid that the knights might return and take revenge on them — they could hear the knights' men at work outside and feared they would return to massacre them.[18] Osbert, one of the servants, tore a piece off his shirt and covered what was left of the archbishop's head. The cathedral had to be cleared before anything could be done, but this would prove difficult given the growing confusion and lamentation. The shock and tears of the people were slowly evolving to a realization that their archbishop had just been martyred. Thomas's Christmas Day prophecy had been fulfilled. Some began to manifest an initial, intense veneration for the new martyr of Canterbury. People started to tear off pieces of their clothes to dip them in Thomas's blood to make relics. Some sick people in the crowd came forward and asked to be blessed with the blood and have it applied to their infirmities. Other enterprising citizens took small glass bottles they had with them and began to collect the blood. This would later be diluted with water and widely distributed.[19]

The monks had to expend some effort to disperse the people and their devotion, finally emptying the cathedral and locking the doors. Thomas's body lay where it fell for some time, alone in the dark. The monks could not escape the inevitable, mournful task of dealing with the body, but they were unsure of what to do. They decided to begin to prepare it for burial. A monk gently took the severed piece of skull, placed it back on Thomas's shattered head, and carefully bound it together with a linen cloth. The monks then examined the body and took off the outer clothes; they would be preserved and later venerated as relics. What remained of the brains and blood were carefully gathered into a silver vessel. In a moment of devotion, Thomas's confessor, Robert, bent down over the body and pulled away part of the archbishop's outer garment to reveal the hair shirt to the monks, who gazed at it in astonishment: The shirt was infested with lice. Some of the monks had been taken aback at the sudden devotion of the people as they were trying to get them out of the cathedral, but now they, too, saw Thomas in a different light. It was a moment of revelation for them and the beginning of devotion among them. They lifted the body onto a bier and carried it before the high altar. Robert of Merton silently began the prayers for the dead.[20] No Mass or Office could be chanted in the cathedral now — it had been desecrated by the murder. Until it was purified and reconsecrated, there would be silence.

Outside, the weather was bad; it would turn out to be a stormy night. That may have provided some relief to the frightened monks — de Broc and his allies would not venture out in such bad weather. Most of the monks retired to their rooms, leaving the body in the cathedral overnight; a small number of them offered a prayerful vigil. The horror of what they had witnessed would remain with them for the rest of their lives, but they were also newly aware that their archbishop had had a hidden life, a penitential life, which had now borne fruit in martyrdom.

A number of them would have to rethink the man and the archbishop, as indeed would many others. Though fear surrounded the monastery and cathedral that night, there was also another feeling — a strange joy and a peace, for what had happened that day would change everything for them and for Canterbury, as indeed it had changed everything for the man they had known as Thomas.

42

The Saint and
the Penitent

The monks slept uneasily that night. They expected Thomas's assassins to return, and events would prove them correct. Though the knights were making other arrangements, Robert de Broc arrived back at the monastery the next morning armed with threats. He too was fearful; he knew the power of a martyr, so he meant to bury Becket once and for all. Meeting the prior and monks, he ordered them to bury the body without any ceremony — otherwise he would seize it, drag it after his horse, and hang it from the gallows before tearing it apart and discarding it in a swamp.[1] The monks heeded the order and proceeded to take Thomas's body down into the crypt where they had decided to lay him to rest.

Richard, prior of Dover, and Walter, abbot of Boxley, had arrived in the meantime to meet Thomas for a conference on the future of the temporary prior of Canterbury, Odo.[2] Instead of greeting the archbishop, they found him slaughtered and themselves in the midst of profound mourning and confusion. They took charge and helped the monks carry out the task of preparing the body for burial. Given the haste required, they could not wash or embalm the body, so they quickly removed the rest of his clothing, discovering his Benedictine habit and his hair shirt; they also found the marks of his penances on his back. They were lost for words; they had not expected this. These revelations posed new questions for them, but now was not the time to reflect on them: Ranulf and his men could return at any moment. They quickly dressed Thomas in his episcopal vestments, put gloves on his hands and his ring on his finger, shod his feet with sandals, and laid his crozier in his arm. They put the pallium around his neck and a miter on his broken head. Finally, his chalice was placed on his breast, over his heart. They prayed the burial rites, then placed the body in a stone sarcophagus, which they sealed. The sarcophagus would be placed directly beneath the high altar in the cathedral, between altars dedicated to Saint John the Baptist and Saint Augustine of Canterbury. Afterward, to mark the site of his martyrdom, the monks put benches over the place in the north transept where Thomas had died.[3]

As the monks turned to the tasks of the day and wondered what would happen next, the people who had crowded around Thomas's body the evening before were spreading the news. The blood that had been collected both on cloth and in bottles was being shared about, and reports began to emerge of healings. One woman who suffered from paralysis had been washed in some of the blood on the evening of the murder; when she emerged from her bath, she could walk again.[4] Other such stories began to filter out, leading locals and people from the surrounding countryside to gather outside the cathedral to try to gain admittance to the crypt to pray at the new martyr's grave.

News of Thomas's murder began to reach all parts of England and the continent, and it was greeted with dismay. The Becket affair had occupied many of the churchmen and crowned heads of Europe; his murder would now send shockwaves throughout the kingdoms and the Church and divide opinions even further. Henry was staying at Argentan, near Sées, when he received word on January 1. When the messenger announced the news, the king froze and began to shake; he suddenly burst into tears and uttered loud wails. Tearing off his clothes, he put on sackcloth, or so the pope was later told. Henry fell into a deep depression, locking himself in his bedchamber, refusing visitors and all food and drink.[5] He was inconsolable, or at least that was what Arnulf of Lisieux relayed to Pope Alexander.

There is little doubt that Henry was deeply distressed at Thomas's murder; the memory of their old friendship may have led him into a genuine state of grief. He was also aware that he bore responsibility for the killing — he had taunted his barons and knights. If not directly, certainly in less than subtle terms, he had indicated that the only way to end the dispute and save his honor was to have Thomas taken out of the equation. But given his nature, he may not have been troubled too much by his conscience. Arnulf's reports are probably exaggerated, and for a reason: Henry's shock may have been more informed by the realization that the whole affair had blown up in his face, and he was now facing very serious consequences. Regardless of how Thomas's murder had happened, he was the one all Europe would look at — he was the one who was responsible for the death of the archbishop. As the details of the murder filtered out, things would look even worse for Henry. The killing had been brutal and had taken place in the cathedral, violating not only a holy place but also the important Christian concept of sanctuary. The three bishops, Roger, Gilbert, and Jocelin, were in serious trouble, too. Their recent lobbying of the king to deal with the archbishop was now seen as inciting Henry to murder; many would now regard them as sharing responsibility.

The pope had yet to be informed. He was now based at Frascati, outside Rome, and the news would take time to reach him. Henry wanted to inform the pope himself to try to steer Alexander's view of the killing. Thomas's friends realized this, and as soon as Herbert and Alexander Llewellyn, now in Paris, heard of the killing, they forced themselves out of their stupor to get a messenger on the road to Italy as quickly as possible. Rather than trust anyone else, faithful Alexander volunteered to go. So began a race down France through Italy as two sets of envoys with competing versions of the murder aimed to get to the pope first.[6] Henry was convinced his envoy would succeed, and so he wrote a letter to Alexander absolving himself of all responsibility.

However, the race made no difference. Pope Alexander had already heard the news before either envoy arrived, and he too had fallen into a state of shock. Consumed with anger and grief, he could not speak to his cardinals about it for more than a week, trying to carry out his duties as he came to terms with the killing. When Alexander Llewellyn arrived ahead of Henry's envoy, the pope was emerging from his depression and intent on dealing ferociously with those responsible. The pope had issued an order that no Englishman was to be granted an audience: The pope was considering his options and would not be swayed by either side in the dispute. When Henry's envoys arrived and discovered what was happening, they grew very worried. There was a real possibility that the pope would excommunicate the king and impose an interdict on his realms. In desperation, they sent a message to the pope indicating that they would submit on Henry's behalf to whatever judgment he made. They also realized that to make excuses would make matters worse — it was time to face up to reality; they accepted that their king had given the knights cause to kill the archbishop.

Pope Alexander thought deeply about his response, and he heeded advice that Thomas, in a moment of insight and charity, had once given him: not to punish Henry too severely, but to try and bring him around. In the end, Alexander excommunicated the four knights. Bishop William of Sens, who was intent on revenge for Thomas's murder, was already preparing to impose an interdict on Henry's continental realms.[7] Bishop William called a council to meet on January 25, 1171, to implement his sanctions, and while Henry organized a large legation to prevent the interdict, his efforts failed.[8] The bishop was unsparing in his denunciation of the king, declaring Henry an enemy to the angels and the whole body of Christ.[9] When he heard of the Bishop of Sens's interdict, Pope Alexander confirmed it and raised it to a papal interdict.[10] As for the king himself, while Alexander stopped short of excommunicating him, he imposed a personal interdict: Henry was not permitted to enter a church or attend Mass. The pope would send legates to the king to hear his confession, absolve him, and impose a penance. Alexander also confirmed the excommunications and censures imposed by Thomas on the three bishops. He permitted an absolution of Gilbert and Jocelin if they swore on the Bible that they had not incited Henry to kill Thomas. As for Roger de Pont L'Évêque, Alexander was not so docile with him: His incitement was well known, and he would pay the price. He would have to languish in his censure for some time — he was not permitted absolution for more than a year and a half.[11] Despite this, Roger and the other two bishops would bear the shame and disgrace of Thomas's murder for the rest of their lives, although for Thomas's supporters, the bishops' punishments were too light.[12] As biographies of the archbishop were written in their lifetimes, the three bishops would attempt to defend themselves, claiming that the archbishop was ultimately responsible for his own demise. But they were fighting a losing battle as devotion to Thomas grew throughout the Church, and his side of the story gained credence and support.

Following the murder, the four knights fled to Saltwood and, with Ranulf and his allies, divided the spoils from Thomas's possessions. The four then escaped to Hugh de Morville's castle in Yorkshire, hiding out while enjoying some hunting on the castle estates. When they were formally served with their excommunications by Pope Alexander, the reality of their deed began to dawn on them, and they realized they were not going to escape the consequences of the murder. Some of them began to show remorse. They remained in Yorkshire for about a year; but then, on advice from Henry and others, made their way to Rome to seek absolution. Henry never arrested them nor subjected them to a trial in his courts. Barlow notes that the king regarded them as his own men who had acted in good faith;[13] the only sanctions the men faced were ecclesiastical.

The knights reached Rome by the spring of 1172 and, after some time, were absolved and had penances imposed: They were to go on Crusade to the Holy Land for fourteen years. While various accounts maintain that the individual knights returned to England, some living out their last days there, and that William de Tracy died in Calabria on his way east, the four are known to have traveled to the Holy Land and were there by Easter 1173, undertaking a penitential pilgrimage to Jerusalem and distributing alms to the poor. At some point, they made their way to Antioch to live out their last days in prayer and fasting. By 1182, all four were dead. It is believed that their bodies were brought back to Jerusalem and buried in front of the Temple Gate. An epitaph on the wall identifying the grave as that of Saint Thomas Becket's murderers was decipherable until the sixteenth century, when the city walls were rebuilt.[14]

The murder would finally see Ranulf de Broc expelled from Saltwood Castle, which was returned to the see of Canterbury and would remain so until it was confiscated by the crown during Henry VIII's usurpation of Church properties. De Broc would remain in Henry's favor, however, and after the failed revolt of the king's sons a few years later, Henry gave him castles and lands for his loyalty to the king. He died in 1179.

Henry would not get off so easily: There was the matter of reconciliation with the Church and restitution. Thomas's murder saw the end of any chance Henry had to impose his will on the Church. Pope Alexander sent legates to carry out the reconciliation and impose penances, and Henry was docile and agreeable in all that was put before him; he had no choice to do otherwise. The legates laid out what was required. He had to swear an oath on the Gospels that he was not complicit in Thomas's murder — while it was humiliating for him in these circumstances, oaths never bothered Henry, as everyone knew at this stage. The legates then chipped away at some of the "ancestral customs." Appeals to Rome could not be refused, for example, but over time the customs became part of life with little opposition from the bishops.[15] Henry was also required to make full restitution to the church at Canterbury and to grant a full amnesty to the exiles. He was also required to perform a number of penitential acts. Due to his claimed interest in taking the cross and going on Crusade, he was charged with sending and maintaining a contingent of two hundred knights in Jerusalem for the defense of the Holy Places; he was also sentenced to go on Crusade himself for a period of at least three years. But Alexander was not finished with him yet: To Henry's annoyance, he had to make a public oath of allegiance to Pope Alexander and his Catholic successors. When Henry had agreed to all this and taken the oaths, young Henry was brought to Caen, where he had to repeat the oaths and accept the same terms as his father.

While England and the Church tried to come to terms with what had happened on that winter afternoon in the cathedral, extraordinary things were happening in Canterbury. News of miracles persisted. The blood of the archbishop, now diluted in water to increase its volume, was being taken to people afflicted with numerous ailments, and many were experiencing healings.[16] The monks at the cathedral were cautious at first, but as the stories continued and those affected arrived to give thanks at the tomb while others came seeking favors, it became clear that a new cultus had begun. Kings, nobles, bishops, and priests struggled with Thomas's life and death, but the ordinary faithful, who had hailed him a hero in life, had no such qualms — now they were calling him a saint. By the time the cathedral was reconsecrated and reopened to the public at Easter 1171, crowds of pilgrims were making their way to Canterbury from all parts of England and beyond. Hesitant at first to open the crypt, the monks relented, and when the pilgrims began to gather around the tomb, the miracles began in earnest.

As devotion to Thomas of Canterbury grew and the cathedral was transformed into a shrine attracting multitudes, the monks realized they had to embrace what was happening before their eyes. They had the plain stone sarcophagus covered with a marble casing to make it a little more pleasing to the eye while securing Thomas's resting place. There were holes in the side of the casing so people could reach in to touch and kiss the sarcophagus. In popular devotion, the tomb of the martyr was beginning to be considered an ark where the faithful could find refuge in their needs. Liturgical ceremonies in the cathedral were increased to meet the demands of the faithful, and formal records of all miracles and healings were kept. Edward Grim wrote and published the first biography in late 1171, giving an eyewitness account of the martyrdom and inspiring other writers — those who had known Thomas and those who had not — to compose their own works. These biographies were disseminated far and wide. Those who saw an opportunity to make money came to Canterbury along with the pilgrims. Inns and hostelries opened up, and souvenir sellers arrived to offer pilgrims mementos of their visit to Canterbury. In the meantime, bottles of the archbishop's diluted blood were being distributed throughout England, and miracles were being reported from all over the kingdom.

But there was another task the monks now knew they had to accomplish, as strange as many who knew Thomas would have considered it: his canonization. Submitting a petition, accompanied by details of Thomas's life and the miracles that had occurred following his death, to Pope Alexander, they may have wondered whether he would be inclined to grant it, given that he had been in the midst of the dispute himself. The pope had had time to reflect deeply on all that had happened and on Thomas's character and actions. While the archbishop had not been perfect and had not always responded well and prudently to events as they unfolded, the pope knew that he had been correct in his struggle and that he had, in the end, served the Church well. Indeed, there was little doubt in the pope's mind that Thomas had died for the liberty of the Church, and this meant that he was a martyr. He was also intrigued by the news that came to him of the miracles; they were testimony enough to the nature of Thomas's death and what God thought about it. When the petition arrived, Alexander wasted no time in granting it. He canonized Thomas on Ash Wednesday, February 21, 1173, while he was staying at Segni, a city in the Lepini Mountains outside Rome.[17]

Pope Alexander's own troubles were not over. Barbarossa would continue to defy him until 1177, when their dispute ended with the Peace of Venice; a final antipope, Innocent III, was an irritant for a few months, from September 1179 to January 1180. Following the Third Lateran Council in 1179, which proved to be one of the most influential of the Middle Ages, Alexander was forced from Rome by the rebellious Roman Commune. He never returned; he died in Civita Castellana on August 30, 1181.

As the miracles continued and the pilgrims came, the cult and shrine of Saint Thomas of Canterbury would grow until his tomb became the third most important shrine in medieval Europe. It was the poor who first came in those winter days of December and January 1170–71; then came the pious and the curious; after that, the clergy, priests before bishops, who tend to be more cautious; and then the dignitaries and the royal. Young Henry came to pay homage to his former tutor and "foster father" in 1172. In his silent prayer at the tomb, he may have asked forgiveness for his refusal to receive Thomas in the last week of his life. But young Henry was now quarreling with his father, and this visit was more of a strike against Henry senior than anything else. In 1173, the monks elected a new archbishop, Roger de Bailleul, another abbot of Bec, but he declined. On April 7, 1174, the monks elected Prior Richard of Dover to the see, and he accepted, serving as Thomas's successor until his death in 1184.

Another drama was required before the dispute between Thomas and Henry was over, and the martyr's allies and the pope were determined to ensure that it happened: a penitential pilgrimage by the king himself to the tomb of the archbishop. Despite the absolution and the sentences he had accepted, in the summer of 1174, everything was falling apart for Henry — he was plagued by various disasters, rebellions, and his wife's political infidelity. It seemed that the blood of Thomas Becket was crying to heaven for vengeance, and heaven was listening. News of the miracles may have annoyed him; indeed, they seemed a fresh wound to his pride. It was bad enough that Thomas had won, but that he had become a saint at Henry's expense was too much. Now a greater humiliation lay in store, and again, it seems, Henry had no choice. On July 12, 1174, Henry traveled to Canterbury on this penitential pilgrimage to make public reparation for what many believed was *his* murder of Archbishop Thomas.[18] Arriving in the city, he was taken to the Church of Saint Dunstan, where before monks, other clergy, and barons he was stripped of his clothes, was dressed in sackcloth, and had ashes put on his head. In his bare feet, he walked the long street that would take him to the cathedral, where he knelt at the door and requested admittance. Once inside, before descending to the crypt, he knelt at the spot where Thomas was murdered by his knights and, in an act of penance, kissed the flagstones.

Led down into the crypt, Henry came to the tomb; once again kneeling, he asked forgiveness. Demonstrating remorse, as required, he lay down across the top of the tomb as the monks tore the sackcloth from his back and, taking out scourges, lashed him, each monk taking his turn. For the moment, obeisance was required; Henry gritted his teeth as he received the strokes of this ritual scourging, not as much from the physical pain as from wounded pride. The king had to be chastened, and he was determined to remain as stoical as possible; not a whimper would escape his mouth. His demeanor needed to be penitent. But Henry Angevin was a survivor; he still lived, and he was king. He would move beyond this ignominious moment with no more Becket to make things difficult — or so he thought.

43
A Solitary End

Henry's humiliation at the tomb of his former friend did not chasten him.[1] After the scourging and the long night vigil in the crypt, he would have been glad to get out into the fresh air and go hunting. Peace would evade this man for a long time to come, and it was not Thomas's fault. Henry's dispute with the archbishop, it would turn out, was not to be the most bitter in his life; it was overshadowed in importance and agony by that with his wife, Eleanor, and his sons, in particular young Henry, Richard, and Geoffrey. In 1173, while he was still dealing with the fallout from Thomas's murder, he found himself in the midst of a revolt: His sons and their mother rebelled against him and tried to stage a coup.[2]

Henry's relationship with his wife had broken down.[3] This was not surprising given the nature and strength of their personalities and their individual ambitions. He had been unfaithful to her, not unusual among kings and lords at that time, and as her sons increasingly felt that their father was treating them abysmally, she took their side in their grievances against him. True issue of their parents, the young Plantagenets, as the royal family was to become known, were ambitious, hungry for power, and dysfunctional. Now that Thomas's influence had worn off, young Henry was just as willful as the others. Jealous and headstrong, each of these young men wanted honor and independence, and a decent income. Often finding themselves in a political limbo, given their father's dominance, the sons reacted badly. Young Henry in particular harbored resentment for his father's patronage of their youngest brother, John, who seemed to be Henry's favorite.[4]

In March 1173, young Henry, followed by Richard and Geoffrey, fled to Paris to confer with King Louis and seek his support for their coup against their father.[5] Having sought to rouse support for her sons' cause,[6] sometime between March and May that year,[7] Eleanor attempted to join them in their rebellion. Fleeing Poitiers, where she was living, disguised as a man,[8] she set off for Paris. But it is almost impossible for a queen to flee in secret, and her attempt failed; Henry, expecting her to take their sons' side, had been waiting for her to try to abscond to join them. Captured in transit, she was sent to her husband, then at Rouen. For the next year, no one knew where she was; Henry kept her out of sight. In July 1174, she accompanied him from Barfleur to England, where they disembarked at Southampton. As he was preparing for his penitential pilgrimage to Canterbury, Henry sent his wife into what became sixteen years of imprisonment, moving her from one castle to the next to prevent attempts to rescue her.[9] In those years, Eleanor would have little contact with her sons and would grow increasingly distant from them. Allowing her very brief periods of release for Christmas and other special occasions, Henry kept a tight rein on her.

Regardless of their mother's fate, the three sons raised a revolt against their father that would drag on for years, leading Henry to conclude that this was God's punishment for his part in Thomas's murder. The revolt extended beyond a family feud as the royal house of France got involved. Louis had lost a great deal of respect for Henry following the archbishop's martyrdom, but his territorial ambitions never needed an excuse to get an airing, and he saw a plum opportunity in Henry's dispute with his sons. The three boys had commended their cause to Louis, and he rose to the occasion.[10] He was not the only one. Henry faced serious opposition, and not just from enemies; even some of his own barons defected to his sons' cause.[11] As Henry was increasingly weakened, and was suspicious of his other barons — he could not be sure whether they were truly loyal[12] — his neighbors were sizing up the possibility of making gains for themselves: England could well be easy pickings. King William of Scotland invaded the north, while Henry's supposed ally Philip, Count of Flanders, took to his ships and invaded the south.[13]

Henry may have thought this was the end of his reign, but stubborn as he was, he would battle to the end, and his persistence paid off. With the help of local militias in England and a tenacious defense in Rouen, he pushed Louis back and forced him to capitulate. After eighteen months of fighting, his sons retreated and sued for peace. In the peace conference that followed, at Montlouis on September 30, 1174, Henry's astuteness inclined him to leniency and gave him the upper hand,[14] a graciousness that surprised his sons.[15] Ironically, he emerged from the revolt as powerful as ever. It is possible that, despite their dispute, Henry commended his cause to Saint Thomas and believed that the archbishop's intercession was a major factor in his victory — a sign, perhaps, that his former friend had forgiven him. Indeed, it was just after his penance at Canterbury that a breakthrough came — the defeat of the invading king of Scots in Northumberland.[16]

With Eleanor imprisoned, Henry continued with his extramarital affairs, one of which would prove more serious than his usual dalliances. He entered into a relationship with Rosamund Clifford, a young woman who was originally his mistress but quickly became much more than that. Though the two met in 1166, their intimate relationship is believed to have begun in 1173.[17] Henry had had many mistresses, but he acknowledged his affair with the "Fair Rosamund" publicly in 1174, and it was said that he was contemplating divorcing Eleanor to marry her. Historians dispute whether children were born to them. The liaison ended sometime before 1176, when Rosamund died. She had been living in Godstow Abbey, not far from Oxford, and is believed to have been only in her late twenties at the time of her death. The story of Henry and Rosamund has fueled the romances of troubadours and the works of painters ever since. One rumor maintained that Eleanor had her killed, either poisoning her or having her mutilated in her bath; there is no evidence to support either claim. It had been suggested that Henry publicly flaunted his mistress to annoy Eleanor or force her into seeking an annulment; if so, he failed. Eleanor remained stoic through it all.

Henry found he, too, would have to embrace stoicism — peace was going to further elude him. Despite the treaty brokered between him and his sons at Montlouis, disputes over rights, finances, and succession continued. Young Henry died in 1183.[18] He had caused his father more concern when, in the summer of 1182, he demanded to have Normandy, or another domain, to support himself.[19] With Henry's refusal came more trouble and another revolt and war in February 1183,[20] which only ended with young Henry's death. Richard was now deemed the heir and was called to come to England to be anointed junior king. While he was happy about that, when Henry informed him that he would have to renounce Aquitaine, which he had been governing quite favorably, Richard refused to do so. He had seen his brother Henry twiddle his thumbs while he was supposedly deputed to govern England. Henry senior was never inclined to renounce power, and Richard was not prepared to concede to that banal role. Things were made worse when Richard discovered that his father was going to depute Aquitaine to the beloved younger son, John.[21] So began another dispute, and more war followed. Once again, the family was divided: Henry's younger son, Geoffrey, took up Richard's cause as he nursed his own grievances against his father. In the midst of the conflict, Henry had tried to get his youngest son, John, to get up and oust Richard from Aquitaine, though John had no army and Henry would not give him one.[22] War and invasions by the brothers, now fighting among themselves, in various territories of their father's realms continued until Henry ordered everyone to England at the end of 1184. A treaty was eventually brokered, and a family reconciliation followed, but tensions were increasing — and Richard still held on to Aquitaine. Henry decided to play his trump card: Having Eleanor brought to Normandy under strict guard, he sent her to Richard to convince him to surrender Aquitaine to her. Richard loved his mother and would be inclined to heed what she had to say, but the stratagem was brilliant. Aquitaine had been Eleanor's inheritance and, had Richard refused to relinquish it, his father told him, then Eleanor would be the one to direct her armies against him and take it by force.[23] Richard relented and accept his fate, albeit reluctantly, at the end of 1184.

Still, there was to be no rest for the king. No sooner had one son had been chastened, another was in trouble — this time the beloved John. He had been governing Ireland for his father, but not very successfully. He had offended the Irish nobles and failed to make alliances with the Anglo-Norman settlers; now he found himself in the midst of a conflict.[24] He had no money, so the mercenaries he had engaged deserted him. Realizing that he had no hope of defeating the Irish, John decided that the best thing to do was flee to his father, returning to England in December 1185, blaming the ambitious lord of Meath, Hugh de Lacy, who had set his sights on establishing an ascendancy in Ireland. De Lacy was assassinated in July 1186, and Henry intended to send John back to Ireland, but the death of his son Geoffrey put pay to that. John was left high and dry.

King Louis VII of France had died in 1180. As his health had declined following Thomas's martyrdom, he too had been concerned with his son's succession. Though unable to attend the coronation himself due to an attack of paralysis, he had his son Philip Augustus anointed and crowned in Reims on November 1, 1179. Louis never recovered; he died in Paris on September 18, 1180, and was buried at Barbeau Abbey, not far from Fontainebleau, which he had founded in 1147. In 1817, his bones, having escaped the destruction of the French Revolution, were transferred to the royal crypt in the Abbey of Saint Denis just outside Paris. Louis had managed to make a pilgrimage to the tomb of his friend Saint Thomas in August 1179 — it was the first time a French monarch had visited England. During his visit, dressed as a simple pilgrim, he left a number of gifts, including the largest gem in existence at that time, the Régale de France. Henry met Louis during this visit and they spent some time together. Louis stayed five days in England before returning to France.[25]

Following his father's death, Philip Augustus, ascended the throne of France as Philip II. Very much his father's son, Philip sought to use troubles afflicting the House of Plantagenet in England to his and France's advantage. Henry II and his son Richard despised each other, and by now there was no chance of reconciliation or even an uneasy peace. Philip was ready to use various tactics to pull Richard from Henry, thereby creating opportunities for territorial gains and satisfying his late father's honor. Philip formed an alliance with Richard in the hope of gaining territory while helping the young Plantagenet overcome his father. On another front, he made a demand for custody of Henry's grandchildren by the late Geoffrey: Philip had been a friend of Geoffrey's, so he maintained that he was concerned for their proper upbringing.[26] In the end, Henry and Richard's dispute reached a crisis point. Henry refused to acknowledge Richard as his heir, driving his son further into the arms of the French king and thus igniting another war. The pope at the time, Clement III, tried desperately to intervene, but to no avail. In 1189, Henry was once again on campaign with his army against his son and the king of France.

The years of war and trouble took their toll on Henry; though robust all his life, his health was by now in decline. As the war with this son continued, he made a strategic mistake, after a military encounter at Le Mans, when he should have retreated to the safety of Normandy, as advised, he declared that he wanted to go to Anjou. He knew his health was failing and suspected that he was reaching the end of his life. Aware of his decline, Richard and Philip pushed their advantage and made important gains. When Henry arrived at his castle at Chinon, in the Loire valley, he collapsed, as did his campaign. A peace conference was called to meet at Ballan near Tours on July 4, 1189. It would prove to be a humiliation for Henry. Unable to get off his horse, he was forced to agree to all the terms offered, though they were thoroughly unsatisfactory to his cause. Included was an acknowledgment of Richard as his successor. Henry did not have the strength to resist. His humiliation was compounded the next day when, back at Chinon in his bed, he learned that his favorite and beloved son, John, had defected to Richard's side. This was the last straw. He turned his face to the wall and cried bitterly.

Henry's health deteriorated quickly. He lapsed into delirium with few moments of lucidity — in those brief episodes, he bade farewell to his friends.[27] In one moment of consciousness, the day after his return, he asked to be taken to the castle chapel. Carried on a litter, he was placed before the altar. He made his confession and received the last rites and Holy Communion; not long after, he died. It was July 6, 1189; he was fifty-six years old. His servants clothed him in his best robes, and the few barons who had remained loyal brought him to the nearby Abbey of Fontevraud. Richard had been informed that his father was dying, but he ignored the news. When word came that his father was dead, he waited until nightfall and then came to the abbey. Standing alone over his father's body, he was silent, looking down on his father's face only once. For a moment, he knelt to offer a short prayer and then, rising, left the abbey to take charge of his new kingdom and to make arrangements to have his mother set free.[28] Henry was interred in a tomb in the nearby Fontevraud Abbey after a requiem Mass. While he had directed that he was to be buried at Grandmont Abbey in the Limousin, the weather was unusually hot that summer, so it was judged unfeasible. Eleanor would be buried with him following her death on April 1, 1204; and even Richard himself would, in time, be laid to rest beside his father following his death in his beloved Aquitaine in 1199 at just forty-one years old. John would succeed to the throne upon Richard's death, and it fell to him to continue Henry's line and history of controversy. The same John would be forced to sign the Magna Carta, one of the most influential documents in legal and constitutional history; whether his father would have approved of it is doubtful. To further shame him in the eyes of his father, John lost Normandy and much of the possessions of the Angevin empire to Philip of France, revealing that the nickname given him many years before, "Lackland," was not entirely inappropriate.[29] He managed to hold on to Ireland.

Epilogue

The number of pilgrims making their way to Canterbury continued to increase in the years after Thomas's canonization. Patronage of the new shrine ensured that it would assume an important role and status in England, and in Europe; despite their dispute in life, even Henry was a proud benefactor. As pilgrims arrived in the city, they would have made their way to the cathedral and, entering it, first paused at the place of martyrdom, before descending to the crypt and queuing up to pray at the tomb of the new martyr. When their turn came, they would kneel down and, reaching in to touch the sarcophagus to get close to the martyr's body, pour out their hearts and their needs, many shedding tears as they unburdened themselves. Watching the endless line of pilgrims one day was Richard de Lucy, one of Thomas's enemies in life. As he stood pondering over the devotion of the people, he turned to one of Thomas's former clerks, Henry of Houghton, and in a state of exasperation asked him how all this was possible. How could Thomas, whom he knew to have been lavish in his lifestyle, severe toward the Church when chancellor, and rigid and stubborn when archbishop, be working such miracles? The clerk may have been just as amazed at the devotion and God's response to it, but he offered Richard an explanation. Thomas had suffered years of exile, he said, many injuries, and then a cruel death; if Saint Peter and the Good Thief could obtain pardon for their sins, he mused, Thomas must surely have atoned for his lesser transgressions.

Six years of hard exile and bitter suffering changed Thomas of Canterbury. The story of his life is one of conversion — not a dramatic moment that changed his entire life, but a gradual turn toward the truth and an embrace of virtue. That is often disputed by historians, including W. L. Warren; in his view, Thomas was fundamentally a proud and self-centered man who sought to prove that nothing was beyond his confidence.[1] Dom David Knowles in his study suggests that Thomas's canonization was due directly to his murder and posthumous fame rather than his personality,[2] though he accepts there was a change in Thomas wrought by suffering, the crucial moment in that "conversion" being the crisis following the council at Northampton.[3] Knowles certainly has a point there. The story of Thomas of Canterbury is the story of a man who came to understand what was required of him as a Christian, as a priest, and as a shepherd of Christ's flock; and though in the end he realized it would cost him his life, he had to take a stand. That realization may have taken time and much suffering before it came to fruition; it was not as dramatic as Saint Paul on the road to Damascus. Thomas knew failure and the power his weakness could have over him, but as he bitterly regretted his weakness and sinfulness, he surrendered to Christian hope and the grace of God. In doing so, he invited the virtue of fortitude to establish a firm root within him. Those who gathered at his tomb realized this, though those close to him may have missed it. It was only in hindsight, as they witnessed the miracles, that Thomas's enemies and friends reassessed what they had seen and heard. The hagiographies that emerged often employed fabulous and pious details to ornament Thomas's life — this did him no favors. He was flesh and blood, passionate, angry, unyielding, and often lonely, but these weaknesses and flaws actually enhanced the man Thomas became, as grace transformed them from barriers to holiness to tools in the defense of the rights of the Church and her people.

The pilgrims praying at Thomas's tomb, often in a pitiful state as they reached in to touch his sarcophagus, were turning to a man they knew could protect them and help them in their illnesses, their difficulties, and their needs. Ambition, politics, and failures aside and stripped away, Thomas Becket emerged as a champion and intercessor for the people. As the rich and powerful struggled to come to terms with the archbishop's life and legacy and God's response to his martyrdom, Thomas himself turned to the poor and the needy from heaven and did what he had learned to do in life: feed and protect the flock. It was fitting. After the Council of Clarendon, Thomas had accused himself of abandoning the flock; now, in death, he was the great advocate for the humble and the poor.

Devotion to Thomas — now inscribed in the Church's Canon of Saints as Saint Thomas of Canterbury, bishop and martyr — spread quickly all over the universal Church. Churches and abbeys were dedicated to him, and shrines were established all over Europe. Relics of his blood, in particular Saint Thomas's Water, were disseminated, and the miracles continued unabated. Following the solemn translation of his body in 1220 from its resting place in the crypt to a magnificent new shrine in the newly built Chapel of the Most Holy Trinity above the sanctuary, bone relics were taken and delivered to many places, including Rome, and from there distributed throughout the world. Pilgrims flocked from all over Europe to pray at the tomb and seek his intercession. In England, various pilgrim routes developed, with spiritual itineraries and wayside shrines to mark the progress of travelers. Inns were built along these roads to cater to pilgrims' needs. Canterbury, no longer just the seat of the archbishop primate of England, became a busy international shrine catering to hundreds of thousands of pilgrims each year. As Geoffrey Chaucer's late-fourteenth-century *Canterbury Tales* reveals, the pilgrimage to Saint Thomas's tomb became iconic. However, though it seemed as if it would never end, the pilgrimage's days were numbered. The dangers that Thomas resisted would never stop harassing the Church.

On November 16, 1538, as he was instituting his new church, Henry VIII issued a proclamation at Westminster in which he declared that Thomas Becket was a traitor to the Kingdom of England. In a symbolic gesture, he summoned Thomas Becket to face charges of treason, but no penitent archbishop arrived at the Palace of Whitehall. In response to

Archbishop Becket's defiance, Henry instructed that his shrine at Canterbury be destroyed. Almost immediately, zealous troops departed for Canterbury and, in an orgy of destruction, tore the shrine to pieces, pulling the bones of the occupant out of the tomb and burning them. The precious metals and stones that had formed the shrine and the many votive offerings that had been left over the centuries were confiscated and found their way into the king's treasury to finance his lavish lifestyle. Thomas had defied the honor of a king; it was now decreed that his life and example were a scandal to England and not worthy of veneration. That Henry VIII's own ambitions resembled his predecessor's, and that he too had executed a former lord chancellor, also called Thomas, for his Catholic faith were other excuses to rid England and her new church of Becket.[4] The riches of the shrine were not to be ignored, either.

Despite the destruction of the shrine, a rumor emerged, one that has persisted to this day: that the monks, hearing of the proclamation, took immediate action. Opening the tomb, they are said to have carefully removed the bones of Saint Thomas and dug a grave in a hidden part of the crypt, laying them to rest there, while replacing them with the skeleton of another who, presumably, would be happy to take the archbishop's place to save the holy relics. In the nineteenth century, during excavations in the crypt, the skeleton of a man with serious injuries to his skull was uncovered, and though it was reburied at the time, many have speculated as to whether these were bones of the martyred archbishop.[5]

Like the poor and the humble, Henry VIII understood Saint Thomas of Canterbury, though with a differing emotion: He feared him. A man intent on power and subjecting everything to himself, including the Church, the Tudor king knew the martyred archbishop was a dangerous man, a stubborn man who would not yield to tyranny even when others discerned that compromise might be the safer path. Often alone and alienated, defamed and attacked, Thomas somehow found the strength to take a stand and dig his heels in. In life his enemies saw arrogance and pride as that which kept him rooted to his cause; others, perhaps, saw foolishness; and in a recent biography, one historian, who harbors great admiration for Thomas, writes that it was an innate rebellious streak.[6] But Henry Tudor understood the archbishop for who he was: a voice of truth and freedom in the face of willfulness, fear, and cowardice. Though he was not perfect and made many mistakes, Thomas could not surrender that which was true, not even to achieve what was called peace. Henry VIII's proclamation summed up all he thought about Thomas, and he did not think much of him — he despised him. However, the proclamation is notable for one curious fact: This king "decanonized" Thomas. Henry's removing Thomas's name and feast from the calendars of the Church of England was akin to the ancient Roman practice of *damnatio memoriae*, often meted out to wicked Romans (Emperor Nero included): the "condemnation of memory," a punishment unto oblivion. Thomas was to be forgotten by Henry's new brand of Christianity: a Christianity free of the shackles of Rome; a new, reformed institution centered on the life of the nation and the monarch; a glory for the kingdom — in short, secularized and obedient to its master, who in turn saw himself as the master of the world. Thomas saw this happen in his lifetime, and now his legacy to the Church is his unremitting call to stay awake so as to detect it in all times.

Thomas of Canterbury, then and now, is the foe of tyranny. He is also the thorn in the side of those shepherds in the Church who, for various reasons, conform to tyranny, or at least try to placate it. In his lifetime, he admonished his brother bishops for their cowardice, and he continues to do so today. This is part of his legacy to the Church: He urges pastors to stand firm, even if it means they may lose their possessions, their places of honor, their reputation among the establishment; even if it means they must lose their lives. Thomas lost everything, even his life, and in return he gained everything. This was why the ordinary faithful could trust him — in the end, Thomas of Canterbury was not a man for himself. He was a man for others.

Thomas should not be relegated to *damnatio memoriae*; his legacy should be alive in the hearts and minds of the faithful, and most particularly in the lives and ministry of bishops. As he challenged believers in life, he continues to do so in death and in glory. In engaging with him, we may unintentionally wrap the man and the events around him in knots of scholarship and complexity. But in the end, his story is not complex at all: It is a story of faith. Thomas's mother taught him at her knee to answer the question, "Who is the master; and will you stand by him?" It is a question Thomas asks of all Christians in every age. Thomas of Canterbury is as significant now as he was in the twelfth century — indeed, even more so as the Church continues to find herself in difficult and hostile relationships with secular governments, and as she is being tempted to conform, for the sake of peace or, worse still, relevance, to ideologies and systems contrary to the Christian faith.

Today in Canterbury Cathedral, a single candle stands on the floor of the Trinity Chapel. Faithfully tended by the Anglican clergy of the cathedral, it marks the spot where Thomas's tomb stood from 1220 to 1538. Outside on the façade of the cathedral, statues of Henry VIII, Edward VI, and Elizabeth I — the architects of the English Reformation — have been added to those of saints and bishops of Canterbury and England. In worldly terms, for now anyway, it seems that Thomas's sacrifice was in vain. What he, Anselm, Theobald, and so many others tried to stop came to be: The Church in England seemed to fall under the complete control of the monarch. Henry II would have been delighted that his successor, the eighth of his name, finally achieved what he had hoped to do. That delight, however, might have been marred by the fact that that same monarch, the eighth of his name, also brought Henry II's line to an end by executing the last surviving Plantagenet in 1541: Margaret Pole, Countess of Salisbury. Henry VIII put Margaret to death not only because she was a threat to the throne, but also because of her refusal to renounce her Catholic Faith and her adherence to Rome. The last of Henry Angevin's line shed her blood in common cause with Thomas.

Blessed Margaret Pole and the many thousands of Catholics who remained faithful to the Church in the midst of the Reformation's religious revolution preserved the legacy and example of Saint Thomas. They continued to celebrate his feast in secret in their homes, without the splendor as in medieval days but with as much fervor and devotion. Recusant priests offered the Mass in his memory as the persecuted Catholics of England invoked his intercession for their cause and their country. Many of these would share in his fate, standing on gallows, accused of stubbornness and treason for their refusal to subject their faith and their Church to the will of the monarch.

Thomas's place is no longer in Canterbury. In the Middle Ages, the pilgrims came to him there, but since the destruction of his shrine — indeed, long before it — he goes out to the faithful wherever they are. There is no longer a central focus for devotion to him, because there is no need for it. As he said to his persecutors in the last moments of his life, so now he says to all: "He who seeks me will find me here." He is with all those who call out to him. Given his universality, it is time for a resurgence of devotion to him, for Catholics, and indeed all Christians, to see in him an advocate, a model, and a friend. It is time for the faithful to reflect on his legacy and see how it can help them and the Church face the difficulties that now assail them. In this context, the historian Anne Duggan notes: "Becket's example, of resistance to an aggressive 'public power' and courage in the face of extreme violence, could be appreciated by men and women across the ages."[7] Thomas's sacrifice continues to resonate in the Church and the world, and we should take note of that.

Today, a stone plaque bearing his name, "THOMAS," marks the spot where he was martyred, an area of the cathedral now dubbed "The Martyrdom." That plaque is fittingly simple and poignant, but yet perhaps a misnomer. In the eyes of many, then and now, the whole Becket affair was a row between a king and a bishop, and it was the bishop's vanity and selfish ambition that led to the awful event that took place at four thirty in the afternoon on December 29, 1170. Modern historians can be hard on Thomas; they see that he betrayed a noble and lawful king who was trying to bring peace to his troubled realm. Thomas was obsessed with himself, many of them believe, and not the common good. Such accusations have been made of many martyrs down the centuries, and indeed of Jesus himself; hence the high priest's decision to offer the rabbi from Nazareth to the Romans for the sake of the people. However, to read this man's life in the light of his faith is to come to understand that for Thomas himself, despite the weaknesses, failures, and ambitions of the younger man, in the end, it was not about Thomas at all: It was about Christ and the Church that Christ founded. Perhaps if he had his way, the name inscribed on that plaque at "The Martyrdom" would not be "THOMAS" at all — it would be "CHRIST."

Arca Sancti Thomae

(Invocation to Saint Thomas of Canterbury)

"He who seeks me will find me here."

O holy Thomas of Canterbury,
graciously hear those who invoke you.
Ark for the poor, *hear us.*
Ark for suppliants, *hear us.*
Ark for the sick, *hear us.*
Ark for the desolate, *hear us.*
Ark for the persecuted, *hear us.*
Ark for faithful souls, *hear us.*
Ark of peace, offering your life
for the love of God and his Church, *hear us.*

O blessed Thomas, may we find shelter

within the ark of your intercession;
hear the prayers of those who turn to you
and commend us to the mercy of God.

May his mercy be poured out upon us
like refreshing rain in the summer heat,
like wine to the thirsty soul,
like oil salving the bitter wound,
that he may touch our hearts
and relieve us of our iniquities
and hear our fervent prayer.

O blessed Thomas, faithful servant of God,
pray that … *(mention your intention here).*

Let us pray:

Eternal Father, through the intercession of your faithful bishop
and martyr, Saint Thomas of Canterbury, pour down upon your
children your blessings and graces in abundance. Hear their
prayers and grant them their needs, and as they seek the aid of
your blessed servant, may they imitate him in his fidelity and
charity, offering their lives to your service for the good of Holy
Mother Church and the salvation of souls. Through Christ our
Lord. Amen.

Acknowledgments

Joseph Pearce, in his biography of G. K. Chesterton,[1] relates how the journalist and writer wrote his landmark study of Saint Thomas Aquinas. Having conceived the idea of the book, he had his secretary acquire a pile of books and, after a quick consultation, announced to the same secretary, "Shall we do a bit of Tommy?"[2] and began to dictate, investing his genius into what is a notable work on the saint and theologian. There is a very different scenario here: There is no genius in this writer, and being no Becket scholar, I have had to do more than a quick consultation. This effort draws on the works of superlative scholars who have spent their lives researching the life and times of the martyred archbishop and sharing the fruits of their work with the world. To them I owe a debt, not just for this book, but for many years of engaging with their works and the insights into Saint Thomas they offer us.

Foremost among these scholars to whom I am indebted is Dom David Knowles, who devoted his life to exploring Thomas's life; Professor Frank Barlow for his incisive biography — in writing, my motto has been: "If in doubt go to Barlow"; Professor Anne Duggan, not only for her biography and articles, but also for her fine translation of Thomas's correspondence, which is an indispensable resource and a good read; Michael Staunton, who has given us vibrant translations from the original biographers; and John Guy, who has not only made Thomas popular again in recent times and allowed us see dimensions of his character in clearer focus, but also has offered us what is, I think, one of the most accessible biographies of the martyr. Of course, though they are long gone, students and devotees of Thomas must acknowledge his original biographers, some of them his friends and witnesses to his life and martyrdom. Though scholars may argue over details, agendas, and veracity, it is because of these biographers that we know so much about the archbishop, his life, and the complexities of his dispute with King Henry.

I sincerely thank all those at OSV for their assistance, in particular Mary Beth Giltner, Sarah Reinhard, and Marla Overholt; a special acknowledgment and thanks to my editor Christina Nichols, who did Trojan work on the manuscript, and Neal Quandt for his fine work on the proofs. As this book is aimed primarily at Catholics so they may come to know again the life and personality of Saint Thomas, to see that his struggle is of relevance to us today, I am grateful to OSV for making this possible.

On a personal level, there are many people who have been part of this journey into Thomas's life and the writing of this book who deserve thanks and, perhaps, apology for my obsessiveness over these last few years. My friend John Walsh has been a fellow pilgrim in exploring so many aspects of the Church and her history; I have learned a great deal from him and his insights. Seamus Bellew, a fine historian, has also helped me engage in the history of Christianity in Ireland and Britain. Thanks to Father John McKeever, with whom I have spent many hours over the years, in seminary and out, exploring and discussing Thomas's life and influence. Thanks to Professor Father Vincent Twomey for his guidance, wise suggestions, and patience. I must acknowledge those who very kindly read the manuscript and asked questions that stopped me in my tracks and got me rethinking: Christopher and Caroline McCamley, Patrick and Rachel Kenny, and Dr. Susan Hegarty, for advice at a crucial point. Thanks to Maria Ugente for her important contribution and her prayers, which have proved vital. Practical help is always necessary when moments are stolen from life and work to write, and in this regard I must acknowledge the help and support of Rosemary Meade, Mary Brennan, and Bernadette Mulligan. To my friend, Father Owen Gorman, ODCS, who has had to endure many hours, perhaps even days, weeks, and months of Becket with great patience, but has been a rock and a wise advisor. Finally, to my family: my mother, Thomas, and Caroline, for their continual support. I remember my late aunt and godmother, Brigid Hogan, who was a Becket to me, equipping me with skills and knowledge to engage in my own disputes. And to my late father, Tom, for so much, and to whom this book is dedicated with gratitude.

Sancte Thoma, hic est quem voluisti, nunc ora pro me!

Notes

INTRODUCTION

1. W. L. Warren, *Henry II* (New Haven and London: Yale University Press, 2000), 451.

2. Ibid., 488.

3. Anne Duggan, *Reputations: Thomas Becket* (London: Arnold, 2004), 213.

4. Erastianism is the belief that the state governs the Church and has supremacy over ecclesiastical matters. The ecclesial communities that emerged at the Reformation where the monarch was head of the Church, for example, are Erastian in nature.

5. G. K. Chesterton, *A Short History of England* (Sevenoaks, Kent: Fisher Press, 1994), 56.

6. Ibid., 56–57.

7. *Becket ou l'honneur de Dieu* (*Becket or The Honor of God*) by Jean Anouilh, was first performed at the Théâtre Montparnasse, Paris, on October 8, 1959. The Broadway premiere was on October 5, 1960.

8. *Becket* (1964), released by Paramount Pictures, was directed by Peter Glenville. It starred Richard Burton as Thomas Becket and Peter O'Toole as Henry II.

9. Following the death of the Anglo-Saxon King Edward the Confessor, in 1066, his cousin William, Duke of Normandy, set his sights on England. Edward's mother had been a Norman, the sister of Richard II, Duke of Normandy, and this connection with the Normans had been used by Edward as he sought advice and assistance during his twenty-four-year reign. As he had died childless, there was initially a dispute over the succession, but it was settled when the Witenagemot of England — a gathering of noblemen — elected Harold Godwinson, Earl of Wessex and Edward's brother-in-law, as king. William of Normandy, however, claimed that King Edward had promised the throne to him and was determined to stake his claim. As he gathered forces in Normandy to invade, Harold was engaged in fighting another who claimed the throne, King Harald III of Norway, who claimed that an earlier English king, Harthacnut (King Edward's half-brother), had made an agreement with the Norwegians that if a king of England died childless, the throne would be united to that of Norway. The Norwegians invaded in September 1066 but were defeated at the Battle of Stamford Bridge on September 25. However, Harold's armies were left in a weakened state, and so when William of Normandy invaded on September 28, they were unable to effectively resist. At the Battle of Hastings, on October 14, 1066, the Anglo-Sax-

ons fell to the Normans and King Harold was killed on the battlefield, reputedly by being struck by an arrow in the eye, as portrayed in the Bayeux Tapestry; in reality it is unknown how the king died. Though the Witenagemot immediately elected Edgar the Ætheling as the new king, William's progress, and subsequent battle at Southwark, led to his victory and succession. A number of revolts occurred in the following years, but by the middle 1170s his throne was secure and a process of "Normanization" began. He confiscated land from Anglo-Saxon nobles who had fought with Harold, redistributing it to Norman lords, ultimately beginning the elimination of the English aristocracy. Norman clerics were appointed to key ecclesiastical offices — by 1096 all diocesan sees and abbacies were held by Normans. Normans began to immigrate to England to avail of opportunities and positions within the new government that were opening up. By the time Saint Thomas was born, the invasion was complete.

10. Jean Anouilh, *Becket* (New York: Riverhead Books, 1995), Playwright's Introduction, xix–xx.

11. *Murder in the Cathedral* by T. S. Eliot was first performed in the chapter house of Canterbury Cathedral on June 15, 1935.

12. Eliot, *Murder in the Cathedral*, Part I, lines 667–668.

13. Ibid., Part II, lines 578–580.

14. John Guy, *Thomas Becket, Warrior, Priest, Rebel, Victim: A 900-Year-Old Story Retold* (London: Penguin, 2013).

15. Frank Barlow, *Thomas Becket* (London: Phoenix Giant, 1986).

16. Anne Duggan, *Thomas Becket* (London: Arnold, 2004).

17. Michael Staunton, ed. and trans., *The Lives of Thomas Becket* (Manchester: Manchester University Press, 2001).

PROLOGUE

1. John Butler, *The Quest for Becket's Bones: The Mystery of the Relics of St. Thomas Becket of Canterbury* (New Haven and London: Yale University Press, 1995), 25.

2. *Recognitio* is the formal canonical process of exhumation and identification of the remains of a saint or candidate for beatification or canonization. Such examinations are carried out to formally identify the remains, determine the state of the body, and do what can be done to ensure preservation of the remains for the future. Relics can also be taken for preparation and distribution.

3. The *Polistorie* of Canterbury, a fourteenth-century French chronicle written by the monk John of Canterbury; and the *Quadrilogus*, a composite of four narrative biogra-

phies of Saint Thomas.

4. The *Icelandic Saga of Thomas* (*Thómas saga Erkibyskups*), written in the fourteenth century and based on Robert of Cricklade's lost biography of the martyr, the biography written by Benet of St. Albans, and the *Quadrilogus*. The *Saga* indicates that the body disintegrated upon being touched, leaving only bones, which were then laid in a chest — the feretory.

5. Butler, 23.

PART I: AMBITION'S SERVANT
1. The Ship

1. Dan Jones, *The Plantagenets: The Kings Who Made England* (London: Harper Press, 2012), 3–8.

2. Ætheling or Adelinus, sometimes rendered Adelin, is an Old English term initially meaning one of good or noble birth, but it had come to identify a prince who is eligible to succeed to the throne. In William's case, it singled him out as the heir apparent to the throne of England.

3. King Henry I of England and Normandy (1068–1135) reigned from 1100 to 1135. The fourth son of King William I (William the Conqueror), he completed the conquest of England by the Normans and established a strong, centralized, and autocratic rule. He was supportive of reform within the Church and was an ardent and generous patron of the Cluniac reform of Western monasticism. He was also an avid collector of relics. While increasingly pious in his old age, he was resistant to the Gregorian Reforms, which sought to loosen secular rulers' influence on the Church and her appointments.

4. Perche was a province in what is now France, situated between the provinces of Normandy, Maine, Orléanais, and Beauce.

5. King Louis VI of France (1081–1137) reigned from 1108 to 1137; a member of the House of Capet, he was called *le Gros* (the Fat), for obvious reasons. In his youth, when he was much slimmer, he was renowned on the battlefield as a warrior. He consolidated his power in France, particularly over the nobles — hence his ability to bring the king of England to heel as a feudal vassal in his capacity as Duke of Normandy.

6. Jones, 6.

7. Ibid., 7.

8. The four Matildas were Matilda the empress and heir apparent; Matilda Fitzroy, Countess of Perche, who perished in the *White Ship* tragedy (her mother was identified only as Edith); Matilda Fitzroy, daughter by an unknown mistress, who married Conan

III, Duke of Brittany; and Matilda Fitzroy, whose mother is also unknown, who became the abbess of the Abbey of Notre Dame in Montivilliers in Normandy. "Fitzroy" was the surname given to the illegitimate children of a king, derived from the French, "fitz" meaning "son of" and "roy" derived from *roi*, French for king. It will have been noted by the reader that Matilda was a very popular name for girls at the time, as was Henry for boys.

9. From Geoffrey's nickname, Richard, Duke of York (1411–1460), his descendant, adopted the family name as Plantagenet in the fifteenth century. The House has been referred to as Plantagenet since then. Historians also refer to Henry II, Richard I "Lion-heart," and John as Angevins, some maintaining that John's son, Henry III, is the first Plantagenet king; others suggest that Henry II was the first.

10. Catherine Hanley, *Matilda: Empress, Queen, Warrior* (New Haven and London: Yale University Press, 2020), 65.

11. Laura Betzig, "The French Connection: Sex and the English Revolution," in Todd K. Shackelford and Ronald D. Hansen, eds., *The Evolution of Sexuality* (Berlin: Springer International, 2015), 86.

12. Hanley, 68–71.

13. For a biography of Henry I, see Judith A. Green, *Henry I: King of England and Duke of Normandy* (Cambridge: Cambridge University Press, 2006).

2. A Boy from London

1. Peter Ackroyd, *London: The Biography* (London: Vintage, 2001), 47.

2. A charter is a grant of authority or rights either to an individual, a group, a region, or city, conferred by one who has superiority over those who receive it, usually a monarch.

3. A fanciful legend maintains that Matilda was, in fact, a Saracen princess whom Gilbert met when on Crusade and converted. This story is baseless, though some early historians accepted it as true.

4. Barlow, 12–13.

5. While the day of Thomas's birth is accepted as December 21, there is a debate among historians regarding the year: 1120 is generally accepted, but 1118 and 1119 are also cited as possibilities. Three of Thomas's most recent biographers, Barlow, Duggan, and Guy, cite 1120 as the most likely year. For 1120, see Barlow, 10; Duggan, 8; Guy, xxii.

6. Prior to the liturgical reforms of the Second Vatican Council, Saint Thomas the Apostle's feast was celebrated on December 21, and it remains so on the calendar of the

Extraordinary Form.

7. See Barlow, 12; Guy, 3.

8. The Benedictine Abbey of Bec lies three miles south of Thierville.

9. Regarding Thomas's sisters: Agnes and Rose (Roheise) would marry and have children. Mary would enter religious life and was appointed abbess of Barking Abbey in Essex in 1173. (See Barlow, 13.)

10. Edward Grim was a clerk at Canterbury at the time of Thomas's martyrdom who not only witnessed the murder, but also was injured trying to prevent it. He wrote the first of Thomas's biographies just a year or so after the saint's death, and it is noted for its detail and meticulous research. This biography is preserved in *Materials for the History of Thomas Becket, Archbishop of Canterbury*, ed. J. C. Robertson and J. B. Sheppard (Cambridge: Cambridge University Press, 1875–1885) 2:353-450 (henceforth *MTB*). An accessible source for extracts from Grim's work is *The Lives of Thomas Becket*, trans. Michael Staunton (Manchester: Manchester University Press, 2001).

11. Grim, 356–358; cited in Staunton, 40–41.

12. Grim, 356–357; Staunton, 40–41.

13. Grim, 357; Staunton, 41.

14. Ibid.

15. Grim, 357–358, Staunton, 41.

16. Guy in his biography, for example, describes Grim's account of visions as a "hagiographer's trick to signal his subject's future greatness" (Guy, 4). Anne Duggan is more complimentary, explaining that if there was any truth in these stories, they were no more than "the kind of childhood stories that circulate in families," mothers' dreams that could be seen as prophetic in retrospect (Duggan, 8).

17. John of Salisbury, *MTB*, 2:302.

18. Barlow, 17.

19. Guy, 11; Barlow, 16; Duggan, 9.

20. Barlow, 17.

21. Guy, 11.

22. Barlow, 17.

23. Guy, 11.

24. Barlow, 18.

25. Ibid.

26. The biography attributed to Roger of Pontigny is now officially known as "Anonymous I" and is preserved in *MTB* volume 4, 1–79. The author claims to have known

Thomas at Pontigny" during the archbishop's exile there from 1164 to 1166, and some identify him as Roger, a monk of the community. Historians are doubtful, however, as the biography, which relies heavily on Edward Grim's work, is sparse on detail about Thomas's stay at the abbey, a period of his life with which a monk of Pontigny would have been very familiar.

27. Barlow, 24; Guy, 12.

28. Guy, 13; Barlow, 19.

29. Guy, 14–16.

30. Herbert of Bosham was one of the most important men in Thomas's life, and his biography is one of the longest, most detailed, and most intimate. The year of Herbert's birth is not known, but he was most likely from Bosham in Sussex. He studied in Paris under the theologian and later bishop Peter Lombard before coming to Canterbury to serve in the archiepiscopal household, probably just before Thomas's consecration. Herbert became a close and trusted clerk, and it was he who was given the task of tutoring the new archbishop in Scripture and theology. Ever faithful, he was at Thomas's side throughout his episcopacy and exile, and it was only through obedience to the archbishop that he was not present at the martyrdom — if he had been, he would have made a spirited defense of the master he loved and served. After the martyrdom, he spent most of his time on the continent and began writing Thomas's biography in 1184. Though it is affectionate and detailed, some scholars are not convinced that the biography is accurate regarding some aspects of the Becket Controversy, but more of a hagiography modeled on the Gospels. Herbert's biography of Saint Thomas is to be found in *MTB* in volume 3, 155–534. The date of his death is unknown, but there are no historical references to him after 1189.

31. Herbert of Bosham, 162.

3. Our Friend Richer

1. Dom David Knowles was a Benedictine and noted historian of Downside Abbey in Somerset, England. His biography of Saint Thomas Becket has been acclaimed. He provides an interesting assessment of Thomas's character in "Archbishop Thomas Becket: A Character Study" in his *The Historian and Character and Other Essays* (Cambridge: Cambridge University Press, 1963).

2. David Knowles, "Archbishop Thomas Becket: A Character Study," 105–106.

3. Guy, 16–17.

4. For a biography of Richer, see Kathleen Thompson, "Aigle, Richer de l'," in the

Oxford Dictionary of National Biography, https://www.oxforddnb.com/view/10.1093/ref: odnb/9780198614128.001.0001/odnb-9780198614128-e-47232.

5. "The Anarchy" was the name given to the period of civil war in England between King Henry I's death in 1135 and King Henry II's accession to the throne in 1153.

6. Barlow, 19.

7. Guy, 19–20.

8. Barlow, 20.

9. John Guy speculates that Matilda may have intervened because she was worried that the friendship was becoming too intimate. Noting that Prior Robert of Merton later wrote ambiguously of the relationship, Guy suggests that Robert was "clearly troubled by Thomas's vulnerability to an older man's subversive influence" (Guy, 20).

10. Guy, 19.

11. Grim, 360; Barlow, 20; Guy, 19.

12. The Constitutions of Clarendon were a set of legislative procedures, known as the "ancestral customs," imposed on the Church in 1164 by Henry II to restrict Church privileges, ecclesiastical courts, and papal authority in England. The Constitutions would become the major source of conflict between Thomas and Henry II. See chapter 25.

4. The Anarchy

1. Jim Bradbury, *Stephen and Matilda: The Civil War of 1139–53* (Stroud: History Press, 2005), 17–18.

2. See chapter 18.

3. Hanley, 54–56.

4. Warren, 14–16.

5. Bradbury, 13.

6. Ibid., 14.

7. Hanley, 85–90.

8. Ibid., 100–101.

9. Ibid., 102–103.

10. See chapter 17.

11. "The Charter of Liberties of Stephen," 1136.

12. Bradbury, 55–62.

13. Ibid., 77.

14. The Battle of Lincoln was, perhaps, the only major battle in the civil war; see Bradbury, 94–109, for an account of the events.

15. King Stephen's wife, Matilda of Boulogne, was a remarkable woman in her own right. Born around 1105, she was the daughter of Eustace III, Count of Boulogne, and Mary of Scotland; her maternal grandmother was Saint Margaret of Scotland. She married Stephen in 1125 and gave him five children. On her father's death, she became Countess of Boulogne but shared governance with her husband. At the time of King Henry I's death and Stephen's rushed journey to England to seize the throne, she was heavily pregnant but as determined as Stephen to stake their claim to the throne. In 1152, she contracted a fever and died at Hedingham Castle in Essex; she was buried in the Cluniac abbey that she and Stephen founded at Faversham in Kent. Her death would prove a serious blow to Stephen in terms of his ambition to govern England.

16. Bradbury, 115–120.

17. Ibid., 124–125.

18. Hanley, 177–181.

19. Hanley, 186–187; Bradbury, 138–139.

20. King David I of Scotland (c. 1085–1153), also known as Saint David of Scotland, reigned from 1124 to 1153. The son of Saint Margaret of Scotland, he was not only a competent monarch but also a devout Catholic and an exemplary husband and father. Married to Maud, the daughter of the Earl of Northampton and Huntingdon, he had a legitimate claim to these lands under his title Prince of the Cumbrians.

21. Hanley, 200–201.

22. FitzEmpress means "son of the Empress." Fitz is an old French term meaning "son of."

5. Paris

1. For Thomas's years in Paris, see Barlow, 20–22; Duggan, 11–12; Guy, 33–38.

2. Guy, 36–37.

3. Duggan, 11–12.

4. Barlow, 20; Guy, 37.

5. *Disputatores* were teachers who taught through the art of dialectic — disputation and reasoning through questions and answers.

6. See M. L. Rampolla, "Melun, Robert de," at *Oxford Dictionary of National Biography*, https://www.oxforddnb.com/view/10.1093/ref:odnb/9780198614128.001.0001/odnb -9780198614128-e-23727.

7. Robert of Melun, *Quaestiones de Epistolis Pauli*, in *Robert de Melun: Oeuvres, Volume 2*, edited by R. M. Martin, 1938, pp. 152–154, in J. H. Burns, ed., *The Cambridge*

History of Medieval Political Thought, c. 350–c. 1450 (Cambridge: Cambridge University Press, 1991), 317.

8. Guy, 35.

9. Ibid.

10. Ibid., 36.

11. Roger of Pontigny, 8.

12. Guy, 40.

13. David Knowles, "Archbishop Thomas Becket" in *The Historian and Character*, 104ff.

14. Barlow, 22.

6. Return of the Wastrel

1. Roger of Pontigny, 8.

2. Guy, 39.

3. As cited in Ibid.

4. Barlow, 26–28; Duggan, 8, 12–13; Guy, 42–43.

5. Roger of Pontigny, 8.

6. *The Haskins Society Journal* 13: 1999. *Studies in Medieval History*: Vol 13, (Woodbridge: 2004), 94ff. David Crouch, *The Reign of King Stephen* (Abingdon: Routledge, 2000), 173ff. Robert B. Patterson, *The Earl, the Kings, and the Chronicler: Robert Earl of Gloucester and the Reigns of Henry I and Stephen* (Oxford: Oxford University Press, 2019), 104ff.

7. David Knowles, *Thomas Becket* (London: A&C Black, 1970), 8; Barlow, 27.

8. Guy, 42.

9. Ibid.

10. Barlow, 29–30; Guy, 46.

7. Theobald

1. Gilbert seems to disappear from the narrative following Thomas's entry into Theobald's service. It is thought Thomas inherited the family property, and after his death, his sister Agnes inherited it. Cf. Walter Besant, *Medieval London: Volume I – Historical and Social* (London: A&C Black, 1906), 7–8.

2. For a biography of Theobald, here summarized, see Frank Barlow, "Theobald" in the Oxford Dictionary of National Biography, https://www.oxforddnb.com/view/10.1093/ref:odnb/9780198614128.001.0001/odnb-9780198614128-e-27168.

3. The pallium is a long, stole-like garment woven from the wool of the lambs of Rome, embroidered with six black crosses, and conferred by the pope upon metropolitan archbishops as a symbol of their authority and their unity with the See of Peter. In theory, an archbishop cannot exercise his authority until the pallium has been conferred upon him. Normally a newly elected archbishop would have to petition the pope to receive it and then travel to Rome, or wherever the pope was, to receive it.

4. Guy, 47.

5. Bradbury, 113.

6. Barlow, "Theobald."

7. Knowles, *Thomas Becket*, 21ff.; Barlow, 30–31; Guy, 48–49.

8. Warren, 404–426.

9. For a comprehensive biography of Theobald, see Avrom Saltman, *Theobald, Archbishop of Canterbury* (London: Athlone Press, 1956).

8. Archiepiscopal Servant

1. William of Canterbury, *MTB* 1, 4. Also, Barlow, 34; Guy, 49–50.

2. Barlow, 33.

3. Ibid.

4. Guy, 51.

5. Ibid., 51–52.

6. See chapter 17.

7. Barlow, 33.

8. Ibid., 31.

9. David Luscombe, "Salisbury, John of," in the Oxford Dictionary of National Biography, https://www.oxforddnb.com/view/10.1093/ref:odnb/9780198614128.001.0001/odnb -9780198614128-e-14849. John of Salisbury was born in Salisbury around 1120. Though little is known of his early life, he was of Anglo-Saxon birth, so his advancement in the Norman-dominated Church was considered remarkable. He studied under Peter Abelard in Paris and later under Robert of Melun and Gilbert de la Porrée, among others. He became acquainted with Saint Bernard of Clairvaux, who recommended him to Theobald. Having served both Theobald and Thomas, he wrote a biography defending the latter following his martyrdom; in reality, it is more of an extended letter than a conventional work of biography. In 1176, he was elected bishop of Chartres. He died in office on October 25, 1180.

John was a prolific writer and theologian; his works reveal a fine mind not only able to clarify and analyze various philosophical and theological positions, but also firmly rooted in common sense. He is the originator of the term "theater of the world," *theatrum mundi*, for an important concept that had its roots in Greek philosophy, which John loved. John saw the life of man on earth as a comedy where each person is inclined to forget his own role and assume that of another. It is only the sages, saints, and prophets, he maintains, who are able to embrace the roles given to them by God. This allows these wise ones to take themselves out of the theater of the world into the realm of God, which John calls *auditorium*, a paradise, to observe the comedy being played out in the world. The concept and term would prove influential in the realm of drama, inspiring William Shakespeare's line in *As You Like It* that "all the world's a stage."

Included among John's many works are letters that offer insights into the crisis surrounding Thomas Becket; a biography of Saint Anselm; and his *Policraticus*, a classic work of medieval political theory that seeks to examine the role and responsibilities of kings toward their subjects. Interestingly, John often referred to himself as Johannes Parvus, "John the Little." John's biography of Saint Thomas is preserved in *MTB*, 2, 302–22.

10. Barlow, 36; Guy, 52. The exact dates of Thomas's study in Bologna and Auxerre are uncertain, as are many events in his life prior to his appointment as royal chancellor; they can only be reckoned. Given that Thomas had completed his study in Bologna and was in Auxerre when called to assist Theobald at the Council of Reims in 1148, it can be reckoned that he was in Bologna in 1147 or thereabouts.

11. Guy, 56.

12. Barlow, 34–35; Guy, 56–57

13. Christopher Norton, *St. William of York* (York: York Medieval Press, 2006), 82ff.; Jean Traux, *Archbishops Ralph d'Escures, William of Corbeil and Theobald of Bec: Heirs of Anselm and Ancestors of Becket* (Farnham: Ashgate, 2012), 152–153.

14. For more information on Saint William of York, see Christopher Norton, *St. William of York*.

15. Guy, 57.

16. Ibid., 58.

17. Letter to Cardinal Boso, December 1167, in *The Correspondence of Thomas Becket, Archbishop of Canterbury: 1162-1170*, Volume 1, edited and translated by Anne Duggan (Oxford: Oxford University Press, 2000), henceforth *CTB*, 719–721.

18. An interdict is a prohibition placed on a person or area forbidding the celebration of the sacraments, usually with the exception of baptism and last rites.

19. Guy, 58.

9. Peace

1. Warren, 33–34.

2. Richard Barber, *Henry II, A Prince Among Princes* (London: Allen Lane, 2015), 23.

3. Warren, 36–37.

4. Jones, 28–30.

5. Bradbury, 177–178.

6. Barlow, 33–34; Guy, 126–128.

7. Barlow, 33–34.

8. Bradbury, 188–189.

9. The treaty is known variously as the Treaty of Wallingford, the Treaty of Winchester, and the Treaty of Westminster. For a brief summary of the treaty, see Bradbury, 189–190.

10. Archdeacon

1. A benefice is a salary taken from a particular church or parish income.

2. Barlow, 36.

3. Ibid., 38.

4. Warren, 53.

5. Ibid.; Jones, 45.

6, "Charte de Henri II" in Charles Bémont, *Chartres de libertés anglaises (1100-1305)* (Paris: A. Picard, 1892), 13–14.

PART II: THE KING'S SERVANT
11. Henry

1. Barber, 4. This short biography, *Henry II: A Prince Among Princes*, provides a good introduction to the life and personality of Henry.

2. Gerald of Wales, as preserved in *English Historical Documents, Volume II, 1042-1189*, trans. and ed. David Douglas and George W. Greenway (London: Eyrie & Spottiswoode, 1953), 388.

3. Warren, 629–630.

4. Barber, 15–16.

5. Warren, 39.

6. Barber, 16.

7. Guy, 80.

8. Ibid., 77–78.

9. Ibid., 81.

10. Warren, 211.

11. Guy, 81.

12. Saint Ælred, born in Hexham, Northumberland, in 1110, was the abbot of the Cistercian Abbey of Rievaulx in Yorkshire. Renowned for his holiness and wisdom, he was the author of numerous works, including the famous *Spiritual Friendship* and *The Mirror of Charity*. He died in 1167. He is regarded as an unofficial patron saint of friendship not only because of his written reflections on friendship but also because of his profound capacity to form authentic friendships immersed in Christian faith and charity. Ælred dedicated three of his books to Henry II.

13. Saint Gilbert, founder of the Gilbertine Order, was born around 1083 in Sempringham in Lincolnshire. Ordained a priest, he turned down high office to found, starting in 1131, simple communities of canons, nuns, sisters, and lay brothers following the Cistercian rule of life. He was accused of helping Thomas flee England in 1164 and was almost sent into exile himself; however, though he was a quiet supporter of the archbishop, he took no active part in the dispute. In later life, he was subject to a revolt by lay brothers in his order, but the pope ruled in Gilbert's favor. He died in 1190.

14. Guy, 80.

15. Ibid., 81.

16. Warren, 119.

17. Henry II is credited with laying the foundations of common law in England. See Paul Brand, "Henry II and the Creation of English Common Law," in Christopher Harper-Bill and Nicholas Vincent, eds., *Henry II: New Interpretations* (Woodbridge: Boydell Press, 2007), 215–241.

18. Amercements are financial penalties imposed by law.

19. Warren, 200–206.

12. Royal Chancellor

1. Duggan, 16; Guy, 74.

2. Warren, 448.

3. See Barlow, 42–43; Duggan, 16–17.

4. Guy, 96–97.

5. Ibid., 99.

6. Destined to play a major role in the tragedy of Thomas of Canterbury, Arnulf of Lisieux was born near Sees in Normandy sometime between 1105 and 1114. Initially

educated at home, he later entered the cathedral school in Sees and later went to Bologna to study canon law. He was elected bishop of Lisieux in 1141. During the schism of 1159–1178, he supported Alexander III's claim, and his main task during those years was to ensure the English king was loyal to Alexander. During the Becket Controversy, he was Henry's man. He eventually fell afoul of the king following the rebellion of Young King Henry in 1173. In 1181, Arnulf resigned as bishop and withdrew to the Abbey of Saint Victor in Paris, where he died on August 31, 1184.

7. Guy, 84.

8. Ibid., 86–87.

9. Warren, 60–61.

10. Ibid., 64.

11. Guy, 88.

12. Duggan, 29.

13. Warren, 65.

14. Ibid., 74–77.

15. Guy, 89.

16. Warren, 80.

17. Ibid.

18. Barlow, 55–57.

19. Guy, 92–93.

20. Barlow, 56; Guy, 93.

21. Barlow, 57.

22. Guy, 94–95.

13. The Trappings of Power

1. Warren notes, interestingly, that Thomas, for all his pomp and munificence, was personally frugal and chaste, p. 449.

2. Guy, 76–77.

3. Ibid., 77.

4. Ibid., 78.

5. Regarding Thomas's chastity: William FitzStephen, *MTB* 3, 21; Edward Grim, *MTB* 2, 365; John of Salisbury, *MTB* 2, 303.

6. Guernes of Pont-Sainte-Maxence, from his work, *La Vie de Saint Thomas Le Martyr, Archévêque de Canterbury,* ed. C. Hippeau (Geneva: Slatkin Reprints, 1969), 11–12, cited in Guy, 123.

7. William FitzStephen was clerk to both Henry and Thomas and witness to Thomas's martyrdom. He wrote his life of the archbishop in the years 1173–1174. His account of Thomas's life as chancellor is detailed and independent. It is preserved in *MTB* 3, 1–154.

8. William FitzStephen, 21.

9. Guernes of Pont-Sainte-Maxence, 12–13; Guy, 123–124.

10. Guy, 123.

11. Barlow, 61.

12. See Barlow, 58; Duggan, 182; Guy, 130–131.

13. Guy, 131–133.

14. Master and Servant

1. William FitzStephen, 25: "*Magis unanimes et amici nunquam duo aliqui fuerunt temporibus Christianis.*"

2. Guy notes that in the beginning of their relationship, Thomas was naïve and inexperienced enough to think that his friendship with Henry was that of "near-equals"; rather, he suggests, it was "a partnership of convenience" (Guy, 118).

3. William FitzStephen, 18–21.

4. Guy, 123.

5. Guy, 125–126.

6. Barlow, 28.

7. Barlow, 51. For accounts of the Battle Abbey case and Thomas's part in it, see Barlow, 50–51; Guy, 100–105.

8. Letter 170, to Pope Alexander III, July 1168, *CTB*, 783.

9. Barlow, 51.

10. John of Salisbury, 304–305.

15. Thomas the Warrior

1. Barlow, 52.

2. For Henry's campaign against Owain of Gwynedd, see Warren, 69–71.

3. For Henry's campaign in Toulouse and Thomas's part in it, see Warren, 82–87; Barlow, 57–58; Guy, 108–112.

4. Guy, 111.

5. Ibid.

6. Ibid., 113.

7. Ibid., 113–115.

8. There is a question of whether this is a wedding or a betrothal, as another ceremony took place at Winchester Cathedral on August 27, 1172, which is also described as a wedding. As indicated above, Margaret appears to have had the status and dignity of young Henry's wife from 1160, and was expected to be crowned with him in June 1170 (see chapter 37). Barlow maintains that they were married in 1160, cf. 67, 204, 210; as do Duggan, 182–183, and Guy, 114. So does Strickland, 30–32. See also Lindsay Diggelmann, "Marriage as Tactical Response: Henry II and the Royal Wedding of 1160," in *The English Historical Review* 119, no. 483 (September 2004): 954–964. Even though a dispensation was given to permit the wedding, Diggelmann notes that the couple were related within the seven forbidden degrees and neither had given consent. She notes that the dispensation had been given regarding the age of the children, not the issue of consanguinity, which Louis could have used to renege on his agreement with Henry if required; however, Louis's new wife, Adela, was related to him within the forbidden degrees.

9. Strickland, 34.

10. Ibid., 35.

16. Thomas of Canterbury

1. See chapter 21.

2. Guy, 134; Barlow, 60–61.

3. Guy, 134–135.

4. Ibid., 136.

5. Letter of Theobald of Canterbury to Thomas Royal Chancellor (1160), *MTB* 5, 9–11.

6. Guy, 136.

7. Letter of Theobald of Canterbury to His Archdeacon (1160), *MTB* 5, 11–12.

8. Guy, 137–138.

9. Frank Barlow notes in his biography of Theobald in the *Oxford Dictionary of National Biography* that Theobald's body was found a little shrunken, but intact and rigid, leading people to hail him as a saint.

10. Barlow, 62.

11. Ibid., 69.

12. Gilbert Foliot was a man destined to play an important role in Thomas's struggle, both in his office as archbishop and in his dispute with Henry. Born around 1110, the son of the steward to the Earl of Huntingdon, he came from an illustrious family that

had provided the Church with a number of high-ranking clerics. Entering religious life as a Cluniac monk, he rose up the ranks, becoming prior of two abbeys. He attended the Second Lateran Council in 1139 and wrote an account of that council in 1143. After the council, he was elected abbot of Gloucester; his family's connections are believed to have influenced his being chosen. He was a good abbot and formed a number of important relationships, most notably with Theobald of Bec and Saint Ælred of Rievaulx, who dedicated a book to him. He was a supporter of Matilda's cause during the Anarchy, and this had a part to play in his being elected bishop of Hereford in 1148. Theobald of Bec is believed to have been instrumental in his elevation, as was Thomas in his being transferred to the see of London in 1163. Following Thomas's martyrdom, he remained as bishop of London and died on February 18, 1187. His role in the Becket Controversy aside, he is renowned for his letters, which were compiled into volumes, and for his sermons, for which he is praised. He also wrote a commentary on the Song of Songs and other works, though his authorship of some works attributed to him is disputed.

13. See Barlow, 68–70; Guy, 139–143.

14. The Lambeth Anonymous, in *MTB* 4, 85–88; also, Barlow, 63; Knowles, *Thomas Becket*, 51; Guy, 139.

15. Guy, 142.

16. Barlow, 70–71; Duggan, 23.

17. Strickland, 39.

18. Barlow, 69–70.

19. Strickland, 48–49; Guy, 143.

20. Barlow, 70–71.

21. Guy, 144–145.

22. William FitzStephen, 36.

23. Barlow, 72.

24. Guy, 147.

25. Ibid., 147–148.

26. See chapter 17.

PART III: THE CHURCH'S SERVANT
17. Of Scepters and Croziers

1. See Eamon Duffy, *Saints and Sinners: A History of the Popes*, 3rd. ed. (New Haven and London: Yale University Press, 2006), 120–121; also, Eamon Duffy, *Ten Popes Who Shook the World* (New Haven and London: Yale University Press, 2011), 60–69.

2. Leo (1002–1054) later became Pope Saint Leo IX (reigned 1049–1054).

3. Duffy, *Saints and Sinners,* 112–117.

4. Ibid., 117.

5. Acclamation was, until the late twentieth century, one of the three means permitted for electing a pope, the others being scrutiny — the normal majority vote by secret ballot in conclave — and election by compromise. Acclamation, which was interpreted as being the work of the Holy Spirit, consisted in the papal electors' unanimously proclaiming one candidate in a spontaneous action without prior consultation or agreement. This dispensed with the need for a ballot. The seven popes elected by acclamation were Pope Saint Fabian (200–250, reigned 236–250); Pope Saint Gregory the Great (c. 540–604, reigned 590–604); Pope Saint Gregory III (c. 690–741, reigned 731–741); Pope Saint Gregory VII (c. 1015–1085, reigned 1073–1085); Pope Gregory XV (1554–1623, reigned 1621–1623); Pope Clement X (1590–1676, reigned 1670–1676); and Blessed Pope Innocent XI (1611–1689, reigned 1676–1689). In his apostolic constitution *Universi Dominici Gregis* (*The Lord's Universal Flock*), 1996, Pope Saint John Paul II abolished election by acclamation and compromise, leaving secret ballot as the only means of choosing a new pope.

6. Warren Carroll, *A History of Christendom Volume 2: The Building of Christendom* (Front Royal, VA: Christendom Press, 1987), 502–503.

7. Duffy, *Saints and Sinners,* 121–122.

8. *The Correspondence of Pope Gregory VII,* trans. Ephraim Emerton (New York: Columbia University Press, 1932), 179.

9. Henry IV (1050–1106) reigned as king of Germany from 1053 to 1105 and as Holy Roman emperor from 1056 to 1105. Born in Saxony, he became king at three and emperor at six, with his mother acting as regent. His whole life was one of governance; a man of extraordinary ability and will, he was one of the most important figures of the eleventh century. He possessed great competence as a soldier, tactician, and diplomat, though this last skill did not prevent his being involved in numerous conflicts, the most noteworthy being with Pope Gregory VII. He was excommunicated five times by three different popes. He was married twice and had six children: three sons and three daughters by his first wife, Bertha, but possibly none by his second wife, Eupraxia of Kiev, daughter of the prince of Kiev. (Though she is believed to have borne a child, the manner of its conception is controversial.) His son Henry succeeded him as king of Germany and Holy Roman emperor. He was buried in the cathedral in Speyer, Germany, which he had enlarged and endowed.

10. Carroll, 505; Duffy, *Saints and Sinners,* 123.

11. Carroll, 506; Duffy, *Saints and Sinners*, 123–124.

12. The office and title of the Holy Roman Emperor was not a strictly hereditary one at this point, but had developed into an elected monarchy. Various princes, dubbed electors, had a right to vote in the election.

13. Carroll, 507; Duffy, *Saints and Sinners*, 124.

14. Carroll, 507.

15. Ibid., 508.

16. Ibid.; Duffy, *Saints and Sinners*, 124.

17. Carroll, 508–509.

18. Ibid., 509–510; Duffy, *Saints and Sinners*, 125.

19. Carroll, 510; Duffy, *Saints and Sinners*, 125.

20. Carroll, 511–512.

21. Ibid., 512–513.

22. Blessed Pope Victor III (c. 1026–1087) reigned from 1086 to 1087. Born Dauferio in Benevento into a noble family, he entered a monastery when he was twenty-one against his widowed mother's will. He became a member of the Benedictine community at Monte Cassino, was elected abbot in 1057, and was made cardinal in 1058. He distinguished himself as abbot and was renowned for his holiness. Though he was in failing health, he was elected pope on May 24, 1086. His short but turbulent papacy ended with his death on September 16, 1087. He was beatified by Pope Leo XIII in 1887.

23. Blessed Pope Urban II (c. 1035–1099) reigned from 1088 to 1099. Born Otho de Lagery in Champagne in France, he was the prior of the Abbey of Cluny when made a cardinal in 1080. He was elected by acclamation on March 12, 1088. While attempting to carry out Pope Saint Gregory's reforms and struggling with the antipope, he was responsible for calling and organizing the First Crusade. A strong and influential pope, he died on July 29, 1099, fourteen days after the crusaders captured Jerusalem. He was beatified by Pope Leo XIII in 1881.

24. Pope Paschal II (1050/1055–1118) reigned from 1099 to 1118. Born Ranierius near Forli in Tuscany, he was a Cluniac monk. Made a cardinal in 1073, he was elected pope on August 13, 1099. His reign would be long for a medieval pope, and though he faced much opposition and suffering, he finally brought the crisis with Henry's antipopes to an end. He also appointed the first bishop to the Americas, sending Erik Gnupsson as bishop to Greenland and Vinland (Newfoundland). He died on January 21, 1118.

25. Warren Carroll, *A History of Christendom Volume 3: The Glory of Christendom* (Front Royal, VA: Christendom Press, 1993), 28–30.

18. Anselm

1. Blessed Lanfranc of Bec (1005/1010–1089) was archbishop of Canterbury from 1070 to 1089. Born in Pavia in Italy, he studied the liberal arts and was a renowned teacher. He renounced this career to enter the Abbey of Bec in 1042, living the first three years of his monastic life as a solitary. His abbot appointed him as teacher, and he served as such until his election as prior and then abbot. He was involved in a debate with Berengar of Tours on the issue of transubstantiation. He had a considerable reputation as a scholar and theologian, and his triumph over Berengar increased his eminence and helped him achieve the office of archbishop of Canterbury. After his death, attempts to have him canonized were made but proved inconclusive, though he was venerated within the Benedictine Order. He was eventually included in the *Roman Martyrology* as a Blessed, and the updated *Martyrology* of 2004 preserves this designation.

2. For a biography of Saint Anselm and his struggles with William II and Henry I, see R. W. Southern, *St. Anselm: A Portrait in a Landscape* (Cambridge University Press, 1990), on which this chapter is based, and also his article "Anselm," in the *Oxford Dictionary of National Biography*, https://www.oxforddnb.com/view/10.1093/ref:odnb/9780198614128.001.0001/odnb-9780198614128-e-572.

3. Frank Barlow, "William II [known as William Rufus]," in *Oxford Dictionary of National Biography*, https://www.oxforddnb.com/view/10.1093/ref:odnb/9780198614128.001.0001/odnb-9780198614128-e-29449.

4. Southern, 189–190.

5. Sally Vaughn, "St. Anselm of Canterbury: The Philosopher-Saint as Politician," *Journal of Medieval History* I (1975): 286.

6. M. T. Clanchy, *England and its Rulers 1066-1272* (London: Fontana Press, 1988), 99.

7. Martin Rule, *The Life and Times of St. Anselm, Archbishop of Canterbury and Primate of the Britains,* vol. 1 (Sydney: Wentworth Press, 2016), 87–90.

8. Vaughn, 293.

9. Southern, 279.

10. Ibid.

11. Ibid., 291.

12. Ibid., 292.

13. Ibid, 293.

14. Clanchy, 102–103.

15. Warren, 412.

16. Sally Vaughn, "St. Anselm and the English Investiture Controversy Reconsidered," in *Journal of Medieval History* 6 (1980) 71.

17. Ibid., 74.

18. Ibid., 76.

19. Ibid., 80.

20. Ibid., 82.

21. Known as Thomas II of York, the archbishop was elected in May 1108; his consecration was delayed because of this dispute. He was eventually consecrated in London on June 27, 1109, and received the pallium on August 1 of that year from the papal legate, Cardinal Ulrich. He remained in office until his death on February 25, 1114. He was renowned for his chastity, though also for his love of food; it is said that the cause of his death was overeating.

22. The Wednesday of Holy Week.

19. Father

1. Saint Augustine of Canterbury, not to be confused with the great theologian Saint Augustine of Hippo, was born in the early sixth century in Italy. He became a monk of the Benedictine monastery of Saint Andrew, founded by Pope Saint Gregory the Great on the Caelian Hill. Following his election to the papacy and his encounter with Angles in Rome, Gregory chose Augustine to lead a missionary effort to convert England to the Faith. Arriving in 595, he found an ally in the queen of Kent, Bertha, a Christian married to the pagan King Ethelbert. Converting the king to Christianity, Augustine carried out a successful mission and established his see at Canterbury, building among other ecclesiastical buildings a cathedral and a Benedictine monastery initially dedicated to Saints Peter and Paul. The cathedral and monastery united, the monks would carry out the daily liturgical offices and many duties within the palace and archdiocese for their archbishop-abbot. Saint Augustine died in 604, but Christianity continued to flourish in England, and his successors — first bishops and then archbishops — presided over the Church in England.

2. Letter 1, *CTB*, 3.

3. Knowles, *Thomas Becket*, 56.

4. Ibid.; Guy, 165ff.

5. Guy, 166–169.

6. Barlow, 76–77.

7. Guy, 148.

8. Barlow, 73; Guy, 148.

9. Barlow, 82–83; Guy, 149.

20. Zeal

1. Thursday of Holy Week, Holy Thursday.

2. Knowles, *Thomas Becket*, 56; Barlow, 79–81.

3. Barlow, 80.

4. John of Salisbury, 306: "*Solitarius agens usque in miraculum lacrymis suffundebatur, et sic in altaris versabatur officio ac si praesentialiter in carne geri cerneret Dominicam passionem*"; Staunton, 67–68.

5. Letter 5, *CTB*, I, 17.

6. Guy, 150.

7. Ibid., 150.

8. Barlow, 114; Guy, 151.

9. Guy, 151.

10. Ibid., 152.

11. Ibid., 153.

12. Barlow, 82.

13. Letter 7, *CTB*, I, 21.

14. Letter 8, *CTB*, I, 23.

15. Guy, 154.

16. I. S. Robinson, *The Papacy, 1073–1198: Continuity and Innovation* (Cambridge University Press, 1990), 139–141.

17. Barlow, 84–85.

18. The *positio*, or *positio super virtutibus*, is the formal biography, account of virtues, and petition submitted to the Congregation for the Causes of Saints as evidence of a candidate's heroic virtue in the appeal to have a person declared Venerable.

19. Guy, 155.

20. Letter 10, *CTB*, I, 27.

21. Guy, 156.

22. Letter 11, *CTB*, I, 29.

23. Guy, 155–156.

24. Barlow, 87.

21. Alexander

1. Francesco Gioia, *The Popes: Twenty Centuries of History* (Vatican City: Libreria

Editrice Vaticana, 2005), 80–81. Rolando is also referred to as Rolando Bandinelli, which is believed to be his surname.

2. F. Donald Logan, *A History of the Church in the Middle Ages*, second edition (Abingdon: Routledge, 2012), 125.

3. Carroll, *The Glory of Christendom*, 87.

4. Letter of Pope Alexander III to Syrus, Archbishop of Genoa, and his suffragans (1159), about his election, in Oliver J. Thatcher and Edgar Holmes McNeal, *A Source Book for Medieval History: Selected Documents Illustrating the History of Europe in the Middle Age* (New York: Charles Scribner's Sons, 1905), 192–194. Also, Carroll, *The Glory of Christendom*, 87–88.

5. Carroll, *The Glory of Christendom*, 88.

6. Cf. Michael Walsh, *The Conclave: A Sometimes Secret and Occasionally Bloody History of Papal Elections* (Lanham: Sheed & Ward, 2003), 77–78.

7. Carroll, *The Glory of Christendom*, 88.

8. Ibid., 89.

9. Carroll, *The Glory of Christendom*, 89; Warren, 90.

10. Robert Somerville, *Pope Alexander III and the Council of Tours (1163)* (Los Angeles: University of California Press, 1977), 3–5.

11. Carroll, *The Glory of Christendom*, 113–114.

22. Woodstock

1. Guy, 156.

2. Roger was claiming lands as tenant (tenant-in-chief) or vassal (vassal-in-chief) of the king. A medieval, feudal concept, it means the tenant held the land directly from the king himself. It was not just a renting agreement, but denoted a relationship of homage to the king in which honor and responsibility were bestowed on one who held the lands.

3. Guy, 156–157.

4. For the council at Woodstock, see Warren, 458–460; Barlow, 88–89; Duggan, 37–38; Guy, 156–162.

5. Guy, 157–158.

6. Ibid., 158

7. Ibid., 173–174.

8. Barlow, 93.

9. Ibid., 93.

10. Guy, 174.

11. Ibid., 174–175.

12. Ibid., 175.

13. Barlow, 93–94.

14. William FitzStephen, 43: *"Nunc ei inde gratiam non habeo."*

23. The Council at Westminster

1. Guy, 158–162.

2. See chapter 8.

3. See Guy, 161. Barlow simply notes that Henry allowed a trial (Barlow, 92). War-ren, in his biography, notes that Henry had conceded trial and punishment in the case of Archdeacon Osbert to the Church courts, a concession he would later have cause to regret (Warren, 464).

4. Warren, 456; Barlow, 95; Guy, 175–176.

5. For an account of the council of Westminster, see *Summa Causae Inter Regem et Thomam, MTB* 4, 201–205, as given in Staunton, 79–83; also Barlow, 95; Duggan, 39–40; Guy, 175–179. As both Staunton and Guy provide the most comprehensive records of the council and the issues, this biography draws on these accounts.

6. Saint Jerome's reflections on "double jeopardy" occur in his commentary on the Book of Nahum and on verse 1:9: "What do you plot against the LORD? He will make a full end; he will not take vengeance twice on his foes" or in the Douay Bible translation: "there shall not rise a double affliction." See Jay A. Sigler, "A History of Double Jeopardy," *The American Journal of Legal History* 7, no. 4 (October 1963): 283–309.

7. *Summa Causae Inter Regem et Thomam*, 204: *"Etiam in omnibus; salvo tamen per omnia et in omnibus ordine nostro."* Also, Herbert of Bosham, 273: *"salvo ordine suo"*; Staunton, 82; Guy, 178.

8. Guy, 178.

9. Strickland, 52; Barlow, 95.

24. A Very Public Quarrel

1. Barlow, 95; Guy, 176.

2. Roger of Pontigny, 27.

3. For the details of this encounter see Roger of Pontigny, *MTB* 4, 27–37; also Staunton, 83–85; and Guy, 179–180.

4. Roger of Pontigny, 28.

5. In medieval England, a villein was a feudal tenant who was subject to a lord to

whom he had to pay rents and service in exchange for the land he occupied. Almost tantamount to a slave in some ways, a villein could not leave the land assigned to him without the lord's permission.

6. Roger of Pontigny, 28: "*Moriar et ego pro Domino meo, cum tempus advenerit.*"

7. Staunton, 84.

8. Guy, 180.

9. Barlow, 96.

10. Ibid.

11. This meeting is detailed by Roger of Pontigny, 30–31; also, Barlow, 96; Guy, 179–180.

12. Barlow, 96–97.

13. Letter 19, *CTB*, I, 50.

14. Barlow, 97–98; Guy, 182–183.

15. Barlow, 98.

16. Guy, 183.

17. Barlow, 98.

18. Guy, 184.

25. The Clarendon Affair

1. Guy, 184.

2. Ibid.

3. For accounts on the council of Clarendon and the constitutions that emerged from it, as described in these chapters, see Barlow, 98–106; Duggan, 44–60; Guy, 186–192; Staunton, 87–96.

4. Matthew Strickland in *Henry the Young King* (New Haven and London: Yale University Press, 2016), 53.

5. Roger of Pontigny, 34–35.

6. Ibid.

7. Ibid., 35. Richard de Hastings served as Grand Prior and Master of the Templars in England from 1155 to 1164; he was appointed with the approval of Henry II. He was well connected with the royal family. During his time in office, the Knights Templar acquired property in London, which would be later known as Temple Bar, and within which they built their famous Temple Church.

8. Ibid., 36.

9. There are a number of translations of this document. The original Latin version

can be found in William of Canterbury's biography of Saint Thomas, *MTB* 1, 18–23; Staunton offers a translation, 91–96. The version here can be sourced at the Avalon Project at the Lillian Goldman Law Library at Yale University at https://avalon.law.yale.edu/medieval/constcla.asp, with some amendments.

10. This article removes the right of the Church to sentence clerks who have been found guilty, but rather establishes a law where the condemned has to be handed over to the civil courts to decide the nature of punishment to be imposed.

11. This article, favoring friends of Henry who have been excommunicated, directs that it is not permissible to require a promise of good behavior from excommunicates as a condition of having the censure lifted.

12. Of the few articles of the constitutions that could be tolerated by Pope Alexander III, this was one of them. It simply states that no layperson can be accused before a bishop without lawful witnesses. However, if the accused is the sort that people would be afraid to come forward to accuse them, the archbishop can direct the sheriff to act and twelve law-abiding people of the neighborhood can swear to testify to the truth about the charge. This is, basically, the formation of a jury to deal with particular cases.

13. Here, Henry is removing the bishops' right to excommunicate offenders who are tenants or servants of the king. They will need his permission to do so. In this article, Henry was getting back at Thomas for the issue of William of Eynsford.

14. This article forbids appeals to the pope unless the king permits them.

15. While this article states that disputes over property shall be adjudicated in the court to which the property pertains, the fact that a jury should decide who owns the property is problematic and open to abuse.

16. This is another article that removes the right of excommunication from the bishops and submits it to the judgment and permission of the king.

17. This insists that the bishops, as they hold lands as tenant-in-chief to the king, must, like all who do so, submit to the judgment of the king and his court unless, if found guilty, a capital judgment may be made against them.

18. This article strikes at the heart of the Gregorian Reforms: The king appoints the bishops, and they swear fealty to him, while in the interim the king receives the income of vacant sees, abbeys, and priories.

19. This article aims to remove the competency of ecclesiastical courts to deal with issues of oaths and perjury, transferring it to the king's courts.

20. This article subjects a candidate for Holy Orders to the will of the peer or lord on whose estate his parents were tenants and/or he was born.

21. This final paragraph was designed to leave room for Henry to devise other ancestral customs by which he could bind the bishops, thereby forcing the Church in England to obey him in any matter and in any way he chose.

26. The Darkest Hour

1. Roger of Pontigny, 37.

2. Ibid.

3. Guy, 192–193.

4. Herbert of Bosham, 289.

5. Ibid., 289–290.

6. Ibid., 290.

7. Ibid., 290–292.

8. Ibid., 292.

9. Guy, 193.

10. Ibid.

11. Knowles, *Thomas Becket*, 93.

12. Guy, 194.

13. Thomas's personal letter of penance is not included in *CTB*. It may have been lost, or it remains in Church archives. Given its nature, it would constitute a confession and could have been disposed of accordingly.

14. Letter 25, *CTB*, I, 79.

15. Barlow, 106; Guy, 194.

16. Letter 27, *CTB*, I, 85.

17. Letter 28, *CTB*, I, 87.

18. Barlow, 106–107.

19. Warren, 212.

20. Barlow, 107.

21. Letter 35, *CTB*, I, 135.

22. *The Letters of John of Salisbury: Volume 2: The Later Letters (1163–1180)*, ed. H. E. Butler, W. J. Millor, and C. N. L. Brooke (Oxford University Press, 1979), 3–15.

23. Barlow, 108.

24. Guy, 197.

25. Barlow, 108.

26. Herbert of Bosham, 294; Guy, 197.

27. Crisis at Northampton

1. Barlow, 108–109; Guy, 197–198.

2. Guy, 199.

3. For accounts of Thomas's trial at Northampton, as described in the following chapters, see William FitzStephen's account in *MTB* 3, 49–68; in Staunton, 100–115; also Barlow, 109–114; Duggan, 61–83; Guy, 199–212; Knowles, 94–100; Warren, 485–489.

28. The Archbishop Goes to War

1. "Protomartyr," from the Greek, means "first martyr."

2. William FitzStephen, 57.

3. William FitzStephen, 64.

4. Guy, 212.

29. Exile

1. Guy, 212.

2. Barlow, 115.

3. Ibid.

4. Ibid.

5. Guy, 212–213.

6. The Fens, also known as Fenland, is an area of marshy land in eastern England covering the counties of Lincolnshire, Cambridgeshire, Norfolk, and parts of Suffolk and Huntingdonshire. It is also known as the "Holy Land of England" due to the large number of cathedrals, monasteries, and religious communities in the area. Saint Gilbert set up his community of monks (Gilbertines) in Sempringham in Lincolnshire.

7. Roger of Pontigny, 55.

8. Herbert of Bosham, 324–325. Also Barlow, 116. Knowles says Thomas left England on the evening of November 2 and arrived at Oye beach as dawn was breaking the next day, a voyage during the night; Knowles, *Thomas Becket*, 100.

9. Guy, 214.

10. Ibid., 215.

11. Herbert of Bosham, 331. The hermitage, "Eldemenstre" or "the old monastery," is now known as Saint-Momelin in the Nord department of France.

12. Barlow, 120.

13. While Thomas was an archbishop, he was also a feudal lord, and as such, he had vassals.

14. Guy, 215–216.

15. Barlow, 120.

16. Ibid., 120–121.

17. Barlow, 121.

18. Guy, 216.

19. Barlow, 121.

20. Peter's Pence was and is an annual contribution made by Catholics throughout the world to the Holy See to assist its mission and meet the expenses of the papacy.

21. Guy, 219. Though he notes the size of Thomas's entourage, as recorded by William FitzStephen, Guy is inclined to think that three hundred knights is hyperbole rather than the actual size of the detachment accompanying the archbishop.

22. For an account of Thomas's audience with Pope Alexander and the cardinals, see Alan of Tewkesbury, *MTB* 2, 336–345, in Staunton, 128–134.

23. One version of this speech is preserved as Letter 37, *CTB*, I, 143. See also Guy, 219–220.

24. A term John of Salisbury used to describe those at the courts of King Stephen and King Henry II who were ambitious and corrupt. Guy, xviii.

25. Barlow, 122.

26. Alan of Tewkesbury, 343.

PART IV: SERVANT OF CHRIST
30. Pontigny

1. Guy, 221.

2. Alan of Tewkesbury and the Icelandic Saga, as cited in Barlow, 123.

3. Guy, 221.

4. Barlow, 124.

5. Barlow, 124.

6. Herbert of Bosham, 373; see Barlow, 124.

7. Guy, 223.

8. Barlow, 124.

9. Knowles, "Archbishop Thomas Becket" in *Historian and Character*, 114–115.

10. Ibid., 116.

11. Guy, 224.

12. Ibid., 224–226.

13. Barlow, 125.

14. Ibid., 126–127.

15. Ibid., 126.

16. Duggan, 101.

17. Barlow, 127.

18. Letter 40, *CTB*, I, 155.

19. Letter 45, *CTB*, I, 183.

20. Guy, 230.

21. Barlow, 136.

22. Barlow, 136, Guy, 230.

23. Guy, 230.

24. Warren, 493; Barlow, 136.

25. Guy, 230.

26. Letter 116, *CTB*, I, 563.

27. Letter 54, *CTB*, I, 225.

31. Vézelay

1. Guy, 234.

2. Ibid., 234–235.

3. Barlow, 142.

4. Letter 69, *CTB*, I, 271.

5. Letter 70, *CTB*, I, 273.

6. Letter 68, *CTB*, I, 271.

7. Guy, 237.

8. Barlow, 145.

9. Letter 74, *CTB*, I, 293.

10. Letter 73, *CTB*, I, 285.

11. Guy, 238.

12. Saint Drausinus, or Drausius, was educated by Saint Anseric of Soissons. He became archdeacon in that diocese and later its bishop. Building a monastery at Rethondes and a convent in Soissons, he sought to nurture consecrated life in his diocese. Much admired for his austerities and his able administration, he was also considered an outstanding preacher. He died around the year 674. His tomb, before which Thomas and many pilgrims had offered night vigils, is now preserved in the Louvre Museum in Paris, where it was placed following the French Revolution.

13. Barlow, 147.

14. For accounts of the excommunications at Vézelay, see Barlow, 147–148; Duggan, 110–114; Guy, 238–239.

15. Jocelin de Bailleul was one of the main clerks who prepared the Constitutions of Clarendon. He was also a senior figure in the household of Henry's wife, Queen Eleanor.

16. Letter 82, *CTB*, I, 329.

17. Duggan, 115.

18. Guy, 239, 243–244.

19. Letter 104, *CTB*, I, 489.

20. Barlow, 149–150.

32. The Legates

1. Grim, 413–414; also Barlow, 157.

2. Barlow, 157.

3. Ibid., 157–158.

4. Ibid., 158.

5. Grim, 417–419; Barlow, 159.

6. Guy, 244.

7. Letter 119, *CTB*, I, 573.

8. A "legate a latere" is a legate of the highest degree, appointed by the pope for a particular mission.

9. Guy, 244–245.

10. Barlow, 171.

11. Guy, 246–248.

12. Ibid., 248.

13. Ibid.

14. Barlow, 173; Guy, 248.

15. Barlow, 174.

33. The Two Kings

1. Guy, 250.

2. Letter 162, *CTB*, I, 755.

3. Barlow, 176.

4. Herbert of Bosham, 418–428.

5. Saint Anthelm of Belley (1107–1178) was born in Chambéry, France. He was first a priest of Belley before entering the Carthusian Abbey of Grande Chartreuse, where he

served as prior. He was appointed bishop of Belley in 1163. A heroic bishop, he was well respected for his wisdom.

6. Barlow, 179.

7. Ibid.

8. Barlow 179–181; Guy, 251–256.

9. Guy, 251.

10. Barlow, 180; Guy, 252.

11. Herbert of Bosham, 423.

34. *Ad Honorem Dei*

1. Guy, 254.

2. Herbert of Bosham, 423.

3. Ibid., 424.

4. Ibid., 425.

5. Herbert of Bosham, 425–426; Staunton, 159–160.

6. Barlow, 181; Guy, 255.

7. Letter 183, *CTB*, II, 821.

8. Letter 186, *CTB*, II, 827.

9. These were the last words of Saint Thomas More before his execution on Tower Hill in London on July 6, 1535. More affirmed his loyalty to King Henry VIII, who had condemned him, but stressed that his first loyalty was to God. There are many parallels between Saint Thomas Becket and Saint Thomas More and their disputes with their respective kings. Both were Londoners, both served as chancellor, and both counted the kings they served as personal friends. Both also refused to sacrifice their fidelity to the Catholic Church to appease the ambitions of their kings.

10. Alan of Tewkesbury, 349: "*Confortamini igitur, et nolite expavescere … Deo nostri curam committimus.*"

11. Ibid., 350.

12. Ibid.

13. Ibid., 350–351.

35. Patience and Impatience

1. Barlow, 182–183.

2. Ibid., 183.

3. Ibid., 183.

4. Ibid., 183–184.

5. Saint Malachy of Armagh (1094–1148) was a reforming archbishop of Armagh who suffered much in trying to bring renewal to the Church in Ireland. Born in the city of Armagh, he studied under the abbot of Armagh and was ordained a priest by Saint Celsus, archbishop of Armagh, in 1119. He worked within his diocese until he was appointed abbot of Bangor Abbey in 1123. In 1132, he succeeded Celsus as archbishop. Due to political intrigue, he was unable to take his see for two years; but when finally enthroned, he carried out a vigorous program of reorganization of the Church in Ireland, bringing it into line with the universal Church. He befriended Saint Bernard, and the two supported each other in the work of reform. Impressed by Bernard's foundations, Malachy introduced the Cistercians into Ireland to help reinvigorate monastic life. Trouble was never far from Malachy, and he eventually resigned as archbishop, remaining as bishop of the smaller Diocese of Down. It was when he was traveling back from Rome to Ireland and staying with Bernard for a short visit that he took ill. On November 2, 1148, he died in the arms of Saint Bernard. Bernard buried him in his own tomb in the abbey church, and he was buried there himself when he died five years later. Malachy was the first Irish saint to be formally canonized.

6. Barlow, 184–185; Duggan, 155–157: Guy, 270–272.

7. Barlow, 184.

8. Ibid., 185–186.

9. Ibid., 185.

10. Letter 208, *CTB*, II, 909.

11. For the mediation of Gratian and Vivian, and the subsequent Council of Montmartre, see Herbert of Bosham, 440–442 and 444–451, and Staunton, 166–172.

12. Duggan, 163.

13. Guy, 273.

14. Ibid., 273–274.

15. Barlow, 189; Duggan, 168.

16. Duggan, 169.

17. Ibid., 170.

18. Guy, 275–276.

36. Montmartre

1. Guy, 277.

2. For an account of this conference, see Barlow, 192–195; Duggan, 176–178; Guy,

277–281.

3. Guy, 278–279.

4. Barlow, 195.

5. Cf. Letter 253, *CTB*, II, 1091.

6. Letter 241, *CTB*, II, 1033.

7. Duggan, 178; Guy, 283.

8. Guy, 283.

37. The Crown Affair

1. Guy, 284.

2. Reginald FitzJocelin (d. 1191) later became bishop of Bath and archbishop-elect of Canterbury. It is unclear whether he was born before or after his father became a priest.

3. Guy, 286.

4. Letter 277, *CTB*, II, 1181.

5. Guy, 286–287.

6. Saint Dunstan (909–988) was archbishop of Canterbury from 959 to 988. He composed the coronation ceremony in 973 for the coronation of King Edgar, and it has formed the basis of every coronation since then, including that of Queen Elizabeth II in 1953.

7. For an account of young Henry's coronation and its reverberations, see Strickland, 84–94.

8. Barlow, 208.

9. Guy, 289.

10. For the peace at Fréteval, see Barlow, 209–211; Duggan, 183–187; Guy, 289–295.

11. Guy, 291.

12. Ibid., 292.

13. Ibid., 293–294.

14. Ibid., 295.

38. Return

1. The origins of the Shrine of Our Lady of Rocamadour, in what is now southwestern France, are shrouded in mystery and myth. The sanctuary is named after Saint Amator, who has been variously identified as Zacchaeus of the Gospels; a hermit; or Amator, fifth-century bishop of Auxerre. Perched on a mountain, the site has hosted a Marian shrine since early in the first Christian millennium. A statue of the Black Madonna is

venerated within the sanctuary.

2. Guy, 297.

3. Barlow, 214.

4. William FitzStephen, 116.

5. Guy, 299.

6. Ibid.

7. Ibid.

8. Letter 318, *CTB*, II, 1321.

9. Letter 320, *CTB*, II, 1333.

10. Letter 318, *CTB*, II, 1321.

11. Barlow, 219.

12. Ibid., 219.

13. Barlow, 223; Guy, 303.

14. Guy, 303.

15. Both Barlow and Duggan indicate that Thomas arrived at Sandwich and went on to Canterbury on December 1, 1170. Knowles says it was December 2. Barlow, 224; Duggan, 197; Knowles, *Thomas Becket*, 136.

16. Barlow, 224.

17. Ibid., 225.

18. Guy, 304.

19. Barlow, 221; William Urry, *Thomas Becket: His Last Days* (Stroud: Sutton Publishing, 1999), 45–46.

39. Christmas

1. Possibly December 2 or 3, 1170.

2. Barlow, 226.

3. Strickland, 104.

4. In a famous incident that occurred a short time before Julius Caesar's assassination in 44 BC, a soothsayer (identified by the historian Suetonius as Spurinna, a haruspex, or practitioner of divination) warned him, "Beware the Ides of March!" The Ides of March is March 15. Though he dismissed her warning, Caesar was murdered by his closest collaborators on that day.

5. Barlow, 228–229.

6. Strickland, 105.

7. Barlow, 229.

8. Guy, 305–306.

9. Barlow, 231–232.

10. Barlow, 234–235; Guy, 307–308.

11. Guy, 308.

12. Ibid., 308–310.

13. Ibid., 309–310.

14. Barlow, 235–237; Guy, 310–311.

15. Barlow, 232–233.

16. Herbert of Bosham, 485: "*Certe si haec cerneres, diceres mox te propheticum illud animal, cui erat facies hominis et facies leonis, oculo ad oculum audisse et vidisse.*"

17. Barlow, 233.

18. Barlow, 233–234; Guy, 307.

19. Letter 328, *CTB*, II, 1358.

20. Letter 329, *CTB*, II, 1360.

40. Alfege

1. Margaret Toynbee, *S. Louis of Toulouse and the Process of Canonisation in the Fourteenth Century* (Manchester: Manchester University Press, 1929), 141–143.

2. Osbern, *Osbern's Life of Alfege,* trans. Frances Shaw (London: St Paul's, 1999), 41.

3. Also known as Thorkell the Tall.

4. Osbern, 55.

5. Ibid., 57–65.

6. Ibid., 65.

7. Ibid., 76–77.

8. Ibid., 13.

9. Barlow, 237–238.

10. For accounts of the knights' interview with Thomas, see Barlow 240–243; Duggan, 209–210; Knowles, 141–144; Guy 313–317; Urry, 100–113.

11. Knowles, *Thomas Becket*, 141.

41. Vespers

1. Grim, 430–438; Staunton, 195–203; Barlow, 239–248; Duggan, 209–213; Guy, 313–321.

2. Grim, 432: "*Hic me reperiet qui quaesierit.*"

3. Benedict of Peterborough, *MTB* 2, 9. Benedict of Peterborough was a monk of Can-

terbury and was a witness to Thomas's martyrdom. Following Thomas's canonization he became prior of the community and then, in 1177, abbot of Peterborough. He wrote his account of Saint Thomas's martyrdom, his "Passio," which also contains accounts of the first miracles that he researched by interviewing those involved. He died in 1193.

4. Guy, 317.

5. According to an ancient custom, sacred spaces, be they cathedrals, churches, or chapels, were deemed to be places of sanctuary and refuge. From early on, the Church recognized the right of asylum and opened her churches to those fleeing persecution. Once inside the church, the fugitive was protected and could not be arrested. Thanks to the Church's influence in society and over legal matters, this right of sanctuary was written into law by the Middle Ages. The process of sanctuary was a formal one. The fugitive had to arrive at the door of the church and formally seek sanctuary of the bishop, abbot, or priest. If sanctuary were granted, all weapons had to be abandoned and left outside. The time of refuge was limited to about a month. In this time, the fugitive had to reflect on how to face the charges against him or her. The laws and custom of sanctuary came to an end in the seventeenth century, so they no longer have legal or ecclesiastical force.

6. Grim, 434: "*Habetis hic dilectum Deo ac vere sanctum martyrem Elfegum; alium vobis divina miseratio providebit; non morabitur.*"

7. Grim, 434–435; Staunton, 199; Urry, 120; Guy, 317–318.

8. Grim, 435: "*Non decet orationis domum, ecclesiam Christi, turrem facere, quae, etsi non claudatur, suis sufficit ad munimen; et nos patiendo potius quam pugnando triumphabimus hostem, qui et pati venimus, non repugnare.*"

9. Ibid., 436: "*Ecce praesto sum in nomine Ejus pati qui me sanguine suo redemit; absit ut propter gladios vestros fugiam, aut a justitia recedam.*"

10. Ibid.: "*Et ego pro Domino meo paratus sum mori, ut in meo sanguine ecclesia libertatem consequatur et pacem; sed meis, sive clerico sive laico, in nomine Dei omnipotentis interdico ne in aliquo noceatis.*"

11. Ibid., 437: "*Cernens igitur martyr invictus horam imminere quae miserae mortalitati finem imponeret, paratam. sibi et promissam a Domino coronam immortalitatis jam proximam fieri, inclinata in modum orantis cervice, junctis pariter et elevatis sursum manibus, Deo et sanctae Mariae et beato martyri Dionysio suam et ecclesiae causam commendavit.*" Also, Guy, 320.

12. Ibid.

13. Guy, 320.

14. Grim, 437: "*Pro nomine Jesu et ecclesiae tuition mortem amplecti paratus sum.*"

15. Guy, 320.

16. Grim, 437.

17. Barlow, 248.

18. Barlow, 248–249; Guy, 321–322.

19. Guy, 321.

20. Ibid.

42. The Saint and the Penitent

1. Guy, 322.

2. Barlow, 249–250.

3. Guy, 322.

4. Saint Thomas's first miracle occurred in the hours after his martyrdom, that same night — "*in ipsa nocte*," as William FitzStephen records. One of the men who had witnessed the martyrdom and afterward gathered some of the archbishop's blood in a bottle, brought it home to his wife who was paralyzed. Drawing a bath for her, some of the martyr's blood was poured into it, and the woman was washed. Her paralysis was healed, and she stepped out of the bath unaided. See William FitzStephen, 149–150.

5. Guy, 323–324.

6. Ibid., 324.

7. Barlow, 253.

8. Ibid.

9. Guy, 325.

10. Ibid.

11. Ibid., 325–326.

12. Barlow, 260.

13. Ibid., 258.

14. Barlow, 258–259; Guy, 334.

15. Warren, 602.

16. In time, the diluted blood would become known as Saint Thomas's Water. See Barlow, 267.

17. Barlow, 268–269; Duggan, 230; Knowles, 154; Guy, 331.

18. Guy, 332–333.

43. A Solitary End

1. John Guy maintains that Henry was not repentant at all. See Guy, 329.

2. Nick Barratt, *The Restless Kings: Henry II, His Sons and the Wars for the Plantagenet Crown* (London: Faber & Faber, 2018) offers a succinct history of Henry's struggles with his children.

3. For a fascinating account of Eleanor's life and her relationship with her husband, see Alison Weir, *Eleanor of Aquitaine: By Wrath of God, Queen of England* (London: Vintage, 2007).

4. Warren, 117–118.

5. Ibid., 118.

6. Weir, 207.

7. Ibid., 208.

8. Warren, 118.

9. Weir, 215ff.

10. Barratt, 145–147.

11. Warren, 122.

12. Ibid., 123.

13. Barratt, 118.

14. Warren, 136; Barratt, 153–154.

15. Strickland, 208.

16. Warren, 135.

17. Ibid., 119.

18. Strickland, 308–310.

19. Warren., 584.

20. Ibid., 591.

21. Ibid., 596.

22. Ibid.

23. Ibid, 598.

24. Ibid., 598–599.

25. Ibid., 147.

26. Barratt, 171.

27. Warren, 626.

28. Ibid.

29. Ibid., 594.

Epilogue

1. Warren, 451.

2. Knowles, "Archbishop Thomas Becket" in *The Historian and Character*, 100.

3. Ibid., 112–113.

4. As previously noted, Saint Thomas More, former lord chancellor of England, was executed at Tower Hill in London on July 6, 1535, for his refusal to accept King Henry VIII's founding of the Church of England.

5. On January 23, 1888, as archaeological investigations were being carried out in the eastern crypt of Canterbury Cathedral, a coffin was found just beneath the surface of the floor, not far from where Thomas had originally been buried in 1170. The coffin contained human bones mixed with earth. Upon examination, the bones were found to be of a middle-aged adult man, possibly about fifty years old. The skull was large and seemed to have sustained a number of injuries, seemingly from an implement similar to a mace or pickaxe. A number of bones were missing. Photographs were taken, and the skeleton was quickly reinterred. Many years of speculation followed, leading eventually to a second exhumation on July 18, 1949. Taken to Cambridge University for examination, the bones were studied for two years. A final report concluded that the bones were those of a mature man, possibly sixty years old at the time of death. He was of average height, about five foot eight. All the damage to the skeleton was postmortem, so not the cause of death. Even if the head injuries had killed this man, they were not consistent with the manner of Thomas's death, which was carefully chronicled by a number of witnesses. There was evidence that the body had been buried elsewhere and reinterred in the crypt. The bones of various animals were also found in the coffin, along with the incomplete upper vertebrae of another human skeleton, facts that had not been noted in the 1888 examination. The report concluded that these were not the bones of Saint Thomas Becket, as no similarities to the saint's physical features or the manner of his death were found, though these bones were those of a man who had lived in the medieval period. For more details, see John Butler, *The Quest for Becket's Bones: The Mystery of the Relics of St. Thomas Becket of Canterbury* (New Haven and London: Yale University Press, 1995).

6. John Guy.

7. Duggan, 269.

ACKNOWLEDGMENTS

1. Joseph Pearce, *Wisdom and Innocence: A Life of G. K. Chesterton* (London: Hodder & Stoughton, 1996).

2. Ibid., 423.

Select Bibliography

Primary Works

Duggan, Anne, ed. and trans. *The Correspondence of Thomas Becket, Archbishop of Canterbury 1162–1170*. 2 vol. Oxford: Oxford University Press, 2000.

Robertson, James Craigie, ed. *Materials for the History of Thomas Becket*. 7 vol. Cambridge: Cambridge University Press, 2012.

Staunton, Michael, ed., trans., annot. *The Lives of Thomas Becket*. Manchester: Manchester University Press, 2001.

Secondary Works
Biographies of Saint Thomas

Barlow, Frank. *Thomas Becket*. London: Phoenix Giant, 1986.

Butler, John. *The Quest for Becket's Bones: The Mystery of the Relics of St. Thomas Becket of Canterbury*. New Haven and London: Yale University Press, 1995.

Duggan, Anne. *Reputations: Thomas Becket*. London: Arnold, 2004.

Guy, John. *Thomas Becket, Warrior, Priest, Rebel, Victim: A 900-Year-Old Story Retold*. London: Penguin, 2013.

Knowles, David. *Thomas Becket*. London: A&C Black, 1970.

Radford, Lewis B. *Thomas of London Before His Consecration*. Cambridge: Cambridge University Press, 1894.

Staunton, Michael. *Thomas Becket and His Biographers*. Woodbridge: Boydell Press, 2006.

Urry, William. *Thomas Becket, His Last Days*. Stroud: Sutton Publishing, 1999.

Secondary Works
General History

Barber, Richard. *Henry II: A Prince Among Princes*. London: Allen Lane, 2015.

Barlow, Frank. *The Feudal Kingdom of England: 1042–1216*. 5th ed. London: Routledge, 1999.

Barratt, Nick. *The Restless Kings: Henry II, His Sons and the Wars for the Plantagenet Crown.* London: Faber & Faber, 2019.

Bradbury, Jim. *Stephen and Matilda: The Civil War of 1139–53.* Stroud: The History Press, 2009.

Carroll, Warren. *A History of Christendom, Volume 2: The Building of Christendom.* Front Royal, VA: Christendom Press, 1987.

_____. *A History of Christendom, Volume 3: The Glory of Christendom.* Front Royal, VA: Christendom Press, 1993.

Chesterton, G. K. *A Short History of England.* Sevenoaks, Kent: Fisher Press, 1994.

Clanchy, M. T. *England and Its Rulers, 1066–1272.* London: Fontana, 1988.

Green, Judith A. *Henry I: King of England and Duke of Normandy.* Cambridge: Cambridge University Press, 2006.

Crouch, David. *The Reign of King Stephen, 1135–1154.* Abingdon: Routledge, 2000.

Duffy, Eamon. *Ten Popes Who Shook the World.* New Haven and London: Yale University Press, 2011.

_____. *Saints and Sinners: A History of the Popes.* 3rd ed. New Haven and London: Yale University Press, 2006.

Hanley, Catherine. *Matilda: Empress, Queen, Warrior.* New Haven and London: Yale University Press, 2020.

Harper-Bill, Christopher, and Nicholas Vincent, eds. *Henry II: New Interpretations.* Woodbridge: Boydell Press, 2007.

Knowles, David. *The Historian and Character.* Cambridge: Cambridge University Press, 1963.

Jones, Dan. *The Plantagenets; The Kings who Made England.* London: Harper Press, 2012.

Logan, F. Donald. *A History of the Church in the Middle Ages.* 2nd ed. Abingdon: Routledge, 2012.

Norton, Christopher. *St William of York.* York: York Medieval Press, 2006.

Patterson, Robert B. *The Earl, the Kings, and the Chronicler: Robert Earl of Gloucester and the Reigns of Henry I and Stephen.* Oxford: Oxford University Press, 2019.

Robinson, I. S. *The Papacy, 1073–1198: Continuity and Innovation.* Cambridge: Cambridge University Press, 1990.

Rule, Martin. *The Life and Times of St. Anselm, Archbishop of Canterbury and Primate of the Britains.* Sydney: Wentworth Press, 2016.

Saltman, Avrom. *Theobald, Archbishop of Canterbury.* London: Athlone Press, 1956.

Shaw, Frances. *Osbern's Life of Alfege.* London: St Paul's, 1999.

Southern, R.W. *St. Anselm: A Portrait in a Landscape.* Cambridge: Cambridge University Press, 1990.

Stanley, Arthur P. *Historical Memorials of Canterbury.* London: John Murray, 1912.

Strickland, Matthew. *Henry the Young King, 1155–1183.* New Haven and London: Yale University Press, 2016.

Traux, Jean. *Archbishops Ralph d'Escures, William of Corbeil and Theobald of Bec: Heirs of Anselm and Ancestors of Becket.* Farnham: Ashgate, 2012.

Warren, W. L. *Henry II.* New Haven and London: Yale University Press, 2000.

Weir, Alison. *Eleanor of Aquitaine: By the Wrath of God, Queen of England.* London: Vintage, 2007.

About the Author

Father John S. Hogan, OCDS, is a priest of the Diocese of Meath in Ireland and a member of the Secular Order of Discalced Carmelites. He has served in parish ministry, teaching, retreats, spiritual direction, and broadcasting. He is founder of the Fraternity of St. Genesius, which prays for and supports those in the theatrical and cinematic arts. He is cohost of EWTN's series *Forgotten Heritage*. As an author he has written on spirituality, saints, and history.

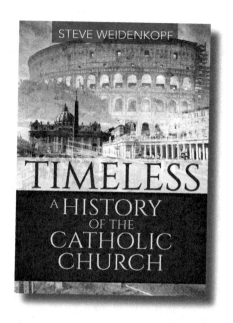